SALEM
WITCHCRAFT

PART THIRD.

THE PHILIP ENGLISH HOUSE. — Page 142.

A M E R I C A N   C L A S S I C S

SALEM WITCHCRAFT

*With an Account of Salem Village
and
A History of Opinions on
Witchcraft and Kindred Subjects*

CHARLES W. UPHAM

Volume II

FREDERICK UNGAR PUBLISHING CO.
New York

Fifth Printing, 1976

ISBN 0-8044-1947-7 Set

ISBN 0-8044-1948-5 Vol. I

ISBN 0-8044-1949-3 Vol. II

Printed in the United States of America

Library of Congress Catalog Card No. 59-10887

WITCH HILL. 1866.

PART THIRD.

—◆—

WITCHCRAFT AT SALEM VILLAGE.

WE left Mr. Parris in the early part of November,
1691, at the crisis of his controversy with the
inhabitants of Salem Village, under circumstances
which seemed to indicate that its termination was
near at hand. The opposition to him had assumed a
form which made it quite probable that it would succeed
in dislodging him from his position. But the end was
not yet. Events were ripening that were to give him a
new and fearful strength, and open a scene in which he
was to act a part destined to attract the notice of the
world, and become a permanent portion of human history. The doctrines of demonology had produced their
full effect upon the minds of men, and every thing was
ready for a final display of their power. The story of
the Goodwin children, as told by Cotton Mather, was
known and read in all the dwellings of the land, and
filled the imaginations of a credulous age. Deputy-
governor Danforth had begun the work of arrests ; and

persons charged with witchcraft, belonging to neighboring towns, were already in prison.

Mr. Parris appears to have had in his family several slaves, probably brought by him from the West Indies. One of them, whom he calls, in his church-record book, "my negro lad," had died, a year or two before, at the age of nineteen. Two of them were man and wife. The former was always known by the name of "John Indian;" the latter was called "Tituba." These two persons may have originated the "Salem witchcraft." They are spoken of as having come from New Spain, as it was then called, — that is, the Spanish West Indies, and the adjacent mainlands of Central and South America, — and, in all probability, contributed, from the wild and strange superstitions prevalent among their native tribes, materials which, added to the commonly received notions on such subjects, heightened the infatuation of the times, and inflamed still more the imaginations of the credulous. Persons conversant with the Indians of Mexico, and on both sides of the Isthmus, discern many similarities in their systems of demonology with ideas and practices developed here.

Mr. Parris's former residence in the neighborhood of the Spanish Main, and the prominent part taken by his Indian slaves in originating the proceedings at the village, may account for some of the features of the transaction.

During the winter of 1691 and 1692, a circle of young girls had been formed, who were in the habit of meeting at Mr. Parris's house for the purpose of practising palmistry, and other arts of fortune-telling, and of becoming experts in the wonders of necromancy, magic, and spiritualism. It consisted, besides the Indian servants, mainly of the following persons : —

Elizabeth, daughter of Mr. Parris, was nine years of age. She seems to have performed a leading part in the first stages of the affair, and must have been a child of remarkable precocity. It is a noticeable fact, that her father early removed her from the scene. She was sent to the town, where she remained in the family of Stephen Sewall, until the proceedings at the village were brought to a close. Abigail Williams, a niece of Mr. Parris, and a member of his household, was eleven years of age. She acted conspicuously in the witchcraft prosecutions from beginning to end. Ann Putnam, daughter of Sergeant Thomas Putnam, the parish clerk or recorder, was twelve years of age. The character and social position of her parents gave her a prominence which an extraordinary development of the imaginative faculty, and of mental powers generally, enabled her to hold throughout. This young girl is perhaps entitled to be regarded as, in many respects, the leading agent in all the mischief that followed. Mary Walcot was seventeen years of age. Her father was Jonathan Walcot (vol. i. p. 225). His first wife, Mary Sibley, to whom he was married in 1664, had died in 1683. She was the mother of Mary. It is a singular fact, and indicates the estimation in which Captain Walcot was held, that, although not a church-member, he filled the office of deacon of the parish for several years before the formation of the church. Mercy Lewis was also seventeen years of age. When quite young, she was, for a time, in the family of the Rev. George Burroughs: and, in 1692, was living as a servant in the family of Thomas Putnam; although, occasionally, she seems to have lived, in the same capacity, with that of John Putnam, Jr., the constable of the village. He was a son of Nathaniel, and resided in the neighborhood of Thomas and Deacon Edward Putnam. Mercy Lewis performed a leading part in the proceedings, had great energy of purpose and capacity of management, and became responsible for much of the crime and horror connected with them. Elizabeth Hubbard, seventeen years of age, who also occupies a bad eminence in the scene, was a niece of Mrs. Dr. Griggs, and lived in her family. Elizabeth Booth and Susannah Sheldon, each eighteen years of age, belonged to families in the neighborhood. Mary Warren, twenty years of age, was a servant in the family of John Procter; and Sarah Churchill, of the same age, was a servant in that of George Jacobs, Sr. These two last were actuated, it is too apparent, by malicious feelings towards the families in which they resided, and contributed largely to the horrible tragedy. The facts to be exhibited will enable every one who carefully considers them, to form an estimate, for himself, of the respective character and conduct of these young persons. It is almost beyond belief that they were wholly actuated by deliberate and cold-blooded malignity. Their crime would, in that view, have been

without a parallel in monstrosity of wickedness, and
beyond what can be imagined of the guiltiest and most
depraved natures. For myself, I am unable to determine how much may be attributed to credulity,
hallucination, and the delirium of excitement, or to
deliberate malice and falsehood.   There is too much
evidence of guile and conspiracy to attribute all their
actions and declarations to delusion ; and their conduct throughout was stamped with a bold assurance
and audacious bearing. With one or two slight and
momentary exceptions, there was a total absence of
compunction or commiseration, and a reckless disregard of the agonies and destruction they were scatter-
ing around them.   They present a subject that justly
claims, and will for ever task, the examination of those
who are most competent to fathom the mysteries of
the human soul, sound its depths, and measure the
extent to which it is liable to become wicked and devilish.   It will be seen that other persons were drawn
to act with these " afflicted children," as they were
called, some from contagious delusion, and some, as
was quite well proved, from a false, mischievous, and
malignant spirit.

Besides the above-mentioned persons, there were
three married women, rather under middle life, who
acted with the afflicted children, — Mrs. Ann Putnam,
the mother of the child of that name ; Mrs. Pope ; and
a woman, named Bibber, who appears to have lived at
Wenham.   Another married woman, — spoken of as
" ancient," — named Goodell, had also been in the

habit of attending their meetings; but she is not named in any of the documents on file, and was probably withdrawn, at an early period, from participating in the transaction.

In the course of the winter, they became quite skilful and expert in the arts they were learning, and gradually began to display their attainments to the admiration and amazement of beholders. At first, they made no charges against any person, but confined themselves to strange actions, exclamations, and contortions. They would creep into holes, and under benches and chairs, put themselves into odd and unnatural postures, make wild and antic gestures, and utter incoherent and unintelligible sounds. They would be seized with spasms, drop insensible to the floor, or writhe in agony, suffering dreadful tortures, and uttering loud and piercing outcries. The attention of the families in which they held their meetings was called to their extraordinary condition and proceedings; and the whole neighborhood and surrounding country soon were filled with the story of the strange and unaccountable sufferings of the " afflicted girls." No explanation could be given, and their condition became worse and worse. The physician of the village, Dr. Griggs, was called in, a consultation had, and the opinion finally and gravely given, that the afflicted children were bewitched. It was quite common in those days for the faculty to dispose of difficult cases by this resort. When their remedies were baffled, and their skill at fault, the patient was said to be " under an evil hand." In all cases, the sage conclusion was received by nurses, and elderly women called in on such occasions, if the symptoms were out of the common course, or did not yield to the prescriptions these persons were in the habit of apply-ing. Very soon, the whole community became excited and alarmed to the highest degree. All other topics were forgotten. The only thing spoken or thought of was the terrible condition of the afflicted children in Mr. Parris's house, or wherever, from time to time, the girls assembled. They were the objects of universal compassion and wonder. The people flocked from all quarters to witness their sufferings, and gaze with awe upon their convulsions. Becoming objects of such notice, they were stimulated to vary and expand the manifestations of the extraordinary influence that was upon them. They extended their operations be-yond the houses of Mr. Parris, and the families to which they belonged, to public places ; and their fits, exclama-tions, and outcries disturbed the exercises of prayer meetings, and the ordinary services of the congrega-tion. On one occasion, on the Lord's Day, March 20th, when the singing of the psalm previous to the sermon was concluded, before the person preaching — Mr. Lawson — could come forward, Abigail Williams cried out, " Now stand up, and name your text." When he had read it, in a loud and insolent voice she ex-claimed, " It's a long text." In the midst of the dis-course, Mrs. Pope broke in, " Now, there is enough of that." In the afternoon of the same day, while re-

ferring to the doctrine he had been expounding in the
preceding service, Abigail Williams rudely ejaculated,
"I know no doctrine you had.   If you did name
one, I have forgot it."   An aged member of the
church was present, against whom a warrant on the
charge of witchcraft had been procured the day before.
Being apprised of the proceeding, Abigail Williams
spoke aloud, during the service, calling by name the
person about to be apprehended, "Look where she
sits upon the beam, sucking her yellow-bird betwixt
her fingers."   Ann Putnam, joining in, exclaimed,
"There is a yellow-bird sitting on the minister's hat,
as it hangs on the pin in the pulpit."   Mr. Lawson
remarks, with much simplicity, that these things, occurring "in the time of public worship, did something
interrupt me in my first prayer, being so unusual."
But he braced himself up to the emergency, and went
on with the service.   There is no intimation that Mr.
Parris rebuked his niece for her disorderly behavior.
As at several other times, the people sitting near Ann
Putnam had to lay hold of her to prevent her proceeding to greater extremities, and wholly breaking up the
meeting.   The girls were supposed to be under an
irresistible and supernatural impulse ; and, instead of
being severely punished, were looked upon with mingled pity, terror, and awe, and made objects of the
greatest attention.   Of course, where members of
the minister's family were countenanced in such proceedings, during the exercises of public worship, on
the Lord's Day, in the meeting-house, it was not

strange that people in general yielded to the excitement. But all did not. Several members of the family of Francis Nurse, Peter Cloyse and wife, and Joseph Putnam, expressed their disapprobation of such doings being allowed, and absented themselves from meeting. Perhaps others took the same course; but whoever did were marked, as the sequel will show.

In the mean while the excitement was worked up to the highest pitch. The families to which several of the "afflicted children" belonged were led to apply themselves to fasting and prayer, on which occasions the neighbors, under the guidance of the minister, would assemble, and unite in invocations to the Divine Being to interpose and deliver them from the snares and dominion of Satan. The "afflicted children" who might be present would not, as a general thing, interrupt the prayers while in progress, but would break out with their wild outcries and convulsive spasms in the intervals of the service. In due time, Mr. Parris sent for the neighboring ministers to assemble at his house, and unite with him in devoting a day to solemn religious services and earnest supplications to the throne of Mercy for rescue from the power of the great enemy of souls. The ministers spent the day in Mr. Parris's house, and the children performed their feats before their eyes. The reverend gentlemen were astounded at what they saw, fully corroborated the opinion of Dr. Griggs, and formally declared their belief that the Evil One had commenced his operations with a bolder front and on a broader scale than ever before in this or any other country.

This judgment of the ministers was quickly made known everywhere; and, if doubt remained in any mind, it was suppressed by the irresistible power of an overwhelming public conviction. Individuals were lost in the universal fanaticism. Society was dissolved into a wild and excited crowd. Men and women left their fields, their houses, their labors and employments, to witness the awful unveiling of the demoniac power, and to behold the workings of Satan himself upon the victims of his wrath.

It must be borne in mind, that it was then an established doctrine in theology, philosophy, and law, that the Devil could not operate upon mortals, or mortal affairs, except through the intermediate instrumentality of human beings in confederacy with him, that is, witches or wizards. The question, of course, in all minds and on all tongues, was, " Who are the agents of the Devil in afflicting these girls ? There must be some among us thus acting, and who are they ? " For some time the girls held back from mentioning names; or, if they did, it was prevented from being divulged to the public. In the mean time, the excitement spread and deepened. At length the people had become so thoroughly prepared for the work, that it was concluded to begin operations in earnest. The continued pressure upon the " afflicted children," the earnest and importunate inquiry, on all sides, " Who is it that bewitches you ? " opened their lips in response, and

they began to select and bring forward their victims.
One after another, they cried out " Good," " Osburn,"
" Tituba." On the 29th of February, 1692, warrants
were duly issued against those persons. It is observable, that the complainants who procured the warrants
in these cases were Joseph Hutchinson, Edward Putnam, Thomas Putnam, and Thomas Preston. This
fact shows how nearly unanimous, at this time, was the
conviction that the sufferings of the girls were the
result of witchcraft. Joseph Hutchinson was a firm-
minded man, of strong common sense, and from his
general character and ways of thinking and acting,
one of the last persons liable to be carried away by a
popular enthusiasm, and was found among the earliest
rescued from it. Thomas Preston was a son-in-law of
Francis Nurse.

As all was ripe for the development of the plot,
extraordinary means were taken to give publicity,
notoriety, and effect to the first examinations. On the
1st of March the two leading magistrates of the
neighborhood, men of great note and influence, whose
fathers had been among the chief founders of the
settlement, and who were Assistants, — that is, members of the highest legislative and judicial body in the
colony, combining with the functions of a senate those
of a court of last resort with most comprehensive
jurisdiction, — John Hathorne and Jonathan Corwin,
entered the village, in imposing array, escorted by
the marshal, constables, and their aids, with all the
trappings of their offices; reined up at Nathaniel In-

gersoll's corner, and dismounted at his door. The whole population of the neighborhood, apprised of the occasion, was gathered on the lawn, or came flocking along the roads. The crowd was so great that it was necessary to adjourn to the meeting-house, which was filled at once by a multitude excited to the highest pitch of indignation and abhorrence towards the prisoners, and of curiosity to witness the novel and imposing spectacle and proceedings. The magistrates took seats in front of the pulpit, facing the assembly; a long table or raised platform being placed before them; and it was announced, that they were ready to enter upon the examination. On bringing in and delivering over the accused parties, the officers who had executed the warrants stated that they " had made diligent search for images and such like, but could find none." After prayer, Constable George Locker produced the body of Sarah Good; and Constable Joseph Herrick, the bodies of Sarah Osburn, and Tituba Mr. Parris's Indian woman. The evidence seems to indicate, that, on these occasions, the prisoners were placed on the platform, to keep them from the contact of the general crowd, and that all might see them.

Sarah Good was first examined, the other two being removed from the house for the time. In complaining of her, and bringing her forward first, the prosecutors showed that they were well advised. There was a general readiness to receive the charge against her, as she was evidently the object of much prejudice in the neighborhood. Her husband, who was a weak, ignorant, and dependent person, had become alienated from her. The family were very poor ; and she and her children had sometimes been without a house to shelter them, and left to wander from door to door for relief. Whether justly or not, she appears to have been subject to general obloquy. Probably there was no one in the country around, against whom popular suspicion could have been more readily directed, or in whose favor and defence less interest could be awakened. She was a forlorn, friendless, and forsaken creature, broken down by wretchedness of condition and ill-repute. The following are the minutes of her examination, as found among the files : —

" *The Examination of Sarah Good before the Worshipful Esqrs. John Hathorne and Jonathan Corwin.*

" Sarah Good, what evil spirit have you familiarity with ? — None.

" Have you made no contracts with the Devil ? — No.

" Why do you hurt these children ? — I do not hurt them. I scorn it.

" Who do you employ then to do it ? — I employ nobody.

" What creature do you employ then ? — No creature : but I am falsely accused.

" Why did you go away muttering from Mr. Parris his house ? — I did not mutter, but I thanked him for what he gave my child.

" Have you made no contract with the Devil ? — No.

" Hathorne desired the children all of them to look upon her, and see if this were the person that hurt them ; and so they all did look upon her, and said this was one of the persons that did torment them. Presently they were all tormented.

" Sarah Good, do you not see now what you have done? Why do you not tell us the truth? Why do you thus torment these poor children? — I do not torment them.

" Who do you employ then? — I employ nobody. I scorn it.

" How came they thus tormented? — What do I know? You bring others here, and now you charge me with it.

" Why, who was it? — I do not know but it was some you brought into the meeting-house with you.

" We brought you into the meeting-house. — But you brought in two more.

" Who was it, then, that tormented the children? — It was Osburn.

" What is it you say when you go muttering away from persons' houses? — If I must tell, I will tell.

" Do tell us then. — If I must tell, I will tell : it is the Commandments. I may say my Commandments, I hope.

" What Commandment is it? — If I must tell you, I will tell : it is a psalm.

" What psalm?

" (After a long time she muttered over some part of a psalm.)

" Who do you serve? — I serve God.

" What God do you serve? — The God that made heaven and earth (though she was not willing to mention the word ' God '). Her answers were in a very wicked, spiteful manner, reflecting and retorting against the authority with base and abusive words ; and many lies she was taken in. It was here said that her husband had said that he was afraid that she either was a witch or would be one very quickly. The worshipful Mr. Hathorne, asked him his reason why he said so of her, whether he had ever seen any thing by her. He answered ' No, not in this nature ; but it was her bad carriage to him : and indeed,' said he, ' I may say with tears, that she is an enemy to all good.' "

The foregoing is in the handwriting of Ezekiel Cheever. The following is in that of John Hathorne : —

" Salem Village, March the 1st, 1692. — Sarah Good, upon examination, denied the matter of fact (viz.) that she ever used any witchcraft, or hurt the abovesaid children, or any of them.

" The abovenamed children, being all present, positively accused her of hurting of them sundry times within this two months, and also that morning. Sarah Good denied that she had been at their houses in said time or near them, or had done them any hurt. All the abovesaid children then present accused her face to face ; upon which they were all dreadfully tortured and tormented for a short space of time ; and, the affliction and tortures being over, they charged said Sarah Good again that she had then so tortured them, and came to them and did it, although she was personally then kept at a considerable distance from them.

" Sarah Good being asked if that she did not then hurt them, who did it ; and the children being again tortured, she looked upon them, and said that it was one of them we brought into the house with us. We asked her who it was : she then answered, and said it was Sarah Osburn, and Sarah Osburn was then under custody, and not in the house ; and the children, being quickly after recovered out of their fit, said that it was Sarah Good and also Sarah Osburn that then did hurt and torment or afflict them, although both of them at the same time at a distance or remote from them personally. There were also sundry other questions put to her, and answers given thereunto by her according as is also given in."

It will be noticed that the examination was conducted in the form of questions put by the magistrate, Hathorne, based upon a foregone conclusion of the prisoner's guilt, and expressive of a conviction, all along on his part, that the evidence of " the afflicted " against her amounted to, and was, absolute demonstration. It will also be noticed, that, severe as was the opinion of her husband in reference to her general conduct, he could not be made to say that he had ever noticed any thing in her of the nature of witchcraft. The torments the girls affected to experience in looking at her must have produced an overwhelming effect on the crowd, as they did on the magistrate, and even on the poor, amazed creature herself. She did not seem to doubt the reality of their sufferings. In this, and in all cases, it must be remembered that the account of the examination comes to us from those who were under the wildest excitement against the prisoners; that no counsel was allowed them; that, if any thing was suffered to be said in their defence by others, it has failed to reach us; that the accused persons were wholly unaccustomed to such scenes and exposures, unsuspicious of the perils of a cross-examination, or of an inquisition conducted with a design to entrap and ensnare; and that what they did say was liable to be misunderstood, as well as misrepresented. We cannot hear their story. All we know is from parties prejudiced, to the highest degree, against them. Sarah Good was an unfortunate and miserable woman in her circumstances and condition : but, from all that appears on the record, making due allowance for the credulity, extravagance, prejudice, folly, or malignity of the witnesses ; giving full effect to every thing that can claim the character of substantial force alleged against her, it is undeniable, that there was not, beyond the afflicted girls, a particle of evidence to sustain the charge on which she was arraigned ; and that, in the worst aspect of her case, she was an object for compassion, rather than punishment. Altogether, the proceedings against her, which terminated with her execution, were cruel and shameful to the highest degree.

On the conclusion of her examination, she was removed from the meeting-house, and Sarah Osburn brought in. Her selection, as one of the persons to be first cried out upon, was judicious. The public mind was prepared to believe the charge against her. Her original name was Sarah Warren. She was married, April 5, 1662, to Robert Prince, who belonged to a leading family, and owned a valuable farm. He died early, leaving her with two young children, James and Joseph.

In the early colonial period, it was the custom for persons who desired to come from the old country to America, but had not the means to defray the expenses of the passage, to let or sell themselves, for a greater or less length of time, to individuals residing here who needed their service. The practice continued

down to the present century. Emigrants who thus
sold themselves for a period of years were called
" redemptioners." Alexander Osburn came over from
Ireland in this character. The widow of Robert Prince
bought out the residue of his time from the person to
whom he was thus under contract, for fifteen pounds,
and employed him to carry on her farm. After a
while, she married him. This, it is probable, gave rise
to some criticism ; and, as her boys grew up, became
more and more disagreeable to them. The marriage,
as was natural, led to unhappy results. In 1720, after
Osburn had been dead some years, a curious case was
brought into court, in which the sons of Robert Prince
testified that Osburn treated their mother and them
with great cruelty and barbarity. They had become
of age before their mother's death, and had signed
their names to a deed conveying away land belonging
to their patrimony. The object of the suit was to invalidate the conveyance by proving that they were compelled by Osburn to sign the deed, he using threats
and violence upon them at the time. There was an
extraordinary conflict of testimony in the trial ; some
witnesses strongly corroborating the accusations of the
Princes, and some equally strong in vindication of
the character of Osburn. It was shown, that, in the
opinion of several of his neighbors, he was an industrious, respectable, and worthy person. It is difficult
to determine the precise merits of the case. After the
death of his wife, Osburn married Ruth, a daughter of
William Cantlebury, and widow of William Sibley.

She was a woman of unquestioned excellence of character, and of a large landed estate. Osburn was her third husband, the first having been Thomas Small. After her marriage to Osburn, he and she joined the church, and were reputable persons in all respects. He was well regarded as a citizen, and often on the parish committee. Neither he nor the widow Sibley appear to have been implicated in the witchcraft proceedings in any other particular than that he testified that his then wife Sarah had not been for some time at meeting. There is no indication that this was volunteer testimony. He and his wife Ruth were among the firmest opponents of Mr. Parris. There is no mention of his having had children by either of his American wives. His son John, who probably came with him to the country, was an inhabitant of the Village; and his name is on the rate-list, for the last time, in 1718, his father having died some years before. The Osborne family, in this part of the country, does not appear to have sprung from this source.

Without attempting to decide where, or in what proportions, the blame is to be laid, the fact is evident, that the marriage of the widow Sarah Prince to Alexander Osburn was an unhappy one. Her mind became depressed, if not distracted. For some time, she had been bedridden. Of course, as she had occupied a respectable social position, and was a woman of property, her case naturally gave rise to scandal. Rumor was busy and gossip rife in reference to her; and it was quite natural that she should have been suggested for the accusing girls to pitch upon. The following is an account of her examination by the magistrates, in the handwriting of John Hathorne : —

" Sarah Osburne, upon examination, denied the matter of fact, viz., that she ever understood or used any witchcraft, or hurt any of the abovesaid children.

" The children above named, being all personally present, accused her face to face; which, being done, they were all hurt, afflicted, and tortured very much; which, being over, and they out of their fits, they said that said Sarah Osburne did then come to them, and hurt them, Sarah Osburne being then kept at a distance personally from them. Sarah Osburne was asked why she then hurt them. She denied it. It being asked of her how she could so pinch and hurt them, and yet she be at that distance personally from them, she answered she did not then hurt them, nor ever did. She was asked who, then, did it, or who she employed to do it. She answered she did not know that the Devil goes about in her likeness to do any hurt. Sarah Osburne, being told that Sarah Good, one of her companions, had, upon examination, accused her, she, notwithstanding, denied the same, according to her examination, which is more at large given in, as therein will appear."

The following is in the handwriting of Ezekiel Cheever : —

" *Sarah Osburn her Examination.*

" What evil spirit have you familiarity with ? — None.

" Have you made no contract with the Devil ? — No : I never saw the Devil in my life.

" Why do you hurt these children ? — I do not hurt them.

" Who do you employ, then, to hurt them?—I employ nobody.

" What familiarity have you with Sarah Good?—None: I have not seen her these two years.

" Where did you see her then?—One day, agoing to town.

" What communications had you with her?—I had none, only ' How do you do?' or so. I do not know her by name.

" What did you call her, then?

" (Osburn made a stand at that; at last, said she called her Sarah.)

" Sarah Good saith that it was you that hurt the children. —I do not know that the Devil goes about in my likeness to do any hurt.

" Mr. Hathorne desired all the children to stand up, and look upon her, and see if they did know her, which they all did; and every one of them said that this was one of the women that did afflict them, and that they had constantly seen her in the very habit that she was now in. Three evidences declared that she said this morning, that she was more like to be bewitched than that she was a witch. Mr. Hathorne asked her what made her say so. She answered that she was frighted one time in her sleep, and either saw, or dreamed that she saw, a thing like an Indian all black, which did pinch her in her neck, and pulled her by the back part of her head to the door of the house.

" Did you never see any thing else?—No.

" (It was said by some in the meeting-house, that she had said that she would never believe that lying spirit any more.)

" What lying spirit is this? Hath the Devil ever deceived you, and been false to you?—I do not know the Devil. I never did see him.

" What lying spirit was it, then ? — It was a voice that I thought I heard.

" What did it propound to you ? — That I should go no more to meeting ; but I said I would, and did go the next sabbath-day.

" Were you never tempted further ? — No.

" Why did you yield thus far to the Devil as never to go to meeting since ? — Alas ! I have been sick, and not able to go.

" Her husband and others said that she had not been at meeting three years and two months."

The foregoing illustrates the unfairness practised by the examining magistrate. He took·for granted, as we shall find to have been the case in all instances, the guilt of the prisoner, and endeavored to entangle her by leading questions, thus involving her in contradiction. By the force of his own assumptions, he had compelled Sarah Good to admit the reality of the sufferings of the girls, and that they must be caused by some one. The amount of what she had said was, that, if caused by one or the other of them, " then it must be Osburn," for she was sure of her own innocence. This expression, to which she was driven in self-exculpation, was perverted by the reporter, Ezekiel Cheever, and by the magistrate, into an indirect confession and a direct accusation of Osburn. In the absence of Good, the magistrate told Osburn that Good had confessed and accused her. This was a misrepresentation of one, and a false and fraudulent trick upon the other. Considering the feeble condition of Sarah Osburn generally, the snares by which she was beset, the distressing and bewildering circumstances in which she was placed, and the infirm state of her reason, as evidenced in her statement of what she saw, or dreamed that she saw and heard, — not having a clear idea which, — her answers, as reported by the prosecutors, show that her broken and disordered mind was essentially truthful and innocent.

Sarah Osburn was removed from the meeting-house, and Tituba brought in and examined, as follows : —

"Tituba, what evil spirit have you familiarity with ? — None.

"Why do you hurt these children ? — I do not hurt them.

"Who is it then ? — The Devil, for aught I know.

"Did you never see the Devil ? — The Devil came to me, and bid me serve him.

"Who have you seen ? — Four women sometimes hurt the children.

"Who were they ? — Goody Osburn and Sarah Good, and I do not know who the others were. Sarah Good and Osburn would have me hurt the children, but I would not.

"(She further saith there was a tall man of Boston that she did see.)

"When did you see them ? — Last night, at Boston.

"What did they say to you ? — They said, 'Hurt the children.'

"And did you hurt them ? — No : there is four women and one man, they hurt the children, and then they lay all upon me ; and they tell me, if I will not hurt the children, they will hurt me.

" But did you not hurt them ? — Yes ; but I will hurt them no more.

" Are you not sorry that you did hurt them ? — Yes.

" And why, then, do you hurt them ? — They say, ' Hurt children, or we will do worse to you.'

" What have you seen ? — A man come to me, and say, ' Serve me.'

" What service ? — Hurt the children : and last night there was an appearance that said, ' Kill the children ; ' and, if I would not go on hurting the children, they would do worse to me.

" What is this appearance you see ? — Sometimes it is like a hog, and sometimes like a great dog.

" (This appearance she saith she did see four times.)

" What did it say to you ? — The black dog said, ' Serve me ; ' but I said, ' I am afraid.' He said, if I did not, he would do worse to me.

" What did you say to it ? — I will serve you no longer. Then he said he would hurt me ; and then he looks like a man, and threatens to hurt me. (She said that this man had a yellow-bird that kept with him.) And he told me he had more pretty things that he would give me, if I would serve him.

" What were these pretty things ? — He did not show me them.

" What else have you seen ? — Two cats ; a red cat, and a black cat.

" What did they say to you ? — They said, ' Serve me.'

" When did you see them ? — Last night ; and they said, ' Serve me ; ' but I said I would not.

" What service ? — She said, hurt the children.

" Did you not pinch Elizabeth Hubbard this morning?
— The man brought her to me, and made pinch her.

" Why did you go to Thomas Putnam's last night, and
hurt his child? — They pull and haul me, and make go.

" And what would they have you do? — Kill her with a
knife.

" (Lieutenant Fuller and others said at this time, when
the child saw these persons, and was tormented by them,
that she did complain of a knife, — that they would have
her cut her head off with a knife.)

" How did you go? — We ride upon sticks, and are there
presently.

" Do you go through the trees or over them? — We see
nothing, but are there presently.

" Why did you not tell your master? — I was afraid:
they said they would cut off my head if I told.

" Would you not have hurt others, if you could? — They
said they would hurt others, but they could not.

" What attendants hath Sarah Good? — A yellow-bird,
and she would have given me one.

" What meat did she give it? — It did suck her between
her fingers.

" Did you not hurt Mr. Curren's child? — Goody Good
and Goody Osburn told that they did hurt Mr. Curren's
child, and would have had me hurt him too; but I did not.

" What hath Sarah Osburn? — Yesterday she had a thing
with a head like a woman, with two legs and wings.

" (Abigail Williams, that lives with her uncle Mr. Parris,
said that she did see the same creature, and it turned into
the shape of Goodie Osburn.)

" What else have you seen with Osburn? — Another
thing, hairy: it goes upright like a man, it hath only two legs.

" Did you not see Sarah Good upon Elizabeth Hubbard,
last Saturday ? — I did see her set a wolf upon her to afflict
her.

" (The persons with this maid did say that she did complain of a wolf. She further said that she saw a cat with
Good at another time.)

" What clothes doth the man go in ? — He goes in black
clothes ; a tall man, with white hair, I think.

" How doth the woman go ? — In a white hood, and a
black hood with a top-knot.

" Do you see who it is that torments these children now ?
— Yes : it is Goody Good ; she hurts them in her own shape.

" Who is it that hurts them now ? — I am blind now : I
cannot see.

" Written by EZEKIEL CHEEVER.

"SALEM VILLAGE, March the 1st, 1692."

Another report of Tituba's examination has been
preserved, and may be found in the second volume of
the collection edited by Samuel G. Drake, entitled the
" Witchcraft Delusion in New England." It is in the
handwriting of Jonathan Corwin, very full and minute,
and shows that the Indian woman was familiar with all
the ridiculous and monstrous fancies then prevalent.
The details of her statement cover nearly the whole
ground of them. While indicating, in most respects,
a mind at the lowest level of general intelligence,
they give evidence of cunning and wariness in the
highest degree. This document is also valuable, as
it affords information about particulars, incidentally
mentioned and thus rescued from oblivion, which

serve to bring back the life of the past. Tituba describes the dresses of some of the witches: " A black
silk hood, with a white silk hood under it, with top-
knots." One of them wore " a serge coat, with a white
cap." The Devil appeared " in black clothes sometimes, sometimes serge coat of other color." She
speaks of the " lean-to chamber " in the parsonage, and
describes an aërial night ride " up " to Thomas Putnam's. " How did you go ? What did you ride
upon ?" asked the wondering magistrate. " I ride
upon a stick, or pole, and Good and Osburn behind
me : we ride taking hold of one another ; don't know
how we go, for I saw no trees nor path, but was presently there when we were up." In both reports, Tituba
describes, quite graphically, the likenesses in which the
Devil appeared to his confederates ; but Corwin gives
the details more fully than Cheever. What the latter
reports of the appearances in which the Devil accompanied Osburn, the former amplifies. " The thing with
two legs and wings, and a face like a woman," " turns "
into a full woman. The " hairy thing " becomes " a
thing all over hairy, all the face hairy, and a long nose,
and I don't know how to tell how the face looks ; is
about two or three feet high, and goeth upright like a
man ; and, last night, it stood before the fire in Mr.
Parris's hall."

It is quite evident that the part played by the Indian
woman on this occasion was pre-arranged. She had,
from the first, been concerned with the circle of
girls in their necromantic operations ; and her state-

ments show the materials out of which their ridiculous and monstrous stories were constructed. She
said that there were four who "hurt the children."
Upon being pressed by the magistrate to tell who they
were, she named Osburn and Good, but did "not know
who the others were." Two others were marked; but
it was not thought best to bring them out until these
three examinations had first been made to tell upon
the public mind. Tituba had been apprised of Elizabeth Hubbard's story, that she had been "pinched"
that morning; and, as well as "Lieutenant Fuller
and others," had heard of the delirious exclamation of
Thomas Putnam's sick child during the night. "Abigail Williams, that lives with her uncle Parris,"
had communicated to the Indian slave the story of
"the woman with two legs and wings." In fact, she
had been fully admitted to their councils, and made
acquainted with all the stories they were to tell. But,
when it became necessary to avoid specifications
touching parties whose names it had been decided not
to divulge at that stage of the business, the wily old
servant escapes further interrogation, "I am blind
now: I cannot see."

Proceedings connected with these examinations were
continued several days. The result appears, in the
handwriting of John Hathorne, as follows: —

"Salem Village, March 1, 169½. — Tituba, an Indian
woman, brought before us by Constable Jos. Herrick, of
Salem, upon suspicion of witchcraft by her committed, according to the complaint of Jos. Hutchinson and Thomas

Putnam, &c., of Salem Village, as appears per warrant granted, Salem, 29th February, 169½. Tituba, upon examination, and after some denial, acknowledged the matter of fact, as, according to her examination given in, more fully will appear, and who also charged Sarah Good and Sarah Osburn with the same.

"Salem Village, March the 1st, 169½. — Sarah Good, Sarah Osburn, and Tituba, an Indian woman, all of Salem Village, being this day brought before us, upon suspicion of witchcraft, &c., by them and every one of them committed; Tituba, an Indian woman, acknowledging the matter of fact, and Sarah Osburn and Sarah Good denying the same before us; but there appearing, in all their examinations, sufficient ground to secure them all. And, in order to further examination, they were all *per mittimus* sent to the jails in the county of Essex.

"Salem, March 2. — Sarah Osburn again examined, and also Tituba, as will appear in their examinations given in. Tituba again acknowledged the fact, and also accused the other two.

"Salem, March 3. — Sarah Osburn, and Tituba, Indian, again examined. The examination now given in. Tituba again said the same.

"Salem, March 5. — Sarah Good and Tituba again examined; and, in their examination, Tituba acknowledged the same she did formerly, and accused the other two above said.

" Salem, March the 7th, 169½. — Sarah Good, Sarah Osburn, and Tituba, an Indian woman, all sent to the jail in Boston, according to their *mittimuses*, then sent to their Majesties' jail-keeper."

It will be noticed that the magistrates did not venture to put into this their final record, what they had unfairly tried to make Sarah Osborn believe, that Sarah Good had been a witness against her. The jail at Ipswich was at a distance of at least ten miles from the village meeting-house, by any road that could then have been travelled. The transferrence of the prisoners day after day must have been very fatiguing to a sick woman like Sarah Osburn. Sarah Good seems to have been able to bear it. Samuel Braybrook, an assistant constable, having charge of her, says, that, on the way to Ipswich, she " leaped off her horse three times ; " that she " railed against the magistrates, and endeavored to kill herself." He further testified, that, at the very time she was performing these feats, Thomas Putnam's daughter, " at her father's house, declared the same." As Braybrook was many miles from Thomas Putnam's house, at the moment when his wonderful daughter exercised this miraculous extent of vision, it would have been more satisfactory to have had some other testimony to the fact. I mention this to show of what stuff the evidence in these cases was made, and the credulity with which every thing was swallowed. The prisoners were put to examination each day.

Osburn and Good steadily maintained their innocence. Tituba all along declared herself guilty, and

accused the other two of having been with her in confederacy with the Devil.   Mr. Parris made the following deposition, in relation to these examinations, to
which he subsequently swore in Court, at the trial of
Sarah Good : —

" THE DEPOSITION OF SAM : PARRIS, aged about thirty
and nine years. — Testifieth and saith, that Elizabeth Parris, Jr., and Abigail Williams, and Ann Putnam, Jr.,
and Elizabeth Hubbard, were most grievously and several
times tortured during the examination of Sarah Good, Sarah
Osburn, and Tituba, Indian, before the magistrates at Salem
Village, 1 March, 1692.   And the said Tituba being the last
of the above said that was examined, they, the above said
afflicted persons, were grievously distressed until the said
Indian began to confess, and then they were immediately
all quiet the rest of the said Indian woman's examination.
Also Thomas Putnam, aged about forty years, and Ezekiel
Cheever, aged about thirty and six years, testify to the whole
of the above said ; and all the three deponents aforesaid
further testify, that, after the said Indian began to confess,
she was herself very much afflicted, and in the face of
authority at the same time, and openly charged the abovesaid Good and Osburn as the persons that afflicted her, the
aforesaid Indian."

By comparing these depositions with the other documents I have presented, it will be seen how admirably
the whole affair was arranged, so far as concerned the
part played by Tituba. She commences her testimony
by declaring her innocence.   The afflicted children
are instantly thrown into torments, which, however,

subside as soon as she begins to confess. Immediately after commencing her confession, and as she proceeds in it, she herself becomes tormented "in the face of authority," before the eyes of the magistrates and the awestruck crowd. Her power to afflict ceases as she breaks loose from her compact with the Devil, who sends some unseen confederate, not then brought to light, to wreak his vengeance upon her for having confessed. Tituba, as well as the girls, showed herself an adept in the arts taught in the circle.

All we know of Sarah Osburn beyond this date are the following items in the Boston jailer's bill "against the country," dated May 29, 1692: "To chains for Sarah Good and Sarah Osburn, 14 shillings:" "To the keeping of Sarah Osburn, from the 7th of March to the 10th of May, when she died, being nine weeks and two days, £1. 3s. 5d."

The only further information we have of Tituba is from Calef, who says, "The account she since gives of it is, that her master did beat her, and otherwise abuse her, to make her confess and accuse (such as he called) her sister-witches; and that whatsoever she said by way of confessing or accusing others was the effect of such usage: her master refused to pay her fees, unless she would stand to what she had said. Calef further states that she laid in jail until finally "sold for her fees." The jailer's charge for her "diet in prison for a year and a month" appears in a shape that corroborates Calef's statements, which were prepared for publication in 1697, and printed in London in 1700.

Although zealously devoted to the work of exposing the enormities connected with the witchcraft prosecutions, there is no ground to dispute the veracity of Calef as to matters of fact. What he says of the declarations of Tituba, subsequent to her examination, is quite consistent with a critical analysis of the details of the record of that examination. It can hardly be doubted, whatever the amount of severity employed to make her act the part assigned her, that she was used as an instrument to give effect to the delusion.

Now let us consider the state of things that had been brought about in the village, and in the surrounding country, at the close of the first week in March, 1692. The terrible sufferings of the girls in Mr. Parris's family and of their associates, for the two preceding months, had become known far and wide. A universal sympathy was awakened in their behalf; and a sentiment of horror sunk deep into all hearts, at the dread demonstration of the diabolical rage in their afflicted and tortured persons. A few, very few, distrusted; but the great majority, ninety-nine in a hundred of all the people, were completely swept into the torrent. Nathaniel Putnam and Nathaniel Ingersoll were entirely deluded, and continued so to the end. Even Joseph Hutchinson was, for a while, carried away. The physicians had all given their opinion that the girls were suffering from an " evil hand." The neighboring ministers, after a day's fasting and prayer, and a scrutinizing inspection of the condition of the afflicted children, had given it, as

the result of their most solemn judgment, that it was
a case of witchcraft. Persons from the neighboring
towns had come to the place, and with their own eyes
received demonstration of the same fact. Mr. Parris
made it the topic of his public prayers and preaching.
The girls, Sunday after Sunday, were under the malign
influence, to the disturbance and affrightment of the
congregation. In all companies, in all families, all
the day long, the sufferings and distraction occurring
in the houses of Mr. Parris, Thomas Putnam, and
others, and in the meeting-house, were topics of excited conversation; and every voice was loud in demanding, every mind earnest to ascertain, who were
the persons, in confederacy with the Devil, thus torturing, pinching, convulsing, and bringing to the last
extremities of mortal agony, these afflicted girls.
Every one felt, that, if the guilty authors of the mischief could not be discovered, and put out of the way,
no one was safe for a moment. At length, when the
girls cried out upon Good, Osburn, and Tituba, there
was a general sense of satisfaction and relief. It was
thought that Satan's power might be checked. The selection of the first victims was well made. They were
just the kind of persons whom the public prejudice
and credulity were prepared to suspect and condemn.
Their examination was looked for with the utmost interest, and all flocked to witness the proceedings.

   In considering the state of mind of the people,
as they crowded into and around the old meeting-
house, we can have no difficulty in realizing the

tremendous effects of what there occurred. It was felt that then, on that spot, the most momentous crisis in the world's history had come. A crime, in comparison with which all other crimes sink out of notice, was being notoriously and defiantly committed in their midst. The great enemy of God and man was let loose among them. What had filled the hearts of mankind for ages, the world over, with dread apprehension, was come to pass; and in that village the great battle, on whose issue the preservation of the kingdom of the Lord on the earth was suspended, had begun. Indeed, no language, no imagery, no conception of ours, can adequately express the feeling of awful and terrible solemnity with which all were overwhelmed. No body of men ever convened in a more highly wrought state of excitement than pervaded that assembly, when the magistrates entered, in all their stern authority, and the scene opened on the 1st of March, 1692. A minister, probably Mr. Parris, began, according to the custom of the times, with prayer. From what we know of his skill and talent in meeting such occasions, it may well be supposed that his language and manner heightened still more the passions of the hour. The marshal, of tall and imposing stature and aspect, accompanied by his constables, brought in the prisoners. Sarah Good, a poverty-stricken, wandering, and wretched victim of ill-fortune and ill-usage, was put to the bar. Every effort was made by the examining magistrate, aided by the officious interference of the marshal, or other deluded or

evil-disposed persons, — who, like him, were permitted
to interpose with charges or abusive expressions, — to
overawe and confound, involve in contradictions, and
mislead the poor creature, and force her to confess
herself guilty and accuse others. In due time, the
" afflicted children " were brought in ; and a scene
ensued, such as no person in that crowd or in that
generation had ever witnessed before. Immediately
on being confronted with the prisoner, and meeting
her eye, they fell, as if struck dead, to the floor; or
screeched in agony ; or went into fearful spasms or
convulsive fits ; or cried out that they were pricked with
pins, pinched, or throttled by invisible hands. They
were severally brought up to the prisoner, and, upon
touching her person, instantly became calm, quiet,
and fully restored to their senses. With one voice
they all declared that Sarah Good had thus tormented
them, by her power as a witch in league with the
Devil. The truth of this charge, in the effect produced by the malign influence proceeding from her,
was thus visible to all eyes. All saw, too, how instantly upon touching her the diabolical effect ceased ;
the malignant fluid passing back, like an electric stream,
into the body of the witch. The spectacle was repeated once and again, the acting perfect, and the delusion consummated. The magistrates and all present
considered the guilt of the prisoner demonstrated, and
regarded her as wilfully and wickedly obstinate in not
at once confessing what her eyes, as well as theirs,
saw. Her refusal to confess was considered as the

highest proof of her guilt. They passed judgment against her, committed her to the marshal, who hurried her to prison, bound her with cords, and loaded her with irons ; for it was thought that no ordinary fastenings could hold a witch. Similar proceedings, with suitable variations, were had with Sarah Osburn and Tituba. The confession of the last-named, the immediate relief thereafter of the afflicted children, and the dreadful torments which Tituba herself experienced, on the spot, from the unseen hand of the Devil wreaking vengeance upon her, put the finishing touch to the delusion. The excitement was kept up, and spread far and wide, by the officers and magistrates riding in cavalcade, day after day, to and from the town and village ; and by the constables, with their assistants, carrying their manacled prisoners from jail to jail in Ipswich, Salem, and Boston.

The point was now reached when the accusers could safely strike at higher game. But time was taken to mature arrangements. Great curiosity was felt to know who the other two were whom Tituba saw in connection with Good and Osburn in their hellish operations. The girls continued to suffer torments and fall in fits, and were constantly urged by large numbers of people, going from house to house to witness their sufferings, to reveal who the witches were that still afflicted them. When all was prepared, they began to cry out, with more or less distinctness ; at first, in significant but general descriptions, and at last calling names. The next victim was also well chosen. An account has been given, in the First Part, of the notoriety which circumstances had attached to Giles Corey. In 1691 he became a member of the church, being then (Vol. I. p. 182) eighty years of age. Four daughters, all probably by his first wife Margaret, the only children of whom there is any mention, were married to John Moulton, John Parker, and Henry Crosby, of Salem, and William Cleaves, of Beverly. On the 11th of April, 1664, Corey was married to Mary Britt, who died, as appears by the inscription on her gravestone in the old Salem burial-ground, Aug. 27, 1684. Martha was his third wife. Her age is unknown. It was entered on the record of the village church, at the time of her admission to it, April 27, 1690; but the figures are worn away from the edge of the page. She was a very intelligent and devout person.

When the proceedings relating to witchcraft began, she did not approve of them, and expressed her want of faith in the "afflicted children." She discountenanced the whole affair, and would not follow the multitude to the examinations; but was said to have spoken freely of the course of the magistrates, saying that their eyes were blinded, and that she could open them. It seemed to her clear that they were violating common sense and the Word of God, and she was confident that she could convince them of their errors. Instead of falling into the delusion, she applied herself with renewed earnestness to keep her own mind under the influence of prayer, and

spent more time in devotion than ever before. Her
husband, however, was completely carried away by
the prevalent fanaticism, believed all he heard, and
frequented the examinations and the exhibitions of
the afflicted children. This disagreement became
quite serious. Her preferring to stay at home, shun-
ning the proceedings, and expressing her disapprobation of what was going on, caused an estrangement
between them. Her peculiar course created comment, in which he and two of his sons-in-law took
part. Some strong expressions were used by him,
because she acted so strangely at variance with everybody else. Her spending so much time on her knees
in devotion was looked upon as a matter of suspicion.
It was said that she tried to prevent him from following up the examinations, and went so far as to remove
the saddle from the horse brought up to convey him
to some meeting at the village connected with the
witchcraft excitement. Angry words, uttered by him,
were heard and repeated. As she was a woman of
notable piety, a professor of religion, and a member
of the church, it was evident that her case, if she were
proceeded against, would still more heighten the panic,
and convulse the public mind. It would give ground
for an idea which the managers of the affair desired
to circulate, that the Devil had succeeded in making
inroads into the very heart of the church, and was
bringing into confederacy with him aged and eminent
church-members, who, under color of their profession,
threatened to extend his influence to the overthrow of

all religion. It was, indeed, established in the popular
sentiments, as a sign and mark of the Devil's coming,
that many professing godliness would join his standard.

For a day or two, it was whispered round that persons in great repute for piety were in the diabolical
confederacy, and about to be unmasked. The name
of Martha Corey, whose open opposition to the proceedings had become known, was passed among the
girls in an under-breath, and caught from one to another among those managing the affair. On the 12th
of March, Edward Putnam and Ezekiel Cheever, having
heard Ann Putnam declare that Goody Corey did
often appear to her, and torture her by pinching and
otherwise, thought it their duty to go to her, and see
what she would say to this complaint; " she being in
church covenant with us." They mounted their horses about " the middle of the afternoon," and first went
to the house of Thomas Putnam to see his daughter
Ann, to learn from her what clothes Goody Corey appeared to her in, in order to judge whether she might
not have been mistaken in the person. The girl told
them, that Goody Corey, knowing that they contemplated making this visit, had just appeared in spirit
to her, but had blinded her so that she could not
tell what clothes she wore. Highly wrought upon by
the extraordinary statement of the girl, which they
received with perfect credulity, the two brethren re-
mounted, and pursued their way. Goody Corey had
heard that her name had been bandied about by the
accusing girls : she also knew that it was one of their

arts to pretend to see the clothes people were wearing at the time their spectres appeared to them. This required, indeed, no great amount of necromancy; as it is not probable that there was much variety in the costume of farmer's wives, at that time, while about their ordinary domestic engagements.

They found her alone in her house. As soon as they commenced conversation, " in a smiling manner she said, ' I know what you are come for; you are come to talk with me about being a witch, but I am none: I cannot help people's talking of me.' " Edward Putnam acknowledged that their visit was in consequence of complaints made against her by the afflicted children. She inquired whether they had undertaken to describe the clothes she then wore. They answered that they had not, and proceeded to repeat what Ann Putnam had said to them about her blinding her so that she could not see her clothes. At this she smiled, no doubt at Ann's cunning artifice to escape having to say what dress she then had on. She declared to the two brethren, that " she did not think that there were any witches." After considerable talk, in which they did not get much to further their purpose, they took their leave. The account of this interview, given by Putnam and Cheever, indicates that Martha Corey was a sensible, enlightened, and sprightly woman, perfectly free from the delusion of the day, courteous in her manners and bearing, and a Christian, well grounded in Scripture.

The two brethren returned forthwith to Thomas

Putnam's house. Ann told them that Goody Corey had not troubled her, nor her spectre appeared, in their absence. She was not inclined to afford them an opportunity to apply the test of the dress. Both the women showed great acuteness and caution. As Corey expected the visit, and had heard that the girls pretended to be able to say what dress persons were wearing, she probably had attired herself in an unusual way on the occasion, to put them at fault, and expose the falseness of their claims to preternatural knowledge ; and Ann Putnam — her sagacity suggesting the risk she was running in the matter of Corey's dress — took refuge in the pretence of blindness. The brethren were too much under delusion to see through the sharp practice of both of them, but considered the fact of Corey's inquiring of them whether Ann described her dress, as, under the circumstances, proof positive against the former.

Wishing to make assurance doubly sure, and to fasten the charge upon Martha Corey, the managers of the affair sent for her to come to the house of Thomas Putnam two days after this conference. Edward Putnam was present, and testified that his niece Ann, immediately upon the entrance of Goodwife Corey, experienced the most dreadful convulsions and tortures and distinctly and positively declared that Corey was the author of her sufferings. This was regarded as conclusive evidence ; and, on the 19th of March, a warrant was issued for her arrest. She was brought to the house of Nathaniel Ingersoll, on Monday the

21st; and the following is the account of her examination, in the handwriting of Mr. Parris. The proceedings took place in the meeting-house at the village.
They were introduced by a prayer from the Rev.
Nicholas Noyes. On some of these occasions Mr.
Hale and perhaps others, but usually Mr. Noyes or
Mr. Parris officiated. We may suppose, from what
we know of their general deportment in connection
with these scenes, that their performances, under the
cover of a devotional exercise, expressed and enforced
a decided prejudgment of the case in hand against
the prisoners, and partook of the character of indictments as much as of prayers.

" *The Examination of Martha Corey.*

" Mr. HATHORNE : You are now in the hands of authority. Tell me, now, why you hurt these persons. — I do not.

" Who doth ? — Pray, give me leave to go to prayer.

" (This request was made sundry times.)

" We do not send for you to go to prayer ; but tell me why
you hurt these. — I am an innocent person. I never had to
do with witchcraft since I was born. I am a gospel woman.

" Do not you see these complain of you ? — The Lord
open the eyes of the magistrates and ministers : the Lord
show his power to discover the guilty.

" Tell us who hurts these children. — I do not know.

" If you be guilty of this fact, do you think you can hide
it ? — The Lord knows.

" Well, tell us what you know of this matter. — Why,
I am a gospel woman; and do you think I can have to do
with witchcraft too ?

" How could you tell, then, that the child was bid to observe what clothes you wore, when some came to speak with you ?

" (Cheever interrupted her, and bid her not begin with a lie ; and so Edward Putnam declared the matter.)

" Mr. HATHORNE :   Who told you that ? — He said the child said.

" CHEEVER : You speak falsely.

" (Then Edward Putnam read again.)

" Mr. HATHORNE : Why did you ask if the child told what clothes you wore ? — My husband told me the others told.

" Who told you about the clothes ?   Why did you ask that question ? — Because I heard the children told what clothes the others wore.

" Goodman Corey, did you tell her ?

" .(The old man denied that he told her so.)

" Did you not say your husband told you so ?

" (No answer.)

" Who hurts these children ?   Now look upon them. — I cannot help it.

" Did you not say you would tell the truth why you asked that question ? how came you to the knowledge ? — I did but ask.

" You dare thus to lie in all this assembly.   You are now before authority.   I expect the truth : you promised it. Speak now, and tell who told you what clothes. — Nobody.

" How came you to know that the children would be examined what clothes you wore ? — Because I thought the child was wiser than anybody if she knew.

" Give an answer : you said your husband told you. — He told me the children said I afflicted them.

" How do you know what they came for ?   Answer me this truly : will you say how you came to know what they came for? — I had heard speech that the children said I troubled them, and I thought that they might come to examine.

"But how did you know it? — I thought they did.

"Did not you say you would tell the truth? who told you what they came for? — Nobody.

"How did you know? — I did think so.

"But you said you knew so.

"(CHILDREN : There is a man whispering in her ear.)

"HATHORNE continued : What did he say to you ? — We must not believe all that these distracted children say.

"Cannot you tell what that man whispered? — I saw nobody.

"But did not you hear? — No.

"(Here was extreme agony of all the afflicted.)

"If you expect mercy of God, you must look for it in God's way, by confession. Do you think to find mercy by aggravating your sins? — A true thing.

"Look for it, then, in God's way. — So I do.

"Give glory to God and confess, then. — But I cannot confess.

"Do not you see how these afflicted do charge you? — We must not believe distracted persons.

"Who do you improve to hurt them? — I improved none.

"Did not you say our eyes were blinded, you would open them? — Yes, to accuse the innocent.

"(Then Crosby gave in evidence.)

"Why cannot the girl stand before you? — I do not know.

"What did you mean by that? — I saw them fall down.

"It seems to be an insulting speech, as if they could not stand before you. — They cannot stand before others.

"But you said they cannot stand before you. Tell me

what was that turning upon the spit by you ? — You believe the children that are distracted. I saw no spit.

" Here are more than two that accuse you for witchcraft. What do you say ? — I am innocent.

" (Then Mr. Hathorne read further of Crosby's evidence.)

" What did you mean by that, — the Devil could not stand before you ?

" (She denied it. Three or four sober witnesses confirmed it.)

" What can I do ? Many rise up against me.

" Why, confess. — So I would, if I were guilty.

" Here are sober persons. What do you say to them ? You are a gospel woman ; will you lie ?

" (Abigail cried out, ' Next sabbath is sacrament-day ; but she shall not come there.')

" I do not care.

" You charge these children with distraction : it is a note of distraction when persons vary in a minute ; but these fix upon you. This is not the manner of distraction. — When all are against me, what can I help it ?

" Now tell me the truth, will you ? Why did you say that the magistrates' and ministers' eyes were blinded, you would open them ?

" (She laughed, and denied it.)

" Now tell us how we shall know who doth hurt these, if you do not ? — Can an innocent person be guilty ?

" Do you deny these words ? — Yes.

" Tell us who hurts these. We came to be a terror to evil-doers. You say you would open our eyes, we are blind. — If you say I am a witch.

" You said you would show us.

" (She denied it.)

" Why do you not now show us ? — I cannot tell : I do not know.

" What did you strike the maid at Mr. Tho. Putnam's with ? — I never struck her in my life.

" There are two that saw you strike her with an iron rod. — I had no hand in it.

" Who had ? Do you believe these children are bewitched ? — They may, for aught I know : I have no hand in it.

" You say you are no witch. Maybe you mean you never covenanted with the Devil. Did you never deal with any familiar ? — No, never.

" What bird was that the children spoke of ?

" (Then witnesses spoke : What bird was it ?)

" I know no bird.

" It may be you have engaged you will not confess ; but God knows. — So he doth.

" Do you believe you shall go unpunished ? — I have nothing to do with witchcraft.

" Why was you not willing your husband should come to the former session here ? — But he came, for all.

" Did not you take the saddle off ? — I did not know what it was for.

" Did you not know what it was for ? — I did not know that it would be to any benefit.

" (Somebody said that she would not have them help to find out witches.)

" Did you not say you would open our eyes ? Why do you not ? — I never thought of a witch.

" Is it a laughing matter to see these afflicted persons ?

" (She denied it. Several prove it.)

" Ye are all against me, and I cannot help it.

" Do not you believe there are witches in the country ? — I do not know that there is any.

" Do not you know that Tituba confessed it ? — I did not hear her speak.

" I find you will own nothing without several witnesses, and yet you will deny for all.

" (It was noted, when she bit her lip, several of the afflicted were bitten. When she was urged upon it that she bit her lip, saith she, What harm is there in it ?)

" (Mr. NOYES : I believe it is apparent she practiseth witchcraft in the congregation : there is no need of images.)

" What do you say to all these things that are apparent ? — If you will all go hang me, how can I help it ?

" Were you to serve the Devil ten years ? Tell how many.

" (She laughed. The children cried there was a yellow-bird with her. When Mr. Hathorne asked her about it, she laughed. When her hands were at liberty, the afflicted persons were pinched.)

" Why do not you tell how the Devil comes in your shape, and hurts these ? You said you would. — How can I know how ?

" Why did you say you would show us ?

" (She laughed again.)

" What book is that you would have these children write in ? — What book ? Where should I have a book ? I showed them none, nor have none, nor brought none.

" (The afflicted cried out there was a man whispering in her ears.)

" What book did you carry to Mary Walcot ? — I carried none. If the Devil appears in my shape —

" (Then Needham said that Parker, some time ago, thought this woman was a witch.)

" Who is your God ? — The God that made me.

" What is his name ? — Jehovah.

" Do you know any other name ? — God Almighty.

" Doth *he* tell you, that you pray to, that *he* is God Almighty ? — Who do I worship but the God that made [me] ?

" How many gods are there ? — One.

" How many persons ? — Three.

" Cannot you say, So there is one God in three blessed persons ?

[The answer is destroyed, being written in the fold of the paper, and wholly worn off.]

" Do not you see these children and women are rational and sober as their neighbors, when your hands are fastened ?

" (Immediately they were seized with fits : and the standers-by said she was squeezing her fingers, her hands being eased by them that held them on purpose for trial.

" Quickly after, the marshal said, ' She hath bit her lip ; ' and immediately the afflicted were in an uproar.)

" [Tell] why you hurt these, or who doth ?

" (She denieth any hand in it.)

" Why did you say, if you were a witch, you should have no pardon ? — Because I am a   woman."

" Salem Village, March the 21st, 1692. — The Reverend Mr. Samuel Parris, being desired to take, in writing, the examination of Martha Corey, hath returned it, as aforesaid.

" Upon hearing the aforesaid, and seeing what we did then see, together with the charges of the persons then present, we committed Martha Corey, the wife of Giles Corey, of Salem Farms, unto the gaol in Salem, as *per mittimus* then given out.

The foregoing is a full copy of the original document. One of Giles Corey's daughters, Deliverance, had married, June 5, 1683, Henry Crosby, who lived on land conveyed to him by her father in the immediate neighborhood. He was the person whose written testimony was read by the magistrate. Its purport seems to have been to prove that Martha Corey had said that the accusing girls could not stand before her, and that the Devil could not stand before her. She had, undoubtedly, great confidence in her own innocence, and in the power of truth and prayer, to silence false accusers, and expressed herself in the forcible language which Parris's report of the examination shows that she was well able to use. It is almost amusing to see how the pride of the magistrates was touched, and their wrath kindled, by what she was reported to have said, "that the magistrates' and ministers' eyes were blinded, and that she would open them." It rankled in Hathorne's breast: he returns to it again and again, and works himself up to a higher degree of resentment on each recurrence. Mr. Noyes's ire was roused, and he, too, put in a stroke. It will be noticed, that she avoided a contradiction of her husband, and could not be brought to give the names of persons from whom she had received information. "If you will all go hang me, how can I help it?" "Ye are all against me." "What can I do, when many rise up against me?" "When all are against me, what can I [say to] help it?" Situated as she was, all that she could do was to give them no advantage, or opportunity to ensnare her, and to avoid compromising others; and it must be allowed that she showed much presence and firmness of mind. Her request, made at the opening of the examination, and at "sundry times," to "go to prayer," somewhat confounded them. She probably was led to make and urge the request particularly in consequence of the tenor of Mr. Noyes's prayer at the opening. She felt that it was no more than fair that there should be a prayer on her side, as well as on the other. It might well be feared, that, if allowed to offer a prayer, coming from a person in her situation, an aged professor, and one accustomed to express herself in devotional exercises, it might produce a deep impression upon the whole assembly. To refuse such a request had a hard look; but, as the magistrates saw, it never would have done to have permitted it. It would have reversed the position of all concerned. The latter part of the examination has the appearance that she was suspected to be unsound on a particular article of the prevalent creed. It is much to be regretted that the abrasion of the paper at the folding has obliterated her last answer to this part of the inquisition. It is singular that Mr. Parris has left the blank in her final answer. Probably she used her customary expression, " I am a gospel woman." The writing, at this point, is very clear and distinct ; and a vacant space is left, just as it is given above.

The fact that Martha Corey was known to be an eminently religious person, and very much given to acts of devotion, constituted a serious obstacle, no doubt, in the way of the prosecutors. Parris's record of the examination shows how they managed to get over it. They gave the impression that her frequent and long prayers were addressed to the Devil.

The disagreement between her and her husband, touching the witchcraft prosecutions, brought him into a very uncomfortable predicament. With his characteristic imprudence of speech, he had probably expressed himself strongly against her unbelief in the sufferings of the girls and her refusal to attend the exhibitions of their tortures, or the examination of persons accused. He was, unquestionably, highly shocked and incensed at her open repudiation of the whole doctrine of witchcraft. Although he had become, in his old age, a professor and a fervently religious man, perhaps he fell back, in his resentment of her course, into his life-long rough phrases, and said that she acted as though the Devil was in her. He might have said that she prayed like a witch. Being entirely carried away by the delusion, he had his own marvellous stories to tell about his cattle's being be-

witched, &c.   His talk, undoubtedly, came to the
ears of the prosecutors ; and they seem to have taken
steps to induce him to come forward as a witness
against her.   The following document is among the
papers : —

"The evidence of Giles Corey testifieth and saith, that
last Saturday, in the evening, sitting by the fire, my wife
asked me to go to bed. I told her I would go to prayer ;
and, when I went to prayer, I could not utter my desires
with any sense, nor open my mouth to speak.

"My wife did perceive it, and came towards me, and said
she was coming to me.

"After this, in a little space, I did, according to my
measure, attend the duty.

"Some time last week, I fetched an ox, well, out of the
woods about noon ; and, he laying down in the yard, I went
to raise him to yoke him ; but he could not rise, but dragged
his hinder parts, as if he had been hip-shot. But after did
rise.

"I had a cat sometimes last week strangely taken on the
sudden, and did make me think she would have died presently. My wife bid me knock her in the head, but I did
not ; and since, she is well.

"Another time, going to duties, I was interrupted for a
space ; but afterward I was helped according to my poor
measure. My wife hath been wont to sit up after I went to
bed : and I have perceived her to kneel down on the hearth,
as if she were at prayer, but heard nothing.

"*At the examination of Sarah* Good and others, my
wife was willing

"March 24, 1692."

The foregoing document does not express the idea
that he thought his wife was a witch. He states what
he observed, and what happened to him and to his
cattle. He evidently supposed they were bewitched,
and that he was obstructed, in going to prayer, in a
strange manner; but he does not, in terms, charge it
upon her. It gives an interesting insight of the inner-
most domestic life of the period, in a farmhouse, and
exhibits striking touches of the character and ways of
these two old people. It illustrates the state of the
imagination prevailing among those who were carried
away by the delusion. If an ox had a sprained muscle,
or a cat a fit of indigestion, it was thought to be the
work of an evil hand. Poor old Giles had come late to
a religious life, and, it is to be feared, was a novice in
prayer. It is no wonder that he was not an adept in
"uttering his desires," and experienced occasionally
some difficulty in arranging and expressing his devotional sentiments.

There is something very singular in the appearance
of the foregoing deposition. Purporting to be a piece
of testimony, it was not given in the usual and regular way. It does not indicate before whom it was
made. It is not attested in the ordinary manner;
apparently, was not sworn to in the presence of persons authorized to act in such cases; was never offered
in court or anywhere. It is a disconnected paper
found among the remnants of the miscellaneous collection in the clerk's office, and is evidently an un-
finished document; the words in Italics, at the close,
being erased by a line running through them.

It is probable that the parties who tried to get the old man to testify against his wife discovered that they could not draw any thing from him to answer their designs, but that there was danger that his evidence would be favorable to her, and gave up the attempt to use him on the occasion. The fact that he would not lend himself to their purposes perhaps led to resentment on their part, which may explain the subsequent proceedings against him.

The document, in its chirography, suggests the idea that it was written by Mr. Noyes, which is not improbable, as Corey was a member of his congregation and church. Noyes was deeply implicated in the prosecutions, and violent in driving them on. The handwriting of the original papers reveals the agency of those who were the most busy in procuring evidence against persons accused. That of Thomas Putnam occurs in very many instances. But Mr. Parris was, beyond all others, the busiest and most active prosecutor. The depositions of the child Abigail Williams, his niece and a member of his family, were written by him, as also a great number of others. He took down most of the examinations, put in a deposition of his own whenever he could, and was always ready to indorse those of others.

It will be remembered, that, when Tituba was put through her examination, she said " four women sometimes hurt the children." She named Good and Osburn, but pretended to have been blinded as to the others. Martha Corey was, in due time, as we

have seen, brought out. The fourth was the venerable
head of a large and prominent family, and a member
of the mother-church in Salem. She had never transferred her relations to the village church, with which,
however, she had generally worshipped, and probably
communed. Being one of the chief matrons of the
place, she was seated in the meeting-house with ladies
of similar age and standing, occupying the same bench
or compartment with the widow of Thomas Putnam,
Sr. The women were seated separately from the
men ; and the only rule applied among them was eminence in years and respectability.

It has always been considered strange and unaccountable, that a person of such acknowledged worth
as Rebecca Nurse, of infirm health and advanced
years, should have been selected among the early victims of the witchcraft prosecutions. Jealousies and
prejudices, such as often infest rural neighborhoods,
may have been engendered, in minds open to such
influences, by the prosperity and growing influence of
her family. It may be that animosities kindled by the
long and violent land controversy, with which many
parties had been incidentally connected, lingered in
some breasts. There are decided indications, that the
passions awakened by the angry contest between the
village and " Topsfield men," and which the collisions
of a half-century had all along exasperated and hardened, may have been concentrated against the Nurses.
Isaac Easty, whose wife was a sister of Rebecca Nurse,
and the Townes, who were her brothers or near kins-

men, were the leaders of the Topsfield men. It is a
significant circumstance, in this connection, that to
one of the most vehement resolutions passed at meetings of the inhabitants of the village, against the
claims of Topsfield, Samuel Nurse, her eldest son,
and Thomas Preston, her eldest son-in-law, entered
their protest on the record; and, on another similar
occasion, her husband Francis Nurse, her son Samuel,
and two of her sons-in-law, Preston and Tarbell, took
the same course. So far as the family sided with
Topsfield in that controversy, it naturally exposed
them to the ill-will of the people of the village. An
analysis of the names and residences of the persons
proceeded against, throughout the prosecutions, will
show to what an extent hostile motives were supplied
from this quarter. The families of Wildes, How,
Hobbs, Towne, Easty, and others who were "cried
out" upon by the afflicted children, occupied lands
claimed by parties adverse to the village. What,
more than all these causes, was sufficient to create a
feeling against the Nurses, is the fact that they were
opposed to the party which had existed from the beginning in the parish composed originally of the friends
of Bayley. To crown the whole, when the excitement
occasioned by the extraordinary doings in Mr. Parris's
family began to display itself, and the "afflicted children" were brought into notice, the members of this
family, with the exception, for a time, of Thomas Preston, discountenanced the whole thing. They absented
themselves from meeting, on account of the disturb-

ances and disorders the girls were allowed to make during the services of worship, in the congregation, on the Lord's Day. Unfriendly remarks, from whatever cause, made in the hearing of the girls, provided subjects for them to act upon. Some persons behind them, suggesting names in this way, whether carelessly or with malicious intent, were guilty of all the misery that was created and blood that was shed.

It became a topic of rumor, that Rebecca Nurse was soon to be brought out. It reached the ears of her friends, and the following document comes in at this point: —

"We whose names are underwritten being desired to go to Goodman Nurse his house, to speak with his wife, and to tell her that several of the afflicted persons mentioned her; and accordingly we went, and we found her in a weak and low condition in body as she told us, and had been sick almost a week. And we asked how it was otherwise with her: and she said she blessed God for it, she had more of his presence in this sickness than sometime she have had, but not so much as she desired; but she would, with the apostle, press forward to the mark; and many other places of Scripture to the like purpose. And then, of her own accord, she began to speak of the affliction that was amongst them, and in particular of Mr. Parris his family, and how she was grieved for them, though she had not been to see them, by reason of fits that she formerly used to have; for people said it was awful to behold: but she pitied them with all her heart, and went to God for them. But she said she heard that there was persons spoke of that were as innocent as she was, she believed; and, after much to this purpose, we told her we heard that she was spoken of also. ' Well,' she said, ' if it be so, the will of the Lord be done:' she sat still a while, being as it were amazed; and then she said, ' Well, as to this thing I am as innocent as the child unborn; but surely,' she said, ' what sin hath God found out in me unrepented of, that he should lay such an affliction upon me in my old age?' and, according to our best observation, we could not discern that she knew what we came for before we told her. ISRAEL PORTER,

ELIZABETH PORTER

" To the substance of what is above, we, if called thereto, are ready to testify on oath. DANIEL ANDREW, PETER CLOYSE."

Elizabeth Porter, who joins her husband in making this statement, was a sister of John Hathorne, the examining magistrate, and the mother-in-law of Joseph Putnam, who was among the very few that condemned the proceedings from the first. She stood, therefore, between the two parties. The character of each of the signers and indorsers of this interesting paper is sufficient proof that its statements are truthful. It cannot but excite the most affecting sensibilities in every breast. This venerable lady, whose conversation and bearing were so truly saint-like, was an invalid of extremely delicate condition and appearance, the mother of a large family, embracing sons, daughters, grandchildren, and one or more great-grandchildren. She was a woman of piety, and simplicity of heart. In all probability, she shared in the popular belief on the subject of witchcraft, and supposed that the sufferings of the children were real, and that they were afflicted by an " evil hand." At the very time that she was sorrowfully sympathizing with them and Mr. Parris's family, and praying for them, they were circulating suspicions against her, and maturing their plans for her destruction.

Rebecca Nurse was a daughter of William Towne, of Yarmouth, Norfolk County, England, where she was baptized, Feb. 21, 1621. Her sister Mary, who married Isaac Easty, was baptized at the same place, Aug. 24, 1634. The records of the First Church at Salem, Sept. 3, 1648, give the baptism of " Joseph and Sarah, children of Sister Towne." Sarah was at that time seven years of age. She became the wife of Edmund Bridges, and afterwards of Peter Cloyse.

On the 23d of March, a warrant was issued, on complaint of Edward Putnam, and Jonathan, son of John Putnam, for the arrest of " Rebecca, wife of Francis Nurse ; " and the next morning, at eight o'clock, she was brought to the house of Nathaniel Ingersoll, in the custody of George Herrick, the marshal of Essex. There were several distinct indictments, four of which, for having practised " certain detestable arts called witchcraft " upon Ann Putnam, Mary Walcot, Elizabeth Hubbard, and Abigail Williams, are preserved. The examination took place forthwith at the meeting-house. The age, character, connections, and appearance of the prisoner, made the occasion one of the extremest interest. Hathorne, the magistrate, began the proceedings by addressing one of the afflicted :

" What do you say? Have you seen this woman hurt you?" The answer was, "Yes, she beat me this morning." Hathorne, addressing another of the afflicted, said, "Abigail, have you been hurt by this woman?" Abigail answered, "Yes." At that point, Ann Putnam fell into a grievous fit, and, while in her spasms, cried out that it was Rebecca Nurse who was thus afflicting her. As soon as Ann's fit was over, and order restored, Hathorne said, "Goody Nurse, here are two, Ann Putnam the child, and Abigail Williams, complain of your hurting them. What do you say to it?" The prisoner replied, "I can say, before my eternal Father, I am innocent, and God will clear my innocency." Hathorne, apparently touched for the moment by her language and bearing, said, " Here is never a one in the assembly but desires it; but, if you be guilty, pray God discover you." Henry Kenney rose up from the body of the assembly to speak. Hathorne permitted the interruption, and said, " Goodman Kenney, what do you say?" Then Kenney complained of the prisoner, " and further said, since this Nurse came into the house, he was seized twice with an amazed condition." Hathorne, addressing the prisoner, said, "Not only these, but the wife of Mr. Thomas Putnam, accuseth you by credible information, and that both of tempting her to iniquity and of greatly hurting her." The prisoner again affirmed her innocence, and said, in answer to the charge of having hurt these persons, that " she had not been able to get out of doors these eight or nine days."

Hathorne then called upon Edward Putnam, who, as the record says, "gave in his relate," which undoubtedly was a statement of his having seen the afflicted in their sufferings, and heard them accuse Rebecca Nurse as their tormentor. Hathorne said, "Is this true, Goody Nurse?" She denied that she had ever hurt them or any one else in her life. Hathorne repeated, "You see these accuse you: is it true?" She answered, "No." He again put the question, "Are you an innocent person relating to this witchcraft?" It seems, from his manner, that he was beginning really to doubt whether she might not be innocent; and perhaps the feeling of the multitude was yielding in her favor.

Here Thomas Putnam's wife cried out, "Did you not bring the black man with you? Did you not bid me tempt God, and die? How oft have you eat and drank your own damnation?" This sudden outbreak, from such a source, accompanied with the wild and apparently supernatural energy and uncontrollable vehemence with which the words were uttered, roused the multitude to the utmost pitch of horror; and the prisoner seems to have been shocked at the dreadful exhibition of madness in the woman and in the assembly. Releasing her hands from confinement, she spread them out towards heaven, and exclaimed, "O Lord, help me!" Instantly, the whole company of the afflicted children "were grievously vexed." After a while, the tumult subsided, and Hathorne again addressed her, "Do you not see what a solemn condition these are in? When your hands are loosed, the persons are afflicted." Then Mary Walcot and Elizabeth Hubbard came forward, and accused her. Hathorne again addressed her, " Here are these two grown persons now accuse. What say you? Do not you see these afflicted persons, and hear them accuse you?" She answered, " The Lord knows I have not hurt them. I am an innocent person." Hathorne continued, " It is very awful to all to see these agonies, and you, an old professor, thus charged with contracting with the Devil by the effects of it, and yet to see you stand with dry eyes where there are so many wet." She answered, " You do not know my heart." Hathorne, " You would do well, if you are guilty, to confess, and give glory to God." — " I am as clear as the child unborn." Hathorne continued, " What uncertainty there may be in apparitions, I know not: yet this with me strikes hard upon you, that you are, at this very present, charged with familiar spirits, — this is your bodily person they speak to; they say now they see these familiar spirits come to your bodily person. Now, what do you say to that?" — " I have none, sir." — " If you have, confess, and give glory to God. I pray God clear you, if you be innocent, and, if you are guilty, discover you; and therefore give me an upright answer. Have you any familiarity with these spirits?" — " No: I have none but with God alone." It looks as if again the magistrate began to open his mind to a fair view of the case. He seems to have sought satisfaction in reference to all the charges

that had been made against her. She was suffering
from infirmities of body, the result not only of age, but
of the burdens of life often pressing down the physical
frame, particularly of those who have borne large families of children. The magistrate had heard some
malignant gossip of this kind, and he asked, "How
came you sick? for there is an odd discourse of that in
the mouths of many." She replied that she suffered
from weakness of stomach. He inquired, more spe-
cifially, "Have you no wounds?" Her answer was,
that her ailments and weaknesses, all her bodily infirmities, were the natural effects of what she had experienced in a long life. "I have none but old age." —
"You do know whether you are guilty, and have
familiarity with the Devil; and now, when you are
here present, to see such a thing as these testify, — a
black man whispering in your ear, and birds about
you, — what do you say to it?" — "It is all false: I
am clear." — "Possibly, you may apprehend you are
no witch; but have you not been led aside by temptations that way?" — "I have not." At this point, it
almost seems that Hathorne was yielding to the moral
effect of the evidence she bore in her deportment and
language, the impress of conscious innocence in her
countenance, and the manifestation of true Christian
purity and integrity in her whole manner and bearing.
Instead of pressing her with further interrogatories,
he gave way to an expression, in the form of a solilo-
quy or ejaculation, "What a sad thing is it, that a
church-member here, and now another of Salem,

should thus be accused and charged!" Upon hearing this rather ambiguous expression of the magistrate, Mrs. Pope fell into a grievous fit.

Mrs. Pope was the wife of Joseph Pope, living with his mother, the widow Gertrude Pope, on the farm shown on the map. She had followed up the meetings of the circle, been a constant witness of the sufferings of the " afflicted children," and attended all the public examinations, until her nervous system was excited beyond restraint, and for a while she went into fits and her imagination was bewildered. She acted with the accusers, and participated in their sufferings. On some occasions, her conduct was wild and extravagant to the highest degree. At the examination of Martha Corey, she was conspicuous for the violence of her actions. In the midst of the proceedings, and in the presence of the magistrates and hundreds of people, she threw her muff at the prisoner; and, that missing, pulled off her shoe, and, more successful this time, hit her square on the head. Hers seems, however, to have been a case of mere delusion, amounting to temporary insanity. That it was not deliberate and cold-blooded imposture is rendered probable by the fact, that she was rescued from the hallucination, and, with her husband, among the foremost to deplore and denounce the whole affair. But, when a woman of her position acted in this manner, on such an occasion, and then went into convulsions, and the whole company of afflicted persons joined in, the confusion, tumult, and frightfulness of the scene can hardly be imagined, certainly it cannot be described in words.

Quiet being restored, Hathorne proceeded: "Tell us, have you not had visible appearances, more than what is common in nature?" — "I have none, nor never had in my life." — "Do you think these suffer voluntary or involuntary?" — "I cannot tell." — "That is strange: every one can judge." — "I must be silent." — "They accuse you of hurting them; and, if you think it is not unwillingly, but by design, you must look upon them as murderers." — "I cannot tell what to think of it." This answer was considered as very aspersive in its bearing upon the witnesses, and she was charged with having called them murderers. Being hard of hearing, she did not always take in the whole import of questions put to her. She denied that she said she thought them murderers; all she said, and that she stood to to the last, was that she could not tell what to make of their conduct. Finally, Hathorne put this question, and called for an answer, "Do you think these suffer against their wills or not?" She answered, "I do not think these suffer against their wills." To this point she was not afraid or unwilling to go, in giving an opinion of the conduct of the accusing girls. Infirm, half deaf, cross-questioned, circumvented, surrounded with folly, uproar, and outrage, as she was, they could not intimidate her to say less, or entrap her to say more.

Then another line of criminating questions was started by the magistrate: "Why did you never visit these afflicted persons?"—"Because I was afraid I should have fits too." On every motion of her body, "fits followed upon the complainants, abundantly and very frequently." As soon as order was again restored, Hathorne, being, as he always was, wholly convinced of the reality of the sufferings of the "afflicted children," addressed her thus, "Is it not an unaccountable case, that, when you are examined, these persons are afflicted?" Seeing that he and the whole assembly put faith in the accusers, her only reply was, "I have got nobody to look to but God." As she uttered these words, she naturally attempted to raise her hands, whereupon "the afflicted persons were seized with violent fits of torture." After silence was again restored, the magistrate pressed his questions still closer. "Do you believe these afflicted persons are bewitched?" She answered, "I do think they are." It will be noticed that there was this difference between Rebecca Nurse and Martha Corey: The latter was an utter heretic on the point of the popular faith respecting witchcraft; she did not believe that there were any witches, and she looked upon the declarations and actions of the "afflicted children" as the ravings of "distracted persons." The former seems to have held the opinions of the day, and had no disbelief in witchcraft: she was willing to admit that the children were bewitched; but she knew her own innocence, and nothing could move her from the consciousness of it. Mr. Hathorne continued, "When this witchcraft came upon the stage, there was no suspicion

of Tituba, Mr. Parris's Indian woman. She professed
much love to that child, — Betty Parris ; but it was her
apparition did the mischief: and why should not you
also be guilty, for your apparition doth hurt also?"
Her answer was, " Would you have me belie myself?"
Weary, probably, of the protracted proceedings, her
head drooped on one side ; and forthwith the necks of
the afflicted children were bent in the same way. This
new demonstration of the diabolical power that proceeded from her filled the house with increased awe,
and spread horrible conviction of her guilt through all
minds. Elizabeth Hubbard's neck was fixed in that
direction, and could not be moved. Abigail Williams
cried out, " Set up Goody Nurse's head, the maid's
neck will be broke." Whereupon, some persons held
the prisoner's head up, and " Aaron Way observed that
Betty Hubbard's was immediately righted." To consummate the effect of the whole proceeding, Mr. Parris, by direction of the magistrates, " read what he
had in characters taken from Mr. Thomas Putnam's
wife in her fits." We shall come to the matter thus
introduced by Mr. Parris, at a future stage of the story.
It is sufficient here to say, that it contained the most
positive and minute declarations that the apparition of
Rebecca Nurse had appeared to her, on several occasions, and horribly tortured her. After hearing Parris's
statement, Hathorne asked the prisoner, " What do you
think of this?" Her reply was, "I cannot help it:
the Devil may appear in my shape." It may be mentioned, that Mrs. Ann Putnam was present during this

examination, and, in the course of it, went into the most dreadful bodily agony, charging it on Rebecca Nurse. Her sufferings were so violent, and held on so long, that the magistrates gave permission to her husband to carry her out of the meeting-house, to free her from the malignant presence of the prisoner. The record of the examination closes thus: —

" Salem Village, March 24th, 169½. — The Reverend Mr. Samuel Parris, being desired to take in writing the examination of Rebecca Nurse, hath returned it as aforesaid.

" Upon hearing the aforesaid, and seeing what we then did see, together with the charges of the persons then present, we committed Rebecca Nurse, the wife of Francis Nurse of Salem Village, unto Her Majesty's jail in Salem, as *per mittimus* then given out, in order to further examination.

The presence of Ann Putnam, the mother, on this occasion ; the statement from her, read by Mr. Parris ; and the terrible sufferings she exhibited, produced, no doubt, a deep effect upon the magistrates and all present. Her social position and personal appearance undoubtedly contributed to heighten it. For two months, her house had been the constant scene of the extraordinary actings of the circle of girls of which her daughter and maid-servant were the leading spirits.

Her mind had been absorbed in the mysteries of spiritualism. The marvels of necromancy and magic had been kept perpetually before it. She had been living in the invisible world, with a constant sense of supernaturalism surrounding her. Unconsciously, perhaps, the passions, prejudices, irritations, and animosities, to which she had been subject, became mixed with the vagaries of an excited imagination; and, laid open to the inroads of delusion as her mind had long been by perpetual tamperings with spiritual ideas and phantoms, she may have lost the balance of reason and sanity. This, added to a morbid sensibility, probably gave a deep intensity to her voice, action, and countenance. The effect upon the excited multitude must have been very great. Although she lived to realize the utter falseness of all her statements, her monstrous fictions were felt by her, at the time, to be a reality.

In concluding his report of this examination, Mr. Parris says, "By reason of great noises by the afflicted and many speakers, many things are pretermitted." He was probably quite willing to avoid telling the whole story of the disgraceful and shocking scenes enacted in the meeting-house that day. Deodat Lawson was present during the earlier part of the proceedings. He says that Mr. Hale began with prayer; that the prisoner "pleaded her innocency with earnestness;" that, at the opening, some of the girls, Mary Walcot among them, declared that the prisoner had never hurt them. Presently, however, Mary Walcot screamed out that she was bitten, and charged it upon Rebecca Nurse. The marks of teeth were produced on her wrist. Lawson says, " It was so disposed that I had not leisure to attend the whole time of examination." The meaning is, I suppose, that he desired to withdraw into the neighboring fields to con over his manuscript, and make himself more able to perform with effect the part he was to act that afternoon. " There was once," he says, " such an hideous screech and noise (which I heard as I walked at a little distance from the meeting-house) as did amaze me ; and some that were within told me the whole assembly was struck with consternation, and they were afraid that those that sat next to them were under the influence of witchcraft." The whole congregation was in an uproar, every one afflicted by and affrighting every other, amid a universal outcry of terror and horror.

As it was a part of the policy of the managers of the business to utterly overwhelm the influence of all natural sentiment in the community, they coupled with this proceeding against a venerable and infirm great-grandmother, another of the same kind against a little child. Immediately after the examination of Rebecca Nurse was concluded, Dorcas, a daughter of Sarah Good, was brought before the magistrates. She was between four and five years old. Lawson says, " The child looked hale and well as other children." A warrant had been issued for her apprehension, the day before, on complaint of Edward and Jonathan Putnam. Herrick the marshal, who was a man that magnified his office, and of much personal pride, did

not, perhaps, fancy the idea of bringing up such a
little prisoner ; and he deputized the operation to
Samuel Braybrook, who, the next morning, made return, in due form, that " he had taken the body of
Dorcas Good," and sent her to the house of Nathaniel
Ingersoll, where she was in custody. It seems that
Braybrook did not like the job, and passed the handling of the child over to still another. Whoever performed the service probably brought her in his arms,
or on a pillion. The little thing could not have
walked the distance from Benjamin Putnam's farm.
When led in to be examined, Ann Putnam, Mary Walcot, and Mercy Lewis, all charged her with biting,
pinching, and almost choking them. The two former
went through their usual evolutions in the presence of
the awe and terror stricken magistrates and multitude.
They showed the marks of her little teeth on their
arms ; and the pins with which she pricked them were
found on their bodies, precisely where, in their shrieks,
they had averred that she was piercing them. The
evidence was considered overwhelming ; and Dorcas
was, *per mittimus*, committed to the jail, where she
joined her mother. By the bill of the Boston jailer,
it appears that they both were confined there : as they
were too poor to provide for themselves, " the country "
was charged with ten shillings for " two blankets for
Sarah Good's child." The mother, we know, was
kept in chains ; the child was probably chained too.
Extraordinary fastenings, as has been stated, were
thought necessary to hold a witch.

There was no longer any doubt, in the mass of the community, that the Devil had effected a lodgement at Salem Village. Church-members, persons of all social positions, of the highest repute and profession of piety, eminent for visible manifestations of devotion, and of every age, had joined his standard, and become his active allies and confederates.

The effect of these two examinations was unquestionably very great in spreading consternation and bewilderment far and wide; but they were only the prelude to the work, to that end, arranged for the day. The public mind was worked to red heat, and now was the moment to strike the blow that would fix an impression deep and irremovable upon it. It was Thursday, Lecture-day; and the public services usual on the occasion were to be held at the meeting-house.

Deodat Lawson had arrived at the village on the 19th of March, and lodged at Deacon Ingersoll's. The fact at once became known; and Mary Walcot immediately went to the deacon's to see him. She had a fit on the spot, which filled Lawson with amazement and horror. His turn of mind led him to be interested in such an excitement; and he had become additionally and specially exercised by learning that the afflicted persons had intimated that the deaths of his wife and daughter, which occurred during his ministry at the village, had been brought about by the diabolical agency of the persons then beginning to be unmasked, and brought to justice. He was prepared to listen to the hints thus thrown out, and was ready to push

the prosecutions on with an earnestness in which
resentment and rage were mingled with the blindest
credulity. After Mary Walcot had given him a specimen of what the girls were suffering, he walked over,
early in the evening, to Mr. Parris's house ; and there
Abigail Williams went into the craziest manifestations,
throwing firebrands about the house in the presence
of her uncle, rushing to the back of the chimney as
though she would fly up through its wide flue, and performing many wonderful works. The next day being
Sunday, he preached ; and the services were interrupted, in the manner already described, by the out-
breaks of the afflicted, under diabolic influence. The
next day, he attended the examination of Martha
Corey. On Wednesday, the 23d, he went up to
Thomas Putnam's, as he says, " on purpose to see his
wife." He " found her lying on the bed, having had a
sore fit a little before: her husband and she both
desired me to pray with her while she was sensible,
which I did, though the apparition said I should not go
to prayer. At the first beginning, she attended ; but,
after a little time, was taken with a fit, yet continued
silent, and seemed to be asleep." She had represented
herself as being in conflict with the shape, or spectre,
of a witch, which, she told Lawson, said he should not
pray on the occasion. But he courageously ventured
on the work. At the conclusion of the prayer, " her
husband, going to her, found her in a fit. He took her
off the bed to sit her on his knees ; but at first she
was so stiff she could not be bended, but she after-

wards sat down." Then she went into that state of
supernatural vision and exaltation in which she was
accustomed to utter the wildest strains, in fervid, extravagant, but solemn and melancholy, rhapsodies : she
disputed with the spectre about a text of Scripture,
and then poured forth the most terrible denunciations
upon it for tormenting and tempting her. She was
evidently a very intellectual and imaginative woman,
and was perfectly versed in all the imagery and lofty
diction supplied by the prophetic and poetic parts of
Scripture. Again she was seized with a terrible fit,
that lasted " near half an hour." At times, her mouth
was drawn on one side and her body strained. At
last she broke forth, and succeeded, after many violent
struggles against the spectre and many convulsions of
her frame, in saying what part of the Bible Lawson
was to read aloud, in order to relieve her. " It is,"
she said, " the third chapter of the Revelation." — " I
did," says Lawson, " something scruple the reading
it." He was loath to be engaged in an affair of that
kind in which the Devil was an actor. At length he
overcame his scruples, and the effect was decisive.
" Before I had near read through the first verse, she
opened her eyes, and was well." Bewildered and
amazed, he went back to Parris's house, and they
talked over the awful manifestations of Satan's power.
The next morning, he attended the examination of
Rebecca Nurse, retiring from it, at an early hour,
to complete his preparation for the service that had
been arranged for him that afternoon.

I say arranged, because the facts in this case prove long-concerted arrangement. He was to preach a sermon that day. Word must have been sent to him weeks before. After reaching the village, every hour had been occupied in exciting spectacles and engrossing experiences, filling his mind with the fanatical enthusiasm requisite to give force and fire to the delivery of the discourse. He could not possibly have written it after coming to the place. He must have brought it in his pocket. It is a thoroughly elaborated and carefully constructed performance, requiring long and patient application to compose it, and exhausting all the resources of theological research and reference, and of artistic skill and finish. It is adapted to the details of an occasion which was prepared to meet it. Not only the sermon but the audience were the result of arrangement carefully made in the stages of preparation and in the elements comprised in it. The preceding steps had all been seasonably and appositely taken, so that, when the regular lecture afternoon came, Lawson would have his voluminous discourse ready, and a congregation be in waiting to hear it, with minds suitably wrought upon by the preceding incidents of the day, to be thoroughly and permanently impressed by it. The occasion had been heralded by a train of circumstances drawing everybody to the spot. The magistrates were already there, some of them by virtue of the necessity of official presence in the earlier part of the day, and others came in from the neighborhood ; the ministers gathered from

the towns in the vicinity ; men and women came from
all quarters, flocking along the highways and the by-
ways, large numbers on horseback, and crowds on
foot.   Probably the village meeting-house, and the
grounds around it, presented a spectacle such as never
was exhibited elsewhere. Awe, dread, earnestness, a
stern but wild fanaticism, were stamped on all countenances, and stirred the heaving multitude to its
depths, and in all its movements and utterances, It
is impossible to imagine a combination of circumstances that could give greater advantage and power
to a speaker, and Lawson was equal to the situation.
No discourse was ever more equal, or better adapted,
to its occasion.   It was irresistible in its power, and
carried the public mind as by storm.

The text is Zechariah, iii. 2 : " And the Lord said
unto Satan, The Lord rebuke thee, O Satan ! even the
Lord that hath chosen Jerusalem rebuke thee : is not
this a brand plucked out of the fire ? " After an
allusion to the rebellion of Satan, and his fall from
heaven with his " accursed legions," and after representing them as filled " with envy and malice against
all mankind," seeking " by all ways and means to
work their ruin and destruction for ever, opposing
to the utmost all persons and things appointed by the
Lord Jesus Christ as means or instruments of their
comfort here or salvation hereafter," he proceeds, in
the manner of those days, to open his text and spread
out his subject, all along exhibiting great ability, skill,
and power, showing learning in his illustrations, draw-

ing aptly and abundantly from the Scriptures, and, at the right points, rising to high strains of eloquence in diction and imagery.

He describes, at great length and with abundant instances ingeniously selected from sacred and profane literature, the marvellous power with which Satan is enabled to operate upon mankind. He says, —

" He is a spirit, and hence strikes at the spiritual part, the most excellent (constituent) part of man. Primarily disturbing and interrupting the animal and vital spirits, he maliciously operates upon the more common powers of the soul by strange and frightful representations to the fancy or imagination ; and, by violent tortures of the body, often threatening to extinguish life, as hath been observed in those that are afflicted amongst us. And not only so, but he vents his malice in diabolical operations on the more sublime and distinguishing faculties of the rational soul, raising mists of darkness and ignorance in the understanding. . . . Sometimes he brings distress upon the bodies of men, by malignant operations in, and diabolical impressions on, the spirituous principle or vehicle of life and motion. . . . There are certainly some lower operations of Satan (whereof there are sundry examples among us), which the bodies and souls of men and women are liable unto. And whosoever hath carefully observed those things must needs be convinced, that the motions of the persons afflicted, both as to the manner and as to the violence of them, are the mere effects of diabolical malice and operations, and that it cannot rationally be imagined to proceed from any other cause whatever. . . . Satan exerts his malice mediately by employing some of mankind and other creatures, and he frequently useth other persons or things, that his designs may be the more undiscernible. Thus he used the serpent in the first temptation (Gen. iii. 1). Hence he contracts and indents with witches and wizards, that they shall be the instruments by whom he may more secretly affect and afflict the bodies and minds of others ; and, if he can prevail upon those that make a visible profession, it may be the better covert unto his diabolical enterprise, and may the more readily pervert others to consenting unto his subjection. So far as we can look into those hellish mysteries, and guess at the administration of that kingdom of darkness, we may learn that witches make witches by persuading one the other to subscribe to a book or articles, &c. ; and the Devil, having them in his subjection, by their consent, he will use their bodies and 'minds, shapes and representations, to affright and afflict others at his pleasure, for the propagation of his infernal kingdom, and accomplishing his devised mischiefs to the souls, bodies, and lives of the children of men, yea, and of the children of God too, so far as permitted and is possible. . . . He insinuates into the society of the adopted children of God, in their most solemn approaches to him, in sacred ordinances, endeavoring to look so like the true saints and ministers of Christ, that, if it were possible, he would deceive the very elect (Matt. xxiv. 24) by his subtilty : for it is certain he never works more like the Prince of darkness than when he looks most like an angel of light ; and, when he most pretends to holiness, he then doth most secretly, and by consequence most surely, undermine it, and those that most excel in the exercise thereof. "

The following is a specimen of the style in which he stirred up the people : —

" The application of this doctrine to ourselves remains now to be attended. Let it be for solemn warning and awakening to all of us that are before the Lord at this time, and to all others of this whole people, who shall come to the knowledge of these direful operations of Satan, which the holy God hath permitted in the midst of us.

" The Lord doth terrible things amongst us, by lengthening the chain of the roaring lion in an extraordinary manner, so that the Devil is come down in great wrath (Rev. xii. 12), endeavoring to set up his kingdom, and, by racking torments on the bodies, and affrightening representations to the minds of many amongst us, to force and fright them to become his subjects. I may well say, then, in the words of the prophet (Mic. vi. 9), ' The Lord's voice crieth to the city,' and to the country also, with an unusual and amazing loudness. Surely, it warns us to awaken out of all sleep, of security or stupidity, to arise, and take our Bibles, turn to, and learn that lesson, not by rote only, but by heart. 1 Pet. v. 8 : ' Be sober, be vigilant ; because your adversary the Devil goes about as a roaring lion, seeking whom amongst you he may distress, delude, and devour.' . . . Awake, awake then, I beseech you, and remain no longer under the dominion of that prince of cruelty and malice, whose tyrannical fury we see thus exerted against the bodies and minds of these afflicted persons ! . . . This warning is directed to all manner of persons, according to their condition of life, both in civil and sacred order ; both high and low, rich and poor, old and young, bond and free. Oh, let the observation of these amazing dispensations of God's unusual and strange Providence quicken us to our duty, at such a time as this, in our respective places and stations, relations and capacities ! The great God hath done such things amongst us as do make the ears of those that hear them to tingle (Jer. xix. 3) ; and serious souls are at a loss to what these things may grow, and what we shall find to be the end of this dreadful visitation, in the permission whereof the provoked God as a lion hath roared, who can but fear? the Lord hath spoken, who can but prophesy? (Amos iii. 8.) The loud trumpet of God, in this thundering providence, is blown in the city, and the echo of it heard through the country, surely then the people must and ought to be afraid (Amos iii. 6). . . . You are therefore to be deeply humbled, and sit in the dust, considering the signal hand of God in singling out this place, this poor village, for the first seat of Satan's tyranny, and to make it (as 'twere the rendezvous of devils, where they muster their infernal forces ; appearing to the afflicted as coming armed to carry on their malicious designs against the bodies, and, if God in mercy prevent not, against the souls, of many in this place. . . . Be humbled also that so many members of this church of the Lord Jesus Christ should be under the influences of Satan's malice in these his operations ; some as the objects of his tyranny on their bodies to that degree of distress which none can be sensible of but those that see and feel it, who are in the mean time also sorely distressed in their minds by frightful representations made by the devils unto them. Other professors and visible members of this church are under the awful accusations and imputations of being the instruments of Satan in his mischievous actings. It cannot but be matter of deep humiliation, to such as are innocent, that the righteous and holy God should permit them to be named in such pernicious and unheard-of practices, and not only so, but that he who cannot but do right should suffer the stain of suspected guilt to be, as it were, rubbed on and soaked in by many sore and amazing circumstances. And it is a matter of soul-abasement to all that are in the bond of God's holy covenant in this place, that Satan's seat should be amongst them, where he attempts to set up his kingdom in opposition to Christ's kingdom, and to take some of the visible subjects of our Lord Jesus, and use at least their shapes and appearances, instrumentally, to afflict and torture other visible subjects of the same kingdom. Surely his design is that Christ's kingdom may be divided against itself, that, being thereby weakened, he may the better take opportunity to set up his own accursed powers and dominions. It calls aloud then to all in this place in the name of the blessed Jesus, and words of his holy apostle (1 Peter v. 6), ' Humble yourselves under the mighty hand of God.'

"It is matter of terror, amazement, and astonishment, to all such wretched souls (if there be any here in the congregation ; and God, of his infinite mercy, grant that none of you may ever be found such!) as have given up their names and souls to the Devil ; who by covenant, explicit or implicit, have bound themselves to be his slaves and drudges, consenting to be instruments in whose shapes he may torment and afflict their fellow-creatures (even of their own kind) to the amazing and astonishing of the standers-by. I would hope I might have spared this use, but I desire (by divine assistance) to declare the whole counsel of God ; and if it come not as conviction where it is so, it may serve for warning, that it may never be so. For it is a most dreadful thing to consider that any should change the service of God for the service of the Devil, the worship of the blessed God for the worship of the cursed enemy of God and man. But, oh! (which is yet a thousand times worse) how shall I name it? if any that are in the visible covenant of

God should break that covenant, and make a league with
Satan ; if any that have sat down and eat at Christ's Table,
should so lift up their heel against him as to have fellowship at the table of devils, and (as it hath been represented
to some of the afflicted) eat of the bread and drink of the
wine that Satan hath mingled. Surely, if this be so, the
poet is in the right, " Audax omnia perpeti. Gens humana
ruit per vetitum nefas : " audacious mortals are grown to a
fearful height of impiety ; and we must cry out in Scripture
language, and that emphatical apostrophe of the Prophet
Jeremy (chap. ii. 12), ' Be astonished, O ye heavens, at this,
and be horribly afraid : be ye very desolate, saith the Lord.'
. . . If you are in covenant with the Devil, the intercession
of the blessed Jesus is against you. His prayer is for the
subduing of Satan's power and kingdom, and the utter confounding of all his instruments. If it be so, then the great
God is set against you. The omnipotent Jehovah, one God
in three Persons ; Father, Son, and Holy Ghost, in their
several distinct operations and all their divine attributes, —
are engaged against you. Therefore KNOW YE that are
guilty of such monstrous iniquity, that He that made you will
not save you, and that He that formed you will show you no
favor (Isa. xxvii. 11). Be assured, that, although you
should now evade the condemnation of man's judgment, and
escape a violent death by the hand of justice ; yet, unless
God shall give you repentance (which we heartily pray for),
there is a day coming when the secrets of all hearts shall be
revealed by Jesus Christ (Rom. ii. 16). Then, then, your sin
will find you out ; and you shall be punished with everlasting destruction from the presence of the Lord, and doomed
to those endless, easeless, and remediless torments prepared
for the Devil and his angels (Matt. xxv. 41). . . . If you

have been guilty of such impiety, the prayers of the people
of God are against you on that account.   It is their duty to
pray daily, that Satan's kingdom may be suppressed, weakened, brought down, and at last totally destroyed ; hence that
all abettors, subjects, defenders, and promoters thereof, may
be utterly crushed and confounded.   They are constrained
to suppress that kindness and compassion that in their
sacred addresses they once bare unto you (as those of their
own kind, and framed out of the same mould), praying with
one consent, as the royal prophet did against his malicious
enemies, the instruments of Satan (Ps. cix. 6), ' Set thou
a wicked man over him, and let Satan stand at his right
hand ' (i.e.), to withstand all that is for his good, and promote
all that is for his hurt ; and (verse 7) ' When he is judged,
let him be condemned, and let his prayer become sin.'

   " Be we exhorted and directed to exercise true spiritual
sympathy with, and compassion towards, those poor, afflicted
persons that are by divine permission under the direful influence of Satan's malicè.   There is a divine precept enjoin-
ing the practice of such duty : Heb. xiii. 3, ' Remember
them that suffer adversity, as being yourselves also in the
body.'   Let us, then, be deeply sensible, and, as the elect of
God, put on bowels of mercy towards those in misery
(Col. iii. 12).   Oh, pity, pity them ! for the hand of the
Lord hath touched them, and the malice of devils hath
fallen upon them.

   " Let us be sure to take unto us and put on the whole
armor of God, and every piece of it ; let none be wanting.
Let us labor to be in the exercise and practice of the whole
company of sanctifying graces and religious duties.   This
important duty is pressed, and the particular pieces of that
armor recited Eph. vi. 11 and 13 to 18.   Satan is repre-

Eng.ᵈ at J.Andrews's by R.Babson

WILLIAM STOUGHTON.

senting his infernal forces; and the devils seem to come
armed, mustering amongst us.   I am this day commanded
to call and cry an alarm unto you : ARM, ARM, ARM ! handle
your arms, see that you are fixed and in a readiness, as
faithful soldiers under the Captain of our salvation, that, by
the shield of faith, ye and we all may resist the fiery darts
of the wicked ; and may be faithful unto death in our
spiritual warfare; so shall we assuredly receive the crown of
life (Rev. ii. 10).   Let us admit no parley, give no quarter : let none of Satan's forces or furies be more vigilant
to hurt us than we are to resist and repress them, in the
name, and by the spirit, grace, and strength of our Lord
Jesus Christ.   Let us ply the throne of grace, in the name
and merit of our Blessed Mediator, taking all possible
opportunities, public, private, and secret, to pour out our
supplications to the God of our salvation.   Prayer is the
most proper and potent antidote against the old Serpent's
venomous operations.   When legions of devils do come
down among us, multitudes of prayers should go up to God.
Satan, the worst of all our enemies, is called in Scripture a
dragon, to note his malice ; a serpent, to note his subtilty ;
a lion, to note his strength.   But none of all these can stand
before prayer.   The most inveterate malice (as that of
Haman) sinks under the prayer of Esther (chap. iv. 16).
The deepest policy (the counsel of Achitophel) withers
before the prayer of David (2 Sam. xv. 31) ; and the
vastest army (an host of a thousand thousand Ethiopians)
ran away, like so many cowards, before the prayer of Asa
(2 Chron. xiv. 9 to 15).

    " What therefore I say unto one I say unto all, in this
important case, PRAY, PRAY, PRAY.

    " To our honored magistrates, here present this day, to

inquire into these things, give me leave, much honored, to offer one word to your consideration. Do all that in you lies to check and rebuke Satan ; endeavoring, by all ways and means that are according to the rule of God, to discover his instruments in these horrid operations. You are concerned in the civil government of this people, being invested with power by their Sacred Majesties, under this glorious Jesus (the King and Governor of his church), for the supporting of Christ's kingdom against all oppositions of Satan's kingdom and his instruments. Being ordained of God to such a station (Rom. xiii. 1), we entreat you, bear not the sword in vain, as ver. 4 ; but approve yourselves a terror of and punishment to evil-doers, and a praise to them that do well (1 Peter ii. 14) ; ever remembering that ye judge not for men, but for the Lord (2 Chron. xix. 6) ; and, as his promise is, so our prayer shall be for you, without ceasing, that he would be with you in the judgment, as he that can and will direct, assist, and reward you. Follow the example of the upright Job (chap. xxix. 16) : Be a father to the poor ; to these poor afflicted persons, in pitiful and painful endeavors to help them ; and the cause that seems to be so dark, as you know not how to determine it, do your utmost, in the use of all regular means, to search it out.

" There is comfort in considering that the Lord Jesus, the Captain of our salvation, hath already overcome the Devil. Christ, that blessed seed of the woman, hath given this cursed old serpent called the Devil and Satan a mortal and incurable bruise on the head (Gen. iii. 15). He was too much for him in a single conflict (Matt. iv.). He opposed his power and kingdom in the possessed. He suffered not the devils to speak, because they knew him (Mark i. 34). He com-

pleted his victory by his death on the cross, and destroyed his
dominion (Heb. ii. 14), that through death he might destroy
death, and him that had the powers of death, that is the
Devil; and by and after his resurrection made show openly
unto the world, that he had spoiled principalities and powers,
triumphing over them (Col. ii. 15). Hence, if we are by
faith united to him, his victory is an earnest and prelibation
of our conquest at last. All Satan's strugglings now are
but those of a conquered enemy. It is no small comfort to
consider, that Job's exercise of patience had its beginning
from the Devil; but we have seen the end to be from the
Lord (James v. 11). That we also may find by experience
the same blessed issue of our present distresses by Satan's
malice, let us repent of every sin that hath been committed,
and labor to practise every duty which hath been neglected.
Then we shall assuredly and speedily find that the kingly
power of our Lord and Saviour shall be magnified, in delivering his poor sheep and lambs out of the jaws and paws of
the roaring lion."

These extended extracts are given from Lawson's
discourse, partly to enable every one to estimate the
effect it must have produced, under the circumstances
of the occasion, but mainly because they present a
living picture of the sentiments, notions, modes of
thinking and reasoning, and convictions, then prevalent. No description given by a person looking back
from our point of view, not having experienced the
delusions of that age, no matter who might attempt
the task, could adequately paint the scene. The
foregoing extracts show better, I think, than any documents that have come down to us, how the subject lay

in the minds of men at that time. They bring before
us directly, without the intervention of any secondary
agency, the thoughts, associations, sentiments, of that
generation, in breathing reality. They carry us back
to the hour and to the spot. Deodat Lawson rises from
his unknown grave, comes forth from the impenetrable
cloud which enveloped the closing scenes of his mortal
career, and we listen to his voice, as it spoke to the
multitudes that gathered in and around the meeting-
house in Salem Village, on Lecture-day, March 24,
1692. He lays bare his whole mind to our immediate
inspection. In and through him, we behold the mind
and heart, the forms of language and thought, the feelings and passions, of the people of that day. We min-
gle with the crowd that hang upon his lips ; we behold
their countenances, discern the passions that glowed
upon their features, and enter into the excitement that
moved and tossed them like a tempest. We are thus
prepared, as we could be in no other way, to comprehend our story.

The sermon answered its end. It re-enforced the
powers that had begun their work. It spread out
the whole doctrine of witchcraft in a methodical, elaborate, and most impressive form. It justified and commended every thing that had been done, and every
thing that remained to be done ; every step in the proceedings ; every process in the examinations ; every kind
of accusation and evidence that had been adduced ;
every phase of the popular belief, however wild and
monstrous ; every pretension of the afflicted children

to preternatural experiences and communications, and every tale of apparitions of departed spirits and the ghosts of murdered men, women, and children, which, engendered in morbid and maniac imaginations, had been employed to fill him and others with horror, inspire revenge, and drive on the general delirium. And it fortified every point by the law and the testimony, by passages and scraps of Scripture, studiously and skilfully culled out, and ingeniously applied. It gave form to what had been vague, and authority to what had floated in blind and baseless dreams of fancy. It crystallized the disordered vagaries, that had been seething in turbulent confusion in the public mind, into a fixed, organized, and permanent shape.

Its publication was forthwith called for. The manuscript was submitted to Increase and Cotton Mather of the North, James Allen and John Bailey of the First, Samuel Willard of the Old South, churches in Boston, and Charles Morton of the church in Charlestown. It was printed with a strong, unqualified indorsement of approval, signed by the names severally of these the most eminent divines of the country. The discourse was dedicated to the "worshipful and worthily honored Bartholomew Gedney, John Hathorne, Jonathan Corwin, Esqrs., together with the reverend Mr. John Higginson, pastor, and Mr. Nicholas Noyes, teacher, of the Church of Christ at Salem," with a preface, addressed to all his "Christian friends and acquaintance, the inhabitants of Salem Village." It was republished in London in 1704, under the immediate direction of its

author. The subject is described as " Christ's Fidelity, the only Shield against Satan's Malignity;" and
the titlepage is enforced by passages of Scripture (Rev.
xii. 12, and Rom. xvi. 20). The interest of the volume is highly increased by an appendix, giving the
substance of notes taken by Lawson on the spot, during the examinations and trials. They are invaluable,
as proceeding from a chief actor in the scenes, who was
wholly carried away by the delusion. They describe,
in marvellous colors, the wonderful manifestations of
diabolical agency in, upon, and through the afflicted
children; resembling, in many respects, reports of
spiritual communications prevalent in our day, although not quite coming up to them. These statements, and the preface to the discourse, are given
in the Appendix to this volume. In a much briefer
form, it was printed by Benjamin Harris, at Boston,
in 1692; and soon after by John Dunton, in London.

Before dismissing Mr. Lawson's famous sermon, our
attention is demanded to a remarkable paragraph in it.
His strong faculties could not be wholly bereft of reason; and he had sense enough left to see, what does
not appear to have occurred to others, that there might
be a re-action in the popular passions, and that some
might be called to account by an indignant public, if
not before a stern tribunal of justice, for the course of
cruelty and outrage they were pursuing, with so high
a hand, against accused persons. He was not entirely
satisfied that the appeal he made in his discourse to

the people to suppress and crush out all vestiges of human feeling, and to stifle compassion and pity in their breasts, would prevail. He foresaw that the friends and families of innocent and murdered victims might one day call for vengeance ; and he attempts to provide, beforehand, a defence that is truly ingenious : —

" Give no place to the Devil by rash censuring of others, without sufficient grounds, or false accusing any willingly. This is indeed to be like the Devil, who hath the title, *Διάβολος*, in the Greek, because he is the calumniator or false accuser. Hence, when we read of such accusers in the latter days, they are, in the original, called *Διάβολοι*, *calumniatores* (2 Tim. iii. 3). It is a time of temptation amongst you, such as never was before : let me entreat you not to be lavish or severe in reflecting on the malice or envy of your neighbors, by whom any of you have been accused, lest, whilst you falsely charge one another, — viz., the relations of the afflicted and relations of the accused, — the grand accuser (who loves to fish in troubled waters) should take advantage upon you. Look at sin, the procuring cause ; God in justice, the sovereign efficient ; and Satan, the enemy, the principal instrument, both in afflicting some and accusing others. And, if innocent persons be suspected, it is to be ascribed to God's pleasure, supremely permitting, and Satan's malice subordinately troubling, by representation of such to the afflicting of others, even of such as have, all the while, we have reason to believe (especially some of them), no kind of ill-will or disrespect unto those that have been complained of by them. This giving place to the Devil avoid ; for it will have uncomfortable and pernicious influence upon the affairs of this place, by letting out peace, and bringing in confusion and every evil work, which we heartily pray God, in mercy, to prevent."

This artifice of statement, speciously covered,— while it outrages every sentiment of natural justice, and breaks every bond of social responsibility,— is found, upon close inspection, to be a shocking imputation against the divine administration. It represents the Deity, under the phrases " sovereign efficient " and " supremely permitting " in a view which affords equal shelter to every other class of criminals, even of the deepest dye, as well as those who were ready and eager to bring upon their neighbors the charge of confederacy with Satan.

The next Sunday — March 27 — was the regular communion-day of the village church ; and Mr. Parris prepared duly to improve the occasion to advance the movement then so strongly under way, and to deepen still more the impression made by the events of the week, especially by Mr. Lawson's sermon. He accordingly composed an elaborate and effective discourse of his own; and a scene was arranged to follow the regular service, which could not but produce important results. An unexpected occurrence — a part not in the programme — took place, which created a sensation for the moment; but it tended, upon the whole, to heighten the public excitement, and, without much disturbing the order, only precipitated a little the progress of events.

It may well be supposed, that the congregation assembled that day with minds awfully solemnized, and altogether in a condition to be deeply affected by the services. A respectable person always prominently noticeable for her devout participation in the worship of the sanctuary, and a member of the church, had, on Monday, after a public examination, been committed to prison, and was there in irons, waiting to be tried for her life for the blackest of crimes, — a confederacy with the enemy of the souls of. men, the archtraitor and rebel against the throne of God. On Thursday, another venerable, and ever before considered pious, matron of a large and influential family, a participant in their worship, and a member of the mother-church, had been consigned to the same fate, to be tried for the same horrible crime. A little child had been proved to have also joined in the infernal league. No one could tell to what extent Satan had lengthened his chain, or who, whether old or young, were in league with him. Every soul was still alive to the impressions made by Mr. Lawson's great discourse, and by the throngs of excited people, including magistrates and ministers, that had been gathered in the village.

The character and spirit of Mr. Parris's sermon are indicated in a prefatory note in the manuscript, " occasioned by dreadful witchcraft broke out here a few weeks past ; and one member of this church, and another of Salem, upon public examination by civil authority, vehemently suspected for she-witches." The running

title is, " Christ knows how many devils there are in
his church, and who they are ; " and the text is John
vi. 70, 71, " Jesus answered them, Have not I chosen
you twelve, and one of you is a devil ? He spake of
Judas Iscariot, the son of Simon ; for he it was that
should betray him, being one of the twelve."

Peter Cloyse was born May 27, 1639. He came to
Salem from York, in Maine, and was one of the original members of the village church. He appears to
have been a person of the greatest respectability and
strength of character. He married Sarah, sister of
Rebecca Nurse, and widow of Edmund Bridges. She
was admitted to the village church, Jan. 12, 1690, being then about forty-eight years of age. It may well
be supposed that she and her family were overwhelmed
with affliction and horror by the proceedings against
her sister. But, as she and her husband were both
communicants, and it was sacrament-day, it was
thought best for them to summon resolution to attend
the service. After much persuasion, she was induced
to go. She was a very sensitive person, and it must
have required a great effort of fortitude. Her mind
was undoubtedly much harrowed by the allusions made
to the events of the week ; and, when Mr. Parris announced his text, and opened his discourse in the
spirit his language indicates, she could bear it no
longer, but rose, and left the meeting. A fresh wind
blowing at the time caused the door to slam after her.
The congregation was probably startled ; but Parris
was not long embarrassed by the interruption, and

she was attended to in due season.   At the close
of the service, the following scene occurred.   I
give it as Parris describes it in his church-record
book : —

"After the common auditory was dismissed, and before
the church's communion at the Lord's Table, the following
testimony against the error of our Sister Mary Sibley, who
had given direction to my Indian man in an unwarrantable
way to find out witches, was read by the pastor : —

"It is altogether undeniable that our great and blessed
God, for wise and holy ends, hath suffered many persons,
in several families, of this little village, to be grievously
vexed and tortured in body, and to be deeply tempted, to
the endangering of the destruction of their souls ; and all
these amazing feats (well known to many of us) to be done
by witchcraft and diabolical operations. It is also well
known, that, when these calamities first began, which was
in my own family, the affliction was several weeks before
such hellish operations as witchcraft were suspected.   Nay,
it was not brought forth to any considerable light, until
diabolical means were used by the making of a cake by
my Indian man, who had his direction from this our sister,
Mary Sibley ; since which, apparitions have been plenty,
and exceeding much mischief hath followed.   But, by these
means (it seems), the Devil hath been raised amongst us,
and his rage is vehement and terrible ; and, when he shall
be silenced, the Lord only knows.   But now that this our
sister should be instrumental to such distress is a great
grief to myself, and our godly honored and reverend neighbors, who have had the knowledge of it.   Nevertheless, I
do truly hope and believe, that this our sister doth truly

fear the Lord; and I am well satisfied from her, that, what she did, she did it ignorantly, from what she had heard of this nature from other ignorant or worse persons. Yet we are in duty bound to protest against such actions, as being indeed a going to the Devil for help against the Devil: we having no such directions from nature, or God's word, it must therefore be, and is, accounted, by godly Protestants who write or speak of such matters, as diabolical; and therefore calls this our sister to deep humiliation for what she has done, and all of us to be watchful against Satan's wiles and devices.

"Therefore, as we, in duty as a church of Christ, are deeply bound to protest against it, as most directly contrary to the gospel, yet, inasmuch as this our sister did it in ignorance as she professeth and we believe, we can continue her in our holy fellowship, upon her serious promise of future better advisedness and caution, and acknowledging that she is indeed sorrowful for her rashness herein.

"Brethren, if this be your mind, that this iniquity should be thus borne witness against, manifest it by your usual sign of lifting up your hands. — The brethren voted generally, or universally : none made any exceptions.

"Sister Sibley, if you are convinced that you herein did sinfully, and are sorry for it, let us hear it from your own mouth. — She did manifest to satisfaction her error and grief for it.

"Brethren, if herein you have received satisfaction, testify it by lifting up your hands. — A general vote passed; no exception made.

"Note. — 25th March, 1692. I discoursed said sister in my study about her grand error aforesaid, and also then read to her what I had written as above to be read to the

church ; and said Sister Sibley assented to the same with
tears and sorrowful confession."

This proceeding was of more importance than appears, perhaps, at first view. It was one of Mr. Parris's most skilful moves. The course pursued by the
" afflicted " persons had, thus far, in reference to
those engaged in the prosecutions, been in the right
direction. But it was manifest, after the exhibitions
they had given, that they wielded a fearful power, too
fearful to be left without control. They could cry
out upon whomsoever they pleased ; and against their
accusations, armed as they were with the power to
fix the charge of guilt upon any one by giving ocular
demonstration that he or she was the author of their
sufferings, there could be no defence. They might
turn, at any moment, and cry out upon Parris or
Lawson, or either or both of the deacons. Nothing
could withstand the evidence of their fits, convulsions, and tortures. It was necessary to have and
keep them under safe control, and, to this end, to
prevent any outsiders, or any injudicious or inter-
meddling people, from holding intimacy with them.
Parris saw this, and, with his characteristic boldness
of action and fertility of resources, at once put a stop
to all trouble, and closed the door against danger,
from this quarter.

Samuel Sibley was a member of the church, and a
near neighbor of Mr. Parris. He was about thirty-
six years of age. His wife Mary was thirty-two years
of age, and also a member of the church. They

were persons of respectable standing and good repute.
Nothing is known to her disadvantage, but her foolish connection with the mystical operations going on
in Mr. Parris's family ; and of this she was heartily
ashamed.   Her penitent sensibility is quite touch-
ingly described by Mr. Parris.   It is true that what
she had done was a trifle in comparison with what
was going on every day in the families of Mr. Parris
and Thomas Putnam : but she had acted " rashly,"
without " advisedness " from the right quarter, under
the lead of " ignorant persons ; " and therefore it was
necessary to make a great ado about it, and hold her
up as a warning to prevent other persons from meddling in such matters.   Her husband was an uncle
of Mary Walcot, one of the afflicted children ; and
it was particularly important to keep their relatives,
and members of their immediate families, from taking
any part or action in connection with them, except
under due " advisedness," and the direction of persons
learned in such deep matters.   The family connections of the Sibleys were extensive, and a blow struck
at that point would be felt everywhere.   The procedure was undoubtedly effectual.   After Mary Sibley
had been thus awfully rebuked and distressingly exposed for dealing with " John Indian," it is not likely
that any one else ever ventured to intermeddle with
the " afflicted," or have any connection, except as
outside spectators, with the marvellous phenomena
of " diabolical operations."   It will be noticed, that,
while Mr. Parris thus waved the sword of disciplinary

vengeance against any who should dare to intrude
upon the forbidden ground, he occupied it himself
without disguise, and maintained his hold upon it.
He asserts the reality of the " amazing feats " practised by diabolical power in their midst, and enforces
in the strongest language the then prevalent views
and pending proceedings.

The operations of the week, including the solemn
censure of Mary Sibley, had all worked favorably for
the prosecutors and managers of the business. The
magistrates, ministers, and whole body of the people,
had become committed; the accusing girls had proved
themselves apt and competent to their work; the public
reason was prostrated, and natural sensibility stunned.
All resisting forces were powerless, and all collateral
dangers avoided and provided against. The movement was fully in hand. The next step was maturely
considered, and, as we shall see, skilfully taken.

It is to be observed, that there was, at this time,
a break in the regular government of Massachusetts.
In the spring of 1689, the people had risen, seized
the royal governor, Sir Edmund Andros, and put
him in prison. They summoned their old charter
governor, Simon Bradstreet, then living in Salem,
eighty-seven years of age, to the chair of state; called
the assistants of 1686 back to their seats, who provided for an election of representatives by the people
of the towns; and the government thus created conducted affairs until the arrival of Sir William Phipps,
in May, 1692, when Massachusetts ceased to be a

colony, and was thenceforth, until 1774, a royal province. During these three years, from May, 1689, to May, 1692, the government was based upon an uprising of the people. It was a period of pure and absolute independence of the crown or parliament of England. Although Bradstreet's faculties were unimpaired and his spirit true and firm, his age prevented his doing much more than to give his loved and venerated name to the daring movement, and to the official service, of the people. The executive functions were, for the most part, exercised by the deputy-governor, Thomas Danforth, who was a person of great ability and public spirit. Unfortunately, at this time he was zealously in favor of the witchcraft prosecutions. Bradstreet was throughout opposed to them. Had time held off its hand, and his physical energies not been impaired, he would undoubtedly have resisted and prevented them. Danforth, it is said by Brattle, came to disapprove of them finally : but he began them by arrests in other towns, months before any thing of the kind was thought of in Salem Village ; and he contributed, prominently, to give destructive and wide-spread power, in an early stage of its development, to the witchcraft delusion here.

After the lapse of a week, preparations were completed to renew operations, and a higher and more commanding character given to them. On Monday, April 4, Captain Jonathan Walcot and Lieutenant Nathaniel Ingersoll went to the town, and, "for themselves and several of their neighbors," exhibited to the assistants

residing there, John Hathorne and Jonathan Corwin,
complaints against "Sarah Cloyse, the wife of Peter
Cloyse of Salem Village, and Elizabeth Procter of
Salem Farms, for high suspicion of sundry acts of
witchcraft." There the plan of proceedings in reference to the above-said parties was agreed upon. It
was the result of consultation; communications probably passing with the deputy-governor in Boston, or
at his residence in Cambridge. On the 8th of April,
warrants were duly issued, ordering the marshal to
bring in the prisoners "on Monday morning next,
being the eleventh day of this instant April, about
eleven of the clock, in the public meeting-house in the
town." It had been arranged, that the examination
should not be, as before, in the ordinary way, before
the two local magistrates, but, in an extraordinary
way, before the highest tribunal in the colony, or a
representation of it. For a preliminary hearing, with
a view merely to commitment for trial, this surely may
justly be characterized as an extraordinary, wholly
irregular, and, in all points of view, reprehensible
procedure. When the day came, the meeting-house,
which was much more capacious than that at the
village, was crowded; and the old town filled with
excited throngs. Upon opening proceedings, lo and
behold, instead of the two magistrates, the government
of the colony was present, in the highest character
it then had as "a council"! The record says, —

  "Salem, April 11, 1692. — At a Council held at Salem,
and present Thomas Danforth, Esq., deputy-governor;

James Russell, John Hathorne, Isaac Addington, Major
Samuel Appleton, Captain Samuel Sewall, Jonathan Corwin, Esquires."

Russell was of Charlestown, Addington and Sewall
of Boston, and Appleton of Ipswich.   Mr. Parris,
" being desired and appointed to write the examination, did take the same, and also read it before the
council in public."   This document has not come
down to us ; but Hutchinson had access to it, and
the substance of it is preserved in his " History of
Massachusetts."

The marshal (Herrick) brought in Sarah Cloyse
and Elizabeth Procter, and delivered them " before
the honorable council : " and the examination was
begun.

The deputy-governor first called to the stand John
Indian, and plied him, as was the course pursued on
all these occasions, with leading questions : —

" John, who hurt you ? — Goody Procter first, and then
Goody Cloyse.

" What did she do to you ? — She brought the book to
me.

" John, tell the truth : who hurts you ?   Have you been
hurt ? — The first was a gentlewoman I saw.

" Who next ? — Goody Cloyse.

" But who hurt you next ? — Goody Procter.

" What did she do to you ? — She choked me, and
brought the book.

" How oft did she come to torment you ? — A good many
times, she and Goody Cloyse.

" Do they come to you in the night, as well as the day?
— They come most in the day.

" Who? — Goody Cloyse and Goody Procter.

" Where did she take hold of you? — Upon my throat, to
stop my breath.

" Do you know Goody Cloyse and Goody Procter? —
Yes: here is Goody Cloyse."

We may well suppose that these two respectable
women must have been filled with indignation, shocked,
and amazed at the statements made by the Indian,
following the leading interrogatories of the Court.
Sarah Cloyse broke out, " When did I hurt thee?"
He answered, "A great many times." She exclaimed,
" Oh, you are a grievous liar!" The Court proceeded
with their questions: —

" What did this Goody Cloyse do to you? — She pinched
and bit me till the blood came.

" How long since this woman came and hurt you? — Yesterday, at meeting.

" At any time before? — Yes: a great many times."

Having drawn out John Indian, the Court turned to
the other afflicted ones: —

" Mary Walcot, who hurts you? — Goody Cloyse.

" What did she do to you? — She hurt me.

" Did she bring the book? — Yes.

" What was you to do with it? — To touch it, and be
well.

" (Then she fell into a fit.)"

This put a stop to the examination for a time; but
it was generally quite easy to bring witnesses out of a

fit, and restore entire calmness of mind. All that was necessary was to lift them up, and carry them to the accused person, the touch of any part of whose body would, in an instant, relieve the sufferer. This having been done, the examination proceeded : —

"Doth she come alone? — Sometimes alone, and sometimes in company with Goody Nurse and Goody Corey, and a great many I do not know.

"(Then she fell into a fit again.)"

She was, probably, restored in the same way as before; but, her part being finished for that stage of the proceeding, another of the afflicted children took the stand : —

"Abigail Williams, did you see a company at Mr. Parris's house eat and drink? — Yes, sir: that was in the sacrament."

I would call attention to the form of the foregoing questions. Hutchinson says that "Mr. Parris was over-officious: most of the examinations, although in the presence of one or more magistrates, were taken by him." He put the questions. They show, on this occasion, a minute knowledge beforehand of what the witnesses are to say, which it cannot be supposed Danforth, Russell, Addington, Appleton, and Sewall, strangers, as they were, to the place and the details of the affair, could have had. The examination proceeded : —

"How many were there? — About forty, and Goody Cloyse and Goody Good were their deacons.

" What was it ? — They said it was our blood, and they had it twice that day."

The interrogator again turned to Mary Walcot, and inquired, —

" Have you seen a white man ? — Yes, sir : a great many times.

" What sort of a man was he ? — A fine grave man ; and, when he came, he made all the witches to tremble.

" (Abigail Williams confirmed the same, and that they had such a sight at Deacon Ingersoll's.)

" Who was at Deacon Ingersoll's then ? — Goody Cloyse, Goody Nurse, Goody Corey, and Goody Good.

" (Then Sarah Cloyse asked for water, and sat down, as one seized with a dying, fainting fit ; and several of the afflicted fell into fits, and some of them cried out, ' Oh ! her spirit has gone to prison to her sister Nurse.')"

The audacious lying of the witnesses ; the horrid monstrousness of their charges against Sarah Cloyse, of having bitten the flesh of the Indian brute, and drank herself and distributed to others, as deacon, at an infernal sacrament, the blood of the wicked creatures making these foul and devilish declarations, known by her to be utterly and wickedly false ; and the fact that they were believed by the deputy, the council, and the assembly, — were more than she could bear. Her soul sickened at such unimaginable depravity and wrong ; her nervous system gave way ; she fainted, and sunk to the floor. The manner in which the girls turned the incident against her shows how they were hardened to all human feeling, and the

cunning art which, on all occasions, characterized their
proceedings. That such an insolent interruption and
disturbance, on their part, was permitted, without rebuke from the Court, is a perpetual dishonor to every
member of it. The scene exhibited at this moment,
in the meeting-house, is worthy of an attempt to imagine. The most terrible sensation was naturally produced, by the swooning of the prisoner, the loudly
uttered and savage mockery of the girls, and their
going simultaneously into fits, screaming at the top of
their voices, twisting into all possible attitudes, stiffened
as in death, or gasping with convulsive spasms of
agony, and crying out, at intervals, "There is the black
man whispering in Cloyse's ear," "There is a yellow-
bird flying round her head." John Indian, on such
occasions, used to confine his achievements to tumbling, and rolling his ugly body about the floor. The
deepest commiseration was felt by all for the "afflicted," and men and women rushed to hold and soothe
them. There was, no doubt, much loud screeching, and
some miscellaneous faintings, through the whole crowd.
At length, by bringing the sufferers into contact with
Goody Cloyse, the diabolical fluid passed back into her,
they were all relieved, and the examination was resumed. Elizabeth Procter was now brought forward.

In the account given, in the First Part, of the population of Salem Village and the contiguous farms, her
husband, John Procter, was introduced to our acquaintance. From what we then saw of him, we are
well assured that he would not shrink from the protec-

tion and defence of his wife. He accompanied her from her arrest to her arraignment, and stood by her side, a strong, brave, and resolute guardian, trying to support her under the terrible trials of her situation, and ready to comfort and aid her to the extent of his power, disregardful of all consequences to himself. The examination proceeded : —

"Elizabeth Procter, you understand whereof you are charged ; viz , to be guilty of sundry acts of witchcraft. What say you to it ? Speak the truth ; and so you that are afflicted, you must speak the truth, as you will answer it before God another day. Mary Walcot, doth this woman hurt you ? — I never saw her so as to be hurt by her.

"Mercy Lewis, does she hurt you ?

"(Her mouth was stopped.)

"Ann Putnam, does she hurt you ?

"(She could not speak.)

"Abigail Williams, does she hurt you ?

"(Her hand was thrust in her own mouth.)

"John, does she hurt you ? — This is the woman that came in her shift, and choked me.

"Did she ever bring the book ? — Yes, sir.

"What to do ? — To write.

"What ? this woman ? — Yes, sir.

"Are you sure of it ? — Yes, sir.

"(Again Abigail Williams and Ann Putnam were spoke to by the Court ; but neither of them could make any answer, by reason of dumbness or other fits.)

"What do you say, Goody Procter, to these things ? — I take God in heaven to be my witness, that I know nothing of it, no more than the child unborn.

" Ann Putnam, doth this woman hurt you? — Yes, sir : a great many times.

" (Then the accused looked upon them, and they fell into fits.)

" She does not bring the book to you, does she ? —Yes, sir, often ; and saith she hath made her maid set her hand to it.

" Abigail Williams, does this woman hurt you? — Yes, sir, often.

" Does she bring the book to you? — Yes.

" What would she have you do with it? — To write in it, and I shall be well."

Turning to the accused, Abigail said, " Did not you tell me that your maid had written?" Goody Procter seems to have been utterly amazed at the conduct and charges of the girls. She knew, of course, that what they said was false ; but perhaps she thought them crazy, and therefore objects of pity and compassion, and felt disposed to treat them kindly, and see whether they could not be recalled to their senses, and restored to their better nature : for Parris, in his account, says that at this point she answered the question thus put to her by Abigail thus : " Dear child, it is not so.   There is another judgment, dear child." But kindness was thrown away upon them ; for Parris says that immediately " Abigail and Ann had fits."   After coming out of them, " they cried out, ' Look you! there is Goody Procter upon the beam.' " Instantly, as we may well suppose, the whole audience looked where they pointed.   Their manner gave assurance that they saw her " on the beam," among the rafters of the meeting-house; but she was invisible to all other eyes. The people, no doubt, were filled with amazement at such supernaturalism. But John Procter, her husband, did not believe a word of it: and it is not to be doubted that he expressed his indignation at the nonsense and the outrage in his usual bold, strong, and unguarded language, which brought down the vengeance of the girls at once on his own head; for Parris, in his report, goes on to say: —

"(By and by, both of them cried out of Goodman Procter himself, and said he was a wizard. Immediately, many if not all of the bewitched had grievous fits.)

"Ann Putnam, who hurt you? — Goodman Procter, and his wife too.

"(Afterwards, some of the afflicted cried, 'There is Procter going to take up Mrs. Pope's feet!' and her feet were immediately taken up.)

"What do you say, Goodman Procter, to these things? — I know not. I am innocent.

"(Abigail Williams cried out, 'There is Goodman Procter going to Mrs. Pope!' and immediately said Pope fell into a fit.)"

At this point, the deputy, or some member of the Court interposed, if I interpret rightly Parris's report, which is here obscurely expressed, inasmuch as he does not say who spoke; but the import of the words indicates that they proceeded from some member of the Court, who was perfectly deceived: —

"You see, the Devil will deceive you: the children could see what you was going to do before the woman was hurt.

I would advise you to repentance, for the Devil is bringing
you out.

" (Abigail Williams cried out again, ' There is Goodman
Procter going to hurt Goody Bibber!' and immediately
Goody Bibber fell into a fit. There was the like of Mary
Walcot, and divers others. Benjamin Gould gave in his
testimony, that he had seen Goodman Corey and his wife,
Procter and his wife, Goody Cloyse, Goody Nurse, and
Goody Griggs in his chamber last Thursday night. Elizabeth Hubbard was in a trance during the whole examination.
During the examination of Elizabeth Procter, Abigail Williams and Ann Putnam both made offer to strike at said
Procter; but, when Abigail's hand came near, it opened, —
whereas it was made up into a fist before, — and came down
exceeding lightly as it drew near to said Procter, and at
length, with open and extended fingers, touched Procter's
hood very lightly. Immediately, Abigail cried out, her fingers, her fingers, her fingers burned; and Ann Putnam took
on most grievously of her head, and sunk down.)"

Hutchinson, after giving Parris's account of this
examination, expresses himself thus : " No wonder the
whole country was in a consternation, when persons of
sober lives and unblemished characters were committed to prison upon such sort of evidence. Nobody
was safe." All things considered, it may perhaps be
said, that, filled as the witchcraft proceedings were
throughout with folly and outrage, there was nothing
worse than this examination, conducted by the deputy-
governor and council, on the 11th of April, 1692, in
the great meeting-house of the First Church in Salem.
It must have been a scene of the wildest disorder, par-

ticularly in the latter part of it. No wonder that the people in general were deluded, when the most learned councillors of the colony countenanced, participated in, and gave effect to, such disorderly procedures in a house of worship, in the presence of a high judicial tribunal, and of the then supreme government of the colony!

Benjamin Gould gave his volunteer testimony without "advisedness," and quite incontinently. He brought out Goodman Corey before the managers were quite ready to fall upon him; and he antedated, by a considerable length of time, any such imputation upon Goody Griggs. It was well for Elizabeth Hubbard to have been in a trance, so that she could not hear the mention of her aunt's name. The council seems to have adjourned to the next day, at the same place, when Mr. Parris "gave further information against said John Procter," which, unfortunately, has not come down to us. The result was, that Sarah Cloyse, John Procter, and Elizabeth his wife, were all committed for trial, and, with Rebecca Nurse, Martha Corey, and Dorcas Good, were sent to the jail in Boston, in the custody of Marshal Herrick.

The proceedings of the 11th and 12th of April produced a great effect in driving on the general infatuation. Judge Sewall, who was present as one of the council, in his diary at this date, says, " Went to Salem, where, in the meeting-house, the persons accused of witchcraft were examined; was a very great assembly; 'twas awful to see how the afflicted persons

were agitated." In the margin is written, apparently
some time afterwards, the interjection " *Væ!* " thrice
repeated, — " Alas, alas, alas! " What perfectly deluded him and Danforth, and everybody else, were the
exhibitions made by the " afflicted children." This is
the grand phenomenon of the witchcraft proceedings
here in 1692. It, and it alone, carried them through.
Those girls, by long practice in " the circle," and day
by day, before astonished and wondering neighbors
gathered to witness their distresses, and especially on
the more public occasions of the examinations, had
acquired consummate boldness and tact. In simula-
tion of passions, sufferings, and physical affections; in
sleight of hand, and in the management of voice and
feature and attitude, — no necromancers have surpassed them. There has seldom been better acting in
a theatre than they displayed in the presence of the
astonished and horror-stricken rulers, magistrates,
ministers, judges, jurors, spectators, and prisoners.
No one seems to have dreamed that their actings and
sufferings could have been the result of cunning or
imposture. Deodat Lawson was a man of talents, had
seen much of the world, and was by no means a simple-
ton, recluse, or novice; but he was wholly deluded by
them. The prisoners, although conscious of their own
innocence, were utterly confounded by the acting of the
girls. The austere principles of that generation forbade, with the utmost severity, all theatrical shows and
performances. But at Salem Village and the old
town, in the respective meeting-houses, and at Deacon

Nathaniel Ingersoll's, some of the best playing ever got up in this country was practised ; and patronized, for weeks and months, at the very centre and heart of Puritanism, by " the most straitest sect" of that solemn order of men. Pastors, deacons, church-members, doctors of divinity, college professors, officers of state, crowded, day after day, to behold feats which have never been surpassed on the boards of any thea-tre ; which rivalled the most memorable achievements of pantomimists, thaumaturgists, and stage-players ; and made considerable approaches towards the best performances of ancient sorcerers and magicians, or modern jugglers and mesmerizers.

The meeting of the council at Salem, on the 11th of April, 1692, changed in one sense the whole charac-ter of the transaction. Before, it had been a Salem affair. After this, it was a Massachusetts affair. The colonial government at Boston had obtruded itself upon the ground, and, of its own will and seeking, ir-regularly, and without call or justification, had taken the whole thing out of the hands of the local author-ities into its own management. Neither the town nor the village of Salem is responsible, as a principal actor, for what subsequently took place. To that meeting of the deputy-governor and his associates in the colonial administration, at an early period of the transaction, the calamities, outrages, and shame that followed must in justice be ascribed. Had it not taken place, the delusion, as in former instances and other places here and in the mother-country, would have remained within its original local limits, and soon disappeared. That meeting, and the proceedings then had, gave to the fanaticism the momentum that drove it on, and extended its destructive influence far and wide.

The next step in the proceedings is one of the most remarkable features in the case. It is, in some points of view, more suggestive of suspicion, that there was, behind the whole, a skilful and cunning management, ingeniously contriving schemes to mislead the public mind, than almost any other part of the transaction. Mary Warren, as has been said, was a servant in the family of John Procter. She was a member of the "circle" that had so long met at Mr. Parris's house or Thomas Putnam's. She was a constant attendant at its meetings, and a leading spirit among the girls. She did not take an open part against her master or mistress at their examination, although she acted with avidity and malignity against them as an accusing witness at their trials, two months afterwards. It is to be noticed, that Ann Putnam and Abigail Williams, at the examination of Elizabeth Procter, April 11, accused her of having induced or compelled "her maid to set her hand to the book."

On the 18th of April, warrants were got out against Giles Corey and Mary Warren, both of Salem Farms; Abigail Hobbs, daughter of William Hobbs, of Topsfield; and Bridget Bishop, wife of Edward Bishop, of Salem, — to be brought in the next forenoon, at about eight o'clock, at the house of Lieutenant Nathaniel

Ingersoll, of Salem Village. How Mary Warren became transformed from an accuser to an accused, from an afflicted person to an afflicter, is the question. It is not easy to fathom the conduct of these girls. They appear to have acted upon a plan deliberately formed, and to have had an understanding with each other. At the same time, occasionally, they had or pretended to have a falling-out, and came into contradiction. This was perhaps a mere blind, to prevent the suspicion of collusion. The accounts given of Mary Warren seem to render it quite certain that she acted with deliberate cunning, and was a guilty conspirator with the other accusers in carrying on the plot from the beginning. No doubt, it frequently occurred to those concerned in it, that suspicions might possibly get into currency that they were acting a part in concert. It was necessary, by all means, to guard against such an idea. This may be the key to interpret the arrest and proceedings against Mary Warren. If it is, the affair, it must be confessed, was managed with great shrewdness and skill. She conducted the stratagem most dexterously. All at once she fell away from the circle, and began to talk against the " afflicted children," and went so far as to say, that they " did but dissemble." Immediately, they cried out upon her, charged her with witchcraft, and had her apprehended. After being carried to prison, she spoke in strong language against the proceedings. Four persons of unquestionable truthfulness, in prison with her, on the same charge, prepared a deposition to this effect: " We heard Mary Warren several times say that the magistrates might as well examine Keysar's daughter that had been distracted many years, and take notice of what she said, as well as any of the afflicted persons. 'For,' said Mary Warren, 'when I was afflicted, I thought I saw the apparitions of a hundred persons;' for she said her head was distempered that she could not tell what she said. And the said Mary told us, that, when she was well again, she could not say that she saw any of the apparitions at the time aforesaid." I will now give the substance of her examination, which commenced on the 19th of April. Mr. Parris was, as usual, requested to take minutes of the proceedings, which have been preserved: —

" *Examination of Mary Warren, at a Court held at Salem Village, by John Hathorne and Jonathan Corwin, Esqrs.*

" (As soon as she was coming towards the bar, the afflicted fell into fits.)

" Mary Warren, you stand here charged with sundry acts of witchcraft. What do you say for yourself? Are you guilty or not? — I am innocent.

" Hath she hurt you? (Speaking to the sufferers.)

" (Some were dumb. Betty Hubbard testified against her, and then said Hubbard fell into a violent fit.)

" You were, a little while ago, an afflicted person; now you are an afflicter. How comes this to pass? — I look up to God, and take it to be a great mercy of God.

" What! do you take it to be a great mercy to afflict others?

" (Now they were all but John Indian grievously afflicted,

and Mrs. Pope also, who was not afflicted before hitherto
this day; and, after a few moments, John Indian fell into
a violent fit also.)"

"Well, here" (Mr. Parris, the reporter, goes on
to say) "was one that just now was a tormenter in
her apparition, and she owns that she had made a
league with the Devil." The marvel was, that, having
before been a sufferer, as one of the afflicted accusers,
she had then, at that moment, appeared in the opposite character, and owned herself to have become a
confederate with the Evil One. Having established
this conviction in the minds of the magistrates and
spectators, the point was reached at which she completed the delusion by appearing to break away from
her bondage to Satan, assume the functions of a confessing and abjuring witch, and retake her place, with
tenfold effect, among the accusing witnesses. The
manner in which she rescued herself from the power
of Satan exhibits a specimen of acting seldom surpassed. The account proceeds thus: —

"Now Mary Warren fell into a fit, and some of the
afflicted cried out that she was going to confess; but Goody
Corey, and Procter and his wife, came in, *in their apparition*,
and struck her down, and said she should tell nothing."

What is given here in *Italics*, as an "*apparition*,"
was of course based upon the declarations of the
accusing witnesses. It was an art they often practised in offering their testimony. They would cry
out, that the Devil, generally in the shape of a black
man, appeared to them at the time, whispering in the

ear of the accused, or sitting on the beams of the meeting-house in which the examinations were generally conducted. On this occasion, they declared that three of the persons, then in jail in some other place, came in their apparitions, forbade Mary Warren's confession, and struck her down. To give full effect to their statement, she went through the process of tumbling down. Although nothing was seen by any other person present, the deception was perfect. The Rev. Mr. Parris wrote it all down as having actually occurred. His record of the transaction goes on as follows : —

" Mary Warren continued a good space in a fit, that she did neither see nor hear nor speak.

" Afterwards she started up, and said, ' I will speak,' and cried out, ' Oh, I am sorry for it, I am sorry for it ! ' and wringed her hands, and fell a little while into a fit again, and then came to speak, but immediately her teeth were set ; and then she fell into a violent fit, and cried out, ' O Lord, help me ! O good Lord, save me ! '

" And then afterwards cried again, ' I will tell, I will tell ! ' and then fell into a dead fit again.

" And afterwards cried, ' I will tell, they did, they did, they did ; ' and then fell into a violent fit again.

" After a little recovery, she cried, ' I will tell, I will tell. They brought me to it ; ' and then fell into a fit again, which fits continuing, she was ordered to be led out, and the next to be brought in, viz., Bridget Bishop.

" Some time afterwards, she was called in again, but immediately taken with fits for a while.

" ' Have you signed the Devil's book ? — No.'

" ' Have you not touched it ? — No.'

" Then she fell into fits again, and was sent forth for air.

" After a considerable space of time, she was brought in again, but could not give account of things by reason of fits, and so sent forth.

" Mary Warren called in afterwards in private, before magistrates and ministers.

" She said, ' I shall not speak a word : but I will, I will speak, Satan! She saith she will kill me. Oh! she saith she owes me a spite, and will claw me off. Avoid Satan, for the name of God, avoid!' and then fell into fits again, and cried, ' Will ye? I will prevent ye, in the name of God.'"

The magistrate inquired earnestly : —

" ' Tell us how far have you yielded ? '

" A fit interrupts her again.

" ' What did they say you should do, and you should be well ? '

" Then her lips were bit, so that she could not speak : so she was sent away."

Mr. Parris, the reporter of the case, adds : —

" Note that not one of the sufferers was afflicted during her examination, after once she began to confess, though they were tormented before."

She was subsequently examined in the prison several times, falling occasionally into fits, and exhibiting the appearance of a long-continued conflict with Satan, who was supposed to be resisting her inclination to confess, and holding her with violence to the contract she had made with him. The magistrates and ministers beheld with amazement and awe what they believed to be precisely a similar scene to that described by the evangelists when the Devil strove against the power of the Saviour and his disciples, and would not quit his hold upon the young man, but " threw him down, and tare him." At length, as in that case, Satan was overcome. After a protracted, most violent, and terrible contest, Mary Warren got released from his clutches, and made a full and circumstantial confession.

Whoever studies carefully the account of Mary Warren's successive examinations can hardly question, I think, that she acted a part, and acted it with wonderful cunning, skill, and effect.

This examination, beginning on Tuesday, the 19th of April, continued after she was committed to prison in Salem, at the jail there, for several days, and was renewed at intervals until the middle of May. After she had thoroughly broken away from Satan, she revealed all that she had seen and heard while associating with him and his confederate subjects : her testimony was implicitly received, and it dealt death and destruction in all directions. It is a circumstance strongly confirming this view, that Mary Warren was soon released from confinement. It was the general practice to keep those, who confessed, in prison, to retain in that way power over them, and prevent their recanting their confessions. She is found, by the papers on file, to have acted afterwards, as a capital witness,

against ten persons, all of whom were convicted, and
seven executed. Besides these, she testified, with the
appearance of animosity and vindictiveness, against her
master John Procter, and her mistress his wife ; thus
contributing to secure the conviction of both, and
the death of the former. In how many more cases
she figured in the same character and to the same
effect is unknown, as the papers in reference to only
a very small proportion of them have come down to
us. The interpretation I give to the course of Mary
Warren exhibits her guilt, and that of those participating in the stratagem, as of the deepest and blackest
dye. But it seems to be the only one which a scrutiny
of the details of her examinations, and of the facts of
the case, allows us to receive. The effect was most
decisive. The course of the accusing children in
crying out against one of their own number satisfied
the public, and convinced still more the magistrates,
that they were truthful, honest, and upright. They
had before given evidence that they paid no regard
to family influence or eminent reputation. They had
now proved that they had no partiality and no favoritism, but were equally ready to bring to light and to
justice any of their own circle who might fall into
the snare of the Evil One, and become confederate
with him. No dramatic artist, no cunning impostor,
ever contrived a more ingenious plot; and no actors
ever carried one out better than Mary Warren and
the afflicted children.

Giles Corey incurred hostility, perhaps, because his

deposition relating to his wife did not come up to the mark required. It is also highly probable, that, though incensed at her conduct at the time, reflection had brought him to his senses; and that the circumstances of her examination and commitment to prison produced a re-action in his mind. If so, he would have been apt to express himself very freely. His examination took place April 19th, in the meeting-house at the Village. The girls acted their usual part, charging him, one by one, with having afflicted them, and proving it on the spot by tortures and sufferings. After they had severally got through, they all joined at once in their demonstrations. The report made by Parris says, "All the afflicted were seized now with fits, and troubled with pinches. Then the Court ordered his hands to be tied." The magistrates lost all control of themselves, and flew into a passion, exclaiming, " What! is it not enough to act witchcraft at other times, but must you do it now, in face of authority?" He seems to have been profoundly affected by the marvellousness of the accusations, and the exhibition of what to him was inexplicable in the sufferings of the girls; and all he could say was, " I am a poor creature, and cannot help it." — " Upon the motion of his head again, they had their heads and necks afflicted." The magistrates, not having recovered their composure, continued to pour their wrath upon him, " Why do you tell such wicked lies against witnesses?" — " One of his hands was let go, and several were afflicted. He held his head on one side,

and then the heads of several of the afflicted were
held on one side. He drew in his cheeks, and the
cheeks of some of the afflicted were sucked in." Goody
Bibber was on hand, and played her accompaniment.
She also uttered malignant charges against him, and
" was suddenly seized with a violent fit." One of
Bibber's statements was that he had called her husband
" damned devilish rogue." Through all this outrage,
Corey was firm in asserting his innocence. His language and manner were serious, and solemnized by
a sense of the helplessness of his situation and the
wicked falsehoods heaped upon him. His disagreement with his wife about the witchcraft proceedings
being well known, the accusers endeavored to make
it out that they had often quarrelled. But he insisted
that the only difference which had before existed between them was a conflict of opinion on one point.
In his family devotions, he used this expression, " living to God and dying to sin." She " found fault " with
the language, and criticised it. He thought it was all
right! The characteristic spirit of the old man was
roused most strikingly by one of the charges. Bibber and others testified that Corey had said he had
seen the Devil in the shape of a black hog and
was very much frightened. He could not stand
under the imputation of cowardice, and lost sight of
every other element in the accusation but that. The
magistrate asked, " What did you see in the cow-
house? Why do you deny it?" — " I saw nothing
but my cattle." — " (Divers witnessed that he told

them he was frighted.) " — " Well, what do you say
to these witnesses? What was it frighted you?" —
" I do not know that ever I spoke the word in my
life."

But while his character retained its manliness, and
his soul was truly insensible to fear, he was very
much oppressed and distressed by his situation. The
share he had, with two of his sons-in-law, in bringing
his wife into her awful condition, and in driving on
the public infatuation at the beginning, was more than
he could endure to think of, and he was charged with
having meditated suicide. Perhaps he had already
formed the purpose afterwards carried into effect, and
may have dropped expressions, under that thought,
which to others might appear to indicate a design of self-
destruction. He was accused of having said that " he
would make away with himself, and charge his death
upon his son." His sons-in-law, Crosby and Parker,
were acting with the crowd that were pursuing him
to his death. Little did it enter the imagination of
any one then, that there was a method by which he
could " make away with himself," leaving the entire
act of the destruction of his life upon his persecutors,
and the sin to be apportioned between him and them
by the All-wise and All-just.

Abigail Hobbs had been a reckless vagrant creature,
wandering through the woods at night like a half-
deranged person; but she had wit enough to see that
there was safety in confession. She pretended to
have committed, by witchcraft, crimes enough to have

hanged her a dozen times. If she had stood to her confession, we should have heard of her no more.

Bridget Bishop's examination filled the intervals of time while Mary Warren was being carried out of the meeting-house to recover from her fits. Both Parris and Ezekiel Cheever took minutes of it, from which the substance is gathered as follows: —

On her coming in, the afflicted persons, at the same moment, severally fell into fits, and were dreadfully tormented. Hathorne addressed her, calling upon her to give an account of the witchcrafts she was " conversant in." She replied, " I take all this people to witness that I am clear." He then asked the children, " Hath this woman hurt you ? " They all cried out that she had. The magistrate continued, " You are here accused by four or five : what do you say to it ? " — " I never saw these persons before, nor I never * was in this place before. I never did hurt them in my life."

At a meeting of the afflicted children and others, some one declared that Bridget Bishop was present " in her shape " or apparition, and, pointing to a particular spot, said, " There, there she is ! " Young Jonathan Walcot, exasperated by his sister's sufferings, struck at the spot with his sword ; whereupon Mary cried out, " You have hit her, you have torn her coat, and I heard it tear." This story had been brought to Hathorne's ears ; and abruptly, as if to take her off her guard,

* The double negative, as often used, merely intensified the negation. See "Measure for Measure," act i. scene 1.

he said, "Is not your coat cut?" She answered, "No." They then examined the coat, and found what they regarded as having been "cut or torn two ways." It was probably the fashion in which the garment was made; for she was in the habit of dressing more artistically than the women of the Village. At any rate, it did not appear like a direct cut of a sword; but Jonathan got over the difficulty by saying that "the sword that he struck at Goody Bishop was not naked, but was within the scabbard." This explained the whole matter, so that Cheever says, in his report, that "the rent may very probably be the very same that Mary Walcot did tell that she had in her coat, by Jonathan's striking at her appearance"! Parris says, with more caution, more indeed than was usual with him, "Upon some search in the Court, a rent, that seems to answer what was alleged, was found."

Hathorne, having heard the scandals they had circulated against her, proceeded: "They say you bewitched your first husband to death." — "If it please Your Worship, I know nothing of it." — "What do you say of these murders you are charged with?" — "I hope I am not guilty of murder." As she said this, she turned up her eyes, probably to give solemnity to her declaration. At the opening of the examination, she looked round upon the people, and called them to witness her innocence. She had found out by this time, that no justice could be expected from them; and feeling, with Rebecca Nurse on a recent similar occasion, "I have got nobody to look to but

God," she turned her eyes heavenward. Instantly, the eyeballs of all the girls were rolled up in their sockets, and fixed. The effect was awful, and still more increased as they went, after a moment or two, into dreadful torments. Hathorne could no longer contain himself, but broke out, " Do you not see how they are tormented ? You are acting witchcraft before us ! What do you say to this ? Why have you not a heart to confess the truth ? " She calmly replied, " I am innocent. I know nothing of it. I am no witch. I know not what a witch is." The " afflicted children " charged her with having tried to persuade them to sign the Devil's book. As she had never before seen one of them, she was indignant at this barefaced falsehood, and, as Cheever says, " shook her head " in her resentment ; which, as he further says, put them all into great torments. Parris represents that in every motion of her head they were tortured. Marshal Herrick, as usual, put in his oar, and volunteered charges against her. She bore herself well through the shocking scene, and did not shrink, at its close, from expressing her unbelief of the whole thing : " I do not know whether there be any witches or no." When she was removed from the place of examination, the accusers all had fits, and broke forth in outcries of agony. After being taken out, one of the constables in charge of her asked her if she was not troubled to see the afflicted persons so tormented ; and she replied, " No." In answer to further questions, she indicated that she could not

tell what to think of them, and did not concern herself about them at all.

Giles Corey, Bridget Bishop, Abigail Hobbs, together
with Mary Warren, were duly committed to prison.

Two days after, April 21, warrants were issued
" against William Hobbs, husbandman, and Deliverance his wife; Nehemiah Abbot, Jr., weaver; Mary
Easty, the wife of Isaac Easty; and Sarah Wilds, the
wife of John Wilds, — all of the town of Topsfield, or
Ipswich; and Edward Bishop, husbandman, and Sarah
his wife, of Salem Village; and Mary Black, a negro of
Lieutenant Nathaniel Putnam's, of Salem Village also;
and Mary English, the wife of Philip English, merchant
in Salem." All of them were to be delivered to the
magistrates for examination at the house of Lieutenant Nathaniel Ingersoll, at about ten o'clock the
next morning, in Salem Village; and were brought
in accordingly.

What the papers on file enable us to glean of these
nine persons is substantially as follows: William
Hobbs was about fifty years of age, and one of the
earliest settlers of the Village, although his residence was on the territory afterwards included in
Topsfield. His daughter Abigail, of whom I have
just spoken, appears from all the accounts to have
acted at this stage of the transaction a most wicked
part, ready to do all the mischief in her power, and
allowing herself to be used to any extent to fasten
the imputation of witchcraft upon others. Several
persons testified that, long before, she had boasted that

she was not afraid of any thing, " for she had sold
herself body and soul to the Old Boy ; " one witness
testified, that, " some time last winter, I was discoursing with Abigail Hobbs about her wicked car-
riages and disobedience to her father and mother,
and she told me she did not care what anybody said to
her, for she had seen the Devil, and had made a covenant or bargain with him ; " another, Margaret Knight,
testified, that, about a year before, " Abigail Hobbs
and her mother were at my father's house, and Abigail Hobbs said to me, ' Margaret, are you baptized ? '
And I said, ' Yes.' Then said she, ' My mother is
not baptized, but I will baptize her ; ' and immediately
took water, and sprinkled in her mother's face, and
said she did baptize her ' in the name of the Father,
Son, and Holy Ghost.' "

She was arrested, and brought to the Village, on the
19th of April. The next day, she began her operations by declaring that " Judah White, a Jersey maid "
that lived with Joseph Ingersoll at Casco, " but now
lives at Boston," appeared to her " in apparition " the
day before, and advised her to " fly, and not to go to
be examined," but, if she did go, " not to confess any
thing : " she described the dress of this " apparition,"
— she " came to her in fine clothes, in a sad-colored
silk mantle, with a top-knot and a hood." — " She confesseth further, that the Devil in the shape of a man
came to her," and charged her to afflict the girls ;
bringing images made of wood in their likeness with
thorns for her to prick into the images, which she

did: whereupon the girls cried out that they were hurt
by her. She further confessed, that, " she was at the
great meeting in Mr. Parris's pasture, when they administered the sacrament, and did eat of the red bread
and drink of the red wine, at the same time." This
confession established her credibility at once; and,
the next day, the warrants were issued for the nine
persons above mentioned, against whom they had
secured in her an effective witness. She had resided
for some time at Casco Bay; and we shall soon see
how matters began in a few days to work in that direction. There are two indictments against this Abigail
Hobbs: one charging her with having made a covenant with " the Evil Spirit, the Devil," at Casco Bay,
in 1688; the other with having exercised the arts of
witchcraft upon the afflicted girls, at Salem Village,
in 1692.

When her unhappy father was brought to examination, he found that his daughter was playing into the
hands of the accusers; and that his wife, overwhelmed
by the horrors of the situation, although for a time
protesting her innocence and lamenting that she had
been the mother of such a daughter, had broken
down and confessed, saying whatever might be put
in her mouth by the magistrates, the girls, or the
crowd. Under these circumstances, he was brought
forward for examination. Parris took minutes of it.
It is to be regretted, that the paper is much dilapidated,
and portions of the lines wholly lost. What is left
shows that the mind of William Hobbs rose superior

to the terrors and powers arrayed against it. The magistrate commenced proceedings by inquiring of the girls, pointing to the prisoner, " Hath this man hurt you? " Several of them answered " Yes." Goody Bibber, who seems generally to have been a very zealous volunteer backer of the girls, on this occasion, for a wonder, answered " No." The magistrate, addressing the prisoner, " What say you? Are you guilty or not? " — Answer : " I can speak in the presence of God safely, as I must look to give account another day, that I am as clear as a new-born babe? " — " Clear of what? " — " Of witchcraft." — " Have you never hurt these? " — " No." Abigail Williams cried out that he " was going to Mercy Lewis! " Whereupon Mercy was seized with a fit. Then Abigail cried out again, " He is coming to Mary Walcot! " and Mary went into her fit. The magistrate, in consternation, appealed to him : " How can you be clear," when your appearance is thus seen producing such effects before our eyes? Then the children went into fits all together, and " hallooed " at the top of their voices, and " shouted greatly." The magistrate then brought up the confession of his wife against him, and expostulated with him for not confessing ; the afflicted, in the mean while, bringing the whole machinery of their convulsions, shrieks, and uproar to bear against him : but he calmly, and in brief terms, denied it.

The circle of accusing girls seems to have been a receptacle, into which all the scandal, gossip, and defamation of the surrounding country was emptied. Some one had told them that William Hobbs was not a regular attendant at meeting. They passed it on to the magistrate, and he put this question to the accused: " When were you at any public religious meeting? " He replied, " Not a pretty while." — " Why so ? " — " Because I was not well: I had a distemper that none knows. " The magistrate said, " Can you act witchcraft here, and, by casting your eyes, turn folks into fits ? " — " You may judge your pleasure. My soul is clear." — " Do you not see you hurt these by your look ? " — " No : I do not know it." After another display of awful sufferings, caused, as they protested, by the mere look of Hobbs, the magistrate, with triumphant confidence, again put it home to him, " Can you now deny it ? " He answered, " I can deny it to my dying day." The magistrate inquired of him for what reason he withdrew from the room whenever the Scriptures were read in his family. He plumply denied it. Nathaniel Ingersoll and Thomas Haynes testified that his daughter had told them so. The confessions of his wife and daughter were over and over again brought up against him, but to no effect. " Who do you worship ? " said the magistrate. " I hope I worship God only." — " Where ? " — " In my heart." The examination failed to confound or embarrass him in the least. He could not be drawn into the expression of any of the feelings which the conduct of his graceless and depraved daughter or his weak and wretched wife must have

excited. He quietly protested that he knew nothing
about witchcraft; and, towards the close, with solemn
earnestness of utterance, declared that his innocence
was known to the " great God in heaven."

He was committed for trial. All that the documents in existence inform us further, in relation to
William Hobbs, is that he remained in prison until
the 14th of the next December, when two of his neighbors, John Nichols and Joseph Towne, in some way
succeeded in getting him bailed out ; they giving bonds
in the sum of two hundred pounds for his appearance at the sessions of the Court the next month.
But it was not, even then, thought wholly safe to
have him come in ; and the fine was incurred. He
appeared at the term in May, the fine was remitted,
and he discharged by proclamation. On the 26th of
March, 1714, he gave evidence in a case of common-
age rights. He was then seventy-two years of age.
Of his wife and daughter, I shall again have occasion
to speak.

For all that is known of the case of Nehemiah
Abbot, we are indebted to Hutchinson, who had
Parris's minutes of the examination before him.
Hutchinson says, that, of " near an hundred " whose
examinations he had seen, he was the only one who,
having been brought before the magistrates, was finally
dismissed by them. Perhaps even this case was not
an exception : for a document on file shows that a
person named Abbot of the same locality was subsequently arrested and imprisoned ; but unfortunately

the Christian name has been obliterated, or from some cause is wanting. It seems, from Hutchinson's minutes, that he protested his innocence in manly and firm declarations. Mary Walcot testified that she had seen his shape. Ann Putnam cried out that she saw him "upon the beam." The magistrates told him that his guilt was certainly proved, and that, if he would find mercy of God, he must confess. "I speak before God," he answered, "that I am clear from this accusation."—"What, in all respects?" —"Yes, in all respects." The girls were struck with dumbness; and Ann Putnam, re-affirming that he was the man that hurt her, "was taken with a fit." Mary Walcot began to waver in her confidence, and Mercy Lewis said, "It is not the man." This unprecedented variance in the testimony of the girls brought matters to a stand; and he was sent out for a time, while others were examined: —

"When he was brought in again, by reason of much people, and many in the windows, so that the accusers could not have a clear view of him, he was ordered to be abroad, and the accusers to go forth to him, and view him in the light, which they did in the presence of the magistrates and many others, discoursed quietly with him, one and all acquitting him; but yet said he was like that man, but he had not the wen they saw in his apparition. Note, he was a hilly-faced man, and stood shaded by reason of his own hair; so that for a time he seemed to some bystanders and observers to be considerably like the person the afflicted did describe."

Such is Parris's statement, as quoted by Hutchinson. What was the real cause or motive of this discrepancy among the witnesses does not appear. The facts, that at first they went into fits in beholding him, were all struck dumb for a while, and Ann Putnam saw him on the beam, were likely to have an unfavorable effect upon the minds of the people, and threatened to explode the delusion. But Ann, with a quickness of wit that never failed to meet any emergency, when Mercy Lewis said it was not the man, cried out in a fit, "Did you put a mist before my eyes?" She conveyed the idea that the power of Satan blinded her, and caused her to mistake the man. This answered the purpose; and, although Abbot got clear, for the time at least, all were more than ever convinced that the Evil One, in misleading Ann, had shown his hand on the occasion.

The examination of Sarah Wildes had no peculiar features. The afflicted children and Goody Bibber saw her apparition sitting on the beam while she was bodily present at the bar, and went through their usual fits and evolutions. She maintained her innocence with dignity and firmness; and the magistrate, prejudging the case against her, rebuked her obstinacy in not confessing, in his accustomed manner.

No account has come down of the examinations of Edward Bishop, or Sarah his wife. He was the third of that name, probably the son of the "Sawyer." His wife Sarah was a daughter of William Wildes of Ipswich, and, it would seem, a sister of John

Wildes, the examination of whose wife has just been mentioned. Some of the evidence indicates that she was a niece of Rebecca Nurse. They all belonged to that class of persons who, under the general appellation of " the Topsfield men," had been in such frequent collision with the people of the Village. Edward Bishop was forty-four years of age, and his wife forty-one. They had a family, at the time of their imprisonment, of twelve children. Sarah Bishop had been dismissed from the church at the Village, and recommended to that at Topsfield, May 25, 1690. They had land in Topsfield, as well as in the Village, and were more intimately connected in social relations with the former than the latter place. They effected their escape from prison, and survived the storm. Mary, the wife of Philip English, was committed to prison. We have no record of her examination.

Mary Black, the negro woman, belonged to Nathaniel Putnam, but lived in the family of his son Benjamin. Her examination shows that she was an ignorant but an innocent person. She knew nothing about the matter, and had no idea what it all meant. To the questions with which the magistrate pressed her, her answers were, "I do not know," "I cannot tell." The only fact brought out against her besides the actings of the girls was this : " Her master saith a man sat down upon the form with her about a twelvemonth ago." Parris, in his minutes, gives this piece of evidence, but does not enlighten us as to its import. The magistrate asked her, " What did the man

say to you?" Her answer was: "He said nothing."
This is all they got out of her; and it is all the light
we have on the mysterious fact, that a man was once
seated, at some time within twelve months, on the
same form or bench with poor Mary Black. The
magistrate asked the girls, "Doth this negro hurt
you?" They said "Yes." — "Why do you hurt
them?" — "I did not hurt them." This question was
put to her, "Do you prick sticks?" perhaps the
meaning was, Do you prick the afflicted children
with sticks? The simple creature evidently did not
know what they were driving at, and answered, "No:
I pin my neckcloth." The examiner asked her,
"Will you take out the pin, and pin it again?" She
did so, and several of the afflicted cried out that they
were pricked. Mary Walcot was pricked in the arm
till the blood came, Abigail Williams was pricked
in the stomach, and Mercy Lewis was pricked in the
foot. It is probable, that, in this case, the girls, as
they often appear to have done, provided themselves
by concert beforehand with pins ready to be stuck
into the assigned parts of their bodies, and managed
to get the queer and unusual question put. The
whole thing has the appearance of being pre-arranged;
and it answered the purpose, filling the crowd with
amazement, and excluding all possible doubt from the
minds of the magistrates. Mary was committed to
prison, where she remained until discharged, in May,
1693, by proclamation from the governor.

Mary Easty, wife of Isaac Easty, and sister of Re-

becca Nurse and Sarah Cloyse, was about fifty-eight
years of age, and the mother of seven children. Her
husband owned and lived upon a large and valuable
farm, which not many years since was the property
and country residence of the late Hon. B. W. Crown-
inshield, and is now in the possession of Thomas
Pierce, Esq. Her examination was accompanied by
the usual circumstances. The girls had fits, and were
speechless at times : the magistrate expostulated with
her for not confessing her guilt, which he regarded
as demonstrated, beyond a question, by the sufferings
of the afflicted. " Would you have me accuse myself ? " — " How far," he continued, " have you complied with Satan ? " — " Sir, I never complied, but
prayed against him all my days. What would you
have me do ? " — " Confess, if you be guilty." — " I
will say it, if it was my last time, I am clear of
this sin." The magistrate, apparently affected by her
manner and bearing, inquired of the girls, " Are you
certain this is the woman ? " They all went into fits ;
and presently Ann Putnam, coming to herself, said
" that was the woman, it was like her, and she told me
her name." The accused clasped her hands together,
and Mercy Lewis's hands were clenched ; she separated her hands, and Mercy's were released ; she inclined her head, and the girls screamed out, " Put up
her head ; for, while her head is bowed, the necks of
these are broken." The magistrate again asked, " Is
this the woman ? " They made signs that they could
not speak ; but afterwards Ann Putnam and others

cried out: "O Goody Easty, Goody Easty, you are the woman, you are the woman!" — "What do you say to this?" — "Why, God will know." — "Nay, God knows now." — "I know he does." — "What did you think of the actions of others before your sisters came out? did you think it was witchcraft?" — "I cannot tell." — "Why do you not think it is witchcraft?" — "It is an evil spirit; but whether it be witchcraft I do not know." She was committed to prison.

It will be noticed that seven out of the nine examined at this time either lived in Topsfield or were intimately connected with the church and people there. The accusing girls had heard them angrily spoken of by the people around them, and availed themselves, as at all times, of existing prejudices, to guide them in the selection of their victim.

The escape of Abbot, and the wavering, in his case and that of Easty, indicated by the magistrates on this occasion, alarmed the prosecutors; and they felt that something must be done to stiffen Hathorne and Corwin to their previous rigid method of procedure. The following letter was accordingly written to them that very day, immediately after the close of the examinations: —

" *These to the Honored John Hathorne and Jonathan Corwin, Esqrs., living at Salem, present.*

"SALEM VILLAGE, this 21st of April, 1692.

" MUCH HONORED, — After most humble and hearty thanks presented to Your Honors for the great care and pains you have already taken for us, — for which you know

we are never able to make you recompense, and we believe
you do not expect it of us ; therefore a full reward will be
given you of the Lord God of Israel, whose cause and interest you have espoused (and we trust this shall add to
your crown of glory in the day of the Lord Jesus) : and
we — beholding continually the tremendous works of Divine
Providence, not only every day, but every hour — thought it
our duty to inform Your Honors of what we conceive you
have not heard, which are high and dreadful, — of a wheel
within a wheel, at which our ears do tingle.   Humbly crav-
ing continually your prayers and help in this distressed case,
— so, praying Almighty God continually to prepare you,
that you may be a terror to evil-doers and a praise to them
that do well, we remain yours to serve in what we are able,

" THOMAS PUTNAM."

What was meant by the "wheel within a wheel,"
the "high and dreadful" things which were making
their ears to tingle, but had not yet been disclosed
to the magistrates, we shall presently see.   On the
30th of April, Captain Jonathan Walcot and Sergeant
Thomas Putnam (the writer of the foregoing letter)
got out a warrant against Philip English, of Salem,
merchant ; Sarah Morrel, of Beverly ; and Dorcas
Hoar, of the same place, widow.   Morrel and Hoar
were delivered by Marshal Herrick, according to the
tenor of the warrant, at 11, A.M., May 2, at the house
of Lieutenant Nathaniel Ingersoll, in Salem Village.
The warrant has an indorsement in these words :
" Mr. Philip English not being to be found.   G. H."
As the records of the examinations of Philip English

and his wife have not been preserved, and only a few
fragments of the testimony relating to their case are
to be found, all that can be said is that the girls and
their accomplices made their usual charges against
them. There are two depositions in existence, however, which afford some explanation of the causes that
exposed Mr. English to hostility, and indicate the kind
of evidence that was brought against him. Having
many landed estates, in various places, and extensive
business transactions, he was liable to frequent questions of litigation. He was involved, at one time, in
a lawsuit about the bounds of a piece of land in
Marblehead. A person named William Beale, of that
town, had taken great interest in it adversely to the
claims of English; and some harsh words passed
between them. A year or two after the affair, Beale
states, " that, as I lay in my bed, in the morning, presently after it was fair light abroad in the room,"
" I saw a dark shade," &c. To his vision it soon
assumed the shape of Philip English. On a previous occasion, when riding through Lynn to get testimony against English in the aforesaid boundary case,
he says, " My nose gushed out bleeding in a most
extraordinary manner, so that it bloodied a handkerchief of considerable bigness, and also ran down
upon my clothes and upon my horse's mane." He
charged it upon English. These depositions were
sworn to in Court, in August, 1692, and January,
1693. How they got there does not appear, as English
was never brought to trial. All that relates to Mr.

English and his wife may be despatched at this point.
On the 6th of May, a warrant was procured at Boston,
" To the marshal-general, or his lawful deputy," to
apprehend Philip English wherever found within the
jurisdiction, and convey him to the " custody of the
marshal of Essex." Jacob Manning, a deputy-mar-
shal, delivered him to the marshal of Essex on the
30th of May ; and he was brought before the magistrates on the next day, and, after examination, committed to prison.   He and his wife effected their
escape from jail, and found refuge in New York
until the proceedings were terminated, when they
returned to Salem, and continued to reside here.
She survived the shock given by the accusation, the
danger to which she had been exposed, and the sufferings of imprisonment, but a short time.   They occupied the highest social position.   He was a merchant,
conducting an extensive business, and had a large
estate ; owning fourteen buildings in the town, a
wharf, and twenty-one sail of vessels.   His dwelling-
house, represented in the frontispiece of this volume,
stood until a recent period, and is remembered by many
of us.   Its site was on the southern side of Essex
Street, near its termination ; comprising the area between English and Webb Streets.   It must have been
a beautiful situation ; commanding at that time a
full, unobstructed view of the Beverly and Marblehead
shores, and all the waters and points of land between
them.   The mansion was spacious in its dimensions,
and bore the marks of having been constructed in the

best style of elegance, strength, and finish. It was indeed a curious and venerable specimen of the domestic architecture of its day. A first-class house then ; in its proportions, arrangements, and attachments, it would compare well with first-class houses now. Mrs. English was a lady of eminent character and culture. Traditions to this effect have come down with singular uniformity through all the old families of the place. She was the only child of Richard Hollingsworth, and inherited his large property. The Rev. William Bentley, D.D., in his "Description of Salem," and whose daily life made him conversant with all that relates to the locality of Mrs. English's residence, says that the officer came to apprehend her in the evening, after she had retired to rest. He was admitted by the servants, and read his warrant in her bedchamber. Guards were placed around the house. To be accused by the afflicted children was then regarded as certain death. "In the morning," says Bentley, "she attended the devotions of her family, kissed her children with great composure, proposed her plan for their education, took leave of them, and then told the officer she was ready to die." Dr. Bentley suggests that unfriendly feelings may have existed against Mr. English in consequence of some controversies he had been engaged in with the town about the title to lands ; that the superior style in which his family lived had subjected them to vulgar prejudice ; that the existence of this feeling becoming known to the "afflicted girls" led them

to cry out against him and his wife. It may be so.
They availed themselves of every such advantage;
and particularly liked to strike high, so as the more
to astound and overawe the public mind.

I find no further mention of Sarah Morrel. She
doubtless shared the fate of those escaping death, — a
long imprisonment. When Dorcas Hoar was brought
in, there was a general commotion among the afflicted,
falling into fits all around. After coming out of them,
they vied with each other in heaping all sorts of accusations upon the prisoner; Abigail Williams and
Ann Putnam charging her with having choked a
woman in Boston; Elizabeth Hubbard crying out that
she was pinching her, "and showing the marks to
the standers by. The marshal said she pinched her
fingers at the time." The magistrate, indignantly
believing the whole, said, "Dorcas Hoar, why do you
hurt these?" — "I never hurt any child in my life."
The girls then charged her with having killed her husband, and with various other crimes. Mary Walcot,
Susanna Sheldon, and Abigail Williams said they
saw a black man whispering in her ear. The spirit
of the prisoner was raised; and she said, "Oh, you
are liars, and God will stop the mouth of liars!" The
anger of the magistrates was roused by this bold outbreak. "You are not to speak after this manner in
the Court." — "I will speak the truth as long as I
live," she fearlessly replied. Parris says, at the close
of his account, "The afflicted were much distressed

during her examination." Of course, she was sent to prison.

Susanna Martin of Amesbury, a widow, was arrested on a warrant dated April 30, and examined at the Village church May 2. She is described as a short active woman, wearing a hood and scarf, plump and well developed in her figure, of remarkable personal neatness. One of the items of the evidence against her was, that, " in an extraordinary dirty season, when it was not fit for any person to travel, she came on foot" to a house at Newbury. The woman of the house, the substance of whose testimony I am giving, having asked, "whether she came from Amesbury afoot," expressed her surprise at her having ventured abroad in such bad walking, and bid her children make way for her to come to the fire to dry herself. She replied " she was as dry as I was," and turned her coats aside; "and I could not perceive that the soles of her shoes were wet. I was startled at it, that she should come so dry; and told her that I should have been wet up to my knees, if I should have come so far on foot." She replied that " she scorned to have a drabbled tail." The good woman who treated Susanna Martin on this occasion with such hospitable kindness received the impression, as appears by the import of her deposition, that, because Martin came into the house so wonderfully dry, she was therefore a witch. The only inference we are likely to draw is, that she was a particularly neat person; careful to pick her

way; and did not wear skirts of the dimensions of
our times.

The language reported by this witness to have been
used by Susanna Martin created in her, at the time,
visible mortification, as well as resentment. A writer
at the period, not by any means inclined to give a representation favorable to the prisoners, reports her expression thus: " She scorned to be drabbled." She
was undoubtedly a woman who spoke her mind freely,
and with strength of expression, as the magistrates
found. From this cause, perhaps, she had shocked
the prejudices and violated the conventional scrupu-
losities then prevalent, to such a degree as to incur
much comment, if not scandal. There had been a
good deal of gossip about her; and, some time before,
she had been proceeded against as a witch. But there
was no ground for any serious charges against her
character. Like Mrs. Ann Hibbens, perhaps the head
and front of her offending was that she had more
wit than her neighbors. She certainly was a strong-
minded woman, as her examination shows. Two reports of it, each in the handwriting of Parris, have
come down to us. They are almost identical, and in
substance as follows: —

On the appearance of the accused, many of the witnesses against her instantly fell into fits. The magistrate inquired of them, —

" Hath this woman hurt you? "

" (Abigail Williams declared that she had hurt her

often. 'Ann Putnam threw her glove at her in a fit,' and the rest were struck dumb at her presence.)

" What! do you laugh at it? said the magistrate. — Well I may at such folly.

" Is this folly to see these so hurt? — I never hurt man, woman, or child.

" (Mercy Lewis cried out, 'She hath hurt me a great many times, and plucks me down.' Then Martin laughed again. Several others cried out upon her, and the magistrate again addressed her.)

" What do you say to this? — I have no hand in witchcraft.

" What did you do? did you consent these should be hurt? — No, never in my life.

" What ails these people? — I do not know.

" But what do you think ails them? — I do not desire to spend my judgment upon it.

" Do you think they are bewitched? — No : I do not think they are.

" Well, tell us your thoughts about them. — My thoughts are mine own when they are in ; but, when they are out, they are another's.

" Who do you think is their master? — If they be dealing in the black art, you may know as well as I.

" What have you done towards the hurt of these? — I have done nothing.

" Why, it is you, or your appearance. — I cannot help it.

" How comes your appearance just now to hurt these? — How do I know?

" Are you not willing to tell the truth? — I cannot tell. He that appeared in Samuel's shape can appear in any one's shape.

" Do you believe these afflicted persons do not say true ? — They may lie, for aught I know.

" May not you lie? — I dare not tell a lie, if it would save my life."

At this point, the marshal declared that " she pinched her hands, and Elizabeth Hubbard was immediately afflicted. Several of the afflicted cried out that they saw her upon the beam " of the meeting-house over their heads ; and there was, no doubt, a scene of frightful excitement. The magistrate, in the depth of his awe and distress, earnestly appealed to the accused, " Pray God discover you, if you be guilty." Nothing daunted, she replied, " Amen, amen. A false tongue will never make a guilty person." A great uproar then arose. The accusers fell into dreadful convulsions, among the rest John Indian, who cried out, " She bites, she bites ! " The magistrate, overcome by the sight of these sufferings, again appealed to her, " Have not you compassion for these afflicted ? " She calmly and firmly answered, " No : I have none." The uproar rose higher. The accusers all declared that they saw the " black man," Satan himself, standing by her side. They pretended to try to approach her, but were suddenly deprived of the power of locomotion. John Indian attempted to rush upon her, but fell sprawling upon the floor. The magistrate again appealed to her : " What is the reason these cannot come near you ? " — " I cannot tell. It may be the Devil bears me more malice than another." — " Do you not see God evidently discovering you?"—"No, not a bit for that."—"All the congregation besides think so."—"Let them think what they will."—"What is the reason these cannot come to you?"—"I do not know but they can, if they will; or else, if you please, I will come to them."—"What was that the black man whispered to you?"—"There was none whispered to me." She was committed to prison.

In the mean while, preparations had been going on to bring upon the stage a more striking character, and give to the excited public mind a greater shock than had yet been experienced. Intimations had been thrown out that higher culprits than had been so far brought to light were in reserve, and would, in due time, be unmasked. It was hinted that a minister had joined the standard of the Arch-enemy, and was leading the devilish confederacy. In the accounts given of the diabolical sacraments, a man in black had been described, but no name yet given. As Charles the Second, while they were hanging the regicides, at the Restoration, was looking about for a preacher to hang, and used Hugh Peters for the occasion; so the "afflicted children," or those acting behind them, wanted a minister to complete the *dramatis personæ* of their tragedy. His connection with the society and its controversies, and the animosities which had thus become attached to him, naturally suggested Mr. Burroughs. He was then pursuing, as usual, a laborious, humble, self-sacrificing ministry, in the midst of perils and privations, away

down in the frontier settlements on the coast of
Maine, and little dreamed of what was brewing, for
his ruin and destruction, in his former parish at the
village. This is what Thomas Putnam had in his
mind when he spoke of a " wheel within a wheel,"
and " the high and dreadful " things not then disclosed that were to make " ears tingle."

It was necessary to be at once cautious and rapid
in their movements, to prevent the public from getting
information which, by reaching the ears of Burroughs,
might put him on his guard. It was no easy thing
to secure him at the great distance of his place of residence. If he should become apprised of what was going
on, his escape into remoter and inaccessible settlements
would have baffled the whole scheme. Nothing therefore was done at the village, but the steps to arrest him
originated at Boston. Elisha Hutchinson, a magistrate there, issued the proper order, addressed to
John Partridge of Portsmouth, Field-marshal of the
provinces of New Hampshire and Maine, dated April
30, 1692, to arrest George Burroughs, " preacher at
Wells ; " he being " suspected of a confederacy with the
Devil." Partridge was directed to deliver him to the
custody of the marshal of Essex, or, not meeting him,
was requested to bring him to Salem, and hand him
over to the magistrates there. The " afflicted children " had begun, shortly before, to use his name.
Abigail Hobbs had resided some years before at
Casco ; and from her they obtained all the scandal
she had heard there, or chose to fabricate to suit the

purpose of the prosecutors. The way in which the minds of the deluded people were worked up against Mr. Burroughs is illustrated in a deposition subsequently made to this effect: —

Benjamin Hutchinson testified, that, on the 21st of April, 1692, about eleven o'clock in the forenoon, Abigail Williams told him that she saw a person whom she described as Mr. George Burroughs, " a little black minister that lived at Casco Bay." Mr. Burroughs was of small stature and dark complexion. She gave an account of his wonderful feats of strength, said that he was a wizard ; and that he " had killed three wives, two for himself and one for Mr. Lawson." She affirmed that she saw him then. Mr. Burroughs, it will be borne in mind, was at this time a hundred miles away, at his home in Maine. Hutchinson asked her where she saw him. She said " There," pointing to a rut in the road made by a cart-wheel. He had an iron fork in his hand, and threw it where she said Burroughs was standing. Instantly she fell into a fit ; and, when she came out of it, said, " ' You have torn his coat, for I heard it tear.' — ' Whereabouts ? ' said I. ' On one side,' said she. Then we came into the house of Lieutenant Ingersoll ; and I went into the great room, and Abigail came in and said, ' There he stands.' I said, ' Where ? where ? ' and presently drew my rapier." Then Abigail said, he has gone, but " ' there is a gray cat.' Then I said, ' Whereabouts ? ' ' There ! ' said she, ' there ! ' Then I struck with my rapier, and she fell into a fit ; and, when it

was over, she said, 'You killed her.'" Poor Hutchinson could not see the cat he had killed any more
than Burroughs's coat he had torn. Abigail explained the mystery to his satisfaction, by saying that
the spectre of Sarah Good had come in at the moment,
and carried away the dead cat. This was all in broad
daylight; it being, as Hutchinson testified, "about
twelve o'clock." The same day, " after lecture, in said
Ingersoll's chamber," Abigail Williams and Mary
Walcot were present. They said that " Goody Hobbs,
of Topsfield, had bit Mary Walcot by the foot." Then
both fell into a fit; and on coming out, " they saw
William Hobbs and his wife go both of them along
the table." Hutchinson instantly stabbed, with his
rapier, " Goody Hobbs on her side," as the two girls
declared. They further said that the room was " full
of them," that is of witches, in their apparitions; then
Hutchinson and Eleazer Putnam " stabbed with their
rapiers at a venture." The girls cried out, that they
" had killed a great black woman of Stonington, and
an Indian who had come with her:" the girls said
further, " The floor is all covered with blood;" and,
rushing to the window, declared that they saw a great
company of witches on a hill, and that three of them
" lay dead" there, — " the black woman, the Indian,
and one more that they knew not." This was about
four o'clock in the afternoon. This evidence was given
and received in court. It shows the audacity with
which the girls imposed upon the credulity of a people
wrought up by their arts to the highest pitch of in-

sane infatuation ; and illustrates a condition of things, at that time and place, that is truly astonishing.

On the evening before Hutchinson was imposed upon, as just described, by Abigail Williams and Mary Walcot, Ann Putnam had made most astonishing disclosures, at her father's house, in his presence and that of Peter Prescott, Robert Morrel, and Ezekiel Cheever. An account of the affair was drawn up by her father, and sworn to by her, in these words : —

" THE DEPOSITION OF ANN PUTNAM, who testifieth and saith, on the 20th of April, 1692, at evening, she saw the apparition of a minister, at which she was grievously affrighted, and cried out, ' Oh, dreadful, dreadful ! here is a minister come ! What ! are ministers witches too ? Whence came you, and what is your name ? for I will complain of you, though you be a minister, if you be a wizard.' Immediately I was tortured by him, being racked and almost choked by him. And he tempted me to write in his book, which I refused with loud outcries, and said I would not write in his book though he tore me all to pieces, but told him it was a dreadful thing that he, which was a minister, that should teach children to fear God, should come to persuade poor creatures to give their souls to the Devil. ' Oh, dreadful, dreadful ! Tell me your name, that I may know who you are.' Then again he tortured me, and urged me to write in his book, which I refused. And then, presently, he told me that his name was George Burroughs, and that he had had three wives, and that he had bewitched the two first of them to death ; and that he killed Mrs. Lawson, because she was so unwilling to go from the Village, and also killed Mr. Lawson's child because he went

to the eastward with Sir Edmon, and preached so to the
soldiers; and that he had bewitched a great many soldiers
to death at the eastward when Sir Edmon was there; and
that he had made Abigail Hobbs a witch, and several
witches more. And he has continued ever since, by times,
tempting me to write in his book, and grievously torturing
me by beating, pinching, and almost choking me several
times a day. He also told me that he was above a witch.
He was a conjurer."

Her father and the other persons present made
oath that they saw and heard all this at the time;
that "they beheld her tortures and perceived her
hellish temptations by her loud outcries, 'I will not,
I will not write, though you torment me all the days
of my life.'" It will be observed that this was the
evening before Thomas Putnam wrote his letter to
the magistrates, preparing them for something "high
and dreadful" that was soon to be brought to light.

A similar scene took place not long afterwards, in
the presence of her father and her uncle Edward, to
which they also testify. It was thus described by
her under oath : —

"THE DEPOSITION OF ANN PUTNAM, who testifieth and
saith, that, on the 8th of May, at evening, I saw the apparition of Mr. George Burroughs, who grievously tortured
me, and urged me to write in his book, which I refused.
He then told me that his two first wives would appear
to me presently, and tell me a great many lies, but I should
not believe them. Then immediately appeared to me the
forms of two women in winding-sheets, and napkins about

their heads, at which I was greatly affrighted ; and they
turned their faces towards Mr. Burroughs, and looked very
red and angry, and told him that he had been a cruel
man to them, and that their blood did cry for vengeance
against him ; and also told him that they should be clothed
with white robes in heaven, when he should be cast into
hell : and immediately he vanished away. And, as soon as
he was gone, the two women turned their faces towards
me, and looked as pale as a white wall ; and told me that
they were Mr. Burroughs's two first wives, and that he had
murdered them. And one of them told me that she was
his first wife, and he stabbed her under the left arm, and
put a piece of sealing-wax on the wound. And she pulled
aside the winding-sheet, and showed me the place ; and also
told me, that she was in the house where Mr. Parris now
lives, when it was done. And the other told me, that Mr.
Burroughs and that wife which he hath now, killed her in
the vessel, as she was coming to see her friends, because
they would have one another. And they both charged me
that I should tell these things to the magistrates before
Mr. Burroughs' face ; and, if he did not own them, they
did not know but they should appear there. This morning,
also, Mrs. Lawson and her daughter Ann appeared to me,
whom I knew, and told me Mr. Burroughs murdered them.
This morning also appeared to me another woman in a
winding-sheet, and told me that she was Goodman Fuller's
first wife, and Mr. Burroughs killed her because there was
some difference between her husband and him."

This was indeed most extraordinary language and
imagery to have been used by a child of twelve years
of age. It is not strange, that, upon a community,

whose fancies and fears had been so long wrought upon, holding their views, the effect was awfully great. The very fact that it was a child that spoke made her declarations seem supernatural. Then, again, they were accompanied with such ocular demonstration, in her terrible bodily sufferings, that none remained in doubt of the truthfulness and reality of what they listened to and beheld. It did not enter their imaginations, for a moment, that there was any deception or imposture, or even delusion, on her part. Her case is truly a problem not easily solved even now. While we are filled with horror and indignation at the thought that she figures as a capital and fatal witness in all the trials, it is impossible not to feel that a wisdom greater than ours is necessary to fathom the dark mystery of the phenomena presented by her and her mother and other accusers, in this monstrous and terrible affair.

These occurrences, happening just before Mr. Burroughs was brought to the village as a prisoner, were bruited from house to house, from mouth to mouth, and worked the people to a state of horrified exasperation against him; and he was met with execration, when, on the 4th of May, Field-marshal Partridge appeared with him at Salem, and delivered him to the jailer there. When we consider the distance and the circumstances of travel at that time, it is evident that the officers charged with the service acted with the greatest promptitude, celerity, and energy. The tradition is, that they found Mr. Burroughs in his humble

home, partaking of his frugal meal; that he was
snatched from the table without a moment's opportunity to provide for his family, or prepare himself for
the journey, and hurried on his way roughly, and
without the least explanation of what it all meant.
As soon as it was known that he was in jail in Salem,
arrangements were commenced for his examination.
The public mind was highly excited; and it was determined to make the occasion as impressive, effective,
and awe-striking as possible. Another "field-day"
was to be had. On the 9th of May, a special session of
the Magistracy was held, — William Stoughton coming
from Dorchester, and Samuel Sewall from Boston, to
sit with Hathorne and Corwin, and give greater
solemnity and severity to the proceedings. Stoughton
presided. The first step in the proceedings was to have
a private hearing, in the presence of the magistrates
and ministers only; and the report of what passed
there gives proof of what is indicated more or less
clearly in several passages in the accounts that have
come down to us in reference to Mr. Burroughs, —
that he was regarded as not wholly sound in doctrine
on points not connected with witchcraft, was treated
with special severity on that account, and made the
victim of bigoted prejudice among his brethren and in
the churches. In this secret inquisition, he was called
to account for not attending the communion service
on one or two occasions; he being a member of the
church at Roxbury. It was also brought against him,
that none of his children but the eldest had been

baptized. What the facts, in these respects, were, it is impossible to say; as we know of them only through the charges of his enemies. After this, he was carried to the place of public meeting; and, as he entered the room, " many, if not all, the bewitched were grievously tortured." After the confusion had subsided, Susanna Sheldon testified that Burroughs' two wives had appeared to her " in their winding-sheets," and said, " That man killed them." He was ordered to look on the witness; and, as he turned to do so, he " knocked down," as the reporter affirms, " all (or most) of the afflicted that stood behind him." Ann Putnam, and the several other " afflicted children," bore their testimony in a similar strain against him, interspersing at intervals, all their various convulsions, outcries, and tumblings. Mercy Lewis had " a dreadful and tedious fit." Walcot, Hubbard, and Sheldon were cast into torments simultaneously. At length, they were " so tortured " that " authority ordered them " to be removed. Their sufferings were greater than the magistrates and people could longer endure to look upon. The question was put to Burroughs, " what he thought of these things." He answered, " it was an amazing and humbling providence, but he understood nothing of it." Throwing aside all the foolish and ridiculous gossip and all the monstrous fables that belong to the accusations against him, and looking at the only known facts in his history, it appears that Mr. Burroughs was a man of ingenuous nature, free from guile, unsuspicious of guile in others ; a disinterested, humble, patient, and generous person. He had suffered much wrong, and endured great hardships in life ; but they had not impaired his readiness to labor and suffer for others. There was no combativeness or vindictiveness in his disposition. Even in the midst of the unspeakable outrages he was experiencing on this occasion, he does not appear to be incensed or irritated, but simply " amazed." To have such horrid crimes laid to him, instead of rousing a violent spirit within him, impressed him with a humbling sense of an inscrutable Providence. There is a remarkable similarity in the manner in which Rebecca Nurse and George Burroughs received the dreadful accusations brought against them. " Surely," she said, " what sin hath God found out in me unrepented of that he should lay such an affliction upon me in my old age ? " His words are, " It is an humbling providence of God." The more we reflect upon this language, and go to the depths of the spirit that suggested it, the more we realize, that, in each case, it arose from a sanctified Christian heart, and is an attestation in vindication and in honor of the sufferers from whose lips it fell, that outweighs all passions and prejudices, reverses all verdicts, and commands the conviction of all fair and honest minds.

After the " afflicted" had been sent out of the room, there was testimony to show that Mr. Burroughs had given proof of physical strength, which, in a man of his small stature, was sure evidence that he was in league with the Devil. Many marvellous statements

were made to this effect, some of the most extravagant of which he denied. He undoubtedly was a
person of great strength. He had cultivated muscular exercise and development while an undergraduate
at Cambridge, and was early celebrated as a gymnast.
After a while, the accusers and afflicted were again
brought in. Abigail Hobbs testified that she was present at a " witch meeting, in the field near Mr. Parris's
house," in which Mr. Burroughs acted a conspicuous
part. Mary Warren swore that " Mr. Burroughs had
a trumpet which he blew to summon the witches to
their feasts " and other meetings " near Mr. Parris's
house." This trumpet had a sound that reached over
the country far and wide, sending its blasts to Andover, and wakening its echoes along the Merrimack, to
Cape Ann, and the uttermost settlements everywhere ;
so that the witches, hearing it, would mount their
brooms, and alight, in a moment, in Mr. Parris's
orchard, just to the north and west of the parsonage ;
but its sound was not heard by any other ears than
those of confederates with Satan. While the girls were
giving their testimony, every once in a while they
would be dreadfully choked, appearing to be in the
last stages of suffocation and strangulation ; and, coming to, at intervals, would charge it upon Burroughs
or other witches, calling them by name ; generally,
however, confining their selection to persons already
apprehended, and not bringing in others until measures were matured. Mr. Burroughs was committed
for trial.

The examination of Mr. Burroughs presented a spectacle, all things considered, of rare interest and curiosity, — the grave dignity of the magistrates ; the plain, dark figure of the prisoner ; the half-crazed, half-demoniac aspect of the girls ; the wild, excited crowd ; the horror, rage, and pallid exasperation of Lawson, Goodman Fuller and others, also of the relatives and friends of Burroughs's two former wives, as the deep damnation of their taking off and the secrets of their bloody graves were being brought to light ; and the child on the stand telling her awful tale of ghosts in winding-sheets, with napkins round their heads, pointing to their death-wounds, and saying that " their blood did cry for vengeance " upon their murderer. The prisoner stands alone : all were raving around him, while he is amazed ; astounded at such folly and wrong in others, and humbly sensible of his own unworthiness ; bowed down under the mysterious Providence, that permitted such things for a season, yet strong and steadfast in conscious innocence and uprightness.

To complete the proceedings against Burroughs at this time, and raise to the highest point the public abhorrence of him, effective use was made of Deliverance Hobbs, the wife of William Hobbs, of whom I have spoken before. She was first examined April 22. During the earlier part of the proceedings, she maintained her integrity and protested her innocence in a manner which shows that her self-possession held good. But the examination was protracted ; her

strength was exhausted; the declarations of the accusers, their dreadful sufferings, the prejudgment of the
case against her by the magistrates, and the combined
influences of all the circumstances around her, broke
her down. Her firmness, courage, and truth fled; and
she began to confess all that was laid to her charge.
The record is interesting as showing how gradually
she was overwhelmed and overcome. But while mentioning the names of others whom she pretended to
have been associated with as witches, she did not speak
of Burroughs. She referred to those who had been
brought out before that date, but not to him. The intended movement against him had not then been
divulged. On the 3d of May, the day before he arrived,
after it was known that officers had been sent to arrest
him, she was examined again. On this occasion, she
charged Burroughs with having been present, and
taken a leading part in witch-meetings, which she had
described in detail, at her first examination, without
mentioning him at all. This proves that the confessing prisoners were apprised of what it was desired
they should say, and that their testimony was prepared for them by the managers of the affair. The
following is one of the confessions made by this woman,
subsequent to her public examination. I give it partly
to show what a flood of falsehood was poured upon
Burroughs, and partly because it will serve as a
specimen of the stuff of which the confessions were
composed : —

" *The First Examination of Deliverance Hobbs in Prison.*
— She continued in the free acknowledging herself to be a
covenant witch : and further confesseth she was warned to
a meeting yesterday morning, and that there was present
Procter and his wife, Goody Nurse, Giles Corey and his wife,
Goody Bishop alias Oliver ; and Mr. Burroughs was their
preacher, and pressed them to bewitch all in the village,
telling them they should do it gradually, and not all at once,
assuring them they should prevail.   He administered the
sacrament unto them at the same time, with red bread and
red wine like blood.   She affirms she saw Osburn, Sarah
Good, Goody Wilds, Goody Nurse : and Goody Wilds distributed the bread and wine ; and a man in a long-crowned
white hat sat next the minister, and they sat seemingly at a
table, and they filled out the wine in tankards.   The notice
of this meeting was given her by Goody Wilds.   She, herself affirms, did not nor would not eat nor drink, but all the
rest did, who were there present ; therefore they threatened
to torment her.   The meeting was in the pasture by Mr.
Parris's house, and she saw when Abigail Williams ran out
to speak with them ; but, by that time Abigail was come a
little distance from the house, this examinant was struck
blind, so that she saw not with whom Abigail spake.   She
further saith, that Goody Wilds, to prevail with her to sign,
told her, that, if she would put her hand to the book, she
would give her some clothes, and would not afflict her any
more.   Her daughter, Abigail Hobbs, being brought in at
the same time, while her mother was present, was immediately taken with a dreadful fit ; and her mother, being
asked who it was that hurt her daughter, answered it was
Goodman Corey, and she saw him and the gentlewoman of
Boston striving to break her daughter's neck."

On the next day, warrants were procured against
George Jacobs, Sr., and his grand-daughter, Margaret
Jacobs. They were forthwith seized and brought in
by Constable Joseph Neal, of Salem, whose return is
as follows: " May 10, 1692. Then I apprehended the
bodies of George Jacobs, Sr., and Margaret, daughter of
George Jacobs, Jr., according to the tenor of the above
warrant." The examinations, on this occasion, were
held at the house of Thomas Beadle, in the town of
Salem. All the preliminary examinations, so far as
existing documents show, were either in the meeting-
house at the village or that of the town ; or at the
house of Nathaniel Ingersoll at the village, or Thomas
Beadle in the town, — both being inns, or places of
public entertainment. Beadle's house was on the south
side of Essex Street, on land now occupied by Nos.
63 and 65. The eastern boundary of the lot was forty-
nine feet from Ingersoll's Lane, now Daniels Street.
Its front on Essex Street was about sixty feet, and its
depth about one hundred and forty-five feet. What is
now No. 65 is on the very spot where Beadle's tavern
stood ; and with the exception of six feet built, as an
addition, on the eastern side, subsequently to 1733, is
probably the identical house. The ground now occupied by No. 63 was then an open space. It appears by
bills of expenses brought " against the country," that
the inn of Samuel Beadle, a brother of Thomas, was
also sometimes used for purposes connected with the
prosecutions. Thomas Beadle's bill amounted to £58.
11s. 5d. ; that of Samuel to £21. The latter, being

near the jail, was probably used for the entertainment
of constables and the keeping of their horses, as well
as other incidental purposes connected with the transportation of prisoners.

A tradition has long prevailed, that the house, still
standing, of Judge Jonathan Corwin, at the western
corner of North and Essex Streets, was used at these
examinations. One form in which this tradition has
come down is probably correct. The grand jury was
often in session while the jury for trials was hearing
cases in the Court-house. There may not have been
suitable accommodations for both in that building.
The confused sounds and commotions incident to the
trials would have been annoying to the grand jury.
The tradition is, that a place was provided and used
temporarily by that body, in the Corwin house, supposed to have been the spacious room at the south-
eastern corner. As the investigations of the grand
jury were not open to the public, its occasional sittings
would not be seriously incompatible with the con-
venience of a family, or detrimental to the grounds or
apartments of a handsome private residence. Indeed,
it would hardly have been allowable or practicable to
have had the examinations before the magistrates in
any other than a public house. They were always frequented by a promiscuous crowd, and generally scenes
of tumultuary disorder.

George Jacobs, Sr., was an aged man. He is represented in the evidence as " very gray-headed ; " and he
must have been quite infirm, for he walked with two

staffs. His hair was in long, thin, white locks; and, as he was uncommonly tall of stature, he must have had a venerable aspect. Perhaps he was the "man in a long-crowned white hat," referred to by Deliverance Hobbs. The examination shows that his faculties were vigorous, his bearing fearless, and his utterances strong and decided. The magistrates began: "Here are them that accuse you of acts of witchcraft." — "Well, let us hear who are they and what are they." When Abigail Williams testified against him, going through undoubtedly her usual operations, he could not refrain from expressing his contempt for the whole thing by a laugh; explaining it by saying, "Because I am falsely accused — your worships all of you, do you think this is true?" They answered, "Nay: what do you think?" "I never did it." — "Who did it?" — "Don't ask me." The magistrates always took it for granted that the pretensions and sufferings of the girls were real, and threw upon the accused the responsibility of explaining them. They continued: "Why should we not ask you? Sarah Churchill accuseth you. There she is." Jacobs was of opinion that it was not for him to explain the actions of the girls, but for the prosecuting party to prove his guilt. "If you can prove that I am guilty, I will lie under it." Then Sarah Churchill, who was a servant in his family, said, "Last night, I was afflicted at Deacon Ingersoll's; and Mary Walcot said it was a man with two staves: it was my master." It seems, that, after the proceedings against Burroughs were over, a meeting of "the circle" took place in the

evening, at Deacon Ingersoll's, at which there was a
repetition of the actings of the girls; and that Mary
Walcot suggested to Churchill to accuse her master.
This shows the way in which the delusion was kept
up. Probably, such meetings were held at one house
or another in the village, and fresh accusations brought
forward, continually.   Jacobs appealed to the magistrates, trying to recall them to a sense of fairness.
" Pray, do not accuse me : I am as clear as your worships. You must do right judgment." Sarah Churchill
charged him with having hurt her ; and the magistrates,
pushing her on to make further charges, said to her,
" Did he not appear on the other side of the river, and
hurt you ? Did not you see him ? " She answered,
" Yes, he did."   Then, turning to him, the magistrates
said, " There, she accuseth you to your face : she char-
geth you that you hurt her twice." — " It is not true.
What would you have me say ? I never wronged no
man in word nor deed." — " Is it no harm to afflict
these ? " — " I never did it." — " But how comes it to
be in your appearance ? " — " The Devil can take any
likeness." — " Not without their consent."   Jacobs
rejected the imputation.   " You tax me for a wizard :
you may as well tax me for a buzzard. I have done no
harm."   Churchill said, " I know you lived a wicked
life."   Jacobs, turning to the magistrates, said, " Let
her make it out."   The magistrates asked her, " Doth
he ever pray in his family ? "   She replied, " Not unless by himself."   The magistrates, addressing him :
' Why do you not pray in your family ? " — " I cannot

read." — " Well, but you may pray for all that. Can
you say the Lord's Prayer ? Let us hear you." The
reporter, Mr. Parris, says, " He missed in several
parts of it, and could not repeat it right after many
trials." The magistrates, addressing her, said, " Were
you not frighted, Sarah Churchill, when the representation of your master came to you ? " — " Yes."
Jacobs exclaimed, " Well, burn me or hang me, I will
stand in the truth of Christ : I know nothing of it."
In answer to an inquiry from the magistrates, he denied
having done any thing to get his son George or grand-
daughter Margaret to " sign the book."

The appearance of the old man, his intrepid bearing,
and the stamp of conscious innocence on all he said,
probably produced some impression on the magistrates,
as they did not come to any decision, but adjourned
the examination to the next day. The girls then
came down from the village in full force, determined to put him through. When he was brought
in, they accordingly, all at once, " fell into the most
grievous fits and screechings." When they sufficiently
came to, the magistrates turned to the girls : " Is this
the man that hurts you ? " They severally answered,
— Abigail Williams : " This is the man," and fell into a
violent fit. Ann Putnam : " This is the man. He hurts
me, and brings the book to me, and would have me
write in the book, and said, if I would write in it,
I should be as well as his grand-daughter." Mercy
Lewis, after much interruptions by fits : " This is the
man : he almost kills me." Elizabeth Hubbard : " He

never hurt me till to-day, when he came upon the table." Mary Walcot, after much interruption by fits: "This is the man: he used to come with two staves, and beat me with one of them." After all this, the magistrates, thinking he could deny it no longer, turn to him, "What do you say? Are you not a witch?" "No: I know it not, if I were to die presently." Mercy Lewis advanced towards him, but, as soon as she got near, "fell into great fits." — "What do you say to this?" cried the magistrates. "Why, it is false. I know not of it any more than the child that was born to-night." The reporter says, "Ann Putnam and Abigail Williams had each of them a pin stuck in their hands, and they said it was this old Jacobs." He was committed to prison.

The following piece of evidence is among the loose papers on file in the clerk's office : —

"THE DEPOSITION OF SARAH INGERSOLL, aged about thirty years. — Saith, that, seeing Sarah Churchill after her examination, she came to me crying and wringing her hands, seemingly to be much troubled in spirit. I asked her what she ailed. She answered, she had undone herself. I asked her in what. She said, in belying herself and others in saying she had set her hand to the Devil's book, whereas, she said, she never did. I told her I believed she had set her hand to the book. She answered, crying, and said, 'No, no, no: I never, I never did.' I asked her then what made her say she did. She answered, because they threatened her, and told her they would put her into the dungeon, and put her along with Mr. Burroughs; and thus several times she followed me up and down, telling me that she had undone herself, in belying herself and others. I asked her why she did not deny she wrote it. She told me, because she had stood out so long in it, that now she durst not. She said also, that, if she told Mr. Noyes but once she had set her hand to the book, he would believe her; but, if she told the truth, and said she had not set her hand to the book a hundred times, he would not believe her.

"SARAH INGERSOLL."

This paper has also the signature of "Ann Andrews."

This incident probably occurred during the examination of George Jacobs; and the bitter compunction of Churchill was in consequence of the false and malignant course she had been pursuing against her old master. It is a relief to our feelings, so far as she is regarded, to suppose so. Bad as her conduct was as one of the accusers, on other occasions after I am sorry to say as well as before, it shows that she was not entirely dead to humanity, but realized the iniquity of which she had been guilty towards him. It is the only instance of which we find notice of any such a remnant of conscience showing itself, at the time, among those perverted and depraved young persons. The reason, why it is probable that this exhibition of Churchill's penitential tears and agonies of remorse occurred immediately after the first day of Jacobs's examination, is this. It was one of the first, if not the first, held at the house of Thomas Beadle. Sarah Ingersoll would not have been likely to have fallen in with her elsewhere. It is evident, from the tenor and purport of the document, that the deponent was not entirely carried away by the prevalent delusion, and probably did not follow up the proceedings generally. But it was quite natural that her attention should have been called to proceedings of interest at Beadle's house, particularly on that first occasion. She lived in the immediate vicinity. The indorsement by Ann Andrews, the daughter of Jacobs, increases the probability that the occurrence was at his examination.

The representatives of the family of John Ingersoll, — a brother of Deacon Nathaniel Ingersoll, — in 1692, occupied a series of houses on the west side of Daniels Street, leading from Essex Street to the harbor. The widow of John's son Nathaniel lived at the corner of Essex and Daniels Streets; the next in order was the widow of his son John; the next, his daughter Ruth, wife of Richard Rose; the next, the widow of his son Richard; the last, his son Samuel, whose house lot extended to the water. Sarah, the witness in this case, was the wife of Samuel, and afterwards became the second wife of Philip English. One of her children appears to have married a son of Beadle. Their immediate proximity to the Beadle house, and consequent intimacy with his family, led them to become conversant with what occurred there; and Sarah Ingersoll was, in that way, likely to meet Churchill, and to have the conversation with her to which she deposes.

This brief deposition of Sarah Ingersoll is, in many particulars, an important and instructive paper. It

exhibits incidentally the means employed to keep the
accusing girls and confessing witnesses from falling
back, and, by overawing them, to prevent their acknowledging the falseness of their testimony.   It shows how
difficult it was to obtain a hearing, if they were disposed to recant.   It presents Mr. Noyes — as all along
there is too much evidence compelling us to admit
— acting a part as bad as that of Parris; and it discloses the fact, that Mr. Burroughs, although not yet
brought to trial, was immured in a dungeon.

No papers are on file, or have been obtained, in
reference to the examination of Margaret Jacobs, which
was at the same time and place with that of her grandfather.   We shall hear of her in subsequent stages of
the transaction.

On the same day — May 10 — that George and Margaret Jacobs were apprehended and examined, a warrant was issued against John Willard, " husbandman,"
to be brought to Thomas Beadle's house in Salem.
On the 12th, John Putnam, Jr., constable, made return
that he had been to " the house of the usual abode of
John Willard, and made search for him, and in several
other houses and places, but could not find him;" and
that " his relations and friends " said, " that, to their
best knowledge, he was fled."   On the 15th, a warrant
was issued to the marshal of Essex, and the constables
of Salem, " or any other marshal, or marshal's constable
or constables within this their majesty's colony or territory of the Massachusetts, in New England," requiring
them to apprehend said Willard, " if he may be found

in your precincts, who stands charged with sundry acts of witchcraft, by him done or committed on the bodies of Bray Wilkins, and Samuel Wilkins, the son of Henry Wilkins," and others, upon complaint made "by Thomas Fuller, Jr., and Benjamin Wilkins, Sr., yeomen; who, being found, you are to convey from town to town, from constable to constable, . . . to be prosecuted according to the direction of Constable John Putnam, of Salem Village, who goes with the same." On the 18th of May, Constable Putnam brought in Willard, and delivered him to the magistrates. He was seized in Groton. There is no record of his examination; but we gather, from the papers on file, the following facts relating to this interesting case: —

It is said that Willard had been called upon to aid in the arrest, custody, and bringing-in of persons accused, acting as a deputy-constable; and, from his observation of the deportment of the prisoners, and from all he heard and saw, his sympathies became excited in their behalf: and he expressed, in more or less unguarded terms, his disapprobation of the proceedings. He seems to have considered all hands concerned in the business — accusers, accused, magistrates, and people — as alike bewitched. One of the witnesses against him deposed, that he said, in a " discourse" at the house of a relative, " Hang them: they are all witches." In consequence of this kind of talk, in which he indulged as early as April, he incurred the ill-will of the parties engaged in the prose cutions; and it was whispered about that he was himself in the diabolical confederacy. He was a grandson of Bray Wilkins; and the mind of the old man became prejudiced against him, and most of his family connections and neighbors partook of the feeling. When Willard discovered that such rumors were in circulation against him, he went to his grandfather for counsel and the aid of his prayers. He met with a cold reception, as appears by the deposition of the old man as follows: —

"When John Willard was first complained of by the afflicted persons for afflicting of them, he came to my house, greatly troubled, desiring me, with some other neighbors, to pray for him. I told him I was then going from home, and could not stay; but, if I could come home before night, I should not be unwilling. But it was near night before I came home, and so I did not answer his desire; but I heard no more of him upon that account. Whether my not answering his desire did not offend him, I cannot tell; but I was jealous, afterwards, that it did."

Willard soon after made an engagement to go to Boston, on election-week, with Henry Wilkins, Jr. A son of said Henry Wilkins, named Daniel, — a youth of seventeen years of age, who had heard the stories against Willard, and believed them all, remonstrated with his father against going to Boston with Willard, and seemed much distressed at the thought, saying, among other things, "It were well if the said Willard were hanged."

Old Bray Wilkins must go to election too; and so

started off on horseback, — the only mode of travel then practicable from Will's Hill to Winnesimit Ferry, —with his wife on a pillion behind him. He was eighty-two years of age, and she probably not much less ; for she had been the wife of his youth. The old couple undoubtedly had an active time that week in Boston. It was a great occasion, and the whole country flocked in to partake in the ceremonies and services of the anniversary. On Election-day, with his wife, he rode out to Dorchester, to dine at the house of his " brother, Lieutenant Richard Way." Deodat Lawson and his new wife, and several more, joined them at table. Before sitting down, Henry Wilkins and John Willard also came in. Willard, perhaps, did not feel very agreeably towards his grandfather, at the time, for having shown an unwillingness to pray with him. The old man either saw, or imagined he saw, a very unpleasant expression in Willard's countenance. " To my apprehension, he looked after such a sort upon me as I never before discerned in any." The long and hard travel, the fatigues and excitements of election-week, were too much for the old man, tough and rugged as he was ; and a severe attack of a complaint, to which persons of his age are often subject, came on. He experienced great sufferings, and, as he expressed it, " was like a man on a rack."

" I told my wife immediately that I was afraid that Willard had done me wrong ; my pain continuing, and finding no relief, my jealousy continued. Mr. Lawson and others there were all amazed, and knew not what to do for me. There was

a woman accounted skilful came hoping to help me, and after
she had used means, she asked me whether none of those
evil persons had done me damage.   I said, I could not say
they had, but I was sore afraid they had.   She answered,
she did fear so too. . . . As near as I remember.   I lay in
this case three or four days at Boston, and afterward, with
the jeopardy of my life (as I thought), I came home."

On his return, he found his grandson, the same
Daniel who had warned Henry Wilkins against going
to Boston with John Willard, on his death-bed, in
great suffering.   Another attack of his own malady
came on.   There was great consternation in the neighborhood, and throughout the village.   The Devil and
his confederates, it was thought, were making an awful
onslaught upon the people at Will's Hill.   Parris and
others rushed to the scene.   Mercy Lewis and Mary
Walcot were carried up to tell who it was that was bewitching old Bray, and young Daniel, and others of the
Wilkinses who had caught the contagion, and were
experiencing or imagining all sorts of bodily ails.
They were taken to the room where Daniel was approaching his death-agonies; and they both affirmed,
that they saw the spectres of old Mrs. Buckley
and John Willard "upon his throat and upon his
breast, and pressed him and choked him;" and the
cruel operation, they insisted upon it, continued until
the boy died.   The girls were carried to the bedroom
of the old man, who was in great suffering; and, when
they entered, the question was put by the anxious and
excited friends in the chamber to Mercy Lewis, whether

she saw any thing. She said, " Yes : they are looking
for John Willard." Presently she pretended to have
caught sight of his apparition, and exclaimed, " There
he is upon his grandfather's belly." This was thought
wonderful indeed ; for, as the old man says in a deposition he drew up afterwards, " At that time I was in
grievous pain in the small of my belly."

Mrs. Ann Putnam had her story to tell about John
Willard. Its substance is seen in a deposition drawn
up about the time, and is in the same vein as her
testimony in other cases ; presenting a problem to
be solved by those who can draw the line between
semi-insane hallucination and downright fabrication.
Her deposition is as follows : —

" That the shape of Samuel Fuller and Lydia Wilkins
this day told me at my own house by the bedside, who appeared in winding-sheets, that, if I did not go and tell Mr.
Hathorne that John Willard had murdered them, they would
tear me to pieces. I knew them when they were living, and
it was exactly their resemblance and shape. And, at the
same time, the apparition of John Willard told me that he
had killed Samuel Fuller, Lydia Wilkins, Goody Shaw, and
Fuller's second wife, and Aaron Way's child, and Ben Fuller's
child ; and this deponent's child Sarah, six weeks old ; and
Philip Knight's child, with the help of William Hobbs ; and
Jonathan Knight's child and two of Ezekiel Cheever's children with the help of William Hobbs ; Anne Eliot and
Isaac Nichols with the help of William Hobbs ; and that if
Mr. Hathorne would not believe them, — that is, Samuel
Fuller and Lydia Wilkins, — perhaps they would appear to

the magistrates.   Joseph Fuller's apparition the same day
also came to me, and told me that Goody Corey had killed
him.   The spectre aforesaid told me, that vengeance, vengeance, was cried by said Fuller.   This relation is true.

"ANN PUTNAM."

It appears by such papers as are to be found relating
to Willard's case, that a coroner's jury was held over the
body of Daniel Wilkins, of which Nathaniel Putnam
was foreman.   It is much to be regretted that the
finding of that jury is lost.   It would be a real
curiosity.   That it was very decisive to the point,
affirmed by Mercy Lewis and Mary Walcot, that Daniel
was choked and strangled by the spectres of John
Willard and Goody Buckley, is apparent from the
manner in which Bray Wilkins speaks of it.   In an
argument between him and some persons who were
expressing their confidence that John Willard was an
innocent man, he sought to relieve himself from responsibility for Willard's conviction by saying, "It
was not I, nor my son Benjamin Wilkins, but the
testimony of the afflicted persons, and the jury concerning the murder of my grandson, Daniel Wilkins,
that would take away his life, if any thing did."   Mr.
Parris, of course, was in the midst of these proceedings
at Will's Hill; attended the visits of the afflicted girls
when they went to ascertain who were the witches
murdering young Daniel and torturing the old man ;
was present, no doubt, at the solemn examinations and
investigations of the sages who sat as a jury of inquest

over the former, and, in all likelihood, made, as usual, a written report of the same. As soon as he got back to his house, he discharged his mind, and indorsed the verdict of the coroner's jury by this characteristic insertion in his church-records: " Dan : Wilkins. Bewitched to death." The very next entry relates to a case of which this obituary line, in Mr. Parris's church-book, is the only intimation that has come down to us, " Daughter to Ann Douglas. By witchcraft, I doubt not." Willard's examination was at Beadle's, on the 18th. With this deluge of accusations and tempest of indignation beating upon him, he had but little chance, and was committed.

While the marshals and constables were in pursuit of Willard, the time was well improved by the prosecutors. On the 12th of May, warrants were issued to apprehend, and bring " forthwith " before the magistrates sitting at Beadle's, " Alice Parker, the wife of John Parker of Salem ; and Ann Pudeator of Salem, widow." Alice, commonly called Elsie, Parker was the wife of a mariner. We know but little of her. We have a deposition of one woman, Martha Dutch, as follows : —

" This deponent testified and saith, that, about two years last past, John Jarman, of Salem, coming in from sea, I (this deponent and Alice Parker, of Salem, both of us standing together) said unto her, ' What a great mercy it was, for to see them come home well ; and through mercy,' I said, ' my husband had gone, and come home well, many times.' And I, this deponent, did say unto the said Parker, that ' I did hope he would come home this voyage well also.' And the said Parker made answer unto me, and said, ' No : never more in this world.' The which came to pass as she then told me ; for he died abroad, as I certainly hear."

Perhaps Parker had information which had not reached the ears of Dutch, or she may have been prone to take melancholy views of the dangers to which seafaring people are exposed. It was a strange kind of evidence to be admitted against a person in a trial for witchcraft.

Samuel Shattuck, who has been mentioned (vol. i. p. 193) in connection with Bridget Bishop, had a long story to tell about Alice Parker. He seems to have been very active in getting up charges of witchcraft against persons in his neighborhood, and on the most absurd and frivolous grounds. Parker had made a friendly call upon his wife ; and, not long after, one of his children fell sick, and he undertook to suspect that it was " under an evil hand." In similar circumstances, he took the same grudge against Bridget Bishop. Alice Parker, hearing that he had been circulating suspicions to that effect against her, went to his house to remonstrate ; an angry altercation took place between them ; and he gave his version of the affair in evidence. There was no one to present the other side. But the whole thing has, not only a one-sided, but an irrelevant character, in no wise bearing upon the point of witchcraft. All the gossip, scandal, and tittle-tattle of the neighborhood for twenty years back, in this case as in others, was raked up, and allowed to be adduced, however utterly remote from the questions belonging to the trial.

The following singular piece of testimony against Alice Parker may be mentioned. John Westgate was at Samuel Beadle's tavern one night with boon companions; among them John Parker, the husband of Alice. She disapproved of her husband's spending his evenings in such company, and in a bar-room; and felt it necessary to put a stop to it, if she could. Westgate says that she " came into the company, and scolded at and called her husband all to nought; whereupon I, the said deponent, took her husband's part, telling her it was an unbeseeming thing for her to come after him to the tavern, and rail after that rate. With that she came up to me, and called me rogue, and bid me mind my own business, and told me I had better have said nothing." He goes on to state, that, returning home one night some time afterwards, he experienced an awful fright. " Going from the house of Mr. Daniel King, when I came over against John Robinson's house, I heard a great noise ; . . . and there appeared a black hog running towards me with open mouth, as though he would have devoured me at that instant time." In the extremity of his terror, he tried to run away from the awful monster ; but, as might have been expected under the circumstances, he tumbled to the ground. " I fell down upon my hip, and my knife run into my hip up to the haft. When I came home, my knife was in my sheath. When I drew it out of the sheath, then immediately the sheath fell all to pieces." And further this deponent testifieth, that, after he got up from his fall, his stocking and shoe was full of blood, and that he was forced to crawl along by the fence all the way home; and the hog followed him, and never left him till he came home. He further stated that he was accompanied all the way by his " stout dog," which ordinarily was much inclined to attack and " worry hogs," but, on this occasion, " ran away from him, leaping over the fence and crying much." In view of all these things, Westgate concludes his testimony thus: " Which hog I then apprehended was either the Devil or some evil thing, not a real hog; and did then really judge, or determine in my mind, that it was either Goody Parker or by her means and procuring, fearing that she is a witch." The facts were probably these: The sheath was broken by his fall, his skin bruised, and some blood got into his stocking and shoe. The knife was never out of the sheath until he drew it; there was no mystery or witchcraft in it. Nothing was ever more natural than the conduct of the dog. When he saw Westgate frightened out of his wits at nothing, trying to run as for dear life when there was no pursuer, staggering and pitching along in a zigzag direction with very eccentric motions, falling heels over head, and then crawling along, holding himself up by the fence, and all the time looking back with terror, and perhaps attempting to express his consternation, the dog could not tell what to make of it; and ran off, as a dog would be likely to have done, jumping over the fences, barking, and uttering the usual canine ejaculations. Dogs sympathize with their masters, and, if there is a frolic or other acting going on, are fond of joining in it. The whole thing was in consequence of Westgate's not having profited by Alice Parker's rebuke, and discontinued his visits by night to Beadle's bar-room. The only reason why he saw the " black hog with the open mouth," and the dog did not see it, and therefore failed to come to his protection, was because he had been drinking and the dog had not.

We find among the papers relating to these transactions many other instances of this kind of testimony; sounds heard and sights seen by persons going home at night through woods, after having spent the evening under the bewildering influences of talk about witches, Satan, ghosts, and spectres; sometimes, as in this case, stimulated by other causes of excitement.

Perhaps some persons may be curious to know the route by which Westgate made out to reach his home, while pursued by the horrors of that midnight experience. He seems to have frequented Samuel Beadle's bar-room. That old Narragansett soldier owned a lot on the west side of St. Peter's Street, occupying the southern corner of what is now Church Street, which was opened ten years afterwards, that is, in 1702, by the name of Epps's Lane. On that lot his tavern stood. He also owned one-third of an acre at the present corner of Brown and St. Peter's Streets, on which he had a stable and barn; so that his grounds were on both sides of St. Peter's Street, — one parcel on the west,

nearly opposite the present front of the church; the
other on the east side of St. Peter's Street, opposite
the south side of the church. From this locality
Westgate started. He probably did not go down
Brown Street, for that was then a dark, unfrequented
lane, but thought it safest to get into Essex Street.
He made his way along that street, passing the Common, the southern side of which, at that time, with the
exception of some house-lots on and contiguous to
the site of the Franklin Building, bordered on Essex
Street. The casualty of his fall; the catastrophe to
his hip, stocking, and shoe ; and the witchery practised
upon his knife and its sheath, — occurred " over against
John Robinson's house," which was on the eastern
corner of Pleasant and Essex Streets. Christopher
Babbage's house, from which he thought the " great
noise " came, was next beyond Robinson's. He crawled
along the fences and the sides of the houses until he
reached the passage-way on the western side of Thomas
Beadle's house, and through that managed to get to
his own house, which was directly south of said Beadle's lot, between it and the harbor.

There is one item in reference to Alice Parker,
which indicates that the zeal of the prosecutors in
her case, as in that of Mr. Burroughs, and perhaps
others, was aggravated by a suspicion that she was
heretical on some points of the prevalent creed of the
day. Parris says that " Mr. Noyes, at the time of her
examination, affirmed to her face, that, he being with
her at a time of sickness, discoursing with her about

witchcraft, whether she were not guilty, she answered, ' if she was as free from other sins as from witchcraft, she would not ask of the Lord mercy.' " The manner of expression in this passage shows that it was thought that there was something very shocking in her answer. Mr. Noyes " affirmed to her face." No doubt it was thought that she denied the doctrine of original and transmitted, or imputed sin.

Ann Pudeator (pronounced Pud-e-tor) was the widow of Jacob Pudeator, and probably about seventy years of age. The name is spelt variously, and was originally, as it is sometimes found, Poindexter. She was a woman of property, owning two estates on the north line of the Common ; that on which she lived comprised what is between Oliver and Winter Streets. She was arrested and brought to examination on the 12th of May. There is ground to conclude, from the tenor of the documents, that she was then discharged. Some people in the town were determined to gratify their spleen against her, and procured her re-arrest. The examination took place on the 2d of July, and she was then committed. The evidence was, if possible, more frivolous and absurd than in other cases. The girls acted their usual parts, giving, on this occasion, a particularly striking exhibition of the transmission of the diabolical virus out of themselves back into the witch by a touch of her body. " Ann Putnam fell into a fit, and said Pudeator was commanded to take her by the wrist, and did ; and said Putnam was well presently. Mary Warren fell into two fits quickly, after

one another; and both times was helped by said
Pudeator's taking her by the wrist."

When well acted, this must have been one of the
most impressive and effective of all the methods employed in these performances. To see a young woman
or girl suddenly struck down, speechless, pallid as in
death; with muscles rigid, eyeballs fixed or rolled back
in their sockets; the stiffened frame either wholly pros-
trate or drawn up into contorted attitudes and shapes,
or vehemently convulsed with racking pains, or drop-
ping with relaxed muscles into a lifeless lump; and to
hear dread shrieks of delirious ravings, — must have
produced a truly frightful effect upon an excited and
deluded assembly. The constables and their assistants
would go to the rescue, lift the body of the sufferer,
and bear it in their arms towards the prisoner. The
magistrates and the crowd, hushed in the deepest
silence, would watch with breathless awe the result of
the experiment, while the officers slowly approached
the accused, who, when they came near, would, in
obedience to the order of the magistrates, hold out a
hand, and touch the flesh of the afflicted one. Instantly the spasms cease, the eyes open, color returns
to the countenance, the limbs resume their position
and functions, and life and intelligence are wholly restored. The sufferer comes to herself, walks back, and
takes her seat as well as ever. The effect upon the
accused person must have been confounding. It is a
wonder that it did not oftener break them down. It
sometimes did. Poor Deliverance Hobbs, when the

process was tried upon her, was wholly overcome, and passed from conscious and calmly asserted innocence to a helpless abandonment of reason, conscience, and herself, exclaiming, " I am amazed! I am amazed! " and assented afterwards to every charge brought against her, and said whatever she was told, or supposed they wished her to say.

On the 14th of May, warrants were issued against Daniel Andrew ; George Jacobs, Jr. ; his wife, Rebecca Jacobs, Sarah Buckley, wife of William Buckley ; and Mary Whittredge, daughter of said Buckley, — all of Salem Village ; Elizabeth Hart, wife of Isaac Hart, of Lynn ; Thomas Farrar, Sr., also of Lynn ; Elizabeth Colson, of Reading ; and Bethiah Carter, of Woburn. There is nothing of special interest among the few papers that are on file relating to Hart, Colson, or Carter. The constable made return that he had searched the houses of Daniel Andrew and George Jacobs, Jr., but could not find them. He brought in forthwith the bodies of Sarah Buckley, Mary Whittredge, and Rebecca Jacobs. Farrar and the rest were brought in shortly afterwards.

Daniel Andrew was one of the leading men of the village, and the warrant against him was proof that soon none would be too high to be reached by the prosecutors. He felt that it was in vain to attempt to resist their destructive power ; and, getting notice in some way of the approach of the constable, with his near neighbor, friend, and connection, George Jacobs,

Jr., effected his escape, and found refuge in a foreign country.

Rebecca, the wife of George Jacobs, Jr., was the victim of a partial derangement. Her daughter Margaret was already in jail. Her husband had escaped by a hurried flight, and his father was in prison awaiting his trial. She was left in a lonely and unprotected condition, in a country but thinly settled, in the midst of woods. The constable came with his warrant for her. She was driven to desperation, and was inclined to resist; but he persuaded her to go with him by holding out the inducement that she would soon be permitted to return. Four young children, one of them an infant, were left in the house; but those who were old enough to walk followed after, crying, endeavoring to overtake her. Some of the neighbors took them into their houses. The imprisonment of a woman in her situation and mental condition was an outrage; but she was kept in irons, as they all were, for eight months. Her mother addressed an humble but earnest and touching petition to the chief-justice of the court at Salem, setting forth her daughter's condition; but it was of no avail. Afterwards, she addressed a similar memorial to " His Excellency Sir William Phips, Knight, Governor, and the Honorable Council sitting at Boston," in the following terms : —

"*The Humble Petition of Rebecca Fox, of Cambridge, showeth,* that, whereas Rebecca Jacobs (daughter of your humble petitioner) has, a long time, — even many months, — now lain in prison for witchcraft, and is well known to be a person crazed, distracted, and broken in mind, your humble petitioner does most humbly and earnestly seek unto Your Excellency and to Your Honors for relief in this case.

" Your petitioner, — who knows well the condition of her poor daughter, — together with several others of good repute and credit, are ready to offer their oaths, that the said Jacobs is a woman crazed, distracted, and broken in her mind; and that she has been so these twelve years and upwards.

" However, for (I think) above this half year, the said Jacobs has lain in prison, and yet remains there, attended with many sore difficulties.

" Christianity and nature do each of them oblige your petitioner to be very solicitous in this matter ; and, although many weighty cases do exercise your thoughts, yet your petitioner can have no rest in her mind till such time as she has offered this her address on behalf of her daughter.

" Some have died already in prison, and others have been dangerously sick ; and how soon others, and, among them, my poor child, by the difficulties of this confinement may be sick and die, God only knows.

" She is uncapable of making that shift for herself that others can do ; and such are her circumstances, on other accounts, that your petitioner, who is her tender mother, has many great sorrows, and almost overcoming burdens, on her mind upon her account ; but, in the midst of all her perplexities and troubles (next to supplicating to a good and merciful God), your petitioner has no way for help but to make this her afflicted condition known unto you. So, not doubting but Your Excellency and Your Honors will readily hear the cries and groans of a poor distressed woman, and grant what help and enlargement you may, your petitioner heartily begs God's gracious presence with you ; and subscribes herself, in all humble manner, your sorrowful and distressed petitioner, REBECCA FOX."

No heed was paid to this petition ; and the unfortunate woman remained in jail until — after the delusion had passed from the minds of the people — a grand jury found a bill against her, on which she was brought to trial, Jan. 3, 1693, and acquitted. There is no more disgraceful feature in all the proceedings than the long imprisonment of this woman, her being brought to trial, and the obdurate deafness to humanity and reason of the chief-justice, the governor, and the council.

No papers are found relating to the examination of Thomas Farrar ; but the following deposition shows the manner in which prosecutions were got up : —

" THE DEPOSITION OF ANN PUTNAM, who testifieth and saith, that, on the 8th of May, 1692, there appeared to me the apparition of an old, gray-headed man, with a great nose, which tortured me, and almost choked me, and urged me to write in his book ; and I asked him what was his name, and from whence he came, for I would complain of him ; and he told me he came from Lynn, and people do call him ' old Father Pharaoh ; ' and he said he was my grandfather, for my father used to call him father : but I told him I would not call him grandfather ; for he was a wizard, and I would complain of him. And, ever since, he hath afflicted me by times, beating me and pinching me and almost choking me, and urging me continually to write in his book."

"We, whose names are underwritten, having been conversant with Ann Putnam, have heard her declare what is above written, — what she said she saw and heard from the apparition of old Pharaoh, — and also have seen her tortures, and perceived her hellish temptations, by her loud outcries, ' I will not write, old Pharaoh, — I will not write in your book.'   THOMAS PUTNAM,
ROBERT MORRELL."

She had heard this person spoken of as " old Father Pharaoh," with his " great nose ;" and, from a mere spirit of mischief, — for the fun of the thing, — cried out upon him. Many of the documents exhibit a levity of spirit among these girls, which show how hardened and reckless they had become. The following depositions are illustrative of this state of mind among them : —

" THE DEPOSITION OF CLEMENT COLDUM, aged sixty years, or thereabout. — Saith that, on the 29th of May, 1692, being at Salem Village, carrying home Elizabeth Hubbard from the meeting behind me, she desired me to ride faster. I asked her why. She said the woods were full of devils, and said, ' There !' and ' There they be !' but I could see none. Then I put on my horse ; and, after I had ridden a while, she told me I might ride softer, for we had outridden them. I asked her if she was not afraid of the Devil. She answered me, ' No : she could discourse with the Devil as well as with me,' and further saith not. This I am ready to testify on oath, if called thereto, as witness my hand.
" CLEMENT COLDUM."

" THE TESTIMONY OF DANIEL ELLIOT, aged twenty-seven years or thereabouts, who testifieth and saith, that I, being at the house of Lieutenant Ingersoll, on the 28th of March, in the year 1692, there being present one of the afflicted persons, who cried out and said, ' There's Goody Procter.' William Raymond, Jr., being there present, told the girl he believed she lied, for he saw nothing. Then Goody Ingersoll told the girl she told a lie, for there was nothing. Then the girl said she did it for sport, — they must have some sport."

Sarah Buckley was examined May 18, and her daughter Mary Whittredge probably on the same day. We have Parris's report of the proceedings in reference to the former. The only witnesses against her were the afflicted children. They performed their grand operation of going into fits, and being carried to the accused and subjected to her touch ; Ann Putnam, Susanna Sheldon, and Mary Warren enacting the part in succession. Sheldon cried out, " There is the black man whispering in her ear ! " The magistrates and all beholders were convinced. She was committed to prison, and remained in irons for eight months before a trial, which resulted in her acquittal. So eminently excellent was the character of Goodwife Buckley, that her arrest and imprisonment led to expressions in her favor as honorable to those who had the courage to utter them as to her. The following certificates were given, previous to her trial, by ministers in the neighborhood : —

" These are to certify whom it may or shall concern, that I have known Sarah, the wife of William Buckley, of Salem Village, more or less, ever since she was brought out of

England, which is above fifty years ago; and, during all that
time, I never knew nor heard of any evil in her carriage, or
conversation unbecoming a Christian : likewise, she was
bred up by Christian parents all the time she lived here at
Ipswich. I further testify, that the said Sarah was admitted
as a member into the church of Ipswich above forty years
since ; and that I never heard from others, or observed by
myself, any thing of her that was inconsistent with her profession or unsuitable to Christianity, either in word, deed,
or conversation, and am strangely surprised that any person
should speak or think of her as one worthy to be suspected
of any such crime that she is now charged with. In testimony hereof I have here set my hand this 20th of June,
1692.   WILLIAM HUBBARD."

    "Being desired by Goodman Buckley to give my testi-
mony to his wife's conversation before this great calamity
befell her, I cannot refuse to bear witness to the truth ; viz.,
that, during the time of her living in Salem for many years
in communion with this church, having occasionally frequent converse and discourse with her, I have never observed
myself, nor heard from any other, any thing that was unsuitable to a conversation becoming the gospel, and have
always looked upon her as a serious, Godly woman.

                                    "JOHN HIGGINSON."

    "Marblehead, Jan. 2, 169⅔. — Upon the same request,
having had the like opportunity by her residence many years
at Marblehead, I can do no less than give the alike testimony
for her pious conversation during her abode in this place
and communion with us.   SAMUEL CHEEVER."

    William Hubbard was the venerable minister of Ips-
wich, described by Hutchinson as " a man of learning,

and of a candid and benevolent mind, accompanied
with a good degree of catholicism." He is described
by another writer as "a man of singular modesty,
learned without ostentation." He will be remembered with honor for his long and devoted service in
the Christian ministry, and as the historian of New
England and of the Indian wars.

John Higginson was worthy of the title of the
"Nestor of the New-England clergy." He was at this
time seventy-six years old, and had been a preacher
of the gospel fifty-five years. For thirty-three years
he had been pastor of the First Church in Salem, of
which his father was the first preacher. No character,
in all our annals, shines with a purer lustre. John
Dunton visited him in 1686, and thus speaks of him:
"All men look to him as a common father; and old
age, for his sake, is a reverend thing. He is eminent
for all the graces that adorn a minister. His very
presence puts vice out of countenance; his conversation is a glimpse of heaven." The fact, that, while his
colleague, Nicholas Noyes, took so active and disastrous a part in the prosecutions, he, at an early stage,
discountenanced them, shows that he was a person of
discrimination and integrity. That he did not conceal
his disapprobation of the proceedings is demonstrated,
not only by the tenor of his attestation in behalf of
Goodwife Buckley, but by the decisive circumstance
that the "afflicted children" cried out against his
daughter Anna, the wife of Captain William Dolliver,
of Gloucester; got a warrant to apprehend her; and

had her brought to the Salem jail, and committed as a witch. They never struck at friends, but were sure to punish all who were suspected to disapprove of the proceedings. How long Mrs. Dolliver remained in prison we are not informed. But it was impossible to break down the influence or independence of Mr. Higginson. It is not improbable that he believed in witchcraft, with all the other divines of his day; but he feared not to bear testimony to personal worth, and could not be brought to co-operate in violence, or fall in with the spirit of persecution. The weight of his character compelled the deference of the most heated zealots, and even Cotton Mather himself was eager to pay him homage. Four years afterwards, he thus writes of him: "This good old man is yet alive; and he that, from a child, knew the Holy Scriptures, does, at those years wherein men use to be twice children, continue preaching them with such a manly, pertinent, and judicious vigor, and with so little decay of his intellectual abilities, as is indeed a matter of just admiration."

Samuel Cheever was a clergyman of the highest standing, and held in universal esteem through a long life.

From passages incidentally given, it has appeared that it was quite common, in those times, to attribute accidents, injuries, pains, and diseases of all kinds, to an " evil hand." It was not confined to this locality. When, however, the public mind had become excited to so extraordinary a degree by circumstances con-

nected with the prosecutions in 1692, this tendency of
the popular credulity was very much strengthened.
Believing that the sufferer or patient was the victim of
the malignity of Satan, and it also being a doctrine
of the established belief that he could not act upon
human beings or affairs except through the instrumental agency of some other human beings in confederacy with him, the question naturally arose, in
every specific instance, Who is the person in this diabolical league, and doing the will of the Devil in this
case ? Who is the witch ? It may well be supposed,
that the suffering person, and all surrounding friends,
would be most earnest and anxious in pressing this
question and seeking its solution. The accusing girls
at the village were thought to possess the power to
answer it. This gave them great importance, gratified their vanity and pride, and exalted them to the
character of prophetesses. They were ready to meet
the calls made upon them in this capacity ; would be
carried to the room of a sick person ; and, on entering
it, would exclaim, on the first return of pain, or difficulty of respiration, or restless motion of the patient,
" There she is ! " There is such a one's appearance,
choking or otherwise tormenting him or her. If the
minds of the accusing girls had been led towards
a new victim, his or her name would be used, and a
warrant issued for his apprehension. If not, then the
name of some one already in confinement would be
used on the occasion. It was also a received opinion,
that, while ordinary fastenings would not prevent a

witch from going abroad, " in her apparition," to any distance to afflict persons, a redoubling of them might. Whenever one of the accusing girls pretended to see the spectres of persons already in jail afflicting any one, orders would forthwith be given to have them more heavily chained. Every once in a while, a wretched prisoner, already suffering from bonds and handcuffs, would be subjected to additional manacles and chains. This was one of the most cruel features in these proceedings. It is illustrated by the following document : —

"THE DEPOSITION OF BENJAMIN HUTCHINSON, who testifieth and saith, that my wife was much afflicted, presently after the last execution, with violent pains in her head and teeth, and all parts of her body ; but, on sabbath day was fortnight in the morning, she being in such excessive misery that she said she believed that she had an evil hand upon her : whereupon I went to Mary Walcot, one of our next neighbors, to come and look to see if she could see anybody upon her ; and, as soon as she came into the house, she said that our two next neighbors, Sarah Buckley and Mary Whittredge, were upon my wife. And immediately my wife had ease, and Mary Walcot was tormented. Whereupon I went down to the sheriff, and desired him to take some course with those women, that they might not have such power to torment : and presently he ordered them to be fettered, and, ever since that, my wife has been tolerable well ; and I believe, in my heart, that Sarah Buckley and Mary Whittredge have hurt my wife and several others by acts of witchcraft.

"Benjamin Hutchinson owned the above-written evidence to be the truth, upon oath, before the grand inquest, 15–7, 1692."

The evidence is quite conclusive, from considerations suggested by the foregoing document, and indications scattered through the papers generally, that all persons committed on the charge of witchcraft were kept heavily ironed, and otherwise strongly fastened. Only a few of the bills of expenses incurred are preserved. Among them we find the following: For mending and putting on Rachel Clenton's fetters; one pair of fetters for John Howard; a pair of fetters each for John Jackson, Sr., and John Jackson, Jr.; eighteen pounds of iron for fetters; for making four pair of iron fetters and two pair of handcuffs, and putting them on the legs and hands of Goodwife Cloyse, Easty, Bromidg, and Green; chains for Sarah Good and Sarah Osburn; shackles for ten prisoners; and one pair of irons for Mary Cox. When we reflect upon the character of the prisoners generally, — many of them delicate and infirm, several venerable for their virtues as well as years, — and that they were kept in this cruelly painful condition from early spring to the middle of the next January, and the larger part to the May of 1693, in the extremes of heat and cold, exposed to the most distressing severities of both, crowded in narrow, dark, and noisome jails under an accumulation of all their discomforts, restraints, privations, exposures, and abominations, our wonder is, not that many of them died, but that all did not break down in body and mind.

Sarah Buckley and her daughter were not brought
to trial until after the power of the prosecution to
pursue to the death had ceased. They were acquitted
in January, 1692. Their goods and chattels had all
been seized by the officers, as was the usual practice, at the time of their arrest. In humble circumstances before, it took their last shilling to meet the
charges of their imprisonment. They, as all others,
were required to provide their own maintenance
while in prison; and, after trial and acquittal, were
not discharged until all costs were paid. Five pounds
had to be raised, to satisfy the claims of the officers of
the court and of the jails, for each of them. The result
was, the family was utterly impoverished. The poor
old woman, with her aged husband, suffered much,
there is reason to fear, from absolute want during all
the rest of their days. Their truly Christian virtues
dignified their poverty, and secured the respect and
esteem of all good men. The Rev. Joseph Green has
this entry in his diary: " Jan. 2, 1702. — Old William
Buckley died this evening. He was at meeting the
last sabbath, and died with the cold, I fear, for want
of comforts and good tending. Lord forgive! He was
about eighty years old. I visited him and prayed
with him on Monday, and also the evening before he
died. He was very poor; but, I hope, had not his
portion in this life." The ejaculation, " Lord forgive!" expresses the deep sense Mr. Green had, of
which his whole ministry gave evidence, of the inexpressible sufferings and wrongs brought upon families

by the witchcraft prosecutions. The case of Sarah
Buckley, her husband and family, was but one of
many. The humble, harmless, innocent people who
experienced that fearful and pitiless persecution had
to drink of as bitter a cup as ever was permitted by an
inscrutable Providence to be presented to human lips.
In reference to them, we feel as an assurance, what
good Mr. Green humbly hoped, that "they had not
their portion in this life." Those who went firmly,
patiently, and calmly through that great trial without
losing love or faith, are crowned with glory and honor.

The examination and commitment of Mary Easty,
on the 21st of April, have already been described. For
some reason, and in a way of which we have no information, she was discharged from prison on the 18th
of May, and wholly released. This seems to have
been very distasteful to the accusing girls. They
were determined not to let it rest so; and put into
operation their utmost energies to get her back to imprisonment. On the 20th of May, Mercy Lewis, being
then at the house of John Putnam, Jr., was taken
with fits, and experienced tortures of unprecedented
severity. The particular circumstances on this occasion, as gathered from various depositions, illustrate
very strikingly the skilful manner in which the girls
managed to produce the desired effect upon the public
mind.

Samuel Abbey, a neighbor, whether sent for or not
we are not informed, went to John Putnam's house
that morning, about nine o'clock. He found Mercy in

a terrible condition, crying out with piteous tones of anguish, " Dear Lord, receive my soul." — " Lord, let them not kill me quite." — " Pray for the salvation of my soul, for they will kill me outright." He was desired to go to Thomas Putnam's house to bring his daughter Ann, " to see if she could see who it was that hurt Mercy Lewis." He found Abigail Williams with Ann, and they accompanied him back to John Putnam's. On the way, they both cried out that they saw the apparition of Goody Easty afflicting Mercy Lewis. When they reached the scene, they exclaimed, " There is Goody Easty and John Willard and Mary Whittredge afflicting the body of Mercy Lewis;" Mercy at the time laboring for breath, and appearing as choked and strangled, convulsed, and apparently at the last gasp. " Thus," says Abbey, " she continued the greatest part of the day, in such tortures as no tongue can express." Mary Walcot was sent for. Upon coming in, she cried out, "There is the apparition of Goody Easty choking Mercy Lewis, pressing upon her breasts with both her hands, and putting a chain about her neck." A message was then despatched for Elizabeth Hubbard. She, too, saw the shape of Goody Easty, " the very same woman that was sent home the other day," aided in her diabolical operations by Willard and Whittredge, " torturing Mercy in a most dreadful manner." Intelligence of the shocking sufferings of Mercy was circulated far and wide, and people hurried to the spot from all directions. Jonathan Putnam, James Darling, Benjamin Hutchinson, and Samuel Braybrook reached the house during the evening, and found Mercy " in a case as if death would have quickly followed." Occasionally, Mercy would have a respite ; and, at such intervals, Elizabeth Hubbard would fill the gap. " These two fell into fits by turns ; the one being well while the other was ill." Each of them continued, all the while, crying out against Goody Easty, uttering in their trances vehement remonstrances against her cruel operations, representing her as bringing their winding-sheets and coffins, and threatening to kill them " if they would not sign to her book." Their acting was so complete that the bystanders seem to have thought that they heard the words of Easty, as well as the responses of the girls ; and that they saw the " winding-sheet, coffin," and " the book." In the general consternation, Marshal Herrick was sent for. What he saw, heard, thought, and did, appears from the following : —

" May 20, 1692. — THE TESTIMONY OF GEORGE HERRICK, aged thirty-four or thereabouts, and JOHN PUTNAM, JR., of Salem Village, aged thirty-five years or thereabouts. — Testifieth and saith, that, being at the house of the above-said John Putnam, both saw Mercy Lewis in a very dreadful and solemn condition, so that to our apprehension she could not continue long in this world without a mitigation of those torments we saw her in, which caused us to expedite a hasty despatch to apprehend Mary Easty, in hopes, if possible, it might save her life ; and, returning the same night to said John Putnam's house about midnight, we found the said Mercy Lewis in a dreadful fit, but her reason was then returned. Again she said, ' What! have you brought me the winding-sheet, Goodwife Easty? Well, I had rather go into the winding-sheet than set my hand to the book ;' but, after that, her fits were weaker and weaker, but still complaining that she was very sick of her stomach. About break of day, she fell asleep, but still continues extremely sick, and was taken with a dreadful fit just as we left her ; so that we perceived life in her, and that was all."

Edward Putnam, after stating that the grievous afflictions and tortures of Mercy Lewis were charged, by her and the other four girls, upon Mary Easty, deposes as follows : —

" I myself, being there present with several others, looked for nothing else but present death for almost the space of two days and a night. She was choked almost to death, insomuch we thought sometimes she had been dead ; her mouth and teeth shut; and all this very often until such time as we understood Mary Easty was laid in irons."

Mercy's fits did not cease immediately upon Easty's being apprehended, but on her being committed to prison and chains by the magistrate in Salem.

An examination of distances, with the map before us, will show the rapidity with which business was despatched on this occasion. Abbey went to John Putnam, Jr.'s house at nine o'clock in the morning of May 20. He was sent to Thomas Putnam's house for Ann, and brought her and Abigail Williams back with him. Mary Walcot was sent for to the house of her father, Captain Jonathan Walcot, and went up at one

o'clock, "about an hour by sun." Then Elizabeth
Hubbard, who lived at the house of Dr. Griggs, "was
carried up to Constable John Putnam's house:"
Jonathan Putnam, James Darling, Benjamin Hutchinson, and Samuel Braybrook got there in the evening, as
they say, "between eight and eleven o'clock." In the
mean time, Marshal Herrick had arrived. Steps were
taken to get out a warrant. John Putnam and Benjamin Hutchinson went to Salem to Hathorne for the
purpose. They must have started soon after eight.
Hathorne issued the warrant forthwith. It is dated
May 20. Herrick went with it to the house of Isaac
Easty, made the arrest, sent his prisoner to the jail
in Salem, and returned himself to John Putnam's
house "about midnight;" staid to witness the apparently mortal sufferings of Mercy until "about break
of day;" returned to Salem; had the examination before Hathorne, at Thomas Beadle's: the whole thing
was finished, Mary Easty in irons, information of the
result carried to John Putnam's, and Mercy's agonies
ceased that afternoon, as Edward Putnam testifies.

I have given this particular account of the circumstances that led to and attended Mary Easty's second
arrest, because the papers belonging to the case afford,
in some respects, a better insight of the state of things
than others, and because they enable us to realize the
power which the accusing girls exercised. The continuance of their convulsions and spasms for such a
length of time, the large number of persons who witnessed and watched them in the broad daylight, and

the perfect success of their operations, show how
thoroughly they had become trained in their arts.   I
have presented the occurrences in the order of time,
so that, by estimating the distances traversed and the
period within which they took place, an idea can be
formed of the vehement earnestness with which men
acted in the " hurrying distractions of amazing afflictions " and overwhelming terrors.   This instance also
gives us a view of the horrible state of things, when
any one, however respectable and worthy, was liable,
at any moment, to be seized, maligned, and destroyed.

Mary Easty had previously experienced the malice
of the persecutors.   For two months she had suffered
the miseries of imprisonment, had just been released,
and for two days enjoyed the restoration of liberty, the
comforts of her home, and a re-union with her family.
She and they, no doubt, considered themselves safe
from any further outrage.   After midnight, she was
roused from sleep by the unfeeling marshal, torn from
her husband and children, carried back to prison,
loaded with chains, and finally consigned to a dreadful
and most cruel death.   She was an excellent and
pious matron.   Her husband, referring to the transaction nearly twenty years afterwards, justly expressed
what all must feel, that it was " a hellish molestation."

One of the most malignant witnesses against Mary
Easty was " Goodwife Bibber."   She obtruded herself
in many of the cases, acting as a sort of outside member of the " accusing circle," volunteering her aid in

carrying on the persecutions. It was an outrage for
the magistrates or judges to have countenanced such
a false defamer. There are, among the papers,
documents which show that she ought to have been
punished as a calumniator, rather than be called to
utter, under oath, lies against respectable people. The
following deposition was sworn to in Court: —

" THE TESTIMONY OF JOSEPH FOWLER, who testifieth that
Goodman Bibber and his wife lived at my house; and I did
observe and take notice that Goodwife Bibber was a woman
who was very idle in her calling, and very much given to
tattling and tale-bearing, making mischief amongst her
neighbors, and very much given to speak bad words, and
would call her husband bad names, and was a woman of a
very turbulent, unruly spirit."

Joseph Fowler lived in Wenham, and was a person
of respectability and influence. His brother Philip
was also a leading man; was employed as attorney
by the Village Parish in its lawsuit with Mr. Parris;
and married a sister of Joseph Herrick. They were
the grandsons of the first Philip, who was an early
emigrant from Wales, settling in Ipswich, where he
had large landed estates. Henry Fowler and his two
brothers, now of Danvers, are the descendants of this
family: one of them, Augustus, distinguished as a
naturalist, especially in the department of ornithology;
the other, Samuel Page Fowler, as an explorer of our
early annals and local antiquities. In 1692, one of
the Fowlers conducted the proceedings in Court

against the head and front of the witchcraft prosecution ; and the other had the courage, in the most
fearful hour of the delusion, to give open testimony in
the defence of its victims. It is an interesting circumstance, that one of the same name and descent, in his
reprint of the papers of Calef and in other publications, has done as much as any other person of our
day to bring that whole transaction under the light of
truth and justice.

John Porter, who was a grandson of the original
John Porter and the original William Dodge and a
man of property and family, with his wife Lydia ;
Thomas Jacobs and Mary his wife ; and Richard Wal-
ker, — all of Wenham, and for a long time neighbors of
this Bibber, — testify, in corroboration of the statement
of Fowler, that she was a woman of an unruly, turbulent spirit, double-tongued, much given to tattling
and tale-bearing, making mischief amongst her neighbors, very much given to speak bad words, often
speaking against one and another, telling lies and
uttering malicious wishes against people. It was
abundantly proved that she had long been known to be
able to fall into fits at any time. One witness said
" she would often fall into strange fits when she was
crossed of her humor ; " and another, " that she could
fall into fits as often as she pleased."

On the 21st of May, warrants were issued against
the wife of William Basset, of Lynn ; Susanna Roots, of
Beverly ; and Sarah, daughter of John Procter of Salem
Farms ; a few days after, against Benjamin, a son of

said John Procter; Mary Derich, wife of Michael Derich, and daughter of William Basset of Lynn; and the
wife of Robert Pease of Salem.   Such papers as relate
to these persons vary in no particular worthy of notice
from those already presented.

On the 28th of May, warrants were issued against
Martha Carrier, of Andover; Elizabeth Fosdick, of Malden; Wilmot Read, of Marblehead; Sarah Rice, of
Reading; Elizabeth How, of Topsfield; Captain John
Alden, of Boston; William Procter, of Salem Farms;
Captain John Flood, of Rumney Marsh; —— Toothaker and her daughter, of Billerica; and —— Abbot,
between Topsfield and Wenham line.   On the 30th,
a warrant was issued against Elizabeth, wife of Stephen Paine, of Charlestown; on the 4th of June,
against Mary, wife of Benjamin Ireson, of Lynn.   Besides these, there are notices of complaints made and
warrants issued against a great number of people in
all parts of the country: Mary Bradbury, of Salisbury;
Lydia and Sarah Dustin, of Reading; Ann Sears, of
Woburn; Job Tookey, of Beverly; Abigail Somes, of
Gloucester; Elizabeth Carey, of Charlestown; Candy,
a negro woman; and many others.   Some of them have
points of interest, demanding particular notice.

The case of Martha Carrier has some remarkable
features.   It has been shown, by passages already
adduced, that every idle rumor; every thing that the
gossip of the credulous or the fertile imaginations of
the malignant could produce; every thing, gleaned from
the memory or the fancy, that could have an unfavora-

ble bearing upon an accused person, however foreign or irrelevant it might be to the charge, was allowed to be brought in evidence before the magistrates, and received at the trials. We have seen that a child under five years of age was arrested, and put into prison. Children were not only permitted, but induced, to become witnesses against their parents, and parents against their children. Husbands and wives were made to criminate each other as witnesses in court. When Martha Carrier was arrested, four of her children were also taken into custody. An indictment against one of them is among the papers. Under the terrors brought to bear upon them, they were prevailed on to be confessors.. The following shows how these children were trained to tell their story : —

" It was asked Sarah Carrier by the magistrates, —

" How long hast thou been a witch ? — Ever since I was six years old.

" How old are you now ? — Near eight years old : brother Richard says I shall be eight years old in November next.

" Who made you a witch ? — My mother : she made me set my hand to a book.

" How did you set your hand to it ? — I touched it with my fingers, and the book was red : the paper of it was white.

" She said she never had seen the black man : the place where she did it was in Andrew Foster's pasture, and Elizabeth Johnson, Jr., was there. Being asked who was there besides, she answered, her aunt Toothaker and her cousin.

Being asked when it was, she said, when she was baptized.

"What did they promise to give you? — A black dog.

"Did the dog ever come to you? — No.

"But you said you saw a cat once: what did that say to you? — It said it would tear me in pieces, if I would not set my hand to the book.

"She said her mother baptized her, and the Devil, or black man, was not there, as she saw; and her mother said, when she baptized her, 'Thou art mine for ever and ever. Amen.'

"How did you afflict folks? — I pinched them.

"And she said she had no puppets, but she went to them that she afflicted. Being asked whether she went in her body or her spirit, she said in her spirit. She said her mother carried her thither to afflict.

"How did your mother carry you when she was in prison? — She came like a black cat.

"How did you know it was your mother? — The cat told me so, that she was my mother. She said she afflicted Phelps's child last Saturday, and Elizabeth Johnson joined with her to do it. She had a wooden spear, about as long as her finger, of Elizabeth Johnson; and she had it of the Devil. She would not own that she had ever been at the witch-meeting at the village. This is the substance.

"SIMON WILLARD."

The confession of another of her children is among the papers. It runs thus: —

"Have you been in the Devil's snare? — Yes.

"Is your brother Andrew ensnared by the Devil's snare? — Yes.

" How long has your brother been a witch? — Near a month.

" How long have you been a witch? — Not long.

" Have you joined in afflicting the afflicted persons? — Yes.

" You helped to hurt Timothy Swan, did you? — Yes.

" How long have you been a witch? — About five weeks.

" Who was in company when you covenanted with the Devil? — Mrs. Bradbury.

" Did she help you afflict? — Yes.

" Who was at the village meeting when you were there? — Goodwife How, Goodwife Nurse, Goodwife Wildes, Procter and his wife, Mrs. Bradbury, and Corey's wife.

" What did they do there? — Eat, and drank wine.

"Was there a minister there? — No, not as I know of.

" From whence had you your wine? — From Salem, I think, it was.

" Goodwife Oliver there? — Yes: I knew her."

In concluding his report of the trial of this wretched woman, whose children were thus made to become the instruments for procuring her death, Dr. Cotton Mather expresses himself in the following language: —

" This rampant hag (Martha Carrier) was the person of whom the confessions of the witches, and of her own children among the rest, agreed that the Devil had promised her that she should be queen of Hell."

It is quite evident that this " rampant hag " had no better opinion of the dignitaries and divines who managed matters at the time than they had of her.

The record of her examination shows that she was not afraid to speak her mind, and in plain terms too. When brought before the magistrates, the following were their questions and her answers. The accusing witnesses having severally made their charges against her, declaring that she had tormented them in various ways, and threatened to cut their throats if they would not sign the Devil's book, which, they said, she had presented to them, the magistrates addressed her in these words: "What do you say to this you are charged with?" She answered, "I have not done it." One of the accusers cried out that she was, at that moment, sticking pins into her. Another declared that she was then looking upon "the black man,"— the shape in which they pretended the Devil appeared. The magistrate asked the accused, "What black man is that?" Her answer was, "I know none." The accusers cried out that the black man was present, and visible to them. The magistrate asked her, "What black man did you see?" Her answer was, "I saw no black man but your own presence." Whenever she looked upon the accusers, they were knocked down. The magistrate, entirely deluded by their practised acting, said to her, "Can you look upon these, and not knock them down?" Her answer was, "They will dissemble, if I look upon them." He continued: "You see, you look upon them, and they fall down." She broke out, "It is false: the Devil is a liar. I looked upon none since I came into the room but you." Susanna Sheldon cried out, in a trance, "I wonder what could

you murder thirteen persons for." At this, her spirit
became aroused: the accusers fell into the most in-
tolerable outcries and agonies. The accused rebuked
the magistrate, charging him with unfairness in not
paying any regard to what she said, and receiving
every thing that the accusers said. "It is a shameful
thing, that you should mind these folks that are out of
their wits;" and, turning to those who were bringing
these false and ridiculous charges against her, she said,
"You lie; I am wronged." The energy and courage
of the prisoner threw the accusers, magistrates, and
the whole crowd into confusion and uproar. The record closes the description of the scene in these words:
"The tortures of the afflicted were so great that there
was no enduring of it, so that she was ordered away,
and to be bound hand and foot with all expedition; the
afflicted, in the mean while, almost killed, to the great
trouble of all spectators, magistrates, and others."

Parris closes his report of this examination as follows: —

"NOTE. — As soon as she was well bound, they all had
strange and sudden ease. Mary Walcot told the magistrates that this woman told her she had been a witch this
forty years."

This shows the sort of communications the girls
were allowed to hold with the magistrates, exciting
their prejudices against accused persons, and filling
their ears with all sorts of exaggerated and false
stories. However much she may have been maligned

by her neighbors, some of whom had long been in the habit of circulating slanders against her, the whole tenor of the papers relating to her shows that she always indignantly repelled the charge of being a witch, and was the last person in the world to have volunteered such a statement as Mary Walcot reported.

The examination of Martha Carrier must have been one of the most striking scenes of the whole drama of the witchcraft proceedings. The village meeting-house presented a truly wild and exciting spectacle. The fearful and horrible superstition which darkened the minds of the people was displayed in their aspect and movements. Their belief, that, then and there, they were witnessing the great struggle between the kingdoms of God and of the Evil One, and that every thing was at stake on the issue, gave an awe-struck intensity to their expression. The blind, unquestioning confidence of the magistrates, clergy, and all concerned in the prosecutions, in the evidence of the accusers; the loud outcries of their pretended sufferings; their contortions, swoonings, and tumblings, excited the usual consternation in the assembly. In addition to this, there was the more than ordinary bold and defiant bearing of the prisoner, stung to desperation by the outrage upon human nature in the abuse practised upon her poor children; her firm and unshrinking courage, facing the tempest that was raised to overwhelm her, sternly rebuking the magistrates, — "It is a shameful thing that you should mind these folks that are out of their wits;"—her whole demeanor, proclaiming her conscious innocence, and proving that she chose chains, the dungeon, and the scaffold, rather than to belie herself. Seldom has a scene in real life, or a picture wrought by the inspiration of genius and the hand of art, in its individual characters or its general grouping, surpassed that presented on this occasion.

Hutchinson has preserved the record of another examination of a different character. An ignorant negro slave woman was brought before the magistrates. She was cunning enough, not only to confess, but to cover herself with the cloak of having been led into the difficulty by her mistress.

"Candy, are you a witch?—Candy no witch in her country. Candy's mother no witch. Candy no witch, Barbados. This country, mistress give Candy witch.

"Did your mistress make you a witch in this country?—Yes: in this country, mistress give Candy witch.

"What did your mistress do to make you witch?—Mistress bring book and pen and ink; make Candy write in it."

Upon being asked what she wrote, she took a pen and ink, and made a mark. Upon being asked how she afflicted people, and where were the puppets she did it with, she said, that, if they would let her go out for a moment, she would show them how. They allowed her to go out, and she presently returned with two pieces of cloth or linen,—one with two knots, the other with one tied in it. Immediately on seeing these articles, the "afflicted children" were "greatly affrighted," and fell into violent fits. When they came to, they declared that the "black man," Mrs. Hawkes, and the negro, stood by the puppets of rags, and pinched them. Whereupon they fell into fits again. "A bit of one of the rags being set on fire," they all shrieked that they were burned, and " cried out dreadfully." Some pieces being dipped in water, they went into the convulsions and struggles of drowning persons ; and one of them rushed out of the room, and raced down towards the river.

Candy and the girls having played their parts so well, there was no escape for poor Mrs. Hawkes but in confession, which she forthwith made. They were both committed to prison. Fortunately, it was not convenient to bring them to trial until the next January, when, the delusion having blown over, they were acquitted.

Besides those already mentioned, there were others, among the victims of this delusion, whose cases excite our tenderest sensibility, and deepen our horror in the contemplation of the scene. It seems, that, some time before the transactions took place in Salem Village, a difficulty arose between two families on the borders of Topsfield and Ipswich, such as often occur among neighbors, about some small matter of property, fences, or boundaries. Their names were Perley and How. A daughter of Perley, about ten years of age, hearing, probably, strong expressions by her parents, became excited against the Hows, and charged the wife of How with bewitching her. She acted much

after the manner of the "afflicted girls" in Salem
Village, which was near the place of her residence.
Very soon the idea became current that Mrs. How
was a witch; and every thing that happened amiss to
any one was laid at her door. She was cried out
against by the "afflicted children" in Salem Village,
and carried before the magistrates for examination on
the 31st of May, 1692. Upon being brought into her
presence, the accusers fell into their usual fits and
convulsions, and charged her with tormenting them.
To the question, put by the magistrates, "What say
you to this charge?" her answer was, "If it was the
last moment I was to live, God knows I am innocent
of any thing in this nature." The papers connected
with her trial bear abundant testimony to the excellent character of this pious and amiable woman. A
person, who had lived near her twenty-four years,
states, in her deposition, "that she had found her a
neighborly woman, conscientious in her dealing, faithful to her promises, and Christianlike in her conversation." Several others join in a deposition to this
effect: "For our own parts, we have been well acquainted with her for above twenty years. We never
saw but that she carried it very well, and that both
her words and actions were always such as well became a good Christian."

The following passages illustrate the wicked arts
sometimes used to bring accusations upon innocent
persons, and give affecting proof of the excellence of
the character and heart of Elizabeth How : —

" THE TESTIMONY OF SAMUEL PHILLIPS, aged about sixty-seven, minister of the word of God in Rowley, who saith that Mr. Payson (minister of God's word also in Rowley) and myself went, being desired, to Samuel Perly, of Ipswich, to see their young daughter, who was visited with strange fits; and, in her fits (as her father and mother affirmed), did mention Goodwife How, the wife of James How, Jr., of Ipswich, as if she was in the house, and did afflict her. When we were in the house, the child had one of her fits, but made no mention of Goodwife How; and, when the fit was over, and she came to herself, Goodwife How went to the child, and took her by the hand, and asked her whether she had ever done her any hurt; and she answered, ' No, never; and, if I did complain of you in my fits, I knew not that I did so.' I further can affirm, upon oath, that young Samuel Perley, brother to the afflicted girl, looked out of a chamber window (I and the afflicted child being without doors together), and said to his sister, ' Say Goodwife How is a witch, — say she is a witch;' and the child spake not a word that way. But I looked up to the window where the youth stood, and rebuked him for his boldness to stir up his sister to accuse the said Goodwife How; whereas she had cleared her from doing any hurt to his sister in both our hearing; and I added, ' No wonder that the child, in her fits, did mention Goodwife How, when her nearest relations were so frequent in expressing their suspicions, in the child's hearing, when she was out of her fits, that the said Goodwife How was an instrument of mischief to the child.' "

Mr. Payson, in reference to the same occasion, deposed as follows: —

" Being in Perley's house some considerable time before
the said Goodwife How came in, their afflicted daughter,
upon something that her mother spake to her with tartness,
presently fell into one of her usual strange fits, during which
she made no mention (as I observed) of the abovesaid How
her name, or any thing relating to her. Some time after, the
said How came in, when said girl had recovered her capacity, her fit being over. Said How took said girl by the
hand, and asked her whether she had ever done her any
hurt. The child answered, ' No ; never,' with several expressions to that purpose."

The bearing of Elizabeth How, under accusations
so cruelly and shamefully fabricated and circulated
against her, exhibits one of the most beautiful pic-
tures of a truly forgiving spirit and of Christlike
love anywhere to be found. Several witnesses say,
" We often spoke to her of some things that were
reported of her, that gave some suspicion of that she
is now charged with ; and she, always professing her
innocency, often desired our prayers to God for her,
that God would keep her in his fear, and support
her under her burden. We have often heard her
speaking of those persons that raised those reports of
her, and we never heard her speak badly of them for
the same ; but, in our hearing, hath often said that
she desired God that he would sanctify that affliction,
as well as others, for her spiritual good." Others testified to the same effect. Simon Chapman, and Mary,
his wife, say that " they had been acquainted with the
wife of James How, Jr., as a neighbor, for this nine or

ten years;" that they had resided in the same house
with her "by the fortnight together;" that they never
knew any thing but what was good in her. They
"found, at all times, by her discourse, she was a
woman of affliction, and mourning for sin in herself
and others; and, when she met with any affliction, she
seemed to justify God and say that it was all better
than she deserved, though it was by false accusations
from men. She used to bless God that she got good
by affliction; for it made her examine her own heart.
We never heard her revile any person that hath accused her with witchcraft, but pitied them, and said,
'I pray God forgive them; for they harm themselves
more than me. Though I am a great sinner, I am
clear of that; and such kind of affliction doth but
set me to examining my own heart, and I find God
wonderfully supporting me and comforting me by his
word and promises.'"

Joseph Knowlton and his wife Mary, who had lived
near her, and sometimes in the same family with her,
testified, that, having heard the stories told about
her, they were led to —

"take special notice of her life and conversation ever since.
And I have asked her if she could freely forgive them that
raised such reports of her. She told me yes, with all her
heart, desiring that God would give her a heart to be more
humble under such a providence; and, further, she said she
was willing to do any good she could to those who had done
unneighborly by her. Also this I have taken notice, that she
would deny herself to do a neighbor a good turn."

The father of her husband, — James How, Sr., aged
about ninety-four years, — in a communication addressed to the Court, declared that —

" he, living by her for about thirty years, hath taken notice
that she hath carried it well becoming her place, as a daughter, as a wife, in all relations, setting aside human infirmities, as becometh a Christian; with respect to myself as a
father, very dutifully; and as a wife to my son, very careful,
loving, obedient, and kind, — considering his want of eyesight, tenderly leading him about by the hand. Desiring
God may guide your honors, . . . I rest yours to serve."

The only evidence against this good woman — be
yond the outcries and fits of the " afflicted children,"
enacted in their usual skilful and artful style — consisted of the most wretched gossip ever circulated in
an ignorant and benighted community.   It came from
people in the back settlements of Ipswich and Topsfield, and disclosed a depth of absurd and brutal superstition, which it is difficult to believe ever existed in
New England.   So far as those living in secluded
and remote localities are regarded, this was the most
benighted period of our history.   Except where, as
in Salem Village, special circumstances had kept up
the general intelligence, there was much darkness
on the popular mind.   The education that came over
with the first emigrants from the mother-country had
gone with them to their graves.   The system of common schools had not begun to produce its fruit in
the thinly peopled outer settlements.   There is no
more disgraceful page in our annals than that which

details the testimony given at the trial, and records the conviction and execution, of Elizabeth How.

But the dark shadows of that day of folly, cruelty, and crime, served to bring into a brighter and purer light virtues exhibited by many persons. We meet affecting instances, all along, of family fidelity and true Christian benevolence. James How, as has been stated, was stricken with blindness. He had two daughters, Mary and Abigail. Although their farm was out of the line of the public-roads, travel very difficult, and they must have encountered many hardships, annoyances, and, it is to be feared, sometimes unfeeling treatment by the way, one of them accompanied their father, twice every week, to visit their mother in her prison-walls. They came on horseback; she managing the bridle, and guiding him by the hand after alighting. Their humble means were exhausted in these offices of reverence and affection. One of the noble girls made her way to Boston, sought out the Governor, and implored a reprieve for her mother; but in vain. The sight of these young women, leading their blind father to comfort and provide for their "honored mother, — as innocent," as they declared her to be, " of the crime charged, as any person in the world," — so faithful and constant in their filial love and duty, relieved the horrors of the scene; and it ought to be held in perpetual remembrance. The shame of that day is not, and will not be, forgotten; neither should its beauty and glory.

The name of Elizabeth How, before marriage, was

Jackson. Among the accounts rendered against the country for expenses incurred in the witchcraft prosecutions are these two items: " For John Jackson, Sr., one pair of fetters, five shillings ; for John Jackson, Jr., one pair of fetters, five shillings." There is also an item for carrying " the two Jacksons " from one jail to another, and back again. No other reference to them is found among the papers. They were, perhaps, a brother and nephew of Elizabeth How. There is reason to suppose that her husband, James How, Jr., was a nephew of the Rev. Francis Dane, of Andover.

The examination of Job Tookey, of Beverly, presents some points worthy of notice. He is described as a " laborer," but was evidently a person, although perhaps inconsiderate of speech, of more than common discrimination, and not wholly deluded by the fanaticism of the times. He is charged with having said that he " would take Mr. Burroughs's part ; " " that he was not the Devil's servant, but the Devil was his." When the girls testified that they saw his shape afflicting persons, he answered, like a sensible man, if they really saw any such thing, " it was not he, but the Devil in his shape, that hurts the people." Susanna Sheldon, Mary Warren, and Ann Putnam, all declared, that, at that very moment while the examination was going on, two men and two women and one child " rose from the dead, and cried, ' Vengeance ! vengeance ! ' " Nobody else saw or heard any thing : but the girls suddenly became dumb ; their eyes were

fixed on vacancy, all looking towards the same spot;
and their whole appearance gave assurance of the
truth of what they said. In a short time, Mary Warren recovered the use of her vocal organs, and exclaimed, " There are three men, and three women, and
two children. They are all in their winding-sheets:
they look pale upon us, but red upon Tookey, — red as
blood." Again, she exclaimed, in a startled and
affrighted manner, " There is a young child under the
table, crying out for vengeance." Elizabeth Booth,
pointing to the same place, was struck speechless.
In this way, the murder of about every one who had
died at Royal Side, for a year or two past, was put
upon Tookey. Some of them were called by name;
the others, the girls pretended not to recognize. The
wrath and horror of the whole community were excited against him, and he was committed to jail, by the
order of the magistrates, — Bartholomew Gedney,
Jonathan Corwin, and John Hathorne.

No character, indeed, however blameless lovely or
venerable, was safe. The malignant accusers struck
at the highest marks, and the consuming fire of popular frenzy was kindled and attracted towards the most
commanding objects. Mary Bradbury is described, in
the indictment against her, as the " wife of Captain
Thomas Bradbury, of Salisbury, in the county of Essex, gentleman." A few of the documents that are
preserved, belonging to her case, will give some idea
what sort of a person she was: —

" *The Answer of Mary Bradbury to the Charge of Witch-craft, or Familiarity with the Devil.*

" I do plead ' Not guilty.' I am wholly innocent of any such wickedness, through the goodness of God that have kept me hitherto. I am the servant of Jesus Christ, and have given myself up to him as my only Lord and Saviour, and to the diligent attendance upon him in all his holy ordinances, in utter contempt and defiance of the Devil and all his works, as horrid and detestable, and, accordingly, have endeavored to frame my life and conversation according to the rules of his holy word; and, in that faith and practice, resolve, by the help and assistance of God, to continue to my life's end.

" For the truth of what I say, as to matter of practice, I humbly refer myself to my brethren and neighbors that know me, and unto the Searcher of all hearts, for the truth and uprightness of my heart therein (human frailties and un-avoidable infirmities excepted, of which I bitterly complain every day).   MARY BRADBURY."

" July 28, 1692. — Concerning my beloved wife, Mary Bradbury, this is what I have to say : We have been married fifty-five years, and she hath been a loving and faithful wife to me. Unto this day, she hath been wonderful laborious, diligent, and industrious, in her place and employment, about the bringing-up of our family (which have been eleven chil-dren of our own, and four grandchildren). She was both prudent and provident, of a cheerful spirit, liberal and char-itable. She being now very aged and weak, and grieved under her affliction, may not be able to speak much for her-self, not being so free of speech as some others may be. I hope her life and conversation have been such amongst her

neighbors as gives a better and more real testimony of her
than can be expressed by words.

"Owned by me,   THO. BRADBURY."

The Rev. James Allin made oath before Robert Pike,
an assistant and magistrate, as follows : —

"I, having lived nine years at Salisbury in the work of
the ministry, and now four years in the office of a pastor, to
my best notice and observation of Mrs. Bradbury, she hath
lived according to the rules of the gospel amongst us ; was a
constant attender upon the ministry of the word, and all the
ordinances of the gospel ; full of works of charity and mercy
to the sick and poor : neither have I seen or heard any thing
of her unbecoming the profession of the gospel."

Robert Pike also affirmed to the truth of Mr. Allin's
statement, from " upwards of fifty years' experience,"
as did John Pike also : they both declared themselves
ready and desirous to give their testimony before the
Court.

One hundred and seventeen of her neighbors — the
larger part of them heads of families, and embracing
the most respectable people of that vicinity — signed
their names to a paper, of which the following is a
copy : —

"Concerning Mrs. Bradbury's life and conversation, we,
the subscribers, do testify, that it was such as became the
gospel : she was a lover of the ministry, in all appearance,
and a diligent attender upon God's holy ordinances, being of
a courteous and peaceable disposition and carriage. Neither
did any of us (some of whom have lived in the town with her

above fifty years) ever hear or ever know that she ever had any difference or falling-out with any of her neighbors, — man, woman, or child, — but was always ready and willing to do for them what lay in her power night and day, though with hazard of her health, or other danger. More might be spoken in her commendation, but this for the present."

Although this aged matron and excellent Christian lady was convicted and sentenced to death, it is most satisfactory to find that she escaped from prison, and her life was saved.

The following facts show the weight which ought to have been attached to these statements. The position, as well as character and age, of Mary [Perkins] Bradbury entitled her to the highest consideration, in the structure of society at that time. This is recognized in the title " Mrs.," uniformly given her. She had been noted, through life, for business capacity, energy, and influence ; and, in 1692, was probably seventy-five years of age, and somewhat infirm in health. Her husband, Thomas Bradbury, had been a prominent character in the colony for more than fifty years. In 1641, he was appointed, by the General Court, Clerk of the Writs for Salisbury, with the functions of a magistrate, to execute all sorts of legal processes in that place. He was a deputy in 1651 and many subsequent years ; a commissioner for Salisbury in 1657, empowered to act in all criminal cases, and bind over offenders, where it was proper, to higher courts, to take testimonies upon oath, and to join persons in marriage. He was required to keep a record of all his

doings. If the parties agreed to that effect, he was
authorized to hear and determine cases of every kind
and degree, without the intervention of a jury. The
towns north of the Merrimac, and all beyond now
within the limits of New Hampshire, constituted the
County of Norfolk; and Thomas Bradbury, for a long
series of years, was one of its commissioners and associate judges. From the first, he was conspicuous
in military matters; having been commissioned by the
General Court, in 1648, Ensign of the trainband in
Salisbury. He rose to its command; and, in the latter
portion of his life, was universally spoken of as " Captain Bradbury." All along, the records of the General
Court, for half a century, demonstrate the estimation
in which he was held; various important trusts
and special services requiring integrity and ability
being from time to time committed to him. His
family was influentially connected. His son William
married the widow of Samuel Maverick, Jr., who was
the son of one of the King's Commissioners in 1664:
she was the daughter of the Rev. John Wheelwright,
a man of great note, intimately related to the celebrated Anne Hutchinson, and united with her by
sympathy in sentiment and participation in exile.

Robert Pike, born in 1616, was a magistrate in 1644.
He was deputy from Salisbury in 1648, and many
times after; Associate Justice for Norfolk in 1650;
and Assistant in 1682, holding that high station, by
annual elections, to the close of the first charter, and
during the whole period of the intervening and insur-

gent government. He was named as one of the council that succeeded to the House of Assistants, when, under the new charter, Massachusetts became a royal province. He was always at the head of military affairs, having been commissioned, by the General Court, Lieutenant of the Salisbury trainband in 1648; and, in the later years of his life, he held the rank and title of major. John Pike, probably his son, resided in Hampton in 1691, and was minister of Dover at his death in 1710.

Surely, the attestations of such men as the Pikes, father and son, and the Rev. James Allin, to the Christian excellence of Mary Bradbury, must be allowed to corroborate fully the declarations of her neighbors, her husband, and herself.

The motives and influences that led to her arrest and condemnation in 1692 demand an explanation. The question arises, Why should the attention of the accusing girls have been led to this aged and most respectable woman, living at such a distance, beyond the Merrimac? A critical scrutiny of the papers in the case affords a clew leading to the true answer.

The wife of Sergeant Thomas Putnam, as has been stated (vol. i. p. 253), was Ann Carr of Salisbury. Her father, George Carr, was an early settler in that place, and appears to have been an enterprising and prosperous person. The ferry for the main travel of the country across the Merrimac was from points of land owned by him, and always under his charge. He was engaged in ship-building, — employing, and

having in his family, young men ; among them a son of
Zerubabel Endicott, bearing the same name.

Among the papers in the case is the following : —

"THE DEPOSITION OF RICHARD CARR, who testifieth and
saith, that, about thirteen years ago, presently after some
difference that happened to be between my honored father,
Mr. George Carr, and Mrs. Bradbury, the prisoner at the bar,
upon a sabbath at noon, as we were riding home, by the
house of Captain Tho : Bradbury, I saw Mrs. Bradbury go
into her gate, turn the corner of, and immediately there
darted out of her gate a blue boar, and darted at my father's
horse's legs, which made him stumble ; but I saw it no more.
And my father said, 'Boys, what do you see?' We both
answered, 'A blue boar.'

"ZERUBABEL ENDICOTT testifieth and saith, that I lived at
Mr. George Carr, now deceased, at the time above mentioned,
and was present with Mr. George Carr and Mr. Richard
Carr. And I also saw a blue boar dart out of Mr. Bradbury's gate to Mr. George Carr's horse's legs, which made
him stumble after a strange manner. And I also saw the
blue boar dart from Mr. Carr's horse's legs in at Mrs. Bradbury's window. And Mr. Carr immediately said, 'Boys,
what did you see?' And we both said, 'A blue boar.' Then
said he, 'From whence came it?' And we said, 'Out of
Mr. Bradbury's gate.' Then said he, 'I am glad you see it
as well as I.' *Jurat in Curia*, Sept. 9, '92."

Stephen Sewall, the clerk of the courts, with his
usual eagerness to make the most of the testimony
against persons accused, adds to the deposition the
following : —

" And they both further say, on their oaths, that Mr. Carr discoursed with them, as they went home, about what had happened, and they all concluded that it was Mrs. Bradbury that so appeared as a blue boar."

At the date of this occurrence, Richard Carr was twenty years of age, and Zerubabel Endicott a lad of of fifteen.

It is not to be wondered at that there was " some difference between " George Carr and Mrs. Bradbury, if he was in the habit of indulging in such talk about her as he took the leading part in on this occasion. He evidently encouraged in his " boys " the absurd imaginations with which their credulity had been stimulated. They were prepared by preconceived notions to witness something preternatural about the premises of Mrs. Bradbury; and, in their jaundiced vision, any animal, moving in and out of the gate, might naturally assume the likeness of a " blue boar." Such ideas circulating in the family, and among the apprentices of Carr, would soon be widely spread. No doubt, Zerubabel, on his visits to his home, told wondrous stories about Mrs. Bradbury. His brother Samuel, then a youth of eighteen, had his imagination filled with them ; and some time after, on a voyage to " Barbadoes and Saltitudos," in which severe storms and various disasters were experienced, attributed them all to Mrs. Bradbury ; and, " in a bright moonshining night, sitting upon the windlass, to which he had been sent forward to look out for land," the wild fancies of his excited imagination took effect. He heard " a

rumbling noise," and thought he saw the legs of some
person. "Presently he was shook, and looked over
his shoulder, and saw the appearance of a woman,
from her middle upwards, having a white cap and
white neckcloth on her, which then affrighted him very
much ; and, as he was turning of the windlass, he saw
the aforesaid two legs." Such superstitious phantasms
seem to be natural to the experiences of sailor-life,
and perhaps still linger in the forecastle and at the
night-watch.

The habit of maligning Mrs. Bradbury as a witch
dated back in the Carr family more than thirteen years,
as the following deposition proves.   I give it precisely
as it is in the original.   As in a few other instances in
this work, the spelling and punctuation are preserved
as curiosities.   Like all the papers in the case, with
one exception, presented in court against Mrs. Bradbury, it is in the handwriting of Sergeant Thomas
Putnam : —

"THE DEPOSITION OF JAMES CARR. who testifieth and
saith that about 20 years agoe one day as I was accidently
att the house of mr wheleright and his daughter the widdow
maverick then liued there : and she then did most curtuously
invite me to com oftener to the house and wondered I was
grown such a stranger.   and with in a few days affter one
evening I went thether againe : and when I came thether
againe : william Bradbery was yr who was then a suter to
the said widdow but I did not know it tell affterwards :
affter I came in the widdow did so corsely treat the sd
william Bradbery that he went away semeing to be angury :

presently affter this I was taken affter a strange maner as if
liueing creaturs did run about euery part of my body redy
to tare me to peaces and so I continewed for about 3 qurters
of a year by times & I applyed myself to doctor Crosbe who
gave me a grate deal of visek but could make non work tho
he steept tobacco in bosit drink he could make non to work
where upon he tould me that he beleved I was behaged :
and I tould him I had thought so a good while : and he
asked me by hom I tould him I did not care for spaking for
one was counted an honest woman : but ho uging I tould
him and he said he did beleve that m^is Bradbery was a grat
deal worss then goody martin : then presently affter this one
night I being a bed & brod awake there came sumthing to
me which I thought was a catt and went to strick it ofe the
bed and was sezed fast that I could not stir hedd nor foot.
but by and coming to my strenth I herd sumthing a coming to
me againe and I prepared my self to strick it : and it coming
upon the bed I did strick at it and I beleve I hit it : and
after that visek would work on me and I beleve in my hart
that m^is Bradbery the prisoner att the barr has often afflec-
ted me by acts of wicthcraft.

"*Jurat in Curia* Sep.^mr 9. 92." *

* In the innumerable depositions written by Thomas Putnam, he is
not so careful to be correct, in his chirography and construction, as in
his parish-records. But, if the reader is inclined to make the experiment, he will find, that, if the above document should be properly
pointed and spelled, according to our fashion at the present day, it
would read well, and is clearly and forcibly put together. Spelling, at
that time, was phonetic, and it enables us to ascertain the then prevalent pronunciation of words. "Corsely," no doubt, shows how the
word was then spoken. "Angury" was, with a large class of words
now dissyllables, then a trisyllable. "Tould," "spaking," and many
other words above, are spelled just as they were then pronounced.

But the whole of George Carr's family did not sympathize in this morbid state of prejudice, or cherish such foolish and malignant fancies, against Mrs. Bradbury. One of the sons, William, had married, Aug. 20, 1672, Elizabeth, daughter of Robert Pike. It appears, by the following deposition, which is in the handwriting of Major Pike, that there had been another love affair between the families, leading to a melancholy result, inflaming still more the morbid and malign prejudice against Mrs. Bradbury; but William repudiated it utterly: —

" THE TESTIMONY OF WILLIAM CARR, aged forty-one, or thereabouts, is that my brother John Carr, when he was young, was a man of as good capacity as most men of his age; but falling in love with Jane True (now wife of Captain

---

" Wicthcraft " is always, I believe, spelled this way by Thomas Putnam. He had not got rid of the old Anglo-Saxon sound of the word " witch," brought by his father from Buckinghamshire, sixty years before, — " wicca."

The condition of medical science and practice, at that period, is curiously illustrated in this paper. It is plain that the distemper of James Carr was purely in the realm of the sensibilities and fancy; and "doctor Crosbe" is not wholly to blame because his " visek " did not " work." A good smart nightmare, with a feeling that he had given a thorough basting to the spectre, in the form of a cat, of the supposed author of his woful and aggravated disappointment in love, was what he needed; and it cured him. "A posset of sack" was Falstaff's refuge, from the plight into which he had been led by " building upon a foolish woman's promise," when he emerged from the Thames and the "buck-basket." Many others, no doubt, in drowning sorrow and mortification, have found it " the sovereignest thing on earth." But, as administered by physicians of the Dr. Crosby school, with tobacco steeped in it, it must have been a " villanous compound."

John March), and my father being persuaded by [   ] of
the family (which I shall not name) not to let him marry
so young, my father would not give him a portion, whereupon the match broke off, which my brother laid so much to
heart that he grew melancholy, and by degrees much crazed,
not being the man, that he was before, to his dying day.

" I do further testify that my said brother was sick about
a fortnight or three weeks, and then died ; and I was present
with him when he died. And I do affirm that he died peace-
ably and quietly, never manifesting the least trouble in the
world about anybody, nor did not say any thing of Mrs.
Bradbury nor anybody else doing him hurt ; and yet I was
with him till the breath and life were out of his body."

The usual form, *jurat in curia*, is written at the foot
of this deposition, but evidently by a much later hand ;
and this leads me to mention the improbability that
any testimony in favor of the accused ever reached
the Court at the trials. They had no counsel: the
attorney-general had prejudged all the cases ; and his
mind and those of the judges repudiated utterly any
thing like an investigation. Every friendly voice was
silenced. The doors were closed against the defence.
Robert Pike, an assistant under the old and a council-
lor under the new government, endeavored in vain to
enter them.

William Carr was a person of great respectability,
and bore the appointment, by the General Court, of
land-surveyor for the towns in the northern part of
the present county of Essex.

The member of the family who — as stated in the

foregoing deposition — prevented the match, all the circumstances seem to indicate, was Mrs. Ann Putnam. She perhaps had experienced the effects of a too early marriage, bringing the burden of life upon the constitution and the character before they are mature enough to bear it. She may have attributed to this cause the troubles and trials with which her cup had been so bitterly filled, and the blasting of the happiness of her youth. Half deranged, as perpetual excitement from the parish quarrels in reference to Mr. Bayley had made her, she may have become morbidly opposed to the equally early marriage of a brother. Added to this was the fact that Henry True had married one of Mrs. Bradbury's daughters, and that Jane True was his sister. It cannot be doubted that she entertained the same ideas about Mrs. Bradbury as her father and brothers, James and Richard ; and, for this reason, also opposed the match of her brother John. Wishing to be relieved from the self-reproach of having caused his derangement and death, when the witchcraft delusion broke out at Salem Village and she became wholly absorbed by it, as all other deaths and misfortunes were ascribed to it, she avowed and maintained the belief, as some had suspected at the time, that the happiness, health, reason, and life of her brother had been destroyed by diabolical agency, practised by Mrs. Bradbury.

In the state of things long subsisting between the Bradbury and Carr families, we find an explanation of the movement made against Mrs. Bradbury. Young

Ann Putnam may have often heard her unpleasantly spoken of by her mother, and it was natural that she should have " cried out against her."

The family of Mrs. Ann Putnam seem to have had constitutional traits that illustrate and explain her own character and conduct. They were excitable and sensitive to an extraordinary degree. Their judgment, reason, and physical systems, were subject to the power of their fancies and affections. One of her brothers, in consequence of being badly coquetted with and jilted by a young widow, was thrown into an awful condition of body and mind " for about three-quarters of a year." The reason, health, and heart of another were broken ; and he sunk into an early grave, in consequence of having been crossed in love. The death of her sister Bayley may have been caused by the unhappy controversies in the village parish. We have seen, and shall see, the all but maniac condition to which excitement brought her own mind. At last, the heaviest blow that can fall upon a fond wife suddenly snapped the brittle cord of her life. These considerations must be borne in mind, while we attempt to explain her conduct, and should throw the weight of pity and charity into the scales, if mortal judgment ventures to estimate her guilt. They are known to the Infinite Mind, and never overlooked by divine mercy.

I have introduced these singular private details to illustrate what the documents all along show, — that the proceedings against persons charged with witchcraft, in 1692, were instigated by all sorts of personal grudges and private piques, many of them of long standing, fomented and kept alive by an unhappy indulgence of unworthy feelings, always ready to mix themselves with popular excitements, and leading all concerned headlong to the utmost extent of mischief and wrong.

The case of Mary Bradbury has been allowed to occupy so large a space, because I desire to disabuse the public mind of a great error on this subject. It has been too much supposed, that the sufferers in the witchcraft delusion were generally of the inferior classes of society, and particularly ignorant and benighted. They were the very reverse. They mostly belonged to families in the better conditions of life, and, many of them, to the highest social level. They were all persons of great moral firmness and rectitude, as was demonstrated by their bearing under persecutions and outrage, and when confronting the terrors of death. Their names do not deserve reproach, and their memories ought to be held in honor.

The following account of the examination of Elizabeth Cary of Charlestown, given by her husband, Captain Cary, a shipmaster, has the highest interest, as written at the time by one who was an eye-witness, and participated in the sufferings of the occasion: —

"May 24. — I having heard, some days, that my wife was accused of witchcraft; being much disturbed at it, by advice went to Salem Village, to see if the afflicted knew her: we arrived there on the 24th of May. It happened to be a day appointed for examination; accordingly, soon after our arrival, Mr. Hathorne and Mr. Corwin, &c., went to the meeting-house, which was the place appointed for that work. The minister began with prayer; and, having taken care to get a convenient place, I observed that the afflicted were two girls of about ten years old, and about two or three others of about eighteen: one of the girls talked most, and could discern more than the rest.

" The prisoners were called in one by one, and, as they came in, were cried out at, &c. The prisoners were placed about seven or eight feet from the justices, and the accusers between the justices and them. The prisoners were ordered to stand right before the justices, with an officer appointed to hold each hand, lest they should therewith afflict them: and the prisoners' eyes must be constantly on the justices; for, if they looked on the afflicted, they would either fall into fits, or cry out of being hurt by them. After an examination of the prisoners, who it was afflicted these girls, &c., they were put upon saying the Lord's Prayer, as a trial of their guilt. After the afflicted seemed to be out of their fits, they would look steadfastly on some one person, and frequently not speak; and then the justices said they were struck dumb, and after a little time would speak again: then the justices said to the accusers, ' Which of you will go and touch the prisoner at the bar?' Then the most courageous would adventure, but, before they had made three steps, would ordinarily fall down as in a fit: the justices ordered that they should be taken up and carried to the prisoner, that she might touch them; and as soon as they were touched by the accused, the justices would say, ' They are well,' before I could discern any alteration, — by which I observed that the justices understood the manner of it.

Thus far I was only as a spectator : my wife also was there
part of the time, but no notice was taken of her by the
afflicted, except once or twice they came to her, and asked
her name.   But I, having an opportunity to discourse Mr.
Hale (with whom I had formerly acquaintance), I took his
advice what I had best do, and desired of him that I might
have an opportunity to speak with her that accused my
wife ; which he promised should be, I acquainting him that
I reposed my trust in him.   Accordingly, he came to me
after the examination was over, and told me I had now an
opportunity to speak with the said accuser, Abigail Williams, a girl eleven or twelve years old ; but that we could
not be in private at Mr. Parris's house, as he had promised
me : we went therefore into the alehouse, where an Indian
man attended us, who, it seems, was one of the afflicted : to
him we gave some cider: he showed several scars, that
seemed as if they had been long there, and showed them
as done by witchcraft, and acquainted us that his wife, who
also was a slave, was imprisoned for witchcraft.   And now,
instead of one accuser, they all came in, and began to tumble
down like swine ; and then three women were called in to
attend them.   We in the room were all at a stand to see
who they would cry out of ; but in a short time they cried out
' Cary ; ' and, immediately after, a warrant was sent from
the justices to bring my wife before them, who were sitting
in a chamber near by, waiting for this.   Being brought
before the justices, her chief accusers were two girls.   My
wife declared to the justices, that she never had any knowledge of them before that day.   She was forced to stand
with her arms stretched out.   I requested that I might hold
one of her hands, but it was denied me : then she desired
me to wipe the tears from her eyes, and the sweat from her

face, which I did; then she desired she might lean herself
on me, saying she should faint.   Justice Hathorne replied
she had strength enough to torment these persons, and she
should have strength enough to stand.   I speaking something against their cruel proceedings, they commanded me
to be silent, or else I should be turned out of the room.
The Indian before mentioned was also brought in, to be
one of her accusers; being come in, he now (when before
the justices) fell down, and tumbled about like a hog, but
said nothing.   The justices asked the girls who afflicted the
Indian: they answered she (meaning my wife), and that
she now lay upon him.   The justices ordered her to touch
him, in order to his cure, but her head must be turned
another way, lest, instead of curing, she should make him
worse by her looking on him, her hand being guided to
take hold of his; but the Indian took hold of her hand, and
pulled her down on the floor in a barbarous manner: then
his hand was taken off, and her hand put on his, and the
cure was quickly wrought.   I being extremely troubled at
their inhuman dealings, uttered a hasty speech, 'That God
would take vengeance on them, and desired that God would
deliver us out of the hands of unmerciful men.'   Then her
mittimus was writ.   I did with difficulty and charge obtain
the liberty of a room, but no beds in it; if there had been,
could have taken but little rest that night.   She was committed to Boston prison; but I obtained a *habeas corpus* to
remove her to Cambridge prison, which is in our county of
Middlesex.   Having been there one night, next morning the
jailer put irons on her legs (having received such a command); the weight of them was about eight pounds: these
irons and her other afflictions soon brought her into con-

vulsion fits, so that I thought she would have died that
night. I sent to entreat that the irons might be taken off;
but all entreaties were in vain, if it would have saved her
life, so that in this condition she must continue. The trials
at Salem coming on, I went thither to see how things were
managed: and finding that the spectre evidence was there
received, together with idle, if not malicious stories, against
people's lives, I did easily perceive which way the rest would
go; for the same evidence that served for one would serve
for all the rest. I acquainted her with her danger; and that,
if she were carried to Salem to be tried, I feared she would
never return. I did my utmost that she might have her
trial in our own county; I with several others petitioning
the judge for it, and were put in hopes of it: but I soon
saw so much, that I understood thereby it was not intended; which put me upon consulting the means of her
escape, which, through the goodness of God, was effected,
and she got to Rhode Island, but soon found herself not
safe when there, by reason of the pursuit after her; from
thence she went to New York, along with some others that
had escaped their cruel hands, where we found his Excellency Benjamin Fletcher, Esq., Governor, who was very
courteous to us. After this, some of my goods were seized
in a friend's hands, with whom I had left them, and myself
imprisoned by the sheriff, and kept in custody half a day,
and then dismissed; but to speak of their usage of the
prisoners, and the inhumanity shown to them at the time
of their execution, no sober Christian could bear. They
had also trials of cruel mockings, which is the more, considering what a people for religion, I mean the profession
of it, we have been; those that suffered being many of

them church members, and most of them unspotted in their
conversation, till their adversary the Devil took up this
method for accusing them.   JONATHAN CARY."

The only account we have, written by one who had
actually experienced, in his own person, what it was
to fall into the hands of those who got up and carried
on the prosecutions, is the following. Captain Alden
had probably been from an early stage in their operations in the eye of the accusing girls. He was meant,
perhaps, by what often fell from them about " the tall
man in Boston." We are left entirely to conjecture
as to the reason why they singled him out, as not one
of them, we may be quite sure, had ever seen him.
It may be that some person who had experienced
discipline under his orders as a naval commander
bore him a grudge, and took pains to suggest his
name to the girls, and provided them with the coarse,
vulgar, and ridiculous scandal they so recklessly
poured out upon him : —

" *An Account how John Alden, Sr., was dealt with at Salem
Village.*

" John Alden, Sr., of Boston, in the county of Suffolk,
mariner, on the twenty-eighth day of May, 1692, was
sent for by the magistrates of Salem, in the county of
Essex, upon the accusation of a company of poor distracted
or possessed creatures or witches ; and, being sent by Mr.
Stoughton, arrived there on the 31st of May, and appeared
at Salem Village before Mr. Gedney, Mr. Hathorne, and
Mr. Corwin.

" Those wenches being present who played their juggling tricks, falling down, crying out, and staring in people's faces, the magistrates demanded of them several times, who it was, of all the people in the room, that hurt them. One of these accusers pointed several times at one Captain Hill, there present, but spake nothing. The same accuser had a man standing at her back to hold her up. He stooped down to her ear: then she cried out, ' Alden, Alden afflicted her.' One of the magistrates asked her if she had ever seen Alden. She answered, ' No.' He asked her how she knew it was Alden. She said the man told her so.

" Then all were ordered to go down into the street, where a ring was made; and the same accuser cried out, ' There stands Alden, a bold fellow, with his hat on before the judges: he sells powder and shot to the Indians and French, and lies with the Indian squaws, and has Indian papooses.' Then was Alden committed to the marshal's custody, and his sword taken from him; for they said he afflicted them with his sword. After some hours, Alden was sent for to the meeting-house in the Village, before the magistrates, who required Alden to stand upon a chair, to the open view of all the people.

" The accusers cried out that Alden pinched them then, when he stood upon the chair, in the sight of all the people, a good way distant from them. One of the magistrates bid the marshal to hold open Alden's hands, that he might not pinch those creatures. Alden asked them why they should think that he should come to that village to afflict those persons that he never knew or saw before. Mr. Gedney bid Alden to confess, and give glory to God. Alden said he hoped he should give glory to God, and hoped he should never gratify the Devil: but appealed to all that ever knew him, if they ever suspected him to be such a person;

and challenged any one that could bring in any thing on their own knowledge, that might give suspicion of his being such an one. Mr. Gedney said he had known Alden many years, and had been at sea with him, and always looked upon him to be an honest man ; but now he saw cause to alter his judgment. Alden answered, he was sorry for that, but he hoped God would clear up his innocency, that he would recall that judgment again ; and added, that he hoped that he should, with Job, maintain his integrity till he died. They bid Alden look upon the accusers, which he did, and then they fell down. Alden asked Mr. Gedney what reason there could be given why Alden's looking upon *him* did not strike *him* down as well ; but no reason was given that I heard. But the accusers were brought to Alden to touch them ; and this touch, they said, made them well. Alden began to speak of the providence of God in suffering these creatures to accuse innocent persons. Mr. Noyes asked Alden why he should offer to speak of the providence of God: God, by his providence (said Mr. Noyes), governs the world, and keeps it in peace ; and so went on with discourse, and stopped Alden's mouth as to that.   Alden told Mr. Gedney that he could assure him that there was a lying spirit in them ; for I can assure you that there is not a word of truth in all these say of me. But Alden was again committed to the marshal, and his *mittimus* written.

"To Boston Alden was carried by a constable : no bail would be taken for him, but was delivered to the prison-keeper, where he remained fifteen weeks ; and then, observing the manner of trials, and evidence then taken, was at length prevailed with to make his escape.

"Per JOHN ALDEN."

Alden made his escape about the middle of September, at the bloodiest crisis of the tragedy, and just before the execution of nine of the victims, including that of Giles Corey. He is understood to have fled to Duxbury, where his relatives secreted him. He made his appearance among them late at night; and, on their asking an explanation of his unexpected visit at that hour, replied that he was flying from the Devil, and the Devil was after him. After a while, when the delusion had abated, and people were coming to their senses, he delivered himself up, and was bound over to the Superior Court at Boston, the last Tuesday in April, 1693, when, no one appearing to prosecute, he, with some hundred and fifty others, was discharged by proclamation, and all judicial proceedings brought to a close. It is to be feared, that ever after, to his dying day, when the subject of his experience on the 31st of May, 1692, was referred to, the old sailor indulged in rather strong expressions in relating his reminiscences of Rev. "Mr. Nicholas Noyes," "Mr. Bartholomew Gedney," and the "wenches" of Salem Village.

Captain John Alden was a son of John Alden, ever memorable as one of the first founders of Plymouth Colony. He had been for more than thirty years a resident of Boston, a member of the church, and in all respects a leading and distinguished man. For some time, he had been commander of the armed vessel belonging to the colony, and was a brave and efficient officer and an able and experienced mariner. He had seen service in French and Indian wars, had acted two years before, that is in 1690, as commissioner in conducting negotiations with the native tribes, and, at a later period, was charged with important trusts as a naval commander. He was a man of large property, and seventy years of age. He was, as well he might be, utterly confounded and amazed in finding himself charged as a principal culprit in the Salem witchcraft. The accusing girls were evidently delighted to get hold of such a notable and doughty character; and their tongues were released, on the occasion, from all restraints of decorum and decency. When the ring was formed around him "in the street," in front of Deacon Ingersoll's door, his sword unbuckled from his side, and such foul and vulgar aspersions cast upon his good name, he felt, no doubt, that it would have been better to have fallen into the hands of savages of the wilderness or pirates on the sea, than of the crowd of audacious girls that hustled him about in Salem Village. It was a relief to his wounded honor, and gave leisure for the workings of his indignant resentment, to escape from them into Boston jail. Not only his old shipmate, Bartholomew Gedney, but, as will be seen, the learned attorney-general, who was present, and witnessed the whole affair, was fully convinced of his guilt.

The wife of an honest and worthy man in Andover was sick of a fever. After all the usual means had failed to check the symptoms of her disease, the idea

became prevalent that she was suffering under an
" evil hand." The husband, pursuant of the advice
of friends, posted down to Salem Village to ascertain
from the afflicted girls who was bewitching his wife.
Two of them returned with him to Andover. Never
did a place receive such fatal visitors. The Grecian
horse did not bring greater consternation to ancient
Ilium. Immediately after their arrival, they succeeded
in getting more than fifty of the inhabitants into
prison, several of whom were hanged. A perfect panic
swept like a hurricane over the place. The idea seized
all minds, as Hutchinson expresses it, that the only
" way to prevent an accusation was to become an
accuser." — " The number of the afflicted increased
every day, and the number of the accused in proportion." In this state of things, such a great acces-
sion being made to the ranks of the confessing
witches, the power of the delusion became irresistibly
strengthened. Mr. Dudley Bradstreet, the magistrate
of the place, after having committed about forty persons to jail, concluded he had done enough, and declined to arrest any more. The consequence was
that he and his wife were cried out upon, and they
had to fly for their lives. They accused his brother,
John Bradstreet, with having " afflicted " a dog. Bradstreet escaped by flight. The dog was executed. The
number of persons who had publicly confessed that
they had entered into a league with Satan, and exercised the diabolical power thus acquired, to the
injury, torment, and death of innocent parties, pro-

duced a profound effect upon the public mind. At the same time, the accusers had everywhere increased in number, owing to the inflamed state of imagination universally prevalent which ascribed all ailments or diseases to the agency of witches, to a mere love of notoriety and a passion for general sympathy, to a desire to be secure against the charge of bewitching others, or to a malicious disposition to wreak vengeance upon enemies. The prisons in Salem, Ipswich, Boston, and Cambridge, were crowded. All the securities of society were dissolved. Every man's life was at the mercy of every other man. Fear sat on every countenance, terror and distress were in all hearts, silence pervaded the streets: all who could, quit the country; business was at a stand; a conviction sunk into the minds of men, that a dark and infernal confederacy had got foot-hold in the land, threatening to overthrow and extirpate religion and morality, and establish the kingdom of the Prince of darkness in a country which had been dedicated, by the prayers and tears and sufferings of its pious fathers, to the Church of Christ and the service and worship of the true God. The feeling, dismal and horrible indeed, became general, that the providence of God was removed from them; that Satan was let loose, and he and his confederates had free and unrestrained power to go to and fro, torturing and destroying whomever he willed. We cannot, by any extent of research or power of imagination, enter fully into the ideas of the people of that day; and it is there-

fore absolutely impossible to appreciate the awful condition of the community at the point of time to which
our narrative has led us.

In the midst of this state of things, the old colony
of Massachusetts was transformed into a royal province, and a new government organized. Sir William
Phips, the governor, arrived at Boston, with the
new charter, on the evening of the 14th of May.
William Stoughton, of Dorchester, superseded Thomas
Danforth as deputy-governor. In the Council, which
took the place of the Assistants, most of the former
body were retained. Bartholomew Gedney had a few
years before been dropped from the board of Assistants.
He was now placed in the Council with John Hathorne,
Jonathan Corwin, Samuel Appleton, and Robert Pike,
of this county. The new government did not interfere
with the proceedings in progress relating to the
witchcraft prosecutions, at the moment. Examinations and commitments went on as before; only the
magistrates, acting on those occasions, were re-enforced
by Mr. Gedney, who presided at their sessions. The
affair had become so formidable, and the public infatuation had reached such a point, that it was difficult
to determine what ought to be done. Sir William
Phips, no doubt, felt that it was beyond his depth,
and yielded himself to the views of the leading men
of his council. Stoughton was in full sympathy with
Cotton Mather, whose interest had been used in procuring his appointment over Danforth. Through him,
Mather acquired, and held for some time, great as-

cendency with the governor. It was concluded best to appoint a special court of Oyer and Terminer for the witchcraft trials. Stoughton, the deputy-governor, was commissioned as chief-justice. Nathaniel Saltonstall of Haverhill; Major John Richards of Boston; Major Bartholomew Gedney of Salem; Mr. Wait Winthrop, Captain Samuel Sewall, and Mr. Peter Sargent, all three of Boston, — were made associate judges. Saltonstall early withdrew from the service; and Jona. than Corwin, of Salem, succeeded to his place on the bench of the special court. A majority of the judges were citizens of Boston.

Jonathan Corwin had been associated with Hathorne in conducting the examinations that have been described. He was a son of George Corwin, who has been noticed in the account of Salem Village.

A shade of illegality rests upon the very existence of this special court. There has always been a question whether the new charter gave to the governor and council power to create it without the concurrence of the House of Representatives. It has been held that such a court could have no other lawful foundation than an act of the General Court. Hutch. inson was evidently of this opinion. This question was a very serious one; for, as that considerate and able historian and eminent judicial officer says, the tribunal that passed sentence in the witchcraft prosecutions was "the most important court to the life of the subject which was ever held in the province." The time required to convene the popular branch of the government is itself, in all cases, an element of safety. In this case, it would have carried the country beyond the period of the delusion, and saved its annals from their darkest and bloodiest page. The condition of things when he arrived, had his counsellors been wise, would have led Sir William Phips forthwith to issue writs of election of deputies, before taking any action whatever. In a free republican government, the executive department ought never to attempt to dispose of difficult matters of vital importance without the joint deliberations and responsibility of the representatives of the people.

So far as the composition of the court is considered, no objection can be made. The justices were all members of the council, and belonged to the highest order, not only of the magistracy, but of society generally. They constituted as respectable a body of gentlemen as could have been collected. Thomas Newton, of Boston, was commissioned to act as attorney-general. The official title of marshal ceasing with the new government, George Corwin was appointed sheriff of the county of Essex. Herrick appears to have continued in the service as deputy. Sheriff Corwin was twenty-six years of age. He was the grandson of the original George Corwin, and the son of John. His mother was grand-daughter of Governor Winthrop of Massachusetts, and daughter of Governor Winthrop of Connecticut. His wife was a daughter of Bartholomew Gedney; so that it appears that two of the judges were his uncles, and one his

father-in-law.   These personal connections may be
borne in mind, as affording ground to believe, that, in
the discharge of his painful duties, he did not act without advice and suggestions from the highest quarter.

The court-house in which the trials were held stood
in the middle of what is now Washington Street, near
where Lynde and Church Streets, which did not then
exist, now enter it, fronting towards Essex Street.
The building was also used as a town-house; Washington Street being, for this reason, then called "Town-
house Lane." Off against the court-house, on the
west side of the lane, was the house of the Rev. Nicholas Noyes, on the site of the residence of the late
Robert Brookhouse.   Opposite to it was the estate
of Edward Bishop, which fronted westerly on "Town-
house Lane" a little over a hundred feet, including
the present Jeffrey Court, and extending a few feet
beyond the corner of the house of Dr. S. M. Cate,
over a portion of Church Street.   Its depth, towards
St. Peter Street, was about three hundred and forty-
five feet.   Edward Bishop held this estate in the right
of his wife Bridget, the widow of Thomas Oliver
who had died about 1679.   Not long after this marriage, Bishop removed to his farm at Royal Side.   In
1685, the "old Oliver house" was either removed or
rebuilt, and a new one erected on the same premises,
which was occupied by tenants in 1692.   These items
are given because they will help to illustrate the
narrative, and enable us to understand points of
evidence in the approaching trial.   It is a curious

circumstance, that the first public victim of the prosecutions, Bridget Bishop, had been the nearest neighbor
and lived directly opposite, to the person who, more
than any other inhabitant of the town, was responsible
for the blood that was shed, — Nicholas Noyes. The
jail, at that time, was on the western side of Prison
Lane, now St. Peter Street, north of the point where
Federal Street now enters it. The meeting-house
stood on what has always been the site of the First
Church. The "Ship Tavern" was on ground the
front of which is occupied, at present, by "West's
Block," nearly opposite the head of Central Street.
It had long been owned and kept by John Gedney,
Sr. Two of his sons, John and Bartholomew, had
married Susanna and Hannah Clarke. John died in
1685. His widow moved into the family of her father-
in-law; and, after his death in 1688, continued to keep
the house. In 1698 she was married to Deliverance
Parkman, and died in 1728. The tavern, in 1692, was
known as the "Widow Gedney's." The estate had an
extensive orchard in the rear, contiguous, along its
northern boundary, to the orchard of Bridget Bishop,
which occupied ground now covered by the Lyceum
building, and one or two others to the east of it.

The Court was opened at Salem in the first week
of June, 1692. In the mean time, the attorney-general,
to prepare for the management of the cases, came to
Salem. He addressed the following letter to Isaac
Addington, Secretary of the province: —

" SALEM, 31st May, 1692.

" WORTHY SIR, — I have herewith sent you the names of the prisoners that are desired to be transmitted by *habeas corpus ;* and have presumed to send you a copy thereof, being more, as I presume, accustomed to that practice than yourself, and beg pardon if I have infringed upon you therein. I fear we shall not this week try all that we have sent for ; by reason the trials will be tedious, and the afflicted persons cannot readily give their testimonies, being struck dumb and senseless, for a season, at the name of the accused. I have been all this day at the Village, with the gentlemen of the council, at the examination of the persons, where I have beheld strange things, scarce credible but to the spectators, and too tedious here to relate ; and, amongst the rest, Captain Alden and Mr. English have their *mittimus.* I must say, according to the present appearances of things, they are as deeply concerned as the rest; for the afflicted spare no person of what quality soever, neither conceal their crimes, though never so heinous. We pray that Tituba the Indian, and Mrs. Thacher's maid, may be transferred as evidence, but desire they may not come amongst the prisoners but rather by themselves ; with the records in the Court of Assistants, 1679, against Bridget Oliver, and the records relating to the first persons committed, left in Mr. Webb's hands by the order of the council. I pray pardon that I cannot now further enlarge ; and, with my cordial service, only add that I am, sir, your most humble servant,

Hutchinson says that there was no colony or province law against witchcraft in force when the trials began ; and that the proceedings were under an act of James the First, passed in 1603. By that act, persons convicted were to be sentenced to " the pains and penalties of death as felons." By the colonial law, conviction of capital crimes did not incapacitate the party affected from disposing of property. In this and other respects, there were points of difference, which caused some inconvenience in carrying out the practice of the mother-country ; and the attorney-general had to supply the want of experience in the local officers.

It may here be mentioned, that no record of the doings of this special court are now to be found, and our only information respecting them is obtained in brief and imperfect statements of writers of the time. Perhaps Hutchinson had the use of the records. He gives the dates of the several sessions of the courts, and of the conviction and execution of the prisoners. Some of the depositions sworn to in court are on file, but without giving in many instances the date when thus offered in the trials. In some cases, they state when they were laid before the grand jury. Only a small part of them are preserved. The matter they contain was, to a considerable extent, brought forward at the preliminary examinations, and has been already adduced. In the following account of the trials, some further use will be made of these depositions.

Bridget Bishop was the only person tried at the first session of the Court. She was brought through

Prison Lane, up Essex Street, by the First Church, into Town-house Lane, to the Court-house. Cotton Mather says,—

" There was one strange thing with which the court was newly entertained. As this woman was under a guard, passing by the great and spacious meeting-house, she gave a look towards the house; and immediately a demon, invisibly entering the meeting-house, tore down a part of it: so that, though there was no person to be seen there, yet the people, at the noise, running in, found a board, which was strongly fastened with several nails, transported into another quarter of the house."

It is probable that the streets were thronged by crowds eager to get a sight of the prisoner; and that the doors, fences, and house-tops were occupied. Some, perhaps, got into the meeting-house; and, in clambering up to the windows, a board may have been put in requisition, and left misplaced. Incredible almost as it is, this circumstance seems, from Mather's language, — " the court was entertained," — to have been brought in evidence at the trial, and regarded as weighty and conclusive proof of Bridget's guilt.

One or two points in the evidence adduced against her, in addition to those mentioned heretofore, deserve consideration. The position taken, at her trial, by the Rev. John Hale of Beverly demands criticism. The charge of witchcraft had been made against her on more than one occasion before; particularly about the year 1687, when she resided near the bounds of Beverly, at Royal Side. A woman in the neighborhood, subject to fits of insanity, had, while passing into one of them, brought the accusation against her ; but, on the return of her reason, solemnly recanted, and deeply lamented the aspersion. In a violent recurrence of her malady, this woman committed suicide. Mr. Hale had examined the case at the time, and exonerated Bridget Bishop, who was a communicant in his church, from the charge made against her by the unhappy lunatic. He was satisfied, as he states, that " Sister Bishop " was innocent, and in no way deserved to be ill thought of. He hoped " better of said Goody Bishop at that time." Without any pretence of new evidence touching the facts of the case, he came into court in 1692, and related them, to the effect and with the intent to make them bear against her. He described the appearance of the throat of the woman, after death, as follows : —

" As to the wounds she died of, I observed three deadly ones ; a piece of her windpipe cut out, and another wound above that through the windpipe and gullet, and the vein they call jugular. So that I then judged and still do apprehend it impossible for her, with so short a pair of scissors, to mangle herself so without some extraordinary work of the Devil or witchcraft."

If this was his impression at the time, it is strange that he did not then say so. But there is no appearance of any criminal proceedings having been had, by the grand jury or otherwise, against " Sister Bishop " on the occasion. On the contrary, Mr. Hale seems to have acquiesced in the opinion, that the derangement of

the woman was aggravated, if not caused, by her being
overmuch given to searching and pondering upon the
dark passages and mysterious imagery of prophecy.
The truth, in all probability, is, that Mr. Hale's suspicion was an after-thought. The effect produced upon
his mental condition by the statements and actings of
the "afflicted children" in 1692 was unconsciously
transferred to 1687. The delusion, in which he was
then fully participating, led him to put a different
interpretation upon the suicidal wounds and horrible
end of the wretched maniac, five or six years before.

A piece of evidence, which illustrates the state of
opinion at that time, relating to our subject, given in
this case, is worthy of notice. Samuel Shattuck was
a hatter and dyer. His house was on the south side
of Essex Street, opposite the western entrance to the
grounds of the North Church. Before her removal to
the village, Bridget Bishop was in the habit of calling
at Shattuck's to have articles of dress dyed. He states
that she treated him and his family politely and kindly;
or, as he characterized her deportment after his mind
had become jaundiced against her, "in a smooth and
flattering manner." He tells his story in a deposition
written by him, and signed and sworn to in Court
by himself and wife, June 2, 1692. It is as follows: —

"Our eldest child, who promised as much health and
understanding, both by countenance and actions, as any
other children of his years, was taken in a very drooping

condition ; and, as she came oftener to the house, he grew
worse and worse. As he would be standing at the door,
would fall out, and bruise his face upon a great step-stone,
as if he had been thrust out by an invisible hand; oftentimes falling, and hitting his face against the sides of the
house, bruising his face in a very miserable manner. . . .
This child taken in a terrible fit, his mouth and eyes
drawn aside, and gasped in such a manner as if he was upon
the point of death. After this, he grew worse in his fits,
and, out of them, would be almost always crying. That,
for many months, he would be crying till nature's strength
was spent, and then would fall asleep, and then awake, and
fall to crying and moaning ; and that his very countenance
did bespeak compassion. And at length, we perceived his
understanding decayed : so that we feared (as it has since
proved) that he would be quite bereft of his wits; for, ever
since, he has been stupefied and void of reason, his fits still
following of him. After he had been in this kind of sickness
some time, he has gone into the garden, and has got upon a
board of an inch thick, which lay flat upon the ground, and we
have called him ; he would come to the edge of the board, and
hold out his hand, and make as if he would come, but could
not till he was helped off the board. . . . My wife has offered
him a cake and money to come to her ; and he has held out
his hand, and reached after it, but could not come till he had
been helped off the board, by which I judge some enchantment kept him on. . . . Ever since, this child hath been followed with grievous fits, as if he would never recover more ;
his head and eyes drawn aside so as if they would never
come to rights more ; lying as if he were, in a manner,
dead ; falling anywhere, either into fire or water, if he be
not constantly looked to ; and, generally, in such an uneasy,

restless frame, almost always running to and fro, acting so strange that I cannot judge otherwise but that he is bewitched : and, by these circumstances, do believe that the aforesaid Bridget Oliver — now called Bishop — is the cause of it : and it has been the judgment of doctors, such as lived here and foreigners, that he is under an evil hand of witchcraft."

The means used to give this direction to the suspicions of Shattuck and his wife are described in the notice of Bridget Bishop, in the First Part of this work.

Shattuck was a son of the sturdy Quaker of that name who, thirty years before, had given the government of the colony so much trouble, and seems to have inherited some of his notions. In his deposition, he mentions, as corroborative proof of Bridget Bishop's being a witch, that she used to bring to his dye-house " sundry pieces of lace," of shapes and dimensions entirely outside of his conceptions of what could be needed in the wardrobe, or for the toilet, of a plain and honest woman. He evidently regarded fashionable and vain apparel as a snare and sign of the Devil.

The imaginations of several persons in Shattuck's immediate neighborhood seem to have been wrought up to a high point against Bridget Bishop. John Cook lived on the south side of the street, directly opposite the eastern entrance to the grounds of the North Church, on its present site. John Bly's house was on a lot contiguous to the rear of Cook's, fronting on Summer Street. One of Cook's sons (John), aged eighteen, testified, that, —

"About five or six years ago, one morning about sun-rising, as I was in bed, before I rose, I saw Goodwife Bishop, *alias* Oliver, stand in the chamber by the window: and she looked on me and grinned on me, and presently struck me on the side of the head, which did very much hurt me ; and then I saw her go out under the end window at a little crevice, about so big as I could thrust my hand into. I saw her again the same day, — which was the sabbath-day, — about noon, walk across the room ; and having, at the time, an apple in my hand, it flew out of my hand into my mother's lap, who sat six or eight foot distance from me, and then she disappeared: and, though my mother and several others were in the same room, yet they affirmed they saw her not."

Bly and his wife Rebecca had a difficulty with Bishop in reference to payment for a hog they had bought of her. The following is from their testimony at her trial. After stating that she came to their house and quarrelled with them about it, they go on to say that the animal —

"was taken with strange fits, jumping up, and knocking her head against the fence, and seemed blind and deaf, and would not eat, neither let her pigs suck, but foamed at the mouth ; which Goody Henderson, hearing of, said she believed she was overlooked, and that they had their cattle ill in such a manner at the Eastward, when they lived there, and used to cure them by giving of them red ochre and milk, which we also gave the sow. Quickly after eating of which, she grew better ; and then, for the space of near two hours together, she, getting into the street, did set off, jumping and running between the house of said deponents and said Bishop's, as if she were stark mad, and, after that, was well again: and we did then apprehend or judge, and do still, that said Bishop had bewitched said sow."

William Stacey testified, that, as he was " agoing to mill," meeting Bishop in the street, some conversation passed between them, and that, —

" being gone about six rods from her, the said Bishop, with a small load in his cart, suddenly the off-wheel slumped or sunk down into a hole upon plain ground ; that this deponent was forced to get one to help him get the wheel out. Afterwards, this deponent went back to look for said hole where his wheel sunk in, but could not find any hole."

Stacey further deposed, that, on another occasion, he —

" met the said Bishop by Isaac Stearns's brick-kiln. After he had passed by her, this deponent's horse stood still with a small load going up the hill ; so that, the horse striving to draw, all his gears and tackling flew in pieces, and the cart fell down."

These mishaps and marvels occurred in Summer Street, near the foot of Chestnut Street, where the ground was then much lower than it is now. Stacey was ascending the street, on his way through High Street to his father's mill, at the South River.

Stacey concluded his testimony as follows : —

" This deponent hath met with several other of her pranks at several times, which would take up a great time to tell of.

" This deponent doth verily believe that the said Bridget Bishop was instrumental to his daughter Priscilla's death.

About two years ago, the child was a likely, thriving child; and suddenly screeched out, and so continued, in an unusual manner, for about a fortnight, and so died in that lamentable manner."

Many of the extraordinary " pranks," charged upon Bridget Bishop, had their scene near to her dwelling-house. John Louder, a servant of John Gedney, Sr., some years before, had a controversy with her about her fowls, " that used to come into our orchard or garden." He swore as follows : —

" Some little time after which, I, going well to bed, about the dead of the night, felt a great weight upon my breast, and, awakening, looked; and, it being bright moonlight, did clearly see said Bridget Bishop, or her likeness, sitting upon my stomach; and, putting my arms off of the bed to free myself from the great oppression, she presently laid hold of my throat, and almost choked me, and I had no strength or power in my hands to resist, or help myself; and, in this condition, she held me to almost day.   Some time after this, my mistress (Susannah Gedney) was in our orchard, and I was then with her; and said Bridget Bishop, being then in her orchard, — which was next adjoining to ours, — my mistress told said Bridget that I said or affirmed that she came, one night, and sat upon my breast, as aforesaid, which she denied, and I affirmed to her face to be true, and that I did plainly see her; upon which discourse with her, she threatened me.   And, some time after that, I, being not very well, stayed at home on a Lord's Day; and, on the afternoon of said day, the doors being shut, I did see a black pig in the room coming towards me; so I went towards it to kick it, and it vanished away."

Louder goes on to say, that, immediately after this, on the same occasion while he was staying at home from meeting, he saw a black thing jump into the window, and it came and stood just before his face " upon the bar." The body of it looked like a monkey, only the feet were like a cock's feet with claws, and the face somewhat more like a man's than a monkey's. He says that he was greatly affrighted, " not being able to speak or help myself by reason of fear, I suppose ; " and that his mysterious visitor made quite a speech to him, representing that it was a messenger sent to say, that, if he would " be ruled by him, he should want for nothing in this world." The virtuous and indignant Louder says that he answered, " You devil, I will kill you ! " and gave it a blow with his fist, but " could feel no substance ; and it jumped out of the window again." It immediately came in by the porch, although the doors were shut, and said, " You had better take my counsel." Hereupon Louder struck at it with a stick, hitting the ground-sill and breaking the stick, but felt no substance. Louder concludes his testimony as follows : —

" The arm with which I struck was presently disenabled. Then it vanished away, and I opened the back-door and went out ; and, going towards the house-end, I espied said Bridget Bishop in her orchard going towards her house, and, seeing her, had no power to set one foot forward, but returned in again : and, going to shut the door, I again did see that or the like creature, that I before did see within doors, in such a posture as it seemed to be agoing to fly at me ;

upon which I cried out, ' The whole armor of God be between me and you.'   So it sprang back and flew over the apple-tree, flinging the dirt with its feet against my stomach, upon which I was struck dumb, and so continued for about three days' time ; and also shook many of the apples off from the tree which it flew over."

Before removing to his farm, Edward and Bridget Bishop made the alterations, before mentioned, on their town estate.   John Bly, Sr., aged fifty-seven years, and William Bly, aged fifteen, were employed in the opera-tion of removing the cellar wall of " the ould house ; " and testified, that they found in holes and crevices of said cellar wall " several puppets made up of rags and hogs' bristles, with headless pins in them with the points outward."

Upon such evidence, Bridget Bishop was condemned, and executed the next week.   The death-warrants, in these trials, were collected together in one envelope, marked as such.   The envelope remains, but its contents have all been abstracted.   The death-warrant of Bridget Bishop was probably overlooked when the others were gathered together.   The consequence is that it has been preserved, and is the only one known to be in existence.

The sheriff seems to have proceeded, immediately after the execution, to the clerk's office, and indorsed his return on the warrant.   When he wrote it, he added, after the word " dead," — " and buried her on the spot."   On its occurring to him that the burying of the body was not mentioned in the warrant, he drew

To George Corwin Gent High Sherriffe of the County
of Essex Greeting—

Whereas Bridgett Bishop al's Oliver the wife of Edwd Bishop
of Salem in the County of Essex Sawyer at a Speciall Court of Oyer and Termin'
Held at Salem the second Day of this instant month of June for the Countyes of Essex
Middlesex and Suffolk before William Stoughton Esqr and his Associates
Justices of the said Court was Indicted and arraigned upon five severall Indictments
for useing practiseing and exerciseing on the Nineteenth
Day of Aprill last past and divers other dayes and times

before and after certaine acts of Witchcraft in and upon the bodyes of Abigail Williams, Ann putnam Junr
Mercy Lewis, Mary Walcott and Elizabeth Hubbard of Salem village
singlewomen whereby their bodyes were hurt, afflicted pined consumed
wasted and tormented contrary to the forme of the statute in that case
provided To which Indictm'ts the said Bridgett Bishop pleaded not guilty
and for tryall thereof put her selfe upon God and her Country whereby
she was found guilty of the ffelonyes and Witchcraft whereof she stood
Indicted and sentence of Death accordingly passed agt her as the Law
directs, Execution whereof yet remaines to be done These are therefore
in the Name of their Maj'ties William and Mary now King & Queen over
England &c to will and Comand you that upon ffryday next being the
Tenth Day of this instant month of June between the houres of Eight &
twelve in the aforenoon of the same day You safely conduct the said Bridgett
Bishop als Oliver from their Maj'ties Gaol in Salem aforesd to the place of
Execution and there cause her to be hanged by the neck untill shee be dead
and of your doings herein make returne to the Clerk of the sd Court and
precept And hereof you are not to faile at your perill And this shall be yor
sufficient Warrant Given under my hand & Seal at Boston the Eighth
of June in the fourth Year of the Reigne of our Soveraigne Lord &
Lady William & Mary now King & Queen over England &c Anno'q Dom 1692

Wm Stoughton

June 10th 1692

According to the within written precept I have taken the
of the within named Bridgett Bishop out of their ...
Goale in Salem and Safely conveyed her to the place pro...
for her Execution and caused ... to be hanged by the
by the neck untill Shee was dead and ~~buried~~ ...
all which was according to the time within Required a...
so & make Returne by me — George Corwin Sherif

his pen through the words; as is seen in the photograph. This superfluous clause, thus partially obliterated, is the only positive evidence we have of the disposal of the bodies at the time. They were undoubtedly all thrown into pits dug among the rocks, on the spot, and hastily covered by the officers having in charge the details of the executions. There were no prayers over their graves, except those uttered by themselves in their last moments.

The descendants of Bridget Bishop are very numerous in Salem; embracing some of our oldest and most respectable families, and branching widely from them. There is no evidence of issue by her first marriage. Thomas Oliver, her second husband, had daughters by a former wife, who were represented in the next generation under the names of Hilliard, Hooper, and Jones. By his wife Bridget, he had but one child, — a daughter, Christian, born May 8, 1667. She married Thomas Mason, and died in 1693; leaving an only child, Susannah, born August 23, 1687. Edward Bishop was her guardian. She married John Becket in 1711, and by him had a son, John, and six daughters, as follows: Susannah, married to David Felt, Elizabeth to William Peele, Sarah to Nathaniel Silsbee, Rebecca to William Fairfield, Eunice to Thorndike Deland, and Hannah to William Cloutman.

After the condemnation of Bridget Bishop, the Court took a recess, and consulted the ministers of Boston and the neighborhood respecting the prosecutions. The response of the reverend gentlemen, while urging,

in general terms, the importance of caution and circumspection in the methods of examination, decidedly
and earnestly recommended that the proceedings should
be vigorously carried on; and they were, indeed, vigorously carried on.

Hutchinson says, that, "at the first trial, there was
no colony or provincial law against witchcraft in force.
The statute of James the First must therefore have
been considered as in force in the province, witchcraft
not being an offence at common law.   Before the ad-
journment, the old colony law, which makes witchcraft a capital offence, was revived with the other local
laws, as they were called, and made a law of the province."   The General Court, which thus revived the
law making witchcraft a capital offence, met, June 8,
two days before the execution of Bridget Bishop. The
proceedings that took place at Salem were thus assumed as a provincial matter, for which the immediate
locality was not responsible, but the legislature, clergy,
and people of the country at large.

The Court met again on Wednesday, the 29th of
June; and, after trial, sentenced to death Sarah Good,
Sarah Wildes, Elizabeth How, Susanna Martin, and
Rebecca Nurse, who were all executed on the 19th of
July.

Calef says, that, at the trial of Sarah Good, —

" One of the afflicted fell in a fit; and, after coming out of
it, cried out of the prisoner for stabbing her in the breast
with a knife, and that she had broken the knife in stabbing
of her.   Accordingly, a piece of the blade of a knife was

found about her. Immediately, information being given to
the Court, a young man was called, who produced a haft and
part of the blade, which the Court, having viewed and compared, saw it to be the same; and, upon inquiry, the young
man affirmed that yesterday he happened to break that knife,
and that he cast away the upper part, — this afflicted person
being then present. The young man was dismissed and she
was bidden by the Court not to tell lies; and was improved
after (as she had been before) to give evidence against the
prisoners."

Hutchinson, in relating this circumstance, refers to
a case tried before Sir Matthew Hale, when a similar
kind of falsehood was proved against an " afflicted "
witness; notwithstanding which he says the person
on trial was found guilty, " and the judge and all the
court were fully satisfied with the verdict."

Sarah Good appears to have been an unfortunate
woman, having been subject to poverty, and consequent sadness and melancholy. But she was not
wholly broken in spirit. Mr. Noyes, at the time of
her execution, urged her very strenuously to confess.
Among other things, he told her " she was a witch,
and that she knew she was a witch." She was conscious of her innocence, and felt that she was oppressed, outraged, trampled upon, and about to be
murdered, under the forms of law; and her indignation
was roused against her persecutors. She could not
bear in silence the cruel aspersion; and, although she
was just about to be launched into eternity, the torrent
of her feelings could not be restrained, but burst upon

the head of him who uttered the false accusation.
"You are a liar," said she. "I am no more a witch
than you are a wizard; and, if you take away my
life, God will give you blood to drink." Hutchinson
says that, in his day, there was a tradition among the
people of Salem, and it has descended to the present
time, that the manner of Mr. Noyes's death strangely
verified the prediction thus wrung from the incensed
spirit of the dying woman. He was exceedingly cor-
pulent, of a plethoric habit, and died of an internal
hemorrhage, bleeding profusely at the mouth.

We have no information relating to the execution of
Elizabeth How. Her gentle, patient, humble, benig-
nant, devout, and tender heart bore her, no doubt, with
a spirit of saint-like love and faith, through the dreadful scenes. We cannot doubt, that, in death as in life,
she forgave, prayed for, and invoked blessing upon her
persecutors. Neither has any thing come down in reference to the deportment of Sarah Wildes or Susanna
Martin. We may take it for granted, that the former
was a patient and humble, but firm and faithful sufferer; and that the latter displayed the great energy
of spirit, and probably the strength of language, for
which she was remarkable. Of the case of Rebecca
Nurse we have more information.

The character, age, and position of this venerable
matron created an impression, which called, to the
utmost, all the arts and efforts of the prosecution to
counteract. Many who had gone fully and earnestly
in support of the proceedings against others paused

and hesitated in reference to her; and large numbers who had been overawed into silence before, bravely came forward in her defence. The character of Nathaniel Putnam has been described. He was a man of extraordinary strength and acuteness of mind, and in all his previous life had been proof against popular excitement. The death of his brother Thomas, seven years before, had left him the head and patriarch of his great family: as such, he was known as "Landlord Putnam." Entire confidence was felt by all in his judgment, and deservedly. But he was a strong religionist, a life-long member of the Church, and extremely strenuous and zealous in his ecclesiastical relations. He was getting to be an old man; and Mr. Parris had wholly succeeded in obtaining, for the time, possession of his feelings, sympathy, and zeal in the management of the Church, and secured his full co-operation in the witchcraft prosecutions. He had been led by Parris to take the very front in the proceedings. But even Nathaniel Putnam could not stand by in silence, and see Rebecca Nurse sacrificed. A curious paper, written by him, is among those which have been preserved : —

"NATHANIEL PUTNAM, Sr., being desired by Francis Nurse, Sr., to give information of what I could say concerning his wife's life and conversation, I, the abovesaid, have known this said aforesaid woman forty years, and what I have observed of her, human frailties excepted, her life and conversation have been according to her profession ; and she hath brought up a great family of children and educated them well, so that there is in some of them apparent savor of godliness. I have known her differ with her neighbors; but I never knew or heard of any that did accuse her of what she is now charged with."

A similar paper was signed by thirty-nine other persons of the village and the immediate vicinity, all of the highest respectability. The men and women who dared to do this act of justice must not be forgotten:—

"We whose names are hereunto subscribed, being desired by Goodman Nurse to declare what we know concerning his wife's conversation for time past, — we can testify, to all whom it may concern, that we have known her for many years; and, according to our observation, her life and conversation were according to her profession, and we never had any cause or grounds to suspect her of any such thing as she is now accused of.

"ISRAEL PORTER.
ELIZABETH PORTER.
EDWARD BISHOP, Sr.
HANNAH BISHOP.
JOSHUA REA.
SARAH REA.
SARAH LEACH.
JOHN PUTNAM.
REBECCA PUTNAM.
JOSEPH HUTCHINSON, Sr.
LYDIA HUTCHINSON.
WILLIAM OSBURN.
HANNAH OSBURN.
JOSEPH HOLTON, Sr.
SARAH HOLTON.
BENJAMIN PUTNAM.
SARAH PUTNAM.
JOB SWINNERTON.
ESTHER SWINNERTON.
JOSEPH HERRICK, Sr.

SAMUEL ABBEY.
HEPZIBAH REA.
DANIEL ANDREW.
SARAH ANDREW.
DANIEL REA.
SARAH PUTNAM.
JONATHAN PUTNAM.
LYDIA PUTNAM.
WALTER PHILLIPS, Sr.
NATHANIEL FELTON, Sr.
MARGARET PHILLIPS.
TABITHA PHILLIPS.
JOSEPH HOULTON, Jr.
SAMUEL ENDICOTT.
ELIZABETH BUXTON.
SAMUEL ABORN, Sr.
ISAAC COOK.
ELIZABETH COOK.
JOSEPH PUTNAM."

An examination of the foregoing names in connection with the history of the Village will show conclusive proof, that, if the matter had been left to the people there, it would never have reached the point to which it was carried. It was the influence of the magistracy and the government of the colony, and the public sentiment prevalent elsewhere, overruling that of the immediate locality, that drove on the storm.

Israel Porter was the head of a great and powerful family. His wife Elizabeth was, as has been stated, a sister of Hathorne, the examining magistrate. Edward and Hannah Bishop were the venerable heads and founders of a large family. They lived in Beverly, and must each have been about ninety years of age. The list contains the names of the heads of the principal families in the village, — such as John and Rebecca Putnam, the Hutchinsons, Ross, Leaches, Moultons, and Herricks; and, in the neighborhood, such as the Feltons, Osbornes, and Samuel Endicott. The most remarkable fact it discloses is that it contains the name of one of the two complainants who procured the warrant against Rebecca Nurse, — Jonathan Putnam, the eldest son of John; and also of his wife Lydia. Subsequent reflection, and the return of his better judgment, satisfied him that he had done a great wrong to an innocent and worthy person ; and he had the manliness to come out in her favor. This document ought to have been effectual in saving the life of Rebecca Nurse. It will for ever vindicate her character, and reflect honor upon each and every name subscribed to it.

One of the most cruel features in the prosecution
of the witchcraft trials, and which was practised in all
countries where they took place, was the examination
of the bodies of the prisoners by a jury of the same
sex, under the direction and in the presence of a sur-
geon or physician. The person was wholly exposed,
and every part subjected to the most searching scrutiny.
The process was always an outrage upon human nature; and in the cases of the victims on this occasion,
many of them of venerable years and delicate feelings,
it was shocking to every natural and instinctive sentiment. There is reason to fear that it was often conducted in a rough, coarse, and brutal manner. Marshal
Herrick testifies, that, "by order of Their Majesties'
justices," he, accompanied by the jail-keeper Dounton,
and Constable Joseph Neal, made an examination of
the body of George Jacobs. In persons of his great
age, there would, in all likelihood, be shrivelled, desic-
cated, and callous places. They found one on the old
man, under his right shoulder. Herrick made oath
that it was a veritable witch teat, and his deposition
describes it as follows: "About a quarter of an inch
long or better, with a sharp point drooping downwards,
so that I took a pin, and run it through the said teat;
but there was neither water, blood, or corruption, nor
any other matter." As proof positive that this was
" the Devil's mark," Herrick and the turnkey testify
that " the said Jacobs was not in the least sensible of
what had been done"!

The mind loathes the thought of handling in this

way refined and sensitive females of matronly character, or persons of either sex, with infirmities of
body rendered sacred by years.   The results of the examination were reduced to written reports, going into
details, and, among other evidences in the trials,
spread before the Court and jury.*

The evidence in the case of Rebecca Nurse was
made up of the usual representations and actings of
the "afflicted children."   Mary Walcot and Abigail
Williams charged her with having committed several
murders; mentioning particularly Benjamin Houlton,
John Harwood, and Rebecca Shepard, and averring that
she was aided therein by her sister Cloyse.   Mr. Parris,
too, gave in a deposition against her; from which it ap-

* A few days before her trial, Rebecca Nurse was subjected to this
inspection and exploration ; and the jury of women found the witch-
mark upon her.   On the 28th of June, two days before the meeting of
the Court, she addressed to that body the following communication : —

" *To the Honored Court of Oyer and Terminer, now sitting in Salem, this 28th
of June, Anno* 1692.

"The humble petition of Rebecca Nurse, of Salem Village, humbly
showeth: That whereas some women did search your petitioner at Salem,
as I did then conceive for some supernatural mark; and then one of the
said women, which is known to be the most ancient, skilful, prudent person
of them all as to any such concern, did express herself to be of a contrary
opinion from the rest, and did then declare that she saw nothing in or about
Your Honor's poor petitioner but what might arise from a natural cause, — I
there rendered the said persons a sufficient known reason as to myself of the
moving cause thereof, which was by exceeding weaknesses, descending partly
from an overture of nature, and difficult exigencies that hath befallen me in
the times of my travails.   And therefore your petitioner humbly prays
that Your Honors would be pleased to admit of some other women to inquire into this great concern, those that are most grave, wise, and skilful;
namely, Mrs. Higginson, Sr., Mrs. Buxton, Mrs. Woodbury, — two of them

pears, that, a certain person being sick, Mercy Lewis
was sent for.   She was struck dumb on entering
the chamber.   She was asked to hold up her hand, if
she saw any of the witches afflicting the patient.
Presently she held up her hand, then fell into a
trance ; and after a while, coming to herself, said
that she saw the spectres of Goody Nurse and Goody
Carrier having hold of the head of the sick man.   Mr.
Parris swore to this statement with the utmost confidence in Mercy's declarations.

The testimony of three persons particularly is required to be given, as illustrating the extraordinary
extent to which the minds of those involved in the
affair were under infatuation or hallucination.

Mrs. Ann Putnam was about thirty years of age.
For six months she had been constantly absorbed in
what was then, as now, regarded as spiritualism.   Her

being midwives, Mrs. Porter, together with such others as may be chosen
on that account, before I am brought to my trial.   All which I hope your
honors will take into your prudent consideration, and find it requisite so to
do; for my life lies now in your hands, under God.   And, being conscious of
my own innocency, I humbly beg that I may have liberty to manifest it to
the world partly by the means abovesaid.

"And your poor petitioner shall evermore pray, as in duty bound, &c."

Her daughters — Rebecca, wife of Thomas Preston ; and Mary, wife
of John Tarbell — presented the following statement : —

"We whose names are underwritten — can testify, if called to it, that
Goody Nurse hath been troubled with an infirmity of body for many years,
which the jury of women seem to be afraid it should be something else."

There is no intimation, in any of the papers, that the petition of the
mother or the deposition of her daughters received the least attention
from the Court.

house had been the scene of a perpetual series of
wonders supposed to be disclosures and manifestations of a supernatural character. Apparitions, spectral shapes of living witches, ghosts of their murdered
victims, and demons generally, were of daily and hourly
occurrence. The dread secrets of the world unknown
had been revealed to her in waking fancies and dreams
by night. An originally sensitive and imaginative
nature had been wrought into a condition in which
her mental faculties were at once enfeebled and exalted. Besides all this, there were the trials to
which her constitution had been subjected by the
experiences of maternity so early begun, and the pressure upon her mind and heart of the anxieties and
cares incident to a large family of young children.
An accumulation of disappointments, vexations, and
consuming griefs, spread like a dark cloud over her
life, — the deaths of her own children, and of her sister
Bayley and her children, and of her sister Baker's children ; and, finally, the long-continued, and constantly
recurring sufferings, tortures, convulsions, fits, and
trances of her daughter Ann, and her servant-woman
Mercy Lewis, under, as she fully believed, a diabolical
hand. — These things must have given to her countenance and tones of voice a wonderful impressive-
ness to all who looked upon or listened to them.. Her
eminent social position, her general reputation, — for
Lawson, who knew her well, calls her " a very sober
and pious woman," so far as he could judge, — the
stamp of profound earnestness marked on all her

language, the glow which morbid excitement long experienced gave to her expression, must have arrested, to a high degree, the attention of the assembled multitude. An air of sadness, in the wild ravings of imagination, pervades her testimony. I present her deposition in full, as one of the phenomena of this strange transaction: —

"THE DEPOSITION OF ANN PUTNAM, the wife of Thomas Putnam, aged about thirty years, who testifieth and saith, that, on the 18th March, 1692, I being wearied out in helping to tend my poor afflicted child and maid, about the middle of the afternoon I lay me down on the bed to take a little rest; and immediately I was almost pressed and choked to death, that, had it not been for the mercy of a gracious God and the help of those that were with me, I could not have lived many moments: and presently I saw the apparition of Martha Corey, who did torture me so as I cannot express, ready to tear me all to pieces, and then departed from me a little while; but, before I could recover strength or well take breath, the apparition of Martha Corey fell upon me again with dreadful tortures, and hellish temptation to go along with her. And she also brought to me a little red book in her hand and a black pen, urging me vehemently to write in her book; and several times that day she did most grievously torture me, almost ready to kill me. And, on the 19th March, Martha Corey again appeared to me; and also Rebecca Nurse, the wife of Francis Nurse, Sr.: and they both did torture me a great many times this day with such tortures as no tongue can express, because I would not yield to their hellish temptations, that, had I not been upheld by an Almighty arm, I could not have lived while night. The 20th March, being sabbath-day, I had a great deal of respite between my fits. 21st March, being the day of the examination of Martha Corey, I had not many fits, though I was very weak; my strength being, as I thought, almost gone: but, on the 22d March, 1692, the apparition of Rebecca Nurse did again set upon me in a most dreadful manner, very early in the morning, as soon as it was well light. And now she appeared to me only in her shift, and brought a little red book in her hand, urging me vehemently to write in her book; and, because I would not yield to her hellish temptations, she threatened to tear my soul out of my body, blasphemously denying the blessed God, and the power of the Lord Jesus Christ to save my soul; and denying several places of Scripture which I told her of, to repel her hellish temptations. And for near two hours together, at this time, the apparition of Rebecca Nurse did tempt and torture me, and also the greater part of this day, with but very little respite. 23d March, am again afflicted by the apparitions of Rebecca Nurse and Martha Corey, but chiefly by Rebecca Nurse. 24th March, being the day of the examination of Rebecca Nurse, I was several times afflicted in the morning by the apparition of Rebecca Nurse, but most dreadfully tortured by her in the time of her examination, insomuch that the honored magistrates gave my husband leave to carry me out of the meeting-house; and, as soon as I was carried out of the meeting-house doors, it pleased Almighty God, for his free grace and mercy's sake, to deliver me out of the paws of those roaring lions, and jaws of those tearing bears, that, ever since that time, they have not had power so to afflict me until this 31st May, 1692. At the same moment that I was hearing my evidence read by the honored magistrates, to take my oath, I was again re-assaulted and tortured by my before-mentioned tormentor, Rebecca Nurse."

" THE TESTIMONY OF ANN PUTNAM, Jr., witnesseth and saith, that, being in the room when her mother was afflicted, she saw Martha Corey, Sarah Cloyse, and Rebecca Nurse, or their apparition, upon her mother."

Mrs. Ann Putnam made another deposition under oath, at the same trial, which shows that she was determined to overwhelm the prisoner by the multitude of her charges. She says that Rebecca Nurse's apparition declared to her that " she had killed Benjamin Houlton, John Fuller, and Rebecca Shepard ; " and that she and her sister Cloyse, and Edward Bishop's wife, had killed young John Putnam's child ; and she further deposed as followeth : —

" Immediately there did appear to me six children in winding-sheets, which called me aunt, which did most grievously affright me ; and they told me that they were my sister Baker's children of Boston ; and that Goody Nurse, and Mistress Carey of Charlestown, and an old deaf woman at Boston, had murdered them, and charged me to go and tell these things to the magistrates, or else they would tear me to pieces, for their blood did cry for vengeance. Also there appeared to me my own sister Bayley and three of her children in winding-sheets, and told me that Goody Nurse had murdered them."

There is in this deposition a passage which illustrates one of the doctrines held at the time on the subject of witchcraft. Mrs. Ann Putnam " testifieth and saith, that, on the first day of June, 1692, the apparition of Rebecca Nurse did again fall upon me, and almost choke me ; and she told me, that, now she was come out of prison, she had power to afflict me, and that now she would afflict me all this day long." The reference here is probably to the fact, that, on the 1st of June, she with many other prisoners was transferred from the jail in Boston to that in Salem ; and that, "all that day long" being outside of prison walls, she had greater power to afflict than when chained in a cell.   This was undoubtedly the received opinion, and it is curiously illustrated in the foregoing passage.

The only breath of disparagement against the character of Goodwife Nurse that can be found in any of the papers is in the following deposition : —

"THE DEPOSITION OF SARAH HOULTON, relict of Benjamin Houlton, deceased, who testifieth and saith, that, about this time three years, my dear and loving husband, Benjamin Houlton, deceased, was as well as ever I knew him in my life till one Saturday morning, that Rebecca Nurse, who now stands charged for witchcraft, came to our house, and fell a railing at him because our pigs got into her field. Though our pigs were sufficiently yoked, and their fence was down in several places, yet all we could say to her could no ways pacify her ; but she continued railing and scolding a great while together, calling to her son Benj. Nurse to go and get a gun and kill our pigs, and let none of them go out of the field, though my poor husband gave her never a misbeholding word.   And, within a short time after this, my poor husband going out very early in the morning, as he was coming in again, he was taken with a strange fit in the entry; being struck blind and stricken down two or three times, so that, when he came to himself, he told me he thought he should never have come into the house any more. And, all summer after, he continued in a languishing condition, being much pained at his stomach, and often struck blind: but, about a fortnight before he died, he was taken with strange and violent fits, acting much like to our poor bewitched persons when we thought they would have died; and the doctor that was with him could not find what his distemper was. And, the day before he died, he was very cheerly; but, about midnight, he was again most violently seized upon with violent fits, till the next night, about midnight, he departed this life by a cruel death.

"*Jurat in Curia.*"

In explanation of the import of this testimony, it is to be observed, that the estate of Benjamin Houlton was contiguous to that of Francis Nurse. They were separated by a fence, which, as in such cases, was required for half its length to be kept in order by one party, the remaining half by the other. What the exact facts were cannot be ascertained, as we have the story of one side only. The widow Houlton appears to have been a tender-hearted, and, for aught we know, good woman. Some years afterwards, she was married, as his second wife, to Benjamin Putnam, — a very respectable person, and, on the death of his father Nathaniel, the head of that branch of the family. He was, for many years, deacon of the church. But she was, it must be conceded, a prejudiced witness; and her judgment for the time was wholly beclouded by the prevalent superstitions. The garden had been, from the days of Townsend Bishop, a choice portion of the Nurse estate. In all farms, it was a most important and valuable item; and was generally under the special care and management of the wife, daughters, and younger lads of the husbandman. Rebecca Nurse was an efficient helpmeet; contributing her whole share to the success of the great enterprise of clearing the estate, as well as in bringing up and educating a large family. It was, no doubt, very provoking to her, as it would be to any one, to have vegetable and flower beds devastated by the ravages of a neighbor's stray pigs. To what extent her "railing and scolding" went, she was not allowed to contribute her statement, to enable us to judge. The affair probably produced considerable gossip, and seems to be alluded to in Nathaniel Putnam's certificate in behalf of Rebecca Nurse. There is reason to believe that the widow Houlton was one of the first to realize what great injustice had been done by her and others to the good name of Rebecca Nurse.

Notwithstanding this evidence, so deeply were the jury impressed with the eminent virtue and true Christian excellence of this venerable woman, that, in spite of the clamors of the outside crowd, the monstrous statements of accusing witnesses, and the strong leaning of the Court against her, the jury brought in a verdict of "Not guilty." Calef, and Hutchinson after him, describe the effect, and what followed: —

" Immediately, all the accusers in the Court, and, suddenly after, all the afflicted out of Court, made an hideous outcry; to the amazement, not only of the spectators, but the Court also seemed strangely surprised. One of the judges expressed himself not satisfied: another of them, as he was going off the bench, said they would have her indicted anew. The chief-justice said he would not impose on the jury, but intimated as if they had not well considered one expression of the prisoner when she was upon trial; viz., that when one Hobbs, who had confessed herself to be a witch, was brought into Court to witness against her, the prisoner, turning her head to her, said, ' What! do you bring her ? She is one of us ;' or words to that effect. This, together with the clamors of the accusers, induced the jury to go out again, after their verdict, ' Not guilty.' "

The foreman of the jury, Thomas Fisk, made this statement on the 4th of July, a few days after the trial : —

" After the honored Court had manifested their dissatisfaction of the verdict, several of the jury declared themselves desirous to go out again, and thereupon the Court gave leave ; but, when we came to consider the case, I could not tell how to take her words as an evidence against her, till she had a further opportunity to put her sense upon them, if she would take it. And then, going into Court, I mentioned the words aforesaid, which by one of the Court were affirmed to have been spoken by her, she being then at the bar, but made no reply nor interpretation of them ; whereupon these words were to me a principal evidence against her."

Upon being informed of the use made of her words, the prisoner put in the following declaration : —

"These presents do humbly show to the honored Court and jury, that I being informed that the jury brought me in guilty upon my saying that Goodwife Hobbs and her daughter were of our company ; but I intended no otherwise than as they were prisoners with us, and therefore did then, and yet do, judge them not legal evidence against their fellow-prisoners. And I being something hard of hearing and full of grief, none informing me how the Court took up my words, and therefore had no opportunity to declare what I intended when I said they were of our company."

It was perfectly natural for her to have spoken of them as "of our company," not only from the fact that they had long been crowded together in the same jails, but as they had accompanied each other in the transferrence from one jail to another, from time to time. A few days before, a large party, of which she was one, had been brought from Boston, spending the whole day together on the route. Sarah Good, John Procter and wife, Susanna Martin, Bridget Bishop, and Alice Parker happen to be mentioned as belonging to it. Calef further states : —

"After her condemnation, the governor saw cause to grant a reprieve, which, when known (and some say immediately upon granting), the accusers renewed their dismal outcries against her ; insomuch that the governor was by some Salem gentlemen prevailed with to recall the reprieve, and she was executed with the rest.

" The testimonials of her Christian behavior, both in the course of her life and at her death, and her extraordinary care in educating her children, and setting them a good example, under the hands of so many, are so numerous, that for brevity they are here omitted."

The extraordinary conduct of " the Salem gentlemen," in preventing the intended exercise of executive discretion and clemency on this occasion, is explained, it is probable, by the fact, stated by Neal in his " History of New England," that there was an organized association of private individuals, a committee of vigilance, in Salem, during the continuance of the delusion, who had undertaken to ferret out and prosecute all suspected persons. He says that many were arrested and thrown into prison by their influence and interference. It is hardly to be doubted, that the persons who busied themselves to prevent the reprieve of Rebecca Nurse acted under the authority and by the direction of this self-constituted body of inquisitors. The agency of such unauthorized and irresponsible combinations is always of questionable expediency. When acting in the same line with an excited populace, they are extremely dangerous.

There is no more disgraceful record in the judicial annals of the country, than that which relates the trial of this excellent woman. The wave of popular fury made a clear breach over the judgment-seat. The loud and malignant outcry of an infatuated mob, inside and outside of the Court-house, instead of being yielded to, ought to have been, not only sternly rebuked, but visited with prompt and exemplary punishment. The judges were not only overcome and intimidated from the faithful discharge of their sacred duty by a clamoring crowd, but they played into their hands. Hutchinson justly remarks, that their conduct was in violation of that rule to execute "law and justice in mercy," which ought always to be written on their hearts. "In a capital case, the Court often refuses a verdict of ' Guilty ;' but rarely, if ever, sends a jury out again upon one of ' Not guilty.' " The statement made by the foreman of the jury, with the subsequent explanation of the prisoner, taken in connection with the ground on which the chief-justice sent the jury out again after rendering their verdict of "Not guilty," made it the duty of the Court and the executive to give to her the benefit of that verdict.

At the trial of her mother, Sarah Nurse — aged twenty-eight years or thereabouts — offered this piece of testimony : that, " being in the Court, this 29th of June, 1692, I saw Goodwife Bibber pull pins out of her clothes, and held them between her fingers, and clasped her hands round her knee ; and then she cried out, and said, Goody Nurse pinched her." In all these trials, Mercy Lewis was a principal witness and actor ; yet we find, among the papers, testimony from the most respectable and reliable persons, that she was not to be trusted. There was also testimony which ought to have broken the force of the depositions of Ann Putnam and her mother. Four days after the examination and commitment of Rebecca Nurse, John

Tarbell and Samuel Nurse went to the house of Thomas Putnam to find out in what way their mother had been made the object of such shocking accusations. They were men whose credibility was never brought in question. Their declarations, on this occasion, were not disputed, and, if not true, might have been overthrown; for there were many witnesses of the facts they stated. Tarbell swore as follows: "Upon discourse of many things, I asked whether the girl that was afflicted did first speak of Goody Nurse, before others mentioned her to her. They said she told them she saw the apparition of a pale-faced woman that sat in her grandmother's seat, but did not know her name. Then I replied and said, ' But who was it that told her that it was Goody Nurse?' Mercy Lewis said it was Goody Putnam that said it was Goody Nurse. Goody Putnam said that it was Mercy Lewis that told her. Thus they turned it upon one another, saying, ' It was you,' and ' It was you that told her.'" Samuel Nurse testified to the same.

There was another piece of evidence, which, though brought against Rebecca Nurse, bears harder, as we read it now, upon Ann Putnam than any one else, and makes it more difficult to palliate her conduct on the supposition of partial insanity. It is, all along, one of the obscure problems of our subject to determine how far delusion may have been accompanied by fraud and imposture. Edward Putnam testified, that "Ann Putnam, Jr., was bitten by Rebecca Nurse, as she said, about two of the clock of the day" after Rebecca

Nurse had been committed to jail, and while she was several miles distant, in Salem ; and the said Nurse also struck said Ann Putnam with her spectral chain, leaving a mark, " being in a kind of a round ring, and three streaks across the ring: she had six blows with a chain in the space of half an hour; and she had one remarkable one, with six streaks across her arm." Edward Putnam swears, "I saw the mark, both of bite and chains." The Court, no doubt, were solemnly impressed by this amazing evidence ; but it is hard to avoid the conclusion that Ann Putnam was guilty of elaborate falsehood and a studied trick.

In the trials at this session, one of the " afflicted children " cried out against the Rev. Samuel Willard, of the Old South Church, in Boston. " She was sent out of Court, and it was told about that she was mistaken in the person." There was surely evidence enough against the honesty and credibility of the accusers to leave the judges without excuse, and justly meriting perpetual condemnation for not paying heed to it.

The case of Rebecca Nurse proves that a verdict could not have been obtained against a person of her character charged with witchcraft in this county, had not the most extraordinary efforts been made by the prosecuting officer, aided by the whole influence of the Court and provincial authorities. The odium of the proceedings at the trials and at the executions cannot fairly be laid upon Salem, or the people of this vicinity.

But nothing can extenuate the infamy that must for ever rest upon the names of certain parties to the proceedings. Not to attempt here to measure the guilt of the accusing witnesses, it may be mentioned that it was the deliberate conviction of the family of Rebecca Nurse, that Mr. Parris, more than all other persons, was responsible for her execution; whether by his officious activity in driving on the prosecution, or in preventing her reprieve, cannot be known. Of the prominent part taken by Mr. Noyes in the cruel treatment of this woman, there is no room for doubt. The records of the First Church in Salem are darkened by the following entry: —

"1692, July 3. — After sacrament, the elders propounded to the church, — and it was, by an unanimous vote, consented to, — that our sister Nurse, being a convicted witch by the Court, and condemned to die, should be excommunicated; which was accordingly done in the afternoon, she being present."

The scene presented on this occasion must have been truly impressive at the time, as it is shocking to us in the retrospect. The action of the church, at the close of the morning service, of course became universally known; and the "great and spacious meeting-house" was thronged by a crowd that filled every nook and corner of its floor, galleries, and windows. The sheriff and his subordinates brought in the prisoner, manacled, and the chains clanking from her aged form. She was placed in the broad aisle. Mr.

Higginson and Mr. Noyes — the elders, as the clergy were then called — were in the pulpit. The two ruling elders — who were lay officers — and the two deacons were in their proper seats, directly below and in front of the pulpit. Mr. Noyes pronounced the dread sentence, which, for such a crime, was then believed to be not merely an expulsion from the church on earth, but an exclusion from the church in heaven. It was meant to be understood as an eternal doom. As it had been proved, in his estimation, beyond a question, that she had given her soul to the Devil, he delivered her over to the great adversary of God and man.

From the dismal cell, which, for but a few days longer, was to hold her body, he proclaimed the transferrence of her soul to —

"A dungeon horrible on all sides round,
    As one great furnace flamed; yet from those flames
    No light, but rather darkness visible;
    Regions of sorrow, doleful shades, where peace
    And rest can never dwell; hope never comes
    That comes to all; but torture without end,
    As far removed from God, and light of heaven,
    As from the centre thrice to the utmost pole."

Language and imagery, exhausting the resources of the divine genius of the greatest of poets, fail to give expression to what was felt to be the import of this fearful sentence. It sunk the recipient of it below the reach of human sympathy. She was regarded, by that blinded multitude, with a horror that cast out pity, and was full of hate. But in our view now, and, as we believe, in the view of God and angels then, she occupied an infinite height above her persecutors. Her mind was serenely fixed upon higher scenes, and filled with a peace which the world could not take away, or its cruel wrongs disturb. She went back to her prison walls, and then to the scaffold, with a pious and humble faith which has not failed to be recorded among men, as it has been rewarded where the wicked cease from troubling, and the weary are at rest.

Calef, as already quoted, gives the impression produced by her demeanor at her death. Hutchinson expresses in the following words the judgment of history and the sense of all coming times : —

" Mr. Noyes, the minister of Salem, a zealous prosecutor, excommunicated the poor old woman, and delivered her to Satan, to whom he supposed she had formally given herself up many years before ; but her life and conversation had been such, that the remembrance thereof, in a short time after, wiped off all the reproach occasioned by the civil or ecclesiastical sentence against her."

It is impossible to close the story of the lot assigned to this good woman by an inscrutable Providence, without again contemplating it in a condensed recapitulation. In her old age, experiencing a full share of all the delicate infirmities which the instincts of humanity require to be treated with careful and reverent tenderness, she was ruthlessly snatched from the bosom of a loving family reared by her pious fidelity in all Christian graces, from the side of the devoted companion of her long life, from a home that was endeared

by every grateful association and comfort; immured in
the most wretched and crowded jails; kept loaded with
irons and bound with cords for months; insulted and
maligned at the preliminary examinations; outraged
in her person by rough and unfeeling handling and
scrutiny; and in her rights, by the most flagrant and
detestable judicial oppression, by which the benefit of
a verdict, given in her favor, had been torn away;
carried to the meeting-house to receive the sentence
of excommunication in a manner devised to harrow
her most sacred sentiments; and finally carted through
the streets by a route every foot of which must have
been distressing to her infirm and enfeebled frame;
made to ascend a rough and rocky path to the place
of execution, and there consigned to the hangman.
Surely, there has seldom been a harder fate.

Her body was probably thrown with the rest into a
hole in the crevices of the rock, and covered hastily
and thinly over by the executioners.   It has been the
constant tradition of the family, that, in some way, it
was recovered; and the spot is pointed out in the burial-
place belonging to the estate, where her ashes rest by
the side of her husband, and in the midst of her
children.   It is certain, that, at least, one other body
was thus exhumed, and taken to its own proper place
of burial.   From the known character of Francis
Nurse and his sons and sons-in-law, we may be sure
that what others could do they did not suffer to remain undone.   It is left to the imagination to present
the details of the sad and secret enterprise.   In the

darkness of midnight, they found and identified the
body, and bore it tenderly in their arms along the
silent roads and by-ways, across fields and over fences,
to the old home, where it was received by the assembled family, mourned over, and cared for ; and, during
that or the ensuing night, deposited, with tears and
prayers, in their own consecrated grounds. Her descendants of successive generations owned and reverently guarded the spot. They own and guard it to-
day. The interesting reminiscences connected with
the early history of the Nurse house have been alluded
to. It has witnessed an extraordinary variety of the
conditions of domestic vicissitude. Scenes rising before the mind in contemplative retrospection, while
gazing upon it, present the extremest contrasts of
human experience. On the evening of the 25th of
October, 1678, Mary and Elizabeth Nurse were married. Such an occurrence was undoubtedly the occasion of the highest joy and gladness in a happy
household. The old mansion shone in light, and
echoed voices of cheer. How altered its aspect!
What darkness and silence brooded over and within
it, while those same daughters waited, watched, and
listened, through the solemn hours of that night of
woe and horror, for the coming of their father, husbands, and brothers, bearing to the home, from which
she had been so cruelly torn, the remains of their
slaughtered mother!

The subsequent history of the house presents a
circumstance of singular interest in connection with

our story.   All the members of the three branches of
the Putnam family, with the exception of Joseph, seem
to have been carried away by the witchcraft delusion,
in its early stages, and were more or less active in
pushing on the prosecutions.   We have seen how fierce
was the maniac testimony of Mrs. Ann Putnam and
her daughter against Rebecca Nurse.   The lapse of
time, by a Providence that wonderfully works its ends,
has repaired the breaches made by folly and wrong.
The descendants of the numerous family of Mrs. Ann
Putnam have disappeared from the scene : none of
them bearing the name are in the village.   The descendants of Deacon Edward Putnam have also scattered in emigration to other places.   Nathaniel and
John, the heads of the other two branches of the
family, although involved in the witchcraft delusion,
each signed papers in favor of Rebecca Nurse ; their
descendants, as well as those of Joseph, are still
numerous in the village, hold their old position of
respectability and influence, and many of them occupy
the lands of their ancestors.   Stephen, the grandson
of Nathaniel, married Miriam, the grand-daughter of
John.   Their son Phinehas, in 1784, bought the Nurse
homestead from Benjamin Nurse, the great-grandson
of Rebecca.   Orin Putnam, the great-grandson of
Phinehas, to whom the estate descends, married in
1836 the daughter of Allen Nurse, a direct descendant
of Rebecca, and placed her at the head of her old an-
cestral homestead.   The children of that marriage,
with their father and grandfather, constitute the family

that dwell in and own the venerable mansion. This singular restoration, suggesting such pleasing sentiments, adds another to the remarkable elements of interest belonging to the history of the Townsend-Bishop House.

The descendants of Francis and Rebecca Nurse are numerous, and have honorably perpetuated the name. Among them may be mentioned the Rev. Peter Nurse, a graduate of Harvard College in 1802, for some years librarian of that institution, an excellent scholar, and long universally respected as a clergyman; and Amos Nurse, a graduate of the same college in 1812, — an eminent physician connected with the medical faculty of Bowdoin College, a man of distinguished talent and influence in public affairs, and senator in Congress from the State of Maine.

The Court met again on the 5th of August, and tried George Burroughs; John Procter and Elizabeth, his wife; George Jacobs, Sr.; John Willard; and Martha Carrier. They were all condemned, and, with the exception of Elizabeth Procter, executed on the 19th of the same month.

Hutchinson describes the trial of Burroughs. After speaking of the evidence of the "afflicted persons" and the confessing witches, he mentions other circumstances which were thought to corroborate it: "One was, that, being a little man, he had performed feats beyond the strength of a giant; viz., had held out a gun of seven feet barrel with one hand, and had carried a barrel full of cider from a canoe to the shore." Burroughs said that an Indian present at the time did the same. Instantly, the accusers said it was "the black man, or the Devil, who," they swore, "looks like an Indian." Another piece of evidence was, that he went from one place to another, on a certain occasion, in a shorter time than was possible had not the Devil helped him. He said, in answer, that another man accompanied him. Their reply to this was, that it was the Devil, using the appearance of another man. So whatever he said was turned against him. Hutchinson says, "Upon the whole, he was confounded, and used many twistings and turnings, which, I think, we cannot wonder at." This fair and judicious writer, like Brattle, appears in the foregoing remark to have adopted the common scandal, put in circulation by parties interested to disparage Mr. Burroughs. The papers in this case, that have come down to us, are more numerous than in reference to many others among the sufferers; and they do not bear such an impression. Mr. Burroughs was astounded at the monstrous folly and falsehood with which he was surrounded. He was a man without guile, and incapable of appreciating such wickedness. He tried, in simplicity and ingenuousness, to explain what was brought against him; and this, probably, was all the "twisting and turning" he exhibited.

Hutchinson had the benefit of consulting all the papers belonging to this and other trials; but neither he nor Calef seems to have noticed one remarkable fact: many of the depositions, how many we cannot

tell, were procured after the trials were over, and sur-
reptitiously foisted in among the papers to bolster up
the proceedings. We find, for instance, the following
deposition : —

" THOMAS GREENSLITT, aged about forty years, being
deposed, testifieth that, about the first breaking-out of this
last Indian war, being at the house of Captain Joshua
Scotto at Black Point, he saw Mr. George Burrows, who
was lately executed at Salem, lift a gun of six-foot barrel
or thereabouts, putting the forefinger of his right hand into
the muzzle of said gun, and that he held it out at arms'
end, only with that finger : and further this deponent testifieth,
that, at the same time, he saw the said Burrows take up a
full barrel of molasses with but two of the fingers of one of
his hands in the bung, and carry it from the stage head to the
door at the end of the stage, without letting it down ; and that
Lieutenant Richard Hunniwell and John Greenslitt were then
present, and some others that are dead. Sept. 15, '92."

Not only the date to this deposition, but its express
language, proves that it could not have been used at the
trial. There is another, to the same effect and of the
same date, that is, nearly a month after Burroughs was
thrown into his grave. There are others of the same
kind. This stamps the management of the prosecutions,
and of those concerned in the charge of the papers,
with an irregularity of the grossest kind, which partakes
strongly of the character of fraud and falsehood.

When it was found that there was beginning to
grow up a want of confidence in " spectre evidence "
and the testimony of the afflicted children, those con-

cerned in the prosecutions became alarmed lest a
re-action of public sentiment might take place. The
persons who had brought Mr. Burroughs to his death
concluded that their best escape from public indignation was to accumulate evidence against him after
he was in his grave, particularly on the point of his
superhuman strength; and they got up these depositions, and caused them to be put among the papers
on file. Great stress was laid, by those who were
interested in damaging his character and suppressing
sympathy in his fate, upon this particular proof of
his having been in confederacy with the Devil. Increase Mather said, that, in his judgment, it was conclusive evidence that he "had the Devil to be his
familiar," and that, had he been on the jury, he could
not, on this account, have concurred in a verdict of
acquittal; and Cotton Mather, feeling the importance
of making the most of Mr. Burroughs's extraordinary
strength, gives way to his tendency to indulge in the
marvellous, as follows: —

"God had been pleased so to leave this George Burroughs, that he had ensnared himself by several instances
which he had formerly given of preternatural strength,
and which were now produced against him. He was a very
puny man, yet he had often done things beyond the strength
of a giant. A gun of about seven-foot barrel, and so heavy
that strong men could not steadily hold it out with both
hands, — there were several testimonies given in by persons
of credit and honor, that he made nothing of taking up
such a gun behind the lock with but one hand, and holding
it out, like a pistol, at arms' end. Yea, there were two

testimonies, that George Burroughs, with only putting the forefinger of his right hand into the muzzle of a heavy gun, a fowling-piece of about six or seven foot barrel, did lift up the gun, and hold it out at arms' end, — a gun which the deponents thought strong men could not with both hands lift up, and hold at the butt end, as is usual."

It is further observable, in reference to the foregoing deposition from Greenslitt, that it was given six days after the condemnation of his mother, Ann Pudeator, and a week before her execution. Cotton Mather says that he "was overpersuaded by others to be out of the way upon George Burroughs's trial," six weeks before. He did not fail, however, to come to Salem to be with his mother at her trial and until her death, and being here was compelled to give his deposition. His mother's life was at the mercy of the prosecutors; and he was tempted, in the vain hope of conciliating that mercy, to gratify them by making the statement about Burroughs a month after his execution, and whom it could not then harm. What he said was probably no more than the truth. It has been found that the power of the human muscles can be cultivated to a surprising extent; and the feats ascribed to Burroughs, without making much allowance for a natural degree of exaggeration, have been fully equalled in our day.

Calef gives the following account of his execution : —

"Mr. Burroughs was carried in a cart with the others, through the streets of Salem, to execution. When he was upon the ladder, he made a speech for the clearing of his innocency, with such solemn and serious expressions as were to the admiration of all present. His prayer (which he concluded by repeating the Lord's Prayer) was so well worded, and uttered with such composedness and such (at least seeming) fervency of spirit, as was very affecting, and drew tears from many, so that it seemed to some that the spectators would hinder the execution. The accusers said the black man stood and dictated to him. As soon as he was turned off, Mr. Cotton Mather, being mounted upon a horse, addressed himself to the people, partly to declare that he (Mr. Burroughs') was no ordained minister, and partly to possess the people of his guilt, saying that the Devil often had been transformed into an angel of light; and this somewhat appeased the people, and the executions went on. When he was cut down, he was dragged by a halter to a hole, or grave, between the rocks, about two feet deep; his shirt and breeches being pulled off, and an old pair of trousers of one executed put on his lower parts: he was so put in, together with Willard and Carrier, that one of his hands, and his chin, and a foot of one of them, was left uncovered."

Cotton Mather, not satisfied with this display of animosity, at a moment when every human heart, however imbittered by prejudice, is hushed for the time in solemn silence, attempts, in an account afterwards given of Mr. Burroughs's trial, to blacken his character by an elaborate dressing-up of the absurd stories told by the accusers, and a perverse misrepresentation of the demeanor of the accused. He relates with apparent glee what was regarded as a wonderful achievement of adroitness on the part of Chief-justice Stoughton in trapping Mr. Burroughs, and putting the laugh upon him in Court.

" It cost the Court a wonderful deal of trouble to hear
the testimonies of the sufferers ; for, when they were going
to give in their depositions, they would for a long while
be taken with fits, that made them quite uncapable of saying
any thing. The chief judge asked the prisoner, who he
thought hindered these witnesses from giving their testimonies ; and he answered, he supposed it was the Devil. The
honorable person then replied, ' How comes the Devil so
loath to have any testimony borne against you ? ' Which
cast him into very great confusion."

From what fell from him, at the preliminary examination, it is evident that it did not occur to him
as a possibility that human nature could be capable
of the guilt of such a wilful fabrication and imposture
on the part of the " afflicted children." He beheld
their sufferings, and he knew his own innocence. He
felt, whatever his theological creed might have been,
that a Devil was required to explain the mystery.
The apparent sufferings of the accusing witnesses convinced Court, jury, and all, of the guilt of the accused.
The logic of the chief-justice was perfectly absurd.
For, if the Devil caused the sufferings, he was an adverse
party to the prisoner. This, however, overthrows the
whole theory of the prosecution, which was that the prisoner and the Devil were in league with each other. But
the judge, jury, and people, all equally blinded and
stupefied by the delusion, did not see it; and they
chuckled over the alleged confusion of the prisoner.
All thoughtful persons will concur in Mr. Burroughs's
opinion, that, if ever a diabolical power had possession

of human beings, it was in the case of the wretched
creatures who enacted the part of the accusing girls
in the witchcraft proceedings. In his account of the
trial, Mather makes statements which show that he
was privy to the fact, that testimony, subsequently
taken, was lodged with the evidence belonging to the
case. The documents prove that it was done to an
extent beyond what he acknowledges.

Considering that none dared to show the least sympathy with the persons on trial, that they had none to
counsel or stand by them, that the public passions
were incensed against them as against no other persons ever charged with crime, — it being vastly more
flagrant than any other crime, a rebellion against
heaven and earth, God and man; a deliberate selling of
the soul to the Arch-enemy of souls for the ruin of all
other souls,   in view of all these things, it is truly astonishing, that, by the documents themselves, proceeding, as in almost all cases they do, from hostile and
imbittered sources, we are compelled to the conviction,
that, in their imprisonments, trials, and deaths, the
victims of this savage delusion manifested — in most
cases eminently, and in all substantially — the marks,
not only of innocent, but of elevated and heroic minds.
A review of what can be gleaned in reference to
Mr. Burroughs at Casco Bay and Salem Village, and
a considerate survey and scrutiny of all that has
reached us from the day of his arrest to the moment
of his death, have left a decided impression, that he
was an able, intelligent, true-minded man; ingenuous,

sincere, humble in his spirit; faithful and devoted as a minister; and active, generous, and disinterested as a citizen. His descendants, under his own name and the names of Newman, Fowle, Holbrook, Fox, Thomas, and others, have been numerous and respectable. The late Isaiah Thomas, LL.D., was one of them.

From the account given of John Procter, in the First Part, it is apparent that he was a person of decided character, and, although impulsive and liable to be imprudent, of a manly spirit, honest, earnest, and bold in word and deed. He saw through the whole thing, and was convinced that it was the result of a conspiracy, deliberate and criminal, on the part of the accusers. He gave free utterance to his indignation at their conduct, and it cost him his life.

A few days before his trial, he made his will. There is no reference in it to his particular situation. His signature to the document is accurately represented among the autographs given in this work. It was written while the manacles were on him. Notwithstanding the danger to which any one was exposed who expressed sympathy for convicted or accused persons, or doubt of their guilt, a large number had the manliness to try to save this worthy and honest citizen. John Wise, one of the ministers of Ipswich, heads the list of petitioners from that place. The document is in his handwriting. Thirty-one others joined in the act, many of them among the most respectable citizens of that town. Mr. Wise was a learned, able, and enlightened man. He had a free spirit, and was perhaps the only minister in the neighborhood or country, who was discerning enough to see the erroneousness of the proceedings from the beginning. The petition is as follows : —

" *The Humble and Sincere Declaration of us, Subscribers, Inhabitants in Ipswich, on the Behalf of our Neighbors, John Procter and his Wife, now in Trouble and under Suspicion of Witchcraft.*

" TO THE HONORABLE COURT OF ASSISTANTS NOW SITTING IN BOSTON.

" *Honored and Right Worshipful,* — The aforesaid John Procter may have great reason to justify the Divine Sovereignty of God under these severe remarks of Providence upon his peace and honor, under a due reflection upon his life past ; and so the best of us have reason to adore the great pity and indulgence of God's providence, that we are not exposed to the utmost shame that the Devil can invent, under the permissions of sovereignty, though not for that sin forenamed, yet for our many transgressions. For we do at present suppose, that it may be a method within the severer but just transactions of the infinite majesty of God, that he sometimes may permit Sathan to personate, dissemble, and thereby abuse innocents and such as do, in the fear of God, defy the Devil and all his works. The great rage he is permitted to attempt holy Job with ; the abuse he does the famous Samuel in disquieting his silent dust, by shadowing his venerable person in answer to the charms of witchcraft ; and other instances from good hands, — may be arguments. Besides the unsearchable footsteps of God's judgments, that are brought to light every morning, that astonish our weaker reasons ; to teach us adoration, trembling, dependence, &c.   But we must not trouble Your Honors by being tedious.   Therefore, being smitten with the notice of what hath happened, we reckon it within the duties of our charity, that teacheth us to do as we would be done by, to offer thus much for the clearing of our neighbors' innocency ; viz., that we never had the least knowledge of such a ne- fandous wickedness in our said neighbors, since they have been within our acquaintance.   Neither do we remember any such thoughts in us concerning them, or any action by them or either of them, directly tending that way, no more than might be in the lives of any other persons of the clear- est reputation as to any such evils.   What God may have left them to, we cannot go into God's pavilion clothed with clouds of darkness round about ; but, as to what we have ever seen or heard of them, upon our consciences we judge them innocent of the crime objected.   His breeding hath been amongst us, and was of religious parents in our place, and, by reason of relations and properties within our town, hath had constant intercourse with us.   We speak upon our personal acquaintance and observation ; and so leave our neighbors, and this our testimony on their behalf, to the wise thoughts of Your Honors.

Jnᵒ WISE.	NATHANILL PERKINS	BENJAMIN MARSHALL
WILLIAM STORY Senᵣ	THOMAS LOVKINE.	JOHN ANDREWS Juᵣ
REINALLD FOSTER	WILLIAM COGSWELL.	WILLIAM BUTLER.
THOS. CHOTE.	THOMAS VARNY.	WILLIAM ANDREWS.
JOHN BURNUM Sᵣ	JOHN FELLOWS.	JOHN ANDREWS.
WILLIAM THOMSONN.	WM. COGSWELL Juᵣ	JOHN CHOTE Seᵣ
THO. LOW Senᵣ	JONATHAN COGSWELL.	JOSEPH PROCTER.
ISAAC FOSTER.	JOHN COGSWELL Jū.	SAMUEL GIDDING
JOHN BURNUM junᵣ	JOHN COGSWELL.	JOSEPH EVLETH
WILLIAM GOODHEW.	THOMAS ANDREWS.	JAMES WHITE.
ISAAC PERKINS.	JOSEPH ANDREWS."	

I have given the names of the men who signed this paper, as copied from the original. It is due to their memory; and their descendants may well be gratified by the testimony thus borne to their courage and justice.

Their neighbors living near the bounds of the village presented the following paper, in the handwriting of Felton, the first signer. From the appearance of the document, it seems that a portion of it, probably containing an equal number of names, has been cut out by scissors.

"We whose names are underwritten, having several years known John Procter and his wife, do testify that we never heard or understood that they were ever suspected to be guilty of the crime now charged upon them; and several of us, being their near neighbors, do testify, that, to our apprehension, they lived Christian-like in their family, and were ever ready to help such as stood in need of their help.

"NATHANIEL FELTON, Sr., and MARY his wife.
SAMUEL MARSH, and PRISCILLA his wife.
JAMES HOULTON, and RUTH his wife.
JOHN FELTON.
NATHANIEL FELTON, Jr.
SAMUEL FRAYLL, and AN his wife.
ZACHARIAH MARSH, and MARY his wife.
SAMUEL ENDECOTT, and HANAH his wife
SAMUEL STONE.
GEORGE LOCKER.
SAMUEL GASKIL, and PROVIDED his wife.
GEORGE SMITH.
EDWARD GASKIL."

In addition to this testimony in their favor, evidence was offered, at their trial, that one of the accusing

witnesses had denied, out of Court, what she had
sworn to in Court; and declared that she must, at the
time, have been " out of her head," and that she had
never intended to accuse them. It was further proved,
that another of the accusing witnesses acknowledged
that she had sworn falsely, and tried to explain away
her testimony in Court, acknowledging that what the
girls said was " for sport. They must have some
sport." But neither the testimony in their favor from
those who had known them through life, nor the palpable and decisive manner in which the evidence
against them had been impeached and exposed, could
open the eyes of the infatuated Court and jury.

After his conviction, he requested, in vain, time
enough to prepare himself for death, and make the
necessary arrangements of his business and for the
welfare of his family; and the statement has come
down to us, that Mr. Noyes refused to pray with him,
unless he would confess himself guilty. The following
letter, addressed by him to the ministers named, in
behalf of himself and fellow-prisoners, gives a truly
shocking account of the outrages connected with the
prosecutions. It illustrates the courage of the writer
in exposing them, and is a sensible and manly appeal
and remonstrance. There is ground for supposing
that the ministers addressed were known not to be
entirely carried away by the delusion. The fact that
Mr. Mather — meaning, of course, Increase Mather —
is the first named, corroborates other evidence that he
was beginning to entertain doubts about the propriety

of the proceedings. Of the Rev. James Allen, much
has been said in connection with the Townsend-Bishop
farm. He had been a clergyman in England, and was
silenced by the Act of Uniformity, in 1662. He came
to New England; and, after officiating as an assistant
to the Rev. Mr. Davenport, in the First Church at Boston, for six years, was ordained as its preacher in 1668.
He was of independent fortune, and subsequently took
a leading part with those opposed to the party that had
favored the witchcraft prosecutions. He must have
known Rebecca Nurse quite intimately, and much of
the influence used in her favor, and which almost saved
her, may be attributed to him; there was a particular
intimacy between him and Increase Mather, and together they held Cotton Mather somewhat in check,
occasionally at least. The Rev. Joshua Moody had
been settled in the ministry at Portsmouth, New
Hampshire. In the maintenance of the principles of
religious liberty he suffered a long imprisonment, and
was afterwards exiled by arbitrary power. He was
then invited to the First Church in Boston, where he
preached from 1684 to 1693, when he returned to
Portsmouth. He died in 1697. By his active exertions, Mr. and Mrs. English were enabled to escape
from the jail at Boston. The Rev. Samuel Willard,
pastor of the Old South Church in Boston, was one of
the most revered and beloved ministers in the country.
His publications were numerous, learned, and valuable;
consisting of discourses, tracts, and volumes. His
" Body of Divinity " is an elaborate and systematic

work, comprising two hundred and fifty lectures on the Assembly's Catechism. That Procter was not in error in supposing Mr. Willard open to reason on the subject is demonstrated by the fact, that the "afflicted girls" were beginning to cry out against this eminent divine. The Rev. John Bailey was one of the ejected ministers who had here sought refuge from oppression in the mother-country. He was a distinguished person, associated with Mr. Allen and Mr. Moody in the ministry of the First Church at Boston. Cotton Mather made him the subject of the strongest eulogium in his "Magnalia." Procter addressed his letter to these persons because he believed them to be superior in wisdom and candid in spirit. It cannot be doubted that the good men did what they could in his behalf, but in vain.

"SALEM PRISON, July 23, 1692.

"*Mr. Mather, Mr. Allen, Mr. Moody, Mr. Willard, and Mr. Bailey.*

"REVEREND GENTLEMEN, — The innocency of our case, with the enmity of our accusers and our judges and jury, whom nothing but our innocent blood will serve, having condemned us already before our trials, being so much incensed and enraged against us by the Devil, makes us bold to beg and implore your favorable assistance of this our humble petition to His Excellency, that if it be possible our innocent blood may be spared, which undoubtedly otherwise will be shed, if the Lord doth not mercifully step in ; the magistrates, ministers, juries, and all the people in general, being

so much enraged and incensed against us by the delusion of
the Devil, which we can term no other, by reason we know,
in our own consciences, we are all innocent persons.   Here
are five persons who have lately confessed themselves to be
witches, and do accuse some of us of being along with them
at a sacrament, since we were committed into close prison,
which we know to be lies.   Two of the five are (Carrier's
sons) young men, who would not confess any thing till they
tied them neck and heels, till the blood was ready to come
out of their noses; and it is credibly believed and reported
this was the occasion of making them confess what they
never did, by reason they said one had been a witch a
month, and another five weeks, and that their mother made
them so, who has been confined here this nine weeks.   My
son, William Procter, when he was examined, because he
would not confess that he was guilty, when he was innocent,
they tied him neck and heels till the blood gushed out at his
nose, and would have kept him so twenty-four hours, if one,
more merciful than the rest, had not taken pity on him, and
caused him to be unbound.

" These actions are very like the Popish cruelties.   They
have already undone us in our estates, and that will not
serve their turns without our innocent blood.   If it cannot
be granted that we can have our trials at Boston, we humbly
beg that you would endeavor to have these magistrates
changed, and others in their room ; begging also and be-
seeching you, that you would be pleased to be here, if not
all, some of you, at our trials, hoping thereby you may be
the means of saving the shedding of our innocent blood.
Desiring your prayers to the Lord in our behalf, we rest,
your poor afflicted servants,

                              "JOHN PROCTER [and others]."

The bitterness of the prosecutors against Procter was so vehement, that they not only arrested, and tried to destroy, his wife and all his family above the age of infancy, in Salem, but all her relatives in Lynn, many of whom were thrown into prison. The helpless children were left destitute, and the house swept of its provisions by the sheriff. Procter's wife gave birth to a child, about a fortnight after his execution. This indicates to what alone she owed her life.

John Procter had spoken so boldly against the proceedings, and all who had part in them, that it was felt to be necessary to put him out of the way. He had denounced the entire company of the accusers, and their revenge demanded his sacrifice. They brought the whole power of their cunning and audacious arts to bear against him, and pursued him to the death with violence and rage. The manly and noble deportment exhibited in his dying hour seems to have made a deep impression on the minds of some, and gave an effectual blow to the delusion. The descendants of John Procter have always understood that his remains were recovered from the spot where the hangman deposited them, and placed in his own grounds, where they rest to-day.

No account has come to us of the deportment of George Jacobs, Sr., at his execution. As he was remarkable in life for the firmness of his mind, so he probably was in death. He had made his will before the delusion arose. It is dated Jan. 29, 1692; and shows that he, like Procter, had a considerable estate.

philip Englisk

Mary Englesk.

John Procter

anne Putnam.

merry Lewis

William Phips —

Tho: Newton

John Hathorne
Jonathan. Corwin ? Assists

Bar⁰ Wise

Nicholas Noyes

Bartholomew Gedney is one of the attesting witnesses, and probably wrote the document. After his conviction, on the 12th of August, he caused another to be written, which, in its provisions, reflects light upon the state of mind produced by the condition in which he found himself. In his infirm old age, he had been condemned to die for a crime of which he knew himself innocent, and which there is some reason to believe he did not think any one capable of committing. He regarded the whole thing as a wicked conspiracy and absurd fabrication. He had to end his long life upon a scaffold in a week from that day. His house was desolated, and his property sequestered. His only son, charged with the same crime, had eluded the sheriff, — leaving his family, in the hurry of his flight, unprovided for — and was an exile in foreign lands. The crazy wife of that son was in prison and in chains, waiting trial on the same charge ; her little children, including an unweaned infant, left in a deserted and destitute condition in the woods. The older children were scattered, he knew not where, while one of them had completed the bitterness of his lot by becoming a confessor, upon being arrested with her mother as a witch. This grand-daughter, Margaret, overwhelmed with fright and horror, bewildered by the statements of the accusers, and controlled probably by the arguments and arbitrary methods of address employed by her minister, Mr. Noyes, — whose peculiar function in these proceedings seems to have been to drive persons accused to make confession — had been betrayed into that position, and became a confessor, and accuser of others. Under these circumstances, the old man made a will, giving to his son George his estates, and securing the succession of them to his male descendants. But, in the mean while, without his then knowing it, Margaret had recalled her confession, as appears from the following documents, which tell their own story: —

"*The Humble Declaration of Margaret Jacobs unto the Honored Court now sitting at Salem showeth,* that, whereas your poor and humble declarant, being closely confined here in Salem jail for the crime of witchcraft, — which crime, thanks be to the Lord! I am altogether ignorant of, as will appear at the great day of judgment, — may it please the honored Court, I was cried out upon by some of the possessed persons as afflicting them; whereupon I was brought to my examination; which persons at the sight of me fell down, which did very much startle and affright me. The Lord above knows I knew nothing in the least measure how or who afflicted them. They told me, without doubt I did, or else they would not fall down at me; they told me, if I would not confess, I should be put down into the dungeon, and would be hanged, but, if I would confess, I should have my life: the which did so affright me, with my own vile, wicked heart, to save my life, made me make the like confession I did, which confession, may it please the honored Court, is altogether false and untrue. The very first night after I had made confession, I was in such horror of conscience that I could not sleep, for fear the Devil should carry me away for telling such horrid lies. I was, may it please the honored Court, sworn to my confession, as I understand since ; but then, at that time, was ignorant of it, not knowing what an oath did mean. The Lord, I hope, in whom I trust, out of the abundance of his mercy, will forgive me my false forswearing myself. What I said was altogether false against my grandfather and Mr. Burroughs, which I did to save my life, and to have my liberty : but the Lord, charging it to my conscience, made me in so much horror, that I could not contain myself before I had denied my confession, which I did, though I saw nothing but death before me ; choosing rather death with a quiet conscience, than to live in such horror, which I could not suffer. Where, upon my denying my confession, I was committed to close prison, where I have enjoyed more felicity in spirit, a thousand times, than I did before in my enlargement. And now, may it please Your Honors, your declarant having in part given Your Honors a description of my condition, do leave it to Your Honors' pious and judicious discretions to take pity and compassion on my young and tender years, to act and do with me as the Lord above and Your Honors shall see good, having no friend but the Lord to plead my cause for me ; not being guilty, in the least measure, of the crime of witchcraft, nor any other sin that deserves death from man. And your poor and humble declarant shall for ever pray, as she is bound in duty, for Your Honors' happiness in this life, and eternal felicity in the world to come. So prays Your Honors' declarant,

MARGARET JACOBS."

The following letter was written by this same young person to her father. Let it be observed that her grandfather had been executed the day before, partly upon her false testimony.

" *From the Dungeon in Salem Prison.*

"AUGUST 20, 1692.

"HONORED FATHER, — After my humble duty remembered to you, hoping in the Lord of your good health, as, blessed be God! I enjoy, though in abundance of affliction, being close confined here in a loathsome dungeon : the Lord look down in mercy upon me, not knowing how soon I shall be put to death, by means of the afflicted persons ; my grandfather having suffered already, and all his estate seized for the king. The reason of my confinement is this : I having, through the magistrates' threatenings, and my own vile and wretched heart, confessed several things contrary to my conscience and knowledge, though to the wounding of my own soul ; (the Lord pardon me for it !) but, oh ! the terrors of a wounded conscience who can bear ? But, blessed be the Lord ! he would not let me go on in my sins, but in mercy, I hope, to my soul, would not suffer me to keep it any longer : but I was forced to confess the truth of all before the magistrates, who would not believe me ; but it is their pleasure to put me in here, and God knows how soon I shall be put to death. Dear father, let me beg your prayers to the Lord on my behalf, and send us a joyful and happy meeting in heaven. My mother, poor woman, is very crazy, and remembers her kind love to you, and to uncle ; viz., D. A. So, leaving you to the protection of the Lord, I rest, your dutiful daughter,   MARGARET JACOBS."

A temporary illness led to the postponement of her trial ; and, before the next sitting of the Court, the delusion had passed away.

The " uncle D. A.," referred to, was Daniel Andrew, their nearest neighbor, who had escaped at the

same time with her father. She calls him " uncle."
He was, it is probable, a brother of John Andrew who
had married Ann Jacobs, sister of her father. Words
of relationship were then used with a wide sense.

Margaret read the recantation of her confession
before the Court, and was, as she says, forthwith
ordered by them into a dungeon. She obtained permission to visit Mr. Burroughs the day before his
execution, acknowledged that she had belied him,
and implored his forgiveness. He freely forgave, and
prayed with her and for her. It is probable, that,
at the same time, she obtained an interview with her
grandfather for the same purpose. At any rate, the
old man heard of her heroic conduct, and forthwith
crowded into the space between two paragraphs in
his will, in small letters closely written (the jailer
probably being the amanuensis), a clause giving a legacy of " ten pounds to be paid in silver " to his grand-
daughter, Margaret Jacobs. There is the usual declaration, that it " was inserted before sealing and
signing." This will having been made after conviction and sentence to death, and having but two
witnesses, one besides the jailer, was not allowed in
Probate, but remains among the files of that Court.
As a link in the foregoing story, it is an interesting
relic. The legacy clause, although not operative, was
no doubt of inexpressible value to the feelings of Margaret : and the circumstance seems to have touched
the heart even of the General Court, nearly twenty
years afterwards ; for they took pains specifically to

provide to have the same sum paid to Margaret, out of the Province treasury.

She was not tried at the time appointed, in consequence, it is stated, of " an imposthume in the head," and finally escaped the fate to which she chose to consign herself, rather than remain under a violated conscience. In judging of her, we cannot fail to make allowance for her " young and tender years," and to sympathize in the sufferings through which she passed. In making confession, and in accusing others, she had done that which filled her heart with horror, in the retrospect, so long as she lived. In recanting it, and giving her body to the dungeon, and offering her life at the scaffold, she had secured the forgiveness of Mr. Burroughs and her aged grandfather, and deserves our forgiveness and admiration. Every human heart must rejoice that this young girl was saved. She lived to be a worthy matron and the founder of a numerous and respectable family.

George Jacobs, Sr., is the only one, among the victims of the witchcraft prosecutions, the precise spot of whose burial is absolutely ascertained.

The tradition has descended through the family, that the body, after having been obtained at the place of execution, was strapped by a young grandson on the back of a horse, brought home to the farm, and buried beneath the shade of his own trees. Two sunken and weather-worn stones marked the spot. There the remains rested until 1864, when they were exhumed. They were enclosed again, and reverently redeposited

THE JACOBS HOUSE.

in the same place. The skull was in a state of considerable preservation. An examination of the jaw-
bones showed that he was a very old man at the time
of his death, and had previously lost all his teeth. The
length of some parts of the skeleton showed that he was
a very tall man. These circumstances corresponded
with the evidence, which was that he was tall of stature; so infirm as to walk with two staffs; with long,
flowing white hair. The only article found, except the
bones, was a metallic pin, which might have been used
as a breastpin, or to hold together his aged locks. It
is an observable fact, that he rests in his own ground
still. He had lived for a great length of time on that
spot; and it remains in his family and in his name
to this day, having come down by direct descent. It is
a beautiful locality: the land descends with a gradual
and smooth declivity to the bank of the river. It is
not much more than a mile from the city of Salem,
and in full view from the main road.

John Willard appears to have been an honest and
amiable person, an industrious farmer, having a comfortable estate, with a wife and three young children.
He was a grandson of Old Bray Wilkins; whether by
blood or marriage, I have not been able to ascertain.
The indications are that he married a daughter of
Thomas or Henry Wilkins, most probably the former,
with both of whom he was a joint possessor of lands.
He came from Groton; and it is for local antiquaries to discover whether he was a relative of the Rev.
Samuel Willard of Boston. If so, the fact would

shed much light upon our story. There is but one
piece of evidence among the papers relating to his
trial that deserves particular notice. It shows the
horrid character of the charges made by the girls
against prisoners at the bar, from their nature incapable of being refuted and which the prisoners knew
to be false, but the Court, jury, and crowd implicitly
believed. It also illustrates the completeness of the
machinery got up by the "accusing girls" to give
effect to their evidence. In addition to the evil gossip
that could be scoured from all the country round,
and to spectres of witches and ghosts of the dead,
they brought into the scene angels and divine beings,
and testified to what they were told by them. "The
shining man," or the white man, was meant, in the following deposition, to be a spirit of this description : —

"The Testimony of Susanna Sheldon, aged eighteen
years or thereabouts. — Testifieth and saith, that, the day of
the date hereof (9th of May, 1692), I saw at Nathaniel Ingersoll's house the apparitions of these four persons, — William
Shaw's first wife, the Widow Cook, Goodman Jones and
his child; and among these came the apparition of John
Willard, to whom these four said, 'You have murdered us.'
These four having said thus to Willard, they turned as red
as blood. And, turning about to look at me, they turned as
pale as death. These four desired me to tell Mr. Hathorne.
Willard, hearing them, pulled out a knife, saying, if I did,
he would cut my throat."

The deponent goes on to say, that these several
apparitions came before her on another occasion, and
the same language and actions took place, and adds : —

" There did appear to me a shining man, who said I should go and tell what I had heard and seen to Mr. Hathorne. This Willard, being there present, told me, if I did, he would cut my throat. At this time and place, this shining man told me, that if I did go to tell this to Mr. Hathorne, that I should be well, going and coming, but I should be afflicted there. Then said I to the shining man, 'Hunt Willard away, and I would believe what he said, that he might not choke me.' With that the shining man held up his hand, and Willard vanished away. About two hours after, the same appeared to me again, and the said Willard with them; and I asked them where their wounds were, and they said there would come an angel from heaven, and would show them. And forthwith the angel came. I asked what the man's name was that appeared to me last, and the angel told his name was Southwick. And the angel lifted up his winding-sheet, and out of his left side he pulled a pitchfork tine, and put it in again, and likewise he opened all the winding-sheets, and showed all their wounds. And the white man told me to tell Mr. Hathorne of it, and I told him to hunt Willard away, and I would; and he held up his hand, and he vanished away."

In the same deposition, this girl testifies that " she saw this Willard suckle the apparitions of two black pigs on his breasts;" that Willard told her he had been a witch twenty years; that she saw Willard and other wizards kneel in prayer " to the black man with a long-crowned hat, and then they vanished away."

Such was the kind of testimony which the Court received with awe-struck and bewildered credulity, and which took away the lives of valuable and blameless men. All we know of the manner of Willard's death is a passage from Brattle, who states that a deep impression was produced by the admirable deportment of the sufferers during the awful scenes before and at their executions ; giving every evidence of conscious innocence and a Christian character and faith, on the part especially of " Procter and Willard, whose whole management of themselves from the jail to the gallows, and whilst at the gallows, was very affecting, and melting to the hearts of some considerable spectators whom I could mention to you : but they are executed, and so I leave them."

On the 9th of September, the Court met again ; and *Martha Corey, Mary Easty, Alice Parker, Ann Pudeator*, Dorcas Hoar, and Mary Bradbury were tried and condemned ; and, on the 17th, *Margaret Scott, Wilmot Reed, Samuel Wardwell, Mary Parker*, Abigail Faulkner, Rebecca Eames, Mary Lacy, Ann Foster, and Abigail Hobbs received the same sentence. Those in Italics were executed Sept. 22, 1692. Of the circumstances in relation to them, in reference to their death and at the time of their execution, but little information has reached us. The following extract from Mr. Parris's church-records presents a striking picture : —

" 11 September, Lord's Day. — Sister Martha Corey — taken into the church 27 April, 1690 — was, after examination upon suspicion of witchcraft, 27 March, 1692, committed to prison for that fact, and was condemned to the gallows for the same yesterday; and was this day in public, by a general consent, voted to be excommunicated out of the church, and Lieutenant Nathaniel Putnam and the two deacons chosen to signify to her, with the pastor, the mind of the church herein. Accordingly, this 14 September, 1692, the three aforesaid brethren went with the pastor to her in Salem Prison; whom we found very obdurate, justifying herself, and condemning all that had done any thing to her just discovery or condemnation. Whereupon, after a little discourse (for her imperiousness would not suffer much) and after prayer, — which she was willing to decline, — the dreadful sentence of excommunication was pronounced against her."

Calef informs us, that "Martha Corey, protesting her innocency, concluded her life with an eminent prayer upon the ladder."

Nothing has reached us particularly relating to the manner of death of Alice or Mary Parker, Ann Pudeator, Margaret Scott, or Wilmot Reed. They all asserted their innocence; and their deportment gave no ground for any unfavorable comment by their persecutors, who were on the watch to turn every act, word, or look of the sufferers to their disparagement. Wilmot Reed probably adhered to the unresisting demeanor which marked her examination. It was all a mystery to her; and to every question she answered, "I know nothing about it." Of Mary Easty it is grateful to have some account. Her own declarations in vindication of her innocence are fortunately preserved; and her noble record is complete in the following documents. The first appears to have been addressed to the Special Court, and was presented immediately before the trial of Mary Easty. No explanation has come down to us why Sarah Cloyse was not then also brought to trial. Circumstances to which we have no clew rescued her from the fate of her sisters.

"*The Humble Request of Mary Easty and Sarah Cloyse to the Honored Court humbly showeth*, that, whereas we two sisters, Mary Easty and Sarah Cloyse, stand now before the honored Court charged with the suspicion of witchcraft, our humble request is — First, that, seeing we are neither able to plead our own cause, nor is counsel allowed to those in our condition, that you who are our judges would please to be of counsel to us, to direct us wherein we may stand in need. Secondly, that, whereas we are not conscious to ourselves of any guilt in the least degree of that crime whereof we are now accused (in the presence of the living God we speak it, before whose awful tribunal we know we shall ere long appear), nor any other scandalous evil or miscarriage inconsistent with Christianity, those who have had the longest and best knowledge of us, being persons of good report, may be suffered to testify upon oath what they know concerning each of us; viz., Mr. Capen, the pastor, and those of the town and church of Topsfield, who are ready to say something which we hope may be looked upon as very considerable in this matter, with the seven children of one of us; viz., Mary Easty: and it may be produced of like nature in reference to the wife of Peter Cloyse, her sister. Thirdly, that the testimony of witches, or such as are afflicted as is supposed by witches, may not be improved to

condemn us without other legal evidence concurring. We
hope the honored Court and jury will be so tender of the
lives of such as we are, who have for many years lived
under the unblemished reputation of Christianity, as not to
condemn them without a fair and equal hearing of what
may be said for us as well as against us. And your poor
suppliants shall be bound always to pray, &c."

The following was presented by Mary Easty to the
judges after she had received sentence of death. It
would be hard to find, in all the records of human suffering and of Christian deportment under them, a
more affecting production. It is a most beautiful
specimen of strong good-sense, pious fortitude and
faith, genuine dignity of soul, noble benevolence, and
the true eloquence of a pure heart; and was evidently
composed by her own hand. It may be said of her —
and there can be no higher eulogium — that she felt
for others more than for herself.

" *The Humble Petition of Mary Easty unto his Excel-*
lency Sir William Phips, and to the Honored Judge and
Bench now sitting in Judicature in Salem, and the Reverend
Ministers, humbly showeth, that, whereas your poor and
humble petitioner, being condemned to die, do humbly beg
of you to take it in your judicious and pious consideration,
that your poor and humble petitioner, knowing my own
innocency, blessed be the Lord for it ! and seeing plainly the
wiles and subtilty of my accusers by myself, cannot but
judge charitably of others that are going the same way of
myself, if the Lord steps not mightily in. I was confined a
whole month upon the same account that I am condemned

now for, and then cleared by the afflicted persons, as some of Your Honors know. And in two days' time I was cried out upon them, and have been confined, and now am condemned to die. The Lord above knows my innocency then, and likewise does now, as at the great day will be known to men and angels. I petition to Your Honors not for my own life, for I know I must die, and my appointed time is set; but the Lord he knows it is that, if it be possible, no more innocent blood may be shed, which undoubtedly cannot be avoided in the way and course you go in. I question not but Your Honors do to the utmost of your powers in the discovery and detecting of witchcraft and witches, and would not be guilty of innocent blood for the world. But, by my own innocency, I know you are in the wrong way. The Lord in his infinite mercy direct you in this great work, if it be his blessed will that no more innocent blood be shed! I would humbly beg of you, that Your Honors would be pleased to examine these afflicted persons strictly, and keep them apart some time, and likewise to try some of these confessing witches; I being confident there is several of them has belied themselves and others, as will appear, if not in this world, I am sure in the world to come, whither I am now agoing. I question not but you will see an alteration of these things. They say myself and others having made a league with the Devil, we cannot confess. I know, and the Lord knows, as will . . . appear, they belie me, and so I question not but they do others. The Lord above, who is the Searcher of all hearts, knows, as I shall answer it at the tribunal seat, that I know not the least thing of witchcraft; therefore I cannot, I dare not, belie my own soul. I beg Your Honors not to deny this my humble petition from a poor, dying, innocent person. And I question not but the Lord will give a blessing to your endeavors."

The parting interview of this admirable woman with her husband, children, and friends, as she was about proceeding to the place of execution, is said to have been a most solemn, affecting, and truly sublime scene. Calef says that her farewell communications, on this occasion, were reported, by persons who listened to them, to have been " as serious, religious, distinct, and affectionate as could well be expressed, drawing tears from the eyes of almost all present."

Ann Pudeator had been formerly the wife of a person named Greenslitt, who left her with five children. Her subsequent husband, Jacob Pudeator, died in 1682, and by will gave her his whole estate, after the payment of legacies, of five pounds each, to her Greenslitt children, who appear to have been living in 1692 at Casco Bay. These provisions, as well as the expressions used by Pudeator, indicate that he regarded her with affection and esteem. The following document is all that we know else of her character particularly, except that she was a kind neighbor, and ever prompt in offices of charity and sympathy.

" *The Humble Petition of Ann Pudeator unto the Honored Judge and Bench now sitting in Judicature in Salem, humbly showeth,* that, whereas your poor and humble petitioner, being condemned to die, and knowing in my own conscience, as I shall shortly answer it before the great God of heaven, who is the Searcher and Knower of all hearts, that the evidence of Jno. Best, Sr., and Jno. Best, Jr., and Samuel Pickworth, which was given in against me in Court, were all of them altogether false and untrue, and, besides the

abovesaid Jno. Best hath been formerly whipped and likewise is recorded for a liar. I would humbly beg of Your
Honors to take it into your judicious and pious consideration, that my life may not be taken away by such false
evidences and witnesses as these be ; likewise, the evidence
given in against me by Sarah Churchill and Mary Warren
I am altogether ignorant of, and know nothing in the least
measure about it, nor nothing else concerning the crime
of witchcraft, for which I am condemned to die, as will be
known to men and angels at the great day of judgment.
Begging and imploring your prayers at the Throne of Grace
in my behalf, and your poor and humble petitioner shall for
ever pray, as she is bound in duty, for Your Honors' health
and happiness in this life, and eternal felicity in the world
to come."

Abigail, the wife of Francis Faulkner, and daughter
of the Rev. Francis Dane, of Andover, who was among
those sentenced on the 17th of September, had been
examined, on the 11th of August, by Hathorne, Corwin, and Captain John Higginson, sitting as magistrates. Upon the prisoner's being brought in, the
afflicted fell down, and went into fits, as usual. The
magistrates asked the prisoner what she had to say.
She replied, "I know nothing of it." The girls then
renewed their performances, declaring that her shape
was at that moment torturing them. The magistrates
asked her if she did not see their sufferings. She
answered, "Yes; but it is the Devil does it in my
shape." Ann Putnam said that her spectre had afflicted her a few days before, pulling her off her horse.

Upon the touch of her person, the sufferings of the
afflicted would cease for a time. The prisoner held
a handkerchief in her hand. The girls would screech
out, declaring that, as she pressed the handkerchief,
they were dreadfully squeezed. She threw the handkerchief on the table; and they said, "There are the
shapes of Daniel Eames and Captain Floyd [two persons then in prison on the charge of witchcraft] sitting
on her handkerchief." Mary Warren enacted the part
of being dragged against her will under the table by
an invisible hand, from whose grasp she was at once
released, upon the prisoner's being made to touch her.
Notwithstanding all this, she protested her innocence,
and was remanded to jail. On the 30th, she was
brought out again. In the mean while, six had been
executed. The usual means were employed to break
her down; but all that was gained was, that she
owned she had expressed her indignation at the conduct of the afflicted, and was much excited against
them "for bringing her kindred out, and she did
wish them ill: and, her spirit being raised, she did
pinch her hands together, and she knew not but
that the Devil might take that advantage; but it
was the Devil, and not she, that afflicted them."
This was the only concession she would make; and
they were puzzled to determine whether it was a confession, or not, — it having rather the appearance of
clearing herself from all implication with the Devil,
and leaving him on their hands — at any rate, they concluded to regard it in the latter sense; and she was

duly convicted, and sentenced to death. Sir William
Phips ordered a reprieve; and, after she had been
thirteen weeks in prison, he directed her to be discharged on the ground of insufficient evidence. This,
I think, is the only instance of a special pardon granted
during the proceedings.

Samuel Wardwell, like most of the accused belonging to Andover, had originally joined the crowd of
the confessors; but he was too much of a man to remain in that company. He took back his confession,
and met his death. While he was speaking to the
people, at the gallows, declaring his innocency, a puff
of tobacco-smoke from the pipe of the executioner,
as Calef informs us, " coming in his face, interrupted
his discourse: those accusers said that the Devil did
hinder him with smoke." The wicked creatures followed their victims to the last with their malignant
outrages. The cart that carried the prisoners, on this
occasion, to the hill, " was for some time at a set:
the afflicted and others said that the Devil hindered
it," &c.

The route by which they were conveyed from the
jail, which was at the north corner of Federal and
St. Peter's Streets, to the gallows, must have been
a cruelly painful and fatiguing one, particularly to infirm and delicate persons, as many of them were. It
was through St. Peter's, up the whole length of Essex,
and thence probably along Boston Street, far towards
Aborn Street; for the hill could only be ascended from
that direction. It must have been a rough and jolting

operation ; and it is not strange that the cart got
" set." It seems that the prisoners were carried in
a single cart. It was a large one, provided probably
for the occasion ; and it is not unlikely that the reason
why some who had been condemned were not executed, was that the cart could not hold them all at
once. They were executed, one in June, five in July,
five in August, and eight in September, with the in-
tention, no doubt, by taking them in instalments, to
extend the acts of the tragedy, from month to month,
indefinitely.

It was necessary for the safety of the accusers and
prosecutors to prevent a revulsion of the public mind,
or even the least diminution of the popular violence
against the supposed witches. As they all protested
their innocence to the moment of death, and exhibited
a remarkably Christian deportment throughout the
dreadful scenes they were called to encounter from
their arrest to their execution, there was reason to
apprehend that the people would gradually be led to
feel a sympathy for them, if not to entertain doubts of
their guilt. To prevent this, and remove any impressions favorable to them that might be made by the
conduct and declarations of the convicts, the prosecutors were on the alert. After the prisoners had been
swung off, on the 22d of September, " turning him to
the bodies, Mr. Noyes said, ' What a sad thing it is
to see eight firebrands of hell hanging there ! ' " It
was the last time his eyes were regaled by such a
sight. There were no more executions on Witch Hill.

Three days before, a life had been taken by the officers of the law in a manner so extraordinary, and marked by features so shocking, that they find no parallel in the annals of America, and will continue to arrest for ever the notice of mankind. The history and character of old Giles Corey have been given in preceding parts of this work. The only papers relating to him, on file as having been sworn to before the Grand Jury, are a few brief depositions. If he had been put on trial, we might have had more. Elizabeth Woodwell testifies, that "she saw Giles Corey at meeting at Salem on a lecture-day, since he has been in prison. He or his apparition came in, and sat in the middlemost seat of the men's seats, by the post. This was the lecture-day before Bridget Bishop was hanged. And I saw him come out with the rest of the people." Mary Walcot, of course, swore to the same. And Mary Warren swore that Corey was hostile to her and afflicted her, because he thought she " caused her master (John Procter) to ask more for a piece of meadow than he (Corey) was willing to give." She also charged him with " afflicting of her " by his spectre while he was in prison, and " described him in all his garments, both of hat, coat, and the color of them, — with a cord about his waist and a white cap on his head, and in chains." There is reason to believe, that, while in prison, he experienced great distress of mind. Although he had been a rough character in earlier life, and given occasion to much scandal by his disregard of public opinion, he always exhibited symptoms of a generous and sensitive nature. His foolish conduct in becoming so passionately engaged in the witchcraft proceedings, at their earliest stage, as to be incensed against his wife because she did not approve of or believe in them, and which led him to utter sentiments and expressions that had been used against her; and so far yielding to the accusers as to allow them to get from him the deposition, which, while it failed to satisfy their demands, it was shameful for him to have been persuaded to give, all these things, which after his own apprehension and imprisonment he had leisure to ponder upon, preyed on his mind. He saw the awful character of the delusion to which he had lent himself; that it had brought his prayerful and excellent wife to the sentence of death, which had already been executed upon many other devout and worthy persons. He knew that he was innocent of the crime of witchcraft, and was now satisfied that all others were. Besides his own unfriendly course towards his wife, two of his four sons-in-law had turned against her. One (Crosby) had testified, and another (Parker) had allowed his name to be used, as an adverse witness. In view of all this, Corey made up his mind, determined on his course, and stood to that determination. He resolved to expiate his own folly by a fate that would satisfy the demands of the sternest criticism upon his conduct; proclaim his abhorrence of the prosecutions; and attest the strength of his feelings towards those of his children who had been false, and those who had been true, to his wife.

He caused to be drawn up what has been called a will, although it is in reality a deed, and was duly recorded as such. Its phraseology is very strongly guarded, and made to give it clear, full, and certain effect. It begins thus: "Know ye, &c., that I, Giles Corey, lying under great trouble and affliction, through which I am very weak in body, but in perfect memory, — knowing not how soon I may depart this life; in consideration of which, and for the fatherly love and affection which I have and do bear unto my beloved son-in-law, William Cleeves, of the town of Beverly, and to my son-in-law, John Moulton, of the town of Salem, as also for divers other good causes and considerations me at the present especially moving;" and proceeds to convey and confirm all his property — "lands, meadow, housing, cattle, stock, movables and immovables, money, apparel, . . . and all other the aforesaid premises, with their appurtenances" — to the said Cleeves and Moulton "for ever, freely and quietly, without any manner of challenge, claim, or demand of me the said Giles Corey, or of any other person or persons whatsoever for me in my name, or by my cause, means, or procurement;" and, in the use of all the language applicable to that end, he warrants and binds himself to defend the aforesaid conveyance and grant to Cleeves and Moulton, their heirs, executors, administrators, and assigns for ever. The document was properly signed, sealed, and delivered in the presence of competent witnesses, whose several signatures are indorsed to that effect. It was duly acknowledged before "Thomas Wade, Justice of the Peace in Essex," and recorded forthwith. This transaction took place in the jail at Ipswich.

His whole property being thus securely conveyed to his faithful sons-in-law, and placed beyond the reach of his own weakness or change of purpose, Corey resolved on a course that would surely try to the utmost the power of human endurance and firmness. He knew, that, if brought to trial, his death was certain. He did not know but that conviction and execution, through the attainder connected with it, might invalidate all attempts of his to convey his property. But it was certain, that, if he should not be brought to trial and conviction, his deed would stand, and nothing could break it, or defeat its effect. He accordingly made up his mind not to be tried. When called into court to answer to the indictment found by the Grand Jury, he did not plead " Guilty," or " Not guilty," but stood mute. How often he was called forth, we are not informed ; but nothing could shake him. No power on earth could unseal his lips.

He knew that he could have no trial that would deserve the name. To have pleaded " Not guilty " would have made him, by his own act, a party to the proceeding, and have been, by implication, an assent to putting his case to the decision of a blind, maddened, and utterly perverted tribunal. He would not, by any act or utterance of his, leave his case with " the country " represented by a jury that embodied the passions of the deluded and infatuated multitude around him. He knew that the gates of justice were closed, and that truth had fled from the scene. He would have no part nor lot in the matter ; refused to recognize the court, made no response to its questions, and was dumb in its presence. He stands alone in the resolute defiance of his attitude. He knew the penalty of suffering and agony he would have to pay ; but he freely and fearlessly encountered it. All that was needed to carry his point was an unconquerable firmness, and he had it. He rendered it impossible to bring him to trial ; and thereby, in spite of the power and wrath of the whole country and its authorities, retained his right to dispose of his property ; and bore his testimony against the wickedness and folly of the hour in tones that reached the whole world, and will resound through all the ages.

When Corey took this ground, the Court found itself in a position of no little difficulty, and was probably at a loss what to do. No information has come to us of the details of the proceedings. If the usages in England on such occasions were adopted, the prisoner was three times brought before the Court, and called to plead ; the consequences of persisting in standing mute being solemnly announced to him at each time. If he remained obdurate, the sentence of *peine forte et dure* was passed upon him ; and, remanded to prison, he was put into a low and dark apartment. He would there be laid on his back on the bare floor, naked for the most part. A weight of iron would be placed upon him, not quite enough to crush him. He would have no sustenance, save only, on the first day, three morsels of the worst bread; and, on the second day, three draughts of standing water that should be nearest to the prison door: and, in this situation, such would be alternately his daily diet till he died, or till he answered. The object of this terrible punishment was to induce the prisoner to plead to the indictment; upon doing which, he would be brought to trial in the ordinary way. The motive that led prisoners to stand mute in England is stated to have been, most generally, to save their property from confiscation. The practice of putting weights upon them, and gradually increasing them, was to force them, by the slowly increasing torture, to yield.

How far the English practice was imitated in the case of Corey will remain for ever among the dread secrets of his prison-house. The tradition is, that the last act in the tragedy was in an open field near the jail, somewhere between Howard-street Burial Ground and Brown Street. It is said that Corey urged the executioners to increase the weight which was crushing him, that he told them it was of no use to expect him to yield, that there could be but one way of ending the matter, and that they might as well pile on the rocks. Calef says, that, as his body yielded to the pressure, his tongue protruded from his mouth, and an official forced it back with his cane. Some persons now living remember a popular superstition, lingering in the minds of some of the more ignorant class, that Corey's ghost haunted the grounds where this barbar-

ous deed was done; and that boys, as they sported in
the vicinity, were in the habit of singing a ditty beginning thus: —

> " 'More weight! more weight!'
> Giles Corey he cried."

For a person of more than eighty-one years of age,
this must be allowed to have been a marvellous exhibition of prowess; illustrating, as strongly as any
thing in human history, the power of a resolute will
over the utmost pain and agony of body, and demon-
strating that Giles Corey was a man of heroic nerve,
and of a spirit that could not be subdued.

It produced a deep effect, as it was feared that it
would. The bearing of all the sufferers at all the
stages of the proceedings, and at their execution, had
told in their favor; but the course of Giles Corey profoundly affected the public mind. This must have
been noticed by the managers of the prosecutions; and
they felt that some extraordinary expedient was necessary to renew, and render more intense than ever, the
general infatuation. From the very beginning, there
had been great skill and adroitness in arranging the
order of incidents, and supplying the requisite excitements at the right moments and the right points.
Some persons — it can only be conjectured who —
had, all along, been behind the scenes, giving direction
and materials to the open actors. This unseen power
was in the village; and the movements it devised
generally proceeded from Thomas Putnam's house, or
the parsonage. It was on hand to meet the contingency

created by Corey's having actually carried out to the
last his resolution to meet a form of death that would,
if any thing could, cause a re-action in the public mind;
and the following stratagem was contrived to turn the
manner of his death into the means of more than ever
blinding and infatuating the people. It was the last
and one of the most artful strokes of policy by the
prosecutors. On the day after the death of Corey, and
two days before the execution of his wife, Mary Easty,
and the six others, Judge Sewall, then in Salem, received a letter from Thomas Putnam to this effect: —

"Last night, my daughter Ann was grievously tormented
by witches, threatening that she should be pressed to death
before Giles Corey; but, through the goodness of a gracious
God, she had at last a little respite. Whereupon there
appeared unto her (she said) a man in a winding-sheet,
who told her that Giles Corey had murdered him by pressing
him to death with his feet; but that the Devil there appeared unto him, and covenanted with him, and promised
him that he should not be hanged. The apparition said God
hardened his heart, that he should not hearken to the advice
of the Court, and so die an easy death; because, as it said,
it must be done to him as he has done to me. The apparition also said that Giles Corey was carried to the Court for
this, and that the jury had found the murder; and that her
father knew the man, and the thing was done before she
was born."

Cotton Mather represented this vision, made to Ann
Putnam, as proof positive of a divine communication
to her, because, as he says, she could not have received

her information from a human source, as everybody
had forgotten the affair long ago; and that she never
could have heard of it, happening, as it did, before she
was born. Bringing up this old matter to meet the effect
produced by Corey's death was indeed a skilful move;
and it answered its purpose probably to a considerable
extent. The man whom Corey was thus charged with
having murdered seventeen years before died in a manner causing some gossip at the time; and a coroner's
jury found that he had been "bruised to death, having
clodders of blood about the heart." Bringing the
affair back to the public mind, with the story of Ann
Putnam's vision, was well calculated to meet and
check any sympathy that might threaten to arise in
favor of Corey. But the trick, however ingenious,
will not stand the test of scrutiny. Mather's statement that everybody had forgotten the transaction,
and that Ann could only have known of it super-
naturally, is wholly untenable; for it was precisely
one of those things that are never forgotten in a
country village: it had always been kept alive as a
part of the gossip of the neighborhood in connection
with Corey; and her own father, as is unwittingly
acknowledged, knew the man, and all about it. Of
course, the girl had heard of it from him and others.
The industry that had ransacked the traditions and
collected the scandal of the whole country, far and
near, for stories that were brought in evidence against
all the prisoners, had not failed to pick up this choice
bit against Corey. The only reason why it had not

before been brought out was because he had not been
on trial. The man who died with "clodders of blood
about his heart," seventeen years before, was an unfortunate and worthless person, who had incurred
punishment for his misconduct while a servant on
Corey's farm, and afterwards at the hands of his own
family : and he does not appear to have mended his
morals upon passing into the spiritual world ; for the
statement of his ghost to Ann Putnam, that the jury
had found Corey guilty of murder, and that the
Court was hindered by some enchantment from proceeding against him, is disproved by the record which
is — as has been mentioned in the First Part, vol. i.
p. 185 — that the man was carried back to his house
by Corey's wife, and died there some time after ; and
the Court did no more than fine Corey for the punishment he had inflicted upon him while in his service,
and which the evidence showed was repeated by his
parents after his return to his own family.

Thomas Putnam's letter and Ann's vision were the
last things of the kind that occurred. The delusion
was approaching its close, and the people were beginning to be restored to their senses.

When it became known that Corey's resolution was
likely to hold out, and that no torments or cruelties of
any kind could subdue his firm and invincible spirit,
Mr. Noyes hurried a special meeting of his church on
a week-day, and had the satisfaction of dealing the
same awful doom upon him as upon Rebecca Nurse.
The entry in the record of the First Church is as
follows : —

" Sept. 18, G. Corey was excommunicated : the cause of it was, that he being accused and indicted for the sin of witchcraft, he refused to plead, and so incurred the sentence and penalty of *pain fort dure;* being undoubtedly either guilty of the sin of witchcraft, or of throwing himself upon sudden and certain death, if he were otherwise innocent."

This attempt to introduce a form of argument into a church act of excommunication is a slight but significant symptom of its having become felt that the breath of reason had begun to raise a ripple upon the surface of the public mind. It increased slowly but steadily to a gale that beat with severity upon Mr. Noyes and all his fellow-persecutors to their dying day.

After the executions, on the 22d of September, the Court adjourned to meet some weeks subsequently ; and it was, no doubt, their expectation to continue from month to month to hold sessions, and supply, each time, new cart-loads of victims to the hangman. But a sudden collapse took place in the machinery, and they met no more. The executive authority intervened, and their functions ceased. The curtain fell unexpectedly, and the tragedy ended. It is not known precisely what caused this sudden change. It is probable, that a revolution had been going on some time in the public mind, which was kept for a while from notice, but at last became too apparent and too serious to be disregarded. It has generally been attributed to the fact, that the girls became over-confident, and struck too high. They had ventured, as we have seen, to cry

out against the Rev. Samuel Willard, but were rebuked and silenced by the Court. Whoever began to
waver in his confidence of the correctness of the proceedings was in danger of being attacked by them;
and, as a general thing, when a person was " cried out
upon," it may be taken as proof that he had spoken
against them. Increase Mather, the president of Harvard College, called by Eliot " the father of the New-
England clergy," was understood not to go so far as
his son Cotton in sustaining the proceedings; and a
member of his family was accused. The wife of Sir
William Phips sympathized with those who suffered
prosecution, and is said to have written an order for
the release of a prisoner from jail. She was cried out
upon. It may have been noticed, that, though Jonathan Corwin sat with Hathorne as an examining
magistrate and assistant, and signed the commitments
of the prisoners, he never took an active part, but was
a silent and passive agent in the scene. He was subsequently raised to the bench; but there is reason
to believe that his mind was not clear as to the correctness of the proceedings. This probably became
known to the accusing girls; for they cried out repeatedly against his wife's t h er, a respectable and
venerable lady in Boston. The accusers, in aiming
at such characters, overestimated their power; and
the tide began to turn against them. But what
finally broke the spell by which they had held the
minds of the whole colony in bondage was their
accusation, in October, of Mrs. Hale, the wife of the

minister of the First Church in Beverly. Her genuine
and distinguished virtues had won for her a reputation,
and secured in the hearts of the people a confidence,
which superstition itself could not sully nor shake.
Mr. Hale had been active in all the previous proceedings ; but he knew the innocence and piety of his wife,
and he stood forth between her and the storm he had
helped to raise : although he had driven it on while
others were its victims, he turned and resisted it when
it burst in upon his own dwelling. The whole community became convinced that the accusers in crying
out upon Mrs. Hale, had perjured themselves, and
from that moment their power was destroyed ; the
awful delusion was dispelled, and a close put to one of
the most tremendous tragedies in the history of real
life. The wildest storm, perhaps, that ever raged in
the moral world, became a calm ; the tide that had
threatened to overwhelm every thing in its fury, sunk
back to its peaceful bed. There are few, if any, other
instances in history, of a revolution of opinion and
feeling so sudden, so rapid, and so complete. The
images and visions that had possessed the bewildered
imaginations of the people flitted away, and left them
standing in the sunshine of reason and their senses ;
and they could have exclaimed, as they witnessed them
passing off, in the language of the great master of the
drama and of human nature, but that their rigid
Puritan principles would not, it is presumed, have
permitted them, even in that moment of rescue and
deliverance, to quote Shakspeare, —

" The earth hath bubbles, as the water has,
  And these are of them.   Whither are they vanished ?
  Into the air ; and what seemed corporal, melted
  As breath into the wind."

Sir William Phips well knew that the public sentiment demanded a stop to be put to the prosecutions.
Besides that many of the people had lost all faith in
the grounds on which they had been conducted, an
influence from the higher orders of society began to
make itself felt.   Hutchinson says, " Although many
such had suffered, yet there remained in prison a
number of women of as reputable families as any in
the towns where they lived, and several persons, of
still superior rank, were hinted at by the pretended
bewitched, or by the confessing witches.   Some had
been publicly named.   Dudley Bradstreet, a justice
of peace, who had been appointed one of President
Dudley's council, and who was son to the worthy old
governor, then living, found it necessary to abscond.
Having been remiss in prosecuting, he had been charged
by some of the afflicted as a confederate.   His brother,
John Bradstreet, was forced to fly also."

The termination of the proceedings was probably
effectually secured by the spirited course of certain
parties in Andover, who, at the first moment of its
appearing that the public sentiment was changing,
commenced actions for slander against the accusers.

The result of the whole matter was, that, while some
of the judges, magistrates, and ministers persisted in
their fanatical zeal, the great body of the people, high
and low, were rescued from the delusion.

While, in the course of our story, we have witnessed some shocking instances of the violation of the most sacred affections and obligations of life, in husbands and wives, parents and children, testifying against each other, and exerting themselves for mutual destruction, we must not overlook the many instances in which filial, parental, and fraternal fidelity and love have shone conspicuously. It was dangerous to befriend an accused person. Procter stood by his wife to protect her, and it cost him his life. Children protested against the treatment of their parents, and they were all thrown into prison. Daniel Andrew, a citizen of high standing, who had been deputy to the General Court, asserted, in the boldest language, his belief of Rebecca Nurse's innocence; and he had to fly the country to save his life. Many devoted sons and daughters clung to their parents, visited them in prison in defiance of a bloodthirsty mob; kept by their side on the way to execution; expressed their love, sympathy, and reverence to the last; and, by brave and perilous enterprise, got possession of their remains, and bore them back under the cover of midnight to their own thresholds, and to graves kept consecrated by their prayers and tears. One noble young man is said to have effected his mother's escape from the jail, and secreted her in the woods until after the delusion had passed away, provided food and clothing for her, erected a wigwam for her shelter, and surrounded her with every comfort her situation would admit of. The poor creature must, however, have endured a great amount of suffering; for one of her larger limbs was fractured in the all but desperate attempt to rescue her from the prison-walls.

The Special Court being no longer suffered to meet, a permanent and regular tribunal, called the Superior Court of Judicature, was established, consisting of the Deputy-governor, William Stoughton, Chief-justice; and Thomas Danforth, John Richards, Wait Winthrop, and Samuel Sewall, associate justices. They held a Court at Salem, in January, 1693. Hutchinson says that, on this occasion, the Grand Jury found about fifty indictments. The following persons were brought to trial : Rebecca Jacobs, Margaret Jacobs, Sarah Buckley, Job Tookey, Hannah Tyler, Candy, Mary Marston, Elizabeth Johnson, Abigail Barker, Mary Tyler, Sarah Hawkes, Mary Wardwell, Mary Bridges, Hannah Post, Sarah Bridges, Mary Osgood, Mary Lacy, Jr., Sarah Wardwell, Elizabeth Johnson, Jr., and Mary Post. The three last were condemned, but not executed : all the rest were acquitted. Considering that the " spectral evidence " was wholly thrown out at these trials, the facts that the grand jury, under the advice of the Court, brought in so many indictments, and that three were actually convicted, are as discreditable to the regular Court as the convictions at the Special Court are to that body. It has been said that the Special Court had not an adequate representation of lawyers in its composition ; and the results of its proceedings have been ascribed to that circumstance. It has been

held up disparagingly in comparison with the regular Court that succeeded it.   But, in fact, the regular
Court consisted of persons all of whom sat in the
Special Court, with the exception of Danforth.   But
his proceedings in originating the arrests for witchcraft in the fall of 1691, and his action when presiding at the preliminary examination of John Procter,
Elizabeth Procter, and Sarah Cloyse, at Salem, April
11, 1692, show that, so far as the permission of gross
irregularities and the admission of absurd kinds of
testimony are concerned, the regular Court gained
nothing by his sitting with it, unless his views had
been thoroughly changed in the mean time.   The truth
is, that the judges, magistrates, and legislature were
as much to blame, in this whole business, as the
ministers, and much more slow to come to their senses,
and make amends for their wrong-doing.

All the facts known to us, and all the statements
that have come down to us, require us to believe, that
none who confessed, and stood to their confession,
were brought to trial.   All who were condemned either
maintained their innocence from the first, or, if persuaded or overcome into a confession, voluntarily took
it back and disowned it before trial.   If this be so,
then the name of every person condemned ought to
be held in lasting honor, as preferring to die rather
than lie, or stand to a lie.   It required great strength
of mind to take back a confession ; relinquish life and
liberty ; go down into a dungeon, loaded with irons ;
and from thence to ascend the gallows.   It relieves

the mind to think, that Abigail Hobbs, wicked and
shocking as her conduct had been towards Mr. Burroughs and others, came to herself, and offered her
life in atonement for her sin.

The Court continued the trials at successive sessions
during the spring, all resulting in acquittals, until in
May, 1693, Sir William Phips, by proclamation, discharged all. Hutchinson says, " Such a jail-delivery
has never been known in New England." The number then released is stated to have been one hundred
and fifty. How many had been apprehended, during
the whole affair, we have no means of knowing.
Twenty, counting Giles Corey, had been executed.
Two at least, Ann Foster and Sarah Osburn, had died
in jail : it is not improbable that others perished
under the bodily and mental sufferings there. We
find frequent expressions indicating that many died
in prison. A considerable number of children, and
some adults whose friends were able to give the heavy
bonds required and had influence enough to secure
the favor, had some time before been removed to
private custody. Quite a considerable number had
succeeded in breaking jail and eluding recapture.
Upon the whole, there must have been several hundreds committed. Even after acquittal by a jury, and
the Governor's proclamation, none were set at liberty
until they had paid all charges ; including board for
the whole time of their imprisonment, jailer's fees,
and fees of Court of all kinds. The families of many
had become utterly impoverished.

The sufferings of the prisoners and of their relatives and connections are perhaps best illustrated by presenting the substance of a few of the petitions for their release, found among the files. The friends of the parties, in these cases, were not in a condition to give the bonds, and they probably remained in jail until the general discharge; and how long after, before the means could be raised to pay all dues, we cannot know.*

* On the 19th of October, 1692, Thomas Hart, of Lynn, presented a memorial to the General Court, stating that his mother, Elizabeth Hart, had then been in Boston jail for nearly six months: "Though, in all this time, nothing has appeared against her whereby to render her deserving of imprisonment or death, . . . being ancient, and not able to undergo the hardship that is inflicted from lying in misery, and death rather to be chosen than a life in her circumstances." He says, that his father is "ancient and decrepit, and wholly unable" to take any steps in her behalf; that he feels "obliged by all Christian duty, as becomes a child to parents," to lay her case before the General Court. "The petitioner having lived from his childhood under the same roof with his mother, he dare presume to affirm that he never saw nor knew any evil or sinful practice wherein there was any show of impiety nor witchcraft by her; and, were it otherwise, he would not, for the world and all the enjoyments thereof, nourish or support any creature that he knew engaged in the drudgery of Satan. It is well known to all the neighborhood, that the petitioner's mother has lived a sober and godly life, always ready to discharge the part of a good Christian, and never deserving of afflictions from the hands of men for any thing of this nature." He humbly prays "for the speedy enlargement of this person so much abused." I present two more petitions. They help to fill up the picture of the sufferings and hardships borne by individuals and families.

"To the Honored General Court now sitting in Boston, the Humble Petition of Nicholas Rist, of Reading, showeth, that whereas Sara Rist, wife of the petitioner, was taken into custody the first day of June last, and, ever

Margaret Jacobs had to remain in jail after the Governor's proclamation had directed the release of all prisoners, because she could not pay the fees and charges. Her grandfather had been executed, and all his furniture, stock, and moveable property seized by the marshal or sheriff. Her father escaped the warrant by a sudden flight from his home under the cover of midnight, and was in exile " beyond the seas ; " her mother and herself taken at the time by the officers serving the warrants against them ; the younger children of the family, left without protection, had dispersed, and been thrown upon the charity of neighbors ; the house had been stripped of its contents, left open, and deserted. She had not a shilling in the world, and knew not where to look for aid.   She

since lain in Boston jail for witchcraft; though, in all this time, nothing has been made appear for which she deserved imprisonment or death: the petitioner has been a husband to the said woman above twenty years, in all which time he never had reason to accuse her for any impiety or witchcraft, but the contrary. She lived with him as a good, faithful, dutiful wife, and always had respect to the ordinances of God while her strength remained; and the petitioner, on that consideration, is obliged in conscience and justice to use all lawful means for the support and preservation of her life; and it is deplorable, that, in old age, the poor decrepit woman should lie under confinement so long in a stinking jail, when her circumstances rather require a nurse to attend her.

" May it, therefore, please Your Honors to take this matter into your prudent consideration, and direct some speedy methods whereby this ancient decrepit person may not for ever lie in such misery, wherein her life is made more afflictive to her than death."

" *The Humble Petition of Thomas Barrett, of Chelmsford, in New England, in behalf of his daughter Martha Sparkes, wife of Henry Sparkes, who is now a soldier in Their Majesties' Service at the Eastern Parts, and so hath been for a considerable time, humbly showeth,* That your petitioner's daughter hath lain in prison in Boston for the space of twelve months and five days, was taken back to prison, and remained there for some time, until a person named Gammon, apparently a stranger, happened to hear of her case, and, touched with compassion, raised the money required, and released her. It was long before the affairs of the Jacobs' family were so far retrieved as to enable them to refund the money to the noble-hearted fisherman. How many others lingered in prison, or how long, we have no means of ascertaining.

In reviewing the proceedings at the examinations and trials, it is impossible to avoid being struck with the infatuation of the magistrates and judges. They acted throughout in the character and spirit of prosecuting officers, put leading and ensnaring questions to the prisoners, adopted a browbeating deportment towards them, and pursued them with undisguised hostility. They assumed their guilt from the first,

being committed by Thomas Danforth, Esq., the late deputy-governor, upon suspicion of witchcraft; since which no evidence hath appeared against her in any such matter, neither hath any given bond to prosecute her, nor doth any one at this day accuse her of any such thing, as your petitioner knows of. That your petitioner hath ever since kept two of her children; the one of five years, the other of two years old, which hath been a considerable trouble and charge to him in his poor and mean condition: besides, your petitioner hath a lame, ancient, and sick wife, who, for these five years and upwards past, hath been so afflicted as that she is altogether rendered uncapable of affording herself any help, which much augments his trouble. Your poor petitioner earnestly and humbly entreats Your Excellency and Honors to take his distressed condition into your consideration; and that you will please to order the releasement of his daughter from her confinement, whereby she may return home to her poor children to look after them, having nothing to pay the charge of her confinement.

"And your petitioner, as in duty bound, shall ever pray.

"Nov. 1, 1692."

and endeavored to force them to confess; treating them as obstinate culprits because they would not. Every kind of irregularity was permitted. The marshal was encouraged in perpetual interference to prejudice the persons on trial, watching and reporting aloud to the Court every movement of their hands or heads or feet. Other persons were allowed to speak out, from the body of the crowd, whatever they chose to say adverse to the prisoner. Accusers were suffered to make private communications to the magistrates and judges before or during the hearings. The presiding officers showed off their smartness in attempts to make the persons on trial before them appear at a disadvantage. In some instances, as in the case of Sarah Good, the magistrate endeavored to deceive the accused by representing falsely the testimony given by another. The people in and around the court-room were allowed to act the part of a noisy mob, by clamors and threatening outcries; and juries were overawed to bring in verdicts of conviction, and rebuked from the bench if they exercised their rightful prerogative without regard to the public passions. The chief-justice, in particular, appears to have been actuated by violent prejudice against the prisoners, and to have conducted the trials, all along, with a spirit that bears the aspect of animosity.

There is one point of view in which he must be held responsible for the blood that was shed, and the infamy that, in consequence, attaches to the proceedings. It may well be contended, that not a conviction would have taken place, but for a notion of his which he arbitrarily enforced as a rule of law. It was a part of the theory relating to witchcraft, that the Devil made use of the spectres, or apparitions, of some persons to afflict others. From this conceded postulate, a division of opinion arose. Some maintained that the Devil could employ only the spectres of persons in league with him; others affirmed, that he could send upon his evil errands the spectres of innocent persons, without their consent or knowledge. The chief-justice held the former opinion, against the judgment of many others, arbitrarily established it as a rule of Court, and peremptorily instructed juries to regard it as binding upon them in making their verdicts. The consequence was that a verdict of "Guilty" became inevitable. But few at that time doubted the veracity of the "afflicted persons," which was thought to be demonstrated to the very senses by their fits and sufferings, in the presence of the Court, jury, and all beholders. When they swore that they saw the shapes of Bridget Bishop, or Rebecca Nurse, or George Burroughs, choking or otherwise torturing a person, the fact was regarded as beyond question.

The prisoners took the ground, that the statements made by the witnesses, even if admitted, were not proof against them; for the Devil might employ the spectres of innocent persons, or of whomsoever he chose, without the knowledge of the persons whose shapes were thus used by him. When Mrs. Ann Putnam swore that she had seen the spectre of Rebecca Nurse afflicting various persons; and that the said spectre acknowledged to her, that " she had killed Benjamin Houlton, and John Fuller, and Rebecca Shepard," — the answer of the prisoner was, " I cannot help it : the Devil may appear in my shape." When the examining magistrate put the question to Susanna Martin, " How comes your appearance to hurt these ? " Martin replied, " I cannot tell. He that appeared in Samuel's shape, a glorified saint, can appear in any one's shape." The Rev. John Wise, in his noble appeal in favor of John Procter, argued to the same point. But the chief-justice was inexorably deaf to all reason ; compelled the jury to receive, as absolute law, that the Devil could not use the shape of an innocent person ; and, as the " afflicted " swore that they saw the shapes of the prisoners actually engaged in the diabolical work, there was no room left for question, and they must return a verdict of " Guilty."

In this way, innocent persons were slaughtered by a dogma in the mind of an obstinate judge. Dogmas have perverted courts and governments in all ages. A fabrication of fancy, an arbitrary verbal proposition, has been exalted above reason, and made to extinguish common sense. The world is full of such dogmas. They mislead the actions of men, and confound the page of history. " The king cannot die " is one of them. It is held as an axiom of political and constitutional truth. So an entire dynasty, crowded with a more glorious life than any other, is struck from the annals of an empire. In the public records of England, the existence of the Commonwealth is ignored ; and the traces of its great events are erased from the archives of the government, which, in all its formulas and official papers, proclaims a lie. A hunted fugitive, wandering in disguise through foreign lands, without a foot of ground on the globe that he could call his own, is declared in all public acts, parliamentary and judicial, and even by those assuming to utter the voice of history, to have actually reigned all the time. In our country and in our day, we are perplexed, and our public men bewildered, by a similar dogma. The merest fabric of human contrivance, a particular form of political society, is impiously clothed with an essential attribute of God alone ; and ephemeral politicians are announcing, as an eternal law of Providence, that " a State cannot die." The mischiefs that result, in the management of human affairs, from enthroning dogmas over reason, truth, and fact, are, as they ever have been, incalculable.

Chief-justice Stoughton appears to have kept his mind chained to his dogma to the last. It rendered him wholly incapable of opening his eyes to the light of truth. He held on to spectral evidence, and his corollary from it, when everybody else had abandoned both. He would not admit that he, or any one concerned, had been in error. He never could bear to hear any persons express penitence or regret for the part they had taken in the proceedings. When the public delusion had so far subsided that it became difficult to procure the execution of a witch, he was disturbed and incensed to such a degree that he abandoned his seat on the bench. During a session of the Court at Charlestown, in January, 1692–3, " word was brought in, that a reprieve was sent to Salem, and had prevented the execution of seven of those that were there condemned, which so moved the chief judge that he said to this effect: ' We were in a way to have cleared the land of them; who it is that obstructs the cause of justice, I know not: the Lord be merciful to the country!' and so went off the bench, and came no more into that Court."

I have spoken of the judges as appearing to be infatuated, not on account of the opinions they held on the subject of witchcraft, for these were the opinions of their age; nor from the peculiar doctrine their chief enforced upon them, for that was entertained by many, and, as a mere theory, was perhaps as logically deducible from the prevalent doctrines as any other. Their infatuation consisted in not having eyes to see, or ears to hear, evidences continually occurring of the untruthful arts and tricks of the afflicted children, of their cunning evasions, and, in some instances, palpable falsehoods. Then, further, there was solid and substantial evidence before them that ought to have made them pause and consider, if not doubt and disbelieve. We find the following paper among the files: —

" THE TESTIMONY OF JOHN PUTNAM, SR., AND REBECCA HIS WIFE, saith that our son-in-law John Fuller, and our daughter Rebecca Shepard, did both of them die a most violent death (and died acting very strangely at the time of their death); further saith, that we did judge then that they both died of a malignant fever, and had no suspicion of withcraft of any, neither can we accuse the prisoner at the bar of any such thing."

When we recall the testimony of Ann Putnam the mother, and find that the afflicted generally charged the death of the above-named persons upon the shape of Rebecca Nurse, we perceive how absolutely Captain John Putnam and his wife discredit their testimony. The opinion of the father and mother of Fuller and Shepard ought to have had weight with the Court. They were persons of the highest standing, and of recognized intelligence and judgment. They were old church-members, and eminently orthodox in all their sentiments. They were the heads of a great family. He had represented the town in the General Court the year before. No man in this part of the country was more noted for strong good sense than Captain John Putnam. This deposition is honorable to their memory, and clears them from all responsibility for the extent to which the afflicted persons were allowed to sway the judgment of the Court. Taken in connection with the paper signed by so large a portion of the best people of the village, in behalf of Rebecca Nurse, it proves that the blame for the shocking proceedings in the witchcraft prosecutions cannot be laid upon the local population, but rests wholly upon the Court and the public authorities.

The Special Court that condemned the persons charged with witchcraft in 1692 is justly open to censure for the absence of all discrimination of evidence, and for a prejudgment of the cases submitted to them. In view of the then existing law and the practice in the mother-country under it, they ought to have the benefit of the admission that they did, in other respects than those mentioned, no more and no worse than was to be expected. And Cotton Mather, in the " Magnalia," vindicates them on this ground : —

" They consulted the precedents of former times, and precepts laid down by learned writers about witchcraft; as, Keeble on the Common Law, chap. ' Conjuration ' (an author approved by the twelve judges of our nation) : also, Sir Matthew Hale's Trials of Witches, printed anno 1682 ; Glanvill's Collection of Sundry Trials in England and Ireland in the years 1658, '61, '63, '64, and '81 ; Bernard's Guide to Jury-men ; Baxter's and R. B., their histories about Witches, and their Discoveries ; Cotton Mather's Memorable Providences relating to Witchcraft, printed 1685."

So far as the medical profession at the time is concerned, it must be admitted that they bear a full share of responsibility for the proceedings. They gave countenance and currency to the idea of witchcraft in the public mind, and were very generally in the habit, when a patient did not do well under their prescriptions, of getting rid of all difficulty by saying that " an evil hand " was upon him. Their opinion to this effect is cited throughout, and appears in a large number of the documents. There were coroners' juries in cases where it was suspected that a person died of witchcraft. It is much to be regretted that none of their verdicts have been preserved. Drawn up by an attending "chirurgeon," they would illustrate the state of professional science at that day, by informing us of the marks, indications, and conditions of the bodily organization by which the traces of the Devil's hand were believed to be discoverable. All we know is that, in particular cases, as that of Bray Wilkins's grandson Daniel, the jury found decisive proof that he had died by "an evil hand."

It is not to be denied or concealed, that the clergy were instrumental in bringing on the witchcraft delusion in 1692. As the supposed agents of the mischief belonged to the supernatural and spiritual world, which has ever been considered their peculiar province, it was thought that the advice and co-operation of ministers were particularly appropriate and necessary. Opposition to prevailing vices and attempts to reform society were considered at that time in the light of a conflict with Satan himself; and he was thought to be the ablest minister who had the greatest power over the invisible enemy, and could most easily and effectively avert his blows, and counteract his baleful influence. This gave the clergy the front in the battle against the hosts of Belial. They were proud of the position, and were stimulated to distinguish themselves in the conflict. Cotton Mather represents that ministers were honored by the special hostility of the great enemy of souls, "more dogged by the Devil than any other men," just as, according to his philosophy,

the lightning struck the steeples of churches more
frequently than other buildings because the Prince
of the Power of the Air particularly hated the places
where the sound of the gospel was heard. There were,
moreover, it is to be feared, ministers whose ambition
to acquire influence and power had been allowed to
become a ruling principle, and who favored the delusion because thereby their object could be most
surely achieved by carrying the people to the greatest extremes of credulity, superstition, and fanatical
blindness.

But justice requires it to be said that the ministers,
as a general thing, did not take the lead after the
proceedings had assumed their most violent aspect,
and the disastrous effects been fully brought to view.
It may be said, on the contrary, that they took the
lead, as a class, in checking the delusion, and rescuing
the public mind from its control. Prior to the time
when they were called upon to give their advice to the
government, they probably followed Cotton Mather:
after that, they seemed to have freed themselves generally from his influence. The names of Dane and
Barnard of Andover, Higginson of Salem, Cheever
of Marblehead, Hubbard and Wise of Ipswich, Payson
and Phillips of Rowley, Allin of Salisbury, and Capen
of Topsfield, appear in behalf of persons accused.
To come forward in their defence shows courage, and
proves that their influence was in the right direction,
even while the proceedings were at their height. Mr.
Hale, of Beverly, abandoned the prosecutions, and ex-

pressed his disapprobation of them, before the government or the Court relaxed the vigor of their operations, as is sufficiently proved by the fact that the " afflicted children " cried out against his wife. Willard, and James Allen, and Moody, and John Bailey, and even Increase Mather, of Boston, openly discountenanced the course things were taking. The latter circulated a letter from his London correspondent, a person whose opinion was entitled to weight, condemning in the strongest terms the doctrine of the chief-justice, as follows : " All that I speak with much wonder that any man, much less a man of such abilities, learning, and experience as Mr. Stoughton, should take up a persuasion that the Devil cannot assume the likeness of an innocent, to afflict another person. In my opinion, it is a persuasion utterly destitute of any solid reason to render it so much as probable." The ministers may have been among the first to bring on the delusion ; but the foregoing facts prove, that, as a profession, they were the first to attempt to check and discountenance the prosecutions. While we are required, in all fairness, to give this credit to the clergy in general, it would be false to the obligations of historical truth and justice to attempt to palliate the conduct of some of them. Whoever considers all that Mr. Parris, according to his own account, said and did, cannot but shrink from the necessity of passing judgment upon him, and find relief in leaving him to that tribunal which alone can measure the extent of human responsibility,

and sound the depths of the heart. Lawson threw
into the conflagration all the combustible materials
his eloquence and talents, heated, it is to be feared,
by resentment, could contribute. Dr. Bentley, in his
" Description and History of Salem" (Mass. Hist.
Coll., 1st series, vol. vi.) says, " Mr. Noyes came out
and publicly confessed his error, never concealed a
circumstance, never excused himself; visited, loved,
blessed, the survivors whom he had injured; asked
forgiveness always, and consecrated the residue of
his life to bless mankind." It is to be hoped that
the statement is correct. There were several points
of agreement between Noyes and Bentley. Both were
men of ability and learning. Like Bentley, Noyes
lived and died a bachelor; and, like him, was a man of
lively and active temperament, and, in the general tenor
of his life, benevolent and disinterested. Perhaps con-
geniality in these points led Bentley to make the statement, just quoted, a little too strong. He wrote more
than a century after the witchcraft proceedings; just
at that point when tradition had become inflated by
all manner of current talk, of fable mixed with fact,
before the correcting and expunging hand of a severe
scrutiny of records and documents had commenced
its work. The drag-net of time had drawn along
with it every thing that anybody had said; but the
process of sifting and discrimination had not begun.
His kindly and ingenuous nature led him to believe,
and prompted him to write down, all that was amiable, and pleasing to a mind like his. So far as the

records and documents give us information, there is reason to apprehend, that Mr. Noyes, like Stoughton, another old bachelor, never recovered his mind from the frame of feeling or conviction in which it was during the proceedings. His name is not found, as are those of other ministers, to any petitions, memorials or certificates, in favor of the sufferers during the trials, or of reparation to their memories or to the feelings of their friends. He does not appear to have taken any part in arresting the delusion or rectifying the public mind.

Of Cotton Mather, more is required to be said. He aspired to be considered the leading champion of the Church, and the most successful combatant against the Satanic powers. He seems to have longed for an opportunity to signalize himself in this particular kind of warfare; seized upon every occurrence that would admit of such a coloring to represent it as the result of diabolical agency; circulated in his numerous publications as many tales of witchcraft as he could collect throughout New and Old England, and repeatedly endeavored to get up cases of the kind in Boston. There is some ground for suspicion that he was instrumental in originating the fanaticism in Salem; at any rate, he took a leading part in fomenting it. And while there is evidence that he endeavored, after the delusion subsided, to escape the disgrace of having approved of the proceedings, and pretended to have been in some measure opposed to them, it can be too clearly shown that he was secretly and cunningly endeavoring to renew them during the next year in his own parish in Boston.*

How blind is man to the future! The state of things which Cotton Mather labored to bring about, in order that he might increase his own influence over an infatuated people, by being regarded by them as mighty

---

* I know nothing more artful and jesuitical than his attempts to avoid the reproach of having been active in carrying on the delusion in Salem and elsewhere, and, at the same time, to keep up such a degree of credulity and superstition in the minds of the people as to render it easy to plunge them into it again at the first favorable moment. In the following passages, he endeavors to escape the odium that had been connected with the prosecutions : —

"The world knows how many pages I have composed and published, and particular gentlemen in the government know how many letters I have written, to prevent the excessive credit of spectral accusations.

"In short, I do humbly but freely affirm it, that there is not a man living in this world, who has been more desirous than the poor man I to shelter my neighbors from the inconveniences of spectral outcries : yea, I am very jealous I have done so much that way as to sin in what I have done ; such have been the cowardice and fearfulness whereunto my regard unto the dissatisfaction of other people has precipitated me. I know a man in the world, who has thought he has been able to convict some such witches as ought to die ; but his respect unto the public peace has caused him rather to try whether he could not renew them by repentance."

In his Life of Sir William Phips, he endeavors to take the credit to himself of having doubted the propriety of the proceedings while they were in progress. This work was published without his name, in order that he might commend himself with more freedom. The advice given by the ministers of Boston and the vicinity to the government has been spoken of. Cotton Mather frequently took occasion to applaud and magnify the merit of this production. In one of his writings, he speaks of " the gracious words " it contained. In his Life of Phips, he thus modestly takes the credit of its authorship to him-

to cast out and vanquish evil spirits, and as able to
hold Satan himself in chains by his prayers and his
piety, brought him at length into such disgrace that
his power was broken down, and he became the object
of public ridicule and open insult. And the excitement that had been produced for the purpose of

self: it was "drawn up, at their (the ministers') desire, by Mr. Mather
the younger, as I have been informed." And, in order the more
effectually to give the impression that he was rather opposed to the
proceedings, he quotes those portions of the paper which recommended
caution and circumspection, leaving out those other passages in which
it was vehemently urged to carry the proceedings on "speedily and
vigorously."

This single circumstance is decisive of the disingenuity of Dr.
Mather. As it was the purpose of the government, in requesting the
advice of the ministers, to ascertain their opinion of the expediency
of continuing the prosecutions, it was a complete and deliberate perversion and falsification of their answer to omit the passages which
encouraged the proceedings, and to record those only which recommended caution and circumspection. The object of Mather in suppressing the important parts of the document has, however, in some
measure been answered. As the "Magnalia," within which his Life of
Phips is embraced, is the usual and popular source of information and
reference respecting the topics of which it treats, the opinion has prevailed, that the Boston ministers, especially "Mr. Mather the younger,"
endeavored to prevent the transactions connected with the trial and
execution of the supposed witches. Unfortunately, however, for the
reputation of Cotton Mather, Hutchinson has preserved the address of
the ministers entire : and it appears that they approved, applauded, and
stimulated the prosecutions ; and that the people of Salem and the
surrounding country were the victims of a delusion, the principal
promoters of which have, to a great degree, been sheltered from reproach by the dishonest artifice, which has now been exposed.

But, like other ambitious and grasping politicans, he was anxious to
have the support of all parties at the same time. After making court
to those who were dissatisfied with the prosecutions, he thus commends
himself to all who approved of them : —

restoring and strengthening the influence of the clerical and spiritual leaders resulted in effects which reduced that influence to a still lower point. The intimate connection of Dr. Mather and other prominent ministers with the witchcraft delusion brought a reproach upon the clergy from which they have not yet recovered.

"And why, after all my unwearied cares and pains to rescue the miserable from the lions and bears of hell which had seized them, and after all my studies to disappoint the devils in their designs to confound my neighborhood, must I be driven to the necessity of an apology? Truly, the hard representations wherewith some ill men have reviled my conduct, and the countenance which other men have given to these representations, oblige me to give mankind some account of my behavior. No Christian can (I say none but evil-workers can) criminate my visiting such of my poor flock as have at any time fallen under the terrible and sensible molestations of evil angels. Let their afflictions have been what they will, I could not have answered it unto my glorious Lord, if I had withheld my just comforts and counsels from them; and, if I have also, with some exactness, observed the methods of the invisible world, when they have thus become observable, I have been but a servant of mankind in doing so: yea, no less a person than the venerable Baxter has more than once or twice, in the most public manner, invited mankind to thank me for that service."

In other passages, he thus continues to stimulate and encourage the advocates of the prosecutions: —

"Wherefore, instead of all apish shouts and jeers at histories which have such undoubted confirmation as that no man that has breeding enough to regard the common laws of human society will offer to doubt of them, it becomes us rather to adore the goodness of God, who does not permit such things every day to befall us all, as he sometimes did permit to befall some few of our miserable neighbors.

"And it is a very glorious thing that I have now to mention: The devils have, with most horrid operations, broke in upon our neighborhood; and God has at such a rate overruled all the fury and malice of those devils, that all the afflicted have not only been delivered, but,

In addition to the designing exertions of ambitious ecclesiastics, and the benevolent and praiseworthy efforts of those whose only aim was to promote a real and thorough reformation of religion, all the passions of our nature stood ready to throw their concentrated energy into the excitement (as they are sure to do, whatever may be its character), so soon as it became sufficiently strong to encourage their action.

The whole force of popular superstition, all the

I hope, also savingly brought home unto God ; and the reputation of no one good person in the world has been damaged, but, instead thereof, the souls of many, especially of the rising generation, have been thereby awakened unto some acquaintance with religion. Our young people, who belonged unto the praying-meetings, of both sexes, apart, would ordinarily spend whole nights, by whole weeks together, in prayers and psalms upon these occasions, in which devotions the devils could get nothing but, like fools, a scourge for their own backs : and some scores of other young people, who were strangers to real piety, were now struck with the lively demonstrations of hell evidently set forth before their eyes, when they saw persons cruelly frighted, wounded and starved by devils, and scalded with burning brimstone, and yet so preserved in this tortured state, as that, at the end of one month's wretchedness, they were as able still to undergo another; so that, of these also, it might now be said, ' Behold, they pray.'   In the whole, the Devil got just nothing, but God got praises, Christ got subjects, the Holy Spirit got temples, the church got additions, and the souls of men got everlasting benefits.   I am not so vain as to say that any wisdom or virtue of mine did contribute unto this good order of things ; but I am so just as to say, I did not hinder this good."

I cannot, indeed, resist the conviction, that, notwithstanding all his attempts to appear dissatisfied, after they had become unpopular, with the occurrences in the Salem trials, he looked upon them with secret pleasure, and would have been glad to have had them repeated in Boston.

fanatical propensities of the ignorant and deluded multitude, united with the best feelings of our nature to
heighten the fury of the storm. Piety was indignant
at the supposed rebellion against the sovereignty of
God, and was roused to an extreme of agitation and
apprehension in witnessing such a daring and fierce
assault by the Devil and his adherents upon the
churches and the cause of the gospel. Virtue was
shocked at the tremendous guilt of those who were
believed to have entered the diabolical confederacy;
while public order and security stood aghast, amidst
the invisible, the supernatural, the infernal, and
apparently the irresistible attacks that were making
upon the foundations of society. In baleful combination with principles, good in themselves, thus
urging the passions into wild operation, there were
all the wicked and violent affections to which humanity is liable. Theological bitterness, personal animosities, local controversies, private feuds, long-cherished
grudges, and professional jealousies, rushed forward,
and raised their discordant voices, to swell the horrible
din; credulity rose with its monstrous and ever-ex-
panding form, on the ruins of truth, reason, and the
senses; malignity and cruelty rode triumphant through
the storm, by whose fury every mild and gentle sentiment had been shipwrecked; and revenge, smiling in
the midst of the tempest, welcomed its desolating
wrath as it dashed the mangled objects of its hate
along the shore.

The treatment of the prisoners, by the administrative and subordinate officers in charge of them, there is reason to apprehend, was more than ordinarily harsh and unfeeling. The fate of Willard prevented expressions of kindness towards them. The crime of which they were accused put them outside of the pale of human charities. All who believed them guilty looked upon them, not only with horror, but hate. To have deliberately abandoned God and heaven, the salvation of Christ and the brotherhood of man, was regarded as detestable, execrable, and utterly and for ever damnable. This was the universal feeling at the time when the fanaticism was at its height; or, if there were any dissenters, they dared not show themselves. What the poor innocent sufferers experienced of cruelty, wrong, and outrage from this cause, it is impossible for words to tell. It left them in prison to neglect, ignominious ill-treatment, and abusive language from the menials having charge of them; it made their trials a brutal mockery; it made the pathway to the gallows a series of insults from an exasperated mob. If dear relatives or faithful friends kept near them, they did it at the peril of their lives, and were forbidden to utter the sentiments with which their hearts were breaking. There was no sympathy for those who died, or for those who mourned.

It may seem strange to us, at this distance of time, and with the intelligence prevalent in this age, that persons of such known, established, and eminent reputation as many of those whose cases have been particularly noticed, could possibly have been imagined guilty of the crime imputed to them. The question arises in every mind, Why did not their characters save them from conviction, and even from suspicion ? The answer is to be found in the peculiar views then entertained of the power and agency of Satan. It was believed that it would be one of the signs of his coming to destroy the Church of Christ, that some of the " elect" would be seduced into his service, — that he would drag captive in his chains, and pervert into Instruments to further his wicked cause, many who stood among the highest in the confidence of Christians. This belief made them more vehement in their proceedings against ministers, church-members, and persons of good repute, who were proved, by the overwhelming evidence of the " afflicted children " and the confessing witches, to have made a compact with the Devil. There is reason to fear that Mr. Burroughs, and all accused persons of the highest reputation before for piety and worth, especially all who had been professors of religion and accredited church-members, suffered more than others from the severity of the judges and executive officers of the law, and from the rage and hatred of the people. It was indeed necessary, in order to keep up the delusion and maintain the authority of the prosecutions, to break down the influence of those among the accused and the sufferers who had stood the highest, and bore themselves the best through the fiery ordeal of the examinations, trials, and executions.

It is indeed a very remarkable fact, which has
justly been enlarged upon by several who have had
their attention turned to this subject, that, of the
whole number that suffered, none, in the final scene,
lost their fortitude for a moment. Many were quite
aged; a majority, women, of whom some, brought up
in delicacy, were wholly unused to rough treatment
or physical suffering. They must have undergone
the most dreadful hardships, suddenly snatched from
their families and homes; exposed to a torrent of
false accusations imputing to them the most odious,
shameful, and devilish crimes; made objects of the
abhorrence of their neighbors, and, through the notoriety of the affair, of the world; carried to and fro,
over rugged roads, from jail to jail, too often by unfeeling sub-officials; immured in crowded, filthy, and
noisome prisons; heavily loaded with chains, in dun-
geons; left to endure insufficient attention to necessary personal wants, often with inadequate food and
clothing; all expressions of sympathy for them withheld and forbidden, — those who ought to have been
their comforters denouncing them in the most awful
language, and consigning them to the doom of excommunication from the church on earth and from
the hope of heaven. Surely, there have been few
cases in the dark and mournful annals of human
suffering and wrong, few instances of "man's inhumanity to man," to be compared with what the victims of this tragedy endured. Their bearing through
the whole, from the arrest to the scaffold, reflects

credit upon our common nature. The fact that Wardwell lost his firmness, for a time, ought not to exclude his name from the honored list. Its claim to be enrolled on it was nobly retrieved by his recantation, and his manly death.

There is one consideration that imparts a higher character to the deportment of these persons than almost any of the tests to which the firmness of the mind of man has ever been exposed. There was nothing outside of the mind to hold it up, but every thing to bear it down. All that they had in this world, all on which they could rest a hope for the next, was the consciousness of their innocence. Their fidelity to this sense of innocence — for a lie would have saved them — their unfaltering allegiance to this consciousness; the preservation of a calm, steadfast, serene mind; their faith and their prayers, rising above the maledictions of a maniac mob, in devotion to God and forgiveness to men, and, as in the case of Martha Corey and George Burroughs, in clear and collected expressions, — this was truly sublime. It was appreciated, at the time, by many a heart melted back to its humanity; and paved the way for the deliverance of the world, we trust for ever, from all such delusions, horrors, and spectacles. The sufferers in 1692 deserve to be held in grateful remembrance for having illustrated the dignity of which our nature is capable; for having shown that integrity of conscience is an armor which protects the peace of the soul against all the powers that can assail it; and for having given an example, that will be seen of all and in all times, of a courage, constancy, and faithfulness of which all are capable, and which can give the victory over infirmities of age, weaknesses and pains of body, and the most appalling combination of outrages to the mind and heart that can be accumulated by the violence and the wrath of man. Superstition and ignorance consigned their names to obloquy, and shrouded them in darkness. But the day has dawned; the shadows are passing away; truth has risen; the reign of superstition is over; and justice will be done to all who have been true to themselves, and stood fast to the integrity of their souls, even to the death.

The place selected for the executions is worthy of notice. It was at a considerable distance from the jail, and could be reached only by a circuitous and difficult route. It is a fatiguing enterprise to get at it now, although many passages that approach it from some directions have since been opened. But it was a point where the spectacle would be witnessed by the whole surrounding country far and near, being on the brow of the highest eminence in the vicinity of the town. As it was believed by the people generally that they were engaged in a great battle with Satan, one of whose titles was "the Prince of the Power of the Air," perhaps they chose that spot to execute his confederates, because, in going to that high point, they were flaunting him in his face, celebrating their triumph over him in his own realm. There is no contemporaneous nor immediately subsequent record, that the executions took place on the spot assigned by tradition; but that tradition has been uniform and continuous, and appears to be verified by a singular item of evidence that has recently come to light. A letter written by the late venerable Dr. Holyoke to a friend at a distance, dated Salem, Nov. 25, 1791, has found its way back to the possession of one of his grand-daughters, which contains the following passage: " In the last month, there died a man in this town, by the name of John Symonds, aged a hundred years lacking about six months, having been born in the famous '92. He has told me that his nurse had often told him, that, while she was attending his mother at the time she lay in with him, she saw, from the chamber windows, those unhappy people hanging on Gallows' Hill, who were executed for witches by the delusion of the times." John Symonds lived and died near the southern end of Beverly Bridge, on the south side of what is now Bridge Street. He was buried from his house, and Dr. Bentley made the funeral prayer, in which he is said to have used this language : " O God ! the man who with his own hands felled the trees, and hewed the timbers, and erected the house in which we are now assembled, was the ancestor of him whose re-mains we are about to inter." It is inferrible from this that Symonds was born in the house from which he was buried. Gallows Hill, now " Witch Hill " is in full view from that spot, and would be from the chamber windows of a house there, at any time, even in the season when intervening trees were in their

fullest foliage, while no other point in that direction
would be discernible.　From the only other locality
of persons of the name of Symonds, at that time,
in North Fields near the North Bridge, Witch Hill
is also visible, and the only point in that direction
that then would have been.

"Witch Hill" is a part of an elevated ledge of
rock on the western side of the city of Salem, broken
at intervals; beginning at Legg's Hill, and trending
northerly.　The turnpike from Boston enters Salem
through one of the gaps in this ridge, which has been
widened, deepened, and graded.　North of the turnpike, it rises abruptly to a considerable elevation, called
"Norman's Rocks."　At a distance of between three
and four hundred feet, it sinks again, making a wide
and deep gulley; and then, about a third of a mile
from the turnpike, it re-appears, in a precipitous and,
at its extremity, inaccessible cliff, of the height of
fifty or sixty feet.　Its southern and western aspect,
as seen from the rough land north of the turnpike, is
given in the headpiece of the Third Part, at the beginning of this volume.　Its sombre and desolate appearance admits of little variety of delineation.　It is
mostly a bare and naked ledge,　At the top of this
cliff, on the southern brow of the eminence, the executions are supposed to have taken place.　The out-
line rises a little towards the north, but soon begins to
fall off to the general level of the country.　From that
direction only can the spot be easily reached.　It is
hard to climb the western side, impossible to clamber

up the southern face. Settlement creeps down from
the north, and has partially ascended the eastern ac-
clivity, but can never reach the brink. Scattered
patches of soil are too thin to tempt cultivation, and
the rock is too craggy and steep to allow occupation.
An active and flourishing manufacturing industry
crowds up to its base ; but a considerable surface at
the top will for ever remain an open space. It is, as
it were, a platform raised high in air.

.A magnificent panorama of ocean, island, headland,
bay, river, town, field, and forest spreads out and
around to view. On a clear summer day, the picture
can scarcely be surpassed. Facing the sun and the
sea, and the evidences of the love and bounty of
Providence shining over the landscape, the last look
of earth must have suggested to the sufferers a wide
contrast between the mercy of the Creator and the
wrath of his creatures. They beheld the face of the
blessed God shining upon them in his works, and they
passed with renewed and assured faith into his more
immediate presence. The elevated rock, uplifted by
the divine hand, will stand while the world stands,
in bold relief, and can never be obscured by the
encroachments of society or the structures of art, —
a fitting memorial of their constancy.

When, in some coming day, a sense of justice, ap-
preciation of moral firmness, sympathy for suffering
innocence, the diffusion of refined sensibility, a dis-
criminating discernment of what is really worthy of
commemoration among men, a rectified taste, a gen-

erous public spirit, and gratitude for the light that surrounds and protects us against error, folly, and fanaticism, shall demand the rearing of a suitable monument to the memory of those who in 1692 preferred death to a falsehood, the pedestal for the lofty column will be found ready, reared by the Creator on a foundation that can never be shaken while the globe endures, or worn away by the elements, man, or time — the brow of Witch Hill. On no other spot could such a tribute be more worthily bestowed, or more conspicuously displayed.

The effects of the delusion upon the country at large were very disastrous. It cast its shadows over a broad surface, and they darkened the condition of generations. The material interests of the people long felt its blight. Breaking out at the opening of the season, it interrupted the planting and cultivating of the grounds. It struck an entire summer out of one year, and broke in upon another. The fields were neglected; fences, roads, barns, and even the meeting-house, went into disrepair. Burdens were accumulated upon the already over-taxed resources of the people. An actual scarcity of provisions, amounting almost to a famine, continued for some time to press upon families. Farms were brought under mortgage or sacrificed, and large numbers of the people were dispersed. One locality in the village, which was the scene of this wild and tragic fanaticism, bears to this day the marks of the blight then brought upon it. Although in the centre of a town exceeding almost

all others in its agricultural development and thrift,
— every acre elsewhere showing the touch of modern
improvement and culture, — the " old meeting-house
road," from the crossing of the Essex Railroad to the
point where it meets the road leading north from Tap-
leyville, has to-day a singular appearance of abandonment. The Surveyor of Highways ignores it. The
old, gray, moss-covered stone walls are dilapidated,
and thrown out of line. Not a house is on either
of its borders, and no gate opens or path leads to
any. Neglect and desertion brood over the contiguous
grounds. Indeed, there is but one house standing
directly on the roadside until you reach the vicinity of
the site of the old meeting-house; and that is owned
and occupied by a family that bear the name and are
the direct descendants of Rebecca Nurse. On both
sides there are the remains of cellars, which declare
that once it was lined by a considerable population.
Along this road crowds thronged in 1692, for weeks
and months, to witness the examinations.

The ruinous results were not confined to the village,
but extended more or less over the country generally.
Excitement, wrought up to consternation, spread everywhere. People left their business and families, and
came from distant points, to gratify their curiosity,
and enable themselves to form a judgment of the character of the phenomena here exhibited. Strangers
from all parts swelled the concourse, gathered to
behold the sufferings of " the afflicted " as manifested
at the examinations; and flocked to the surrounding

eminences and the grounds immediately in front of Witch Hill, to catch a view of the convicts as they approached the place selected for their execution, offered their dying prayers, and hung suspended high in air. Such scenes always draw together great multitudes. None have possessed a deeper, stronger, or stranger attraction; and never has the dread spectacle been held out to view over a wider area, or from so conspicuous a spot. The assembling of such multitudes so often, for such a length of time, and from such remote quarters, must have been accompanied and followed by wasteful, and in all respects deleterious, effects. The continuous or frequently repeated sessions of the magistrates, grand jury, and jury of trials; and the attendance of witnesses summoned from other towns, or brought from beyond the jurisdiction of the Province, and of families and parties interested specially in the proceedings, — must have occasioned an extensive and protracted interruption of the necessary industrial pursuits of society, and heavily increased the public burdens.

The destruction dealt upon particular families extended to so many as to constitute in the aggregate a vast, wide-spread calamity.*

* The following is a statement of the loss inflicted upon the estate of George Jacobs, Sr. The property of the son was utterly destroyed.

" *An Account of what was seized and taken away from my Father's Estate, George Jacobs, Sr., late of Salem, deceased, by Sheriff Corwin and his Assistants in the year* 1692.

" When my said father was executed, and I was forced to fly out of the country, to my great damage and distress of my family, my wife and

The facts that belong to the story of the witchcraft delusion of 1692, or that may in any way explain or illustrate it, so far as they can be gathered from the imperfect and scattered records and papers that have come down to us, have now been laid before you. But there are one or two inquiries that force themselves upon thoughtful minds, which demand consideration before we close the subject.

daughter imprisoned, — viz , my wife eleven months, and my daughter seven months in prison, — it cost them twelve pounds money to the officers, besides other charges.

Five cows, fair large cattle, £3 per cow	£15	00	0
Eight loads of English hay taken out of the barn, 35s. per load .	14	0	0
A parcel of apples that made 24 barrels cider to halves; viz., 12 barrels cider, 8s. per barrel	4	16	0
Sixty bushels of Indian corn, 2s. 6d. per bushel	7	10	0
A mare	2	0	0
Two good feather beds, and furniture, rugs, blankets, sheets, bolsters and pillows	10	0	0
Two brass kettles, cost	6	0	0
Money, 12s.; a large gold thumb ring, 20s.	1	12	0
Five swine	3	15	0
A quantity of pewter which I cannot exactly know the worth, perhaps	3	0	0
	67	13	0
Besides abundance of small things, meat in the house, fowls, chairs, and other things took clear away . . . . . above	12	0	0
	79	13	0

" GEORGE JACOBS."

When Edward Bishop and his wife Sarah were arrested, household goods which were valued by the sheriff himself at ten pounds, — he refusing that sum for their restitution, — six cows, twenty-four swine, forty-six sheep, were taken from his farm. The imprisonment of himself and wife (prior to their escape) aggregated thirty-seven weeks. Ten shillings a week for board, and other charges and prison fees

What are we to think of those persons who commenced and continued the accusations,—the "afflicted children" and their associates?

In some instances and to some extent, the steps
they took and the testimony they bore may be explained by referring to the mysterious energies of the
imagination, the power of enthusiasm, the influence
of sympathy, and the general prevalence of credulity,

amounting to five pounds, were assessed upon his estate, and taken by
distraint. A family of twelve children was left without any to direct
or care for them, and the product of the farm for that year wholly
cut off.

There were taken from the estate of Samuel Wardwell, who was
executed, five cows, a heifer and yearling, a horse, nine hogs, eight
loads of hay, six acres of standing corn, and a set of carpenters' tools.
From the estate of Dorcas Hoar, a widow, there were taken two
cows, an ox and mare, four pigs, bed, bed-curtains and bedding, and
other household stuff.

Persons apprehended were made to pay all charges of every kind
for their maintenance, fuel, clothes, expenses of transportation from
jail to jail, and inexorable court and prison fees. The usual fee to the
clerk of the courts was £1. 17s. 5d., sometimes more; sometimes, although very rarely, a little less. He must have received a large
amount of money in the aggregate that year. The prisoners were
charged for every paper that was drawn up. If a reprieve was obtained, there was a fee. When discharged, there was a fee. The
expenses of the executions, even hangmen's fees, were levied on the
families of the sufferers. Abraham Foster, whose mother died in
prison, to get her body for burial, had to pay £2. 10s.

When the value of money at that time is considered, and we bear
in mind that most of the persons apprehended were farmers, who
have but little cash on hand, and that these charges were levied on
their stock, crops, and furniture in their absence, and in the unrestrained exercise of arbitrary will, by the sheriff or constables, we
can judge how utterly ruinous the operation must have been.

ignorance, superstition, and fanaticism at the time; and it is not probable, that, when they began, they had any idea of the tremendous length to which they were finally led on.

It was perhaps their original design to gratify a love of notoriety or of mischief by creating a sensation and excitement in their neighborhood, or, at the worst, to wreak their vengeance upon one or two individuals who had offended them. They soon, however, became intoxicated by the terrible success of their imposture, and were swept along by the frenzy they had occasioned. It would be much more congenial with our feelings to believe, that these misguided and wretched young persons early in the proceedings became themselves victims of the delusion into which they plunged every one else. But we are forbidden to form this charitable judgment by the manifestations of art and contrivance, of deliberate cunning and cool malice, they exhibited to the end. Once or twice they were caught in their own snare; and nothing but the blindness of the bewildered community saved them from disgraceful exposure and well-deserved punishment. They appeared as the prosecutors of every poor creature that was tried, and seemed ready to bear testimony against any one upon whom suspicion might happen to fall. It is dreadful to reflect upon the enormity of their wickedness, if they were conscious of imposture throughout. It seems to transcend the capabilities of human crime. There is, perhaps, a slumbering element in the heart of man, that sleeps for ever in the bosom of the innocent and good, and requires the perpetration of a great sin to wake it into action, but which, when once aroused, impels the transgressor onward with increasing momentum, as the descending ball is accelerated in its course. It may be that crime begets an appetite for crime, which, like all other appetites, is not quieted but inflamed by gratification.

Their precise moral condition, the degree of guilt to be ascribed, and the sentence to be passed upon them, can only be determined by a considerate review of all the circumstances and influences around them.

For a period embracing about two months, they had been in the habit of meeting together, and spending the long winter evenings, at Mr. Parris's house, practising the arts of fortune-telling, jugglery, and magic. What they had heard in the traditions and fables of a credulous and superstitious age, — stories handed down in the interior settlements, circulated in companies gathered around the hearths of farmhouses, indulging the excitements of terrified imaginations; filling each other's minds with wondrous tales of second-sight, ghosts and spirits from the unseen world, together with what the West-Indian or South-American slaves could add, — was for a long time the food of their fancies. They experimented continually upon what was the spiritualism of their day, and grew familiar with the imagery and the exhibitions of the marvellous. The prevalent notions concerning witchcraft operations and spectral manifestations came into full effect among them. Living in the constant contemplation of such things, their minds became inflamed and bewildered ; and, at the same time, they grew expert in practising and exhibiting the forms of pretended supernaturalism, the conditions of diabolical distraction, and the terrors of demonology. Apparitions rose before them, revealing the secrets of the past and of the future. They beheld the present spectres of persons then bodily far distant. They declared in language, fits, dreams, or trance, the immediate operations upon themselves of the Devil, by the agency of his confederates. Their sufferings, while thus under " an evil hand," were dreadful to behold, and soon drew wondering and horror-struck crowds around them.

At this point, if Mr. Parris, the ministers, and magistrates had done their duty, the mischief might have been stopped. The girls ought to have been rebuked for their dangerous and forbidden sorceries and divinations, their meetings broken up, and all such tamperings with alleged supernaturalism and spiritualism frowned down. Instead of this, the neighboring ministers were summoned to meet at Mr. Parris's house to witness the extraordinary doings of the girls, and all they did was to indorse, and pray over, them. Countenance was thus given to their pretensions, and the public confidence in the reality of their statements established. Magistrates from the town, church-members, leading people, and people of all sorts, flocked to witness the awful power of Satan, as displayed in the tortures and contortions of the "afflicted children;" who became objects of wonder, so far as their feats were regarded, and of pity in view of their agonies and convulsions.

The aspect of the evidence rather favors the supposition, that the girls originally had no design of accusing, or bringing injury upon, any one. But the ministers at Parris's house, physicians and others, began the work of destruction by pronouncing the opinion that they were bewitched. This carried with it, according to the received doctrine, a conviction that there were witches about; for the Devil could not act except through the instrumentality of beings in confederacy with him. Immediately, the girls were beset by everybody to say who it was that bewitched them. Yielding to this pressure, they first cried out upon such persons as might have been most naturally suggested to them, — Sarah Good, apparently without a regular home, and wandering with her children from house to house for shelter and relief; Sarah Osburn, a melancholy, broken-minded, bed-ridden person; and Tituba, a slave, probably of mixed African and Indian blood. At the examination of these persons, the girls were first brought before the public, and the awful power in their hands revealed to them. The success with which they acted their parts; the novelty of the scene; the ceremonials of the occasion, the magistrates in their imposing dignity and authority, the trappings of the marshal and his officers, the forms of proceeding, — all which they had never seen

before ; the notice taken of them ; the importance attached to them ; invested the affair with a strange
fascination in their eyes, and awakened a new class
of sentiments and ideas in their minds. A love
of distinction and notoriety, and the several passions
that are gratified by the expression by others of sympathy, wonder, and admiration, were brought into
play. The fact that all eyes were upon them, with
the special notice of the magistrates, and the entire
confidence with which their statements were received,
flattered and beguiled them. A fearful responsibility had been assumed, and they were irretrievably
committed to their position. While they adhered to
that position, their power was irresistible, and they
were sure of the public sympathy and of being
cherished by the public favor. If they faltered, they
would be the objects of universal execration and of the
severest penalties of law for the wrongs already done
and the falsehoods already sworn to. There was no
retracing their steps ; and their only safety was in continuing the excitement they had raised. New victims
were constantly required to prolong the delusion,
fresh fuel to keep up the conflagration ; and they
went on to cry out upon others. With the exception
of two of their number, who appear to have indulged
spite against the families in which they were servants,
there is no evidence that they were actuated by private
grievances or by animosities personal to themselves.
They were ready and sure to wreak vengeance upon
any who expressed doubts about the truth of their

testimony, or the propriety of the proceedings; but, beyond this, they were very indifferent as to whom they should accuse. They were willing, as to that matter, to follow the suggestions of others, and availed themselves of all the gossip and slander and unfriendly talk in their families that reached their ears. It was found, that a hint, with a little information as to persons, places, and circumstances, conveyed to them by those who had resentments and grudges to gratify, would be sufficient for the purpose. There is reason to fear, that there were some behind them, giving direction to the accusations, and managing the frightful machinery, all the way through. The persons who were apprehended had, to a considerable extent, been obnoxious, and subject to prejudice, in connection with quarrels and controversies related in Part I., vol. i. They were "Topsfield men," or the opponents of Bayley or of Parris, or more or less connected with some other feuds. As further proof that the girls were under the guidance of older heads, it is obvious, that there was, in the order of the proceedings, a skilful arrangement of times, sequences, and concurrents, that cannot be ascribed to them. No novelist or dramatist ever laid his plot deeper, distributed his characters more artistically, or conducted more methodically the progress of his story.

In the mean while, they were becoming every day more perfect in the performance of their parts; and their imaginative powers, nervous excitability, and flexibility and rapidity of muscular action, were kept under constant stimulus, and attaining a higher development. The effect of these things, so long continued in connection with the perpetual pretence, becoming more or less imbued with the character of belief, of their alliance and communion with spiritual beings and manifestations, may have unsettled, to some extent, their minds. Added to this, a sense of the horrid consequences of their actions, accumulating with every pang they inflicted, the innocent blood they were shedding, and the depths of ruin into which they were sinking themselves and others, not only demoralized, but to some extent, perhaps, crazed them. It is truly a marvel that their physical constitutions did not break down under the exhausting excitements, the contortions of frame, the force to which the bodily functions were subjected in trances and fits, and the strain upon all the vital energies, protracted through many months. The wonder, however, would have been greater, if the mental and moral balance had not thereby been disturbed.

Perpetual conversance with ideas of supernaturalism; daily and nightly communications, whether in the form of conscious imposture or honest delusion, with the spiritual world, continued through a great length of time, — as much at least as the exclusive contemplation of any one idea or class of ideas, — must be allowed to be unsalutary. Whatever keeps the thoughts wholly apart from the objects of real and natural life, and absorbs them in abstractions, cannot be favorable to the soundness of the faculties or the tone of the

mind.   This must especially be the effect, if the subjects thus monopolizing the attention partake of the
marvellous and mysterious.   When these things are
considered, and the external circumstances of the
occasion, the wild social excitement, the consternation,
confusion, and horror, that were all crowded and heaped
up and kept pressing upon the soul without intermission for months, the wonder is, indeed, that not
only the accusers, prosecutors, and sufferers, but the
whole people, did not lose their senses.   Never was
the great boon of life, a sound mind in a sound body,
more liable to be snatched away from all parties.   The
depositions of Ann Putnam, Sr., have a tinge of sadness ; — a melancholy, sickly mania running through
them.   Something of the kind is, perhaps, more or less
discernible in the depositions of others.

Let us, then, relieve our common nature from the
load of the imputation, that, in its normal state, it is
capable of such inconceivable wickedness, by giving to
these wretched persons the benefit of the supposition
that they were more or less deranged.   This view
renders the lesson they present more impressive and
alarming.   Sin in all cases, when considered by a
mind that surveys the whole field, is itself insanity.
In the case of these accusers, it was so great as to
prove, by its very monstrousness, that it had actually
subverted their nature and overthrown their reason.
They followed their victims to the gallows, and jeered,
scoffed, insulted them in their dying hours.   Sarah
Churchill, according to the testimony of Sarah Inger-

soll, on one occasion came to herself, and manifested the symptoms of a restored moral consciousness: but it was a temporary gleam, a lucid interval; and she passed back into darkness, continuing, as before, to revel in falsehood, and scatter destruction around her. With this single exception, there is not the slightest appearance of compunction or reflection among them. On the contrary, they seem to have been in a frivolous, sportive, gay frame of thought and spirits. There is, perhaps, in this view of their conduct and demeanor, something to justify the belief that they were really demented. The fact that a large amount of skilful art and adroit cunning was displayed by them is not inconsistent with the supposition that they had become partially insane; for such cunning and art are often associated with insanity.

The quick wit and ready expedients of the "afflicted children" are very remarkable. They were prompt with answers, if any attempted to cross-examine them, extricated themselves most ingeniously if ever brought into embarrassment, and eluded all efforts to entrap or expose them. Among the papers is a deposition, the use of which at the trials is not apparent. It does not purport to bear upon any particular case. Joseph Hutchinson was a firm-minded man, of strong common sense. He could not easily be deceived; and, although he took part in the proceedings at the beginning, soon became opposed to them. It looks as if, by close questions put to the child, Abigail Williams, on some occasion of his casually meeting her, he had tried to expose the falseness of her accusations, and that he was made to put the conversation into the shape of a deposition. It is as follows: —

"THE DEPOSITION OF JOSEPH HUTCHINSON, aged fifty-nine years, do testify as followeth: "Abigail Williams, I have heard you speak often of a book that has been offered to you. She said that there were two books: one was a short, thick book; and the other was a long book. I asked her what color the book was of. She said the books were as red as blood. I asked her if she had seen the books opened. She said she had seen it many times. I asked her if she did see any writing in the book. She said there were many lines written; and, at the end of every line, there was a seal. I asked her, who brought the book to her. She told me that it was the black man. I asked her who the black man was. She told me it was the Devil. I asked her if she was not afraid to see the Devil. She said, at the first she was, and did go from him; but now she was not afraid, but could talk with him as well as she could with me."

There is an air of ease and confidence in the answers of Abigail, which illustrates the promptness of invention and assurance of their grounds which the girls manifested on all occasions. They were never at a loss, and challenged scrutiny. Hutchinson gained no advantage, and no one else ever did, in an encounter with them.

Whatever opinion may be formed of the moral or mental condition of the "afflicted children," as to their sanity and responsibility, there can be no doubt that they were great actors. In mere jugglery and

sleight of hand, they bear no mean comparison with
the workers of wonders, in that line, of our own day.
Long practice had given them complete control over
their countenances, intonations of voice, and the entire
muscular and nervous organization of their bodies; so
that they could at will, and on the instant, go into fits
and convulsions, swoon and fall to the floor, put their
frames into strange contortions, bring the blood to the
face, and send it back again. They could be deadly
pale at one moment, at the next flushed; their hands
would be clenched and held together as with a vice;
their limbs stiff and rigid or wholly relaxed; their
teeth would be set; they would go through the par-
oxysms of choking and strangulation, and gasp for
breath, bringing froth and blood from the mouth; they
would utter all sorts of screams in unearthly tones;
their eyes remain fixed, sometimes bereft of all light
and expression, cold and stony, and sometimes kindled
into flames of passion; they would pass into the state
of somnambulism, without aim or conscious direction
in their movements, looking at some point, where was
no apparent object of vision, with a wild, unmeaning
glare.   There are some indications that they had
acquired the art of ventriloquism; or they so wrought
upon the imaginations of the beholders, that the sounds
of the motions and voices of invisible beings were believed to be heard. They would start, tremble, and
be pallid before apparitions, seen, of course, only by
themselves; but their acting was so perfect that all
present thought they saw them too.   They would

address and hold colloquy with spectres and ghosts;
and the responses of the unseen beings would be audible to the fancy of the bewildered crowd.   They would
follow with their eyes the airy visions, so that others
imagined they also beheld them.   This was surely a
high dramatic achievement.   Their representations
of pain, and every form and all the signs and marks of
bodily suffering, — as in the case of Ann Putnam's
arm, and the indentations of teeth on the flesh in many
instances, — utterly deceived everybody; and there
were men present who could not easily have been imposed upon.   The Attorney-general was a barrister fresh
from Inns of Court in London.   Deodat Lawson had
seen something of the world; so had Joseph Herrick.
Joseph Hutchinson was a sharp, stern, and sceptical
observer.   John Putnam was a man of great practical
force and discrimination; so was his brother Nathaniel,
and others of the village.   Besides, there were many
from Boston and elsewhere competent to detect a trick;
but none could discover any imposture in the girls.
Sarah Nurse swore that she saw Goody Bibber cheat in
the matter of the pins; but Bibber did not belong to the
·village, and was a bungling interloper.   The accusing
girls showed extraordinary skill, ingenuity, and fancy
in inventing the stories to which they testified, and
seemed to have been familiar with the imagery which
belonged to the literature of demonology.   This has
led some to suppose that they must have had access to
books treating the subject.   Our fathers abhorred, with
a perfect hatred, all theatrical exhibitions.   It would

have filled them with horror to propose going to a play. But unwittingly, week after week, month in and month out, ministers, deacons, brethren, and sisters of the church rushed to Nathaniel Ingersoll's, to the village and town meeting-houses, and to Thomas Beadle's Globe Tavern, and gazed with wonder, awe, and admiration upon acting such as has seldom been surpassed on the boards of any theatre, high or low, ancient or modern.

There is another aspect that perplexes and confounds the judgments of all who read the story. It is this: As it is at present the universal opinion that the whole of this witchcraft transaction was a delusion, having no foundation whatever but in the imaginations and passions; and as it is now certain, that all the accused, both the condemned and the pardoned, were entirely innocent, — how can it be explained that so many were led to confess themselves guilty? The answer to this question is to be found in those general principles which have led the wisest legislators and jurists to the conclusion, that, although on their face and at first thought, they appear to be the very best kind of evidence, yet, maturely considered, confessions made under the hope of a benefit, and sometime even without the impulses of such a hope, are to be received with great caution and wariness. Here were fifty-five persons, who declared themselves guilty of a capital, nay, a diabolical crime, of which we know they were innocent. It is probable that the motive of self-preservation influenced most of them. An awful death was in immediate prospect. There was no escape from the wiles of the accusers. The delusion had obtained full possession of the people, the jury, and the Court. By acknowledging a compact with Satan, they could in a moment secure their lives and liberty. It was a position which only the firmest minds could safely occupy. The principles and the prowess of ordinary characters could not withstand the temptation and the pressure. They yielded, and were saved from an impending and terrible death.

As these confessions had a decisive effect in precipitating the public mind into the depths of its delusion, gave a fatal power to the accusers, and carried the proceedings to the horrible extremities which have concentrated upon them the attention of the world, they assume an importance in the history of the affair that demands a full and thorough exposition. At the examination of Ann Foster, at Salem Village, on the 15th of July, 1692, the following confession was, " after a while," extorted from her. It was undoubtedly the result of the overwhelming effect of the horrors of her condition upon a distressed and half-crazed mind. It shows the staple materials of which confessions were made, and the forms of absurd superstition with which the imaginations of people were then filled : —

The Devil appeared to her in the shape of a bird at several times, — such a bird as she never saw the like before ; and she had had this gift (viz., of striking the afflicted down with her eye) ever since. Being asked why she thought that bird was the Devil, she answered, because he came

white and vanished away black; and that the Devil told
her she should have this gift, and that she must believe him,
and told her she should have prosperity : and she said that
he had appeared to her three times, and always as a bird,
and the last time about half a year since, and sat upon
a table, — had two legs and great eyes, and that it was the
second time of his appearance that he promised her prosperity.   She further stated, that it was Goody Carrier
that made her a witch.   She told her, that, if she would not
be a witch, the Devil would tear her to pieces, and carry
her away, — at which time she promised to serve the Devil;
that she was at the meeting of the witches at Salem Village;
that Goody Carrier came, and told her of the meeting, and
would have her go : so they got upon sticks, and went said
journey, and, being there, did see Mr. Burroughs, the minister, who spake to them all; that there were then twenty-
five persons met together; that she tied a knot in a rag,
and threw it into the fire to hurt Timothy Swan, and that
she did hurt the rest that complained of her by squeezing
puppets like them, and so almost choked them; that she
and Martha Carrier did both ride on a stick or pole when
they went to the witch-meeting at Salem Village, and that
the stick broke as they were carried in the air above the
tops of the trees, and they fell : but she did hang fast about
the neck of Goody Carrier, and they were presently at the
village; that she had heard some of the witches say that
there were three hundred and five in the whole country,
and that they would ruin that place, the village; that there
were also present at that meeting two men besides Mr.
Burroughs, the minister, and one of them had gray hair;
and that the discourse among the witches at the meeting
in Salem Village was, that they would afflict there to set
up the Devil's kingdom.

The confession of which the foregoing is the substance appears to have been drawn out at four several
examinations on different days, during which she was
induced by the influences around her to make her
testimony more and more extravagant at each successive examination. Her daughter, Mary Lacy, called
Goody Lacy, was brought up on the charge of witchcraft at the same time ; and, upon finding the mother
confessing, she saw that her only safety was in confessing also.   When confronted, the daughter cried
out to the mother, " We have forsaken Jesus Christ,
and the Devil hath got hold of us.   How shall we
get clear of this Evil One ? "   She proceeded to say
that she had accompanied her mother and Goody
Carrier, all three riding together on the pole, to
Salem Village.   She then made the following statement : " About three or four years ago, she saw Mistress
Bradbury, Goody Howe, and Goody Nurse baptized by
the old Serpent at Newbury Falls ; that he dipped
their heads in the water, and then said they were his,
and he had power over them ; that there were six baptized at that time, who were some of the chief or higher
powers, and that there might be near about a hundred in company at that time."   It being asked her
" after what manner she went to Newbury Falls," she
answered, " the Devil carried her in his arms."
She said, that, " if she did take a rag, and roll it up
together, and imagine it to represent such and such
a person, then that, whatsoever she did to that rag so
rolled up, the person represented thereby would be

in like manner afflicted." Her daughter, also named Mary Lacy, followed the example of her mother and grandmother, and made confession.

An examination of the confessions shows, that, when accused persons made up their minds to confess, they saw, that, to make their safety secure, it was necessary to go the whole length of the popular superstition and fanaticism. In many instances, they appear to have fabricated their stories with much ingenuity and tact, making them tally with the statements of tho accusers, adding points and items that gave an air of truthfulness, and falling in with current notions and fancies. They were undoubtedly under training by the girls, and were provided with the materials of their testimony. Their depositions are valuable, inasmuch as they enable us to collect about the whole of the notions then prevalent on the subject. If, in delivering their evidences, any prompting was needed, the accusers were at their elbows, and helped them along in their stories. If, in any particular, they were in danger of contradicting themselves or others, they were checked or diverted. In one case, a confessing witch was damaging her own testimony, whereupon one of the afflicted cried out that she saw the shapes or apparitions of other witches interfering with her utterance. The witness took the hint, pretended to have lost the power of expressing herself, and was removed from the stand.

In some cases, the confessing witches showed great adroitness, and knowledge of human nature. When a leading minister was visiting them in the prison, one of them cried out as he passed her cell, calling him by name, " Oh! I remember a text you preached on in England, twenty years since, from these words : ' Your sin will find you out ; ' for I find it to be true in my own case." This skilful compliment, showing the power of his preaching making an impression which time could not efface, was no doubt flattering to the good man, and secured for her his favorable influence.

Justice requires that their own explanation of the influences which led them to confess should not be withheld.

The following declaration of six women belonging to Andover is accompanied by a paper signed by more than fifty of the most respectable inhabitants of that town, testifying to their good character, in which it is said that " by their sober, godly, and exemplary conversation, they have obtained a good report in the place, where they have been well esteemed and approved in the church of which they are members : " —

" We whose names are underwritten, inhabitants of Andover, when as that horrible and tremendous judgment, beginning at Salem Village, in the year 1692, by some called witchcraft, first breaking forth at Mr. Parris's house, several young persons, being seemingly afflicted, did accuse several persons for afflicting them ; and many there believing it so to be, we being informed, that, if a person was sick, the afflicted person could tell what or who was the cause of that sickness : John Ballard of Andover, his wife being

sick at the same time, he, either from himself, or by the advice of others, fetched two of the persons called the afflicted
persons from Salem Village to Andover, which was the beginning of that dreadful calamity that befell us in Andover,
believing the said accusations to be true, sent for the said
persons to come together to the meeting-house in Andover,
the afflicted persons being there. After Mr. Barnard had
been at prayer, we were blindfolded, and our hands were
laid upon the afflicted persons, they being in their fits, and
falling into their fits at our coming into their presence, as
they said; and some led us, and laid our hands upon them;
and then they said they were well, and that we were guilty
of afflicting them. Whereupon we were all seized as prisoners, by a warrant from the justice of the peace, and forthwith
carried to Salem; and by reason of that sudden surprisal,
we knowing ourselves altogether innocent of that crime, we
were all exceedingly astonished and amazed, and conster-
nated and affrighted, even out of our reason; and our
nearest and dearest relations, seeing us in that dreadful
condition, and knowing our great danger, apprehended there
was no other way to save our lives, as the case was then
circumstanced, but by our confessing ourselves to be such
and such persons as the afflicted represented us to be, they,
out of tenderness and pity, persuaded us to confess what we
did confess. And, indeed, that confession that it is said we
made was no other than what was suggested to us by some
gentlemen, they telling us that we were witches, and they
knew it, and we knew it, which made us think that it was
so; and, our understandings, our reason, our faculties almost
gone, we were not capable of judging of our condition; as
also the hard measures they used with us rendered us incapable of making our defence, but said any thing, and

every thing which they desired, and most of what we said was but in effect a consenting to what they said. Some time after, when we were better composed, they telling us what we had confessed, we did profess that we were innocent and ignorant of such things ; and we hearing that Samuel Wardwell had renounced his confession, and was quickly after condemned and executed, some of us were told we were going after Wardwell.

> "MARY OSGOOD.
> MARY TYLER.
> DELIVERANCE DANE.
> ABIGAIL BARKER.
> SARAH WILSON.
> HANNAH TYLER."

The means employed, and the influences brought to bear upon persons accused, were, in many cases, such as wholly to overpower them, and to relieve their confessions, to a great extent, of a criminal character. They were scarcely responsible moral agents. In the month of October, Increase Mather came to Salem, to confer with the confessing witches in prison. The result of his examinations is preserved in a document of which he is supposed to have been the author. The following extracts afford some explanation of the whole subject : —

"Goodwife Tyler did say, that, when she was first apprehended, she had no fears upon her, and did think that nothing could have made her confess against herself. But since, she had found, to her great grief, that she had wronged the truth, and falsely accused herself. She said that, when she was brought to Salem, her brother Bridges rode with her ; and that, all along the way from Andover to Salem, her brother kept telling her that she must needs be a witch, since the afflicted accused her, and at her touch were raised out of their fits, and urging her to confess herself a witch. She as constantly told him that she was no witch, that she knew nothing of witchcraft, and begged him not to urge her to confess. However, when she came to Salem, she was carried to a room, where her brother on one side, and Mr. John Emerson on the other side, did tell her that she was certainly a witch, and that she saw the Devil before her eyes at that time (and, accordingly, the said Emerson would attempt with his hand to beat him away from her eyes); and they so urged her to confess, that she wished herself in any dungeon, rather than be so treated. Mr. Emerson told her, once and again, ' Well, I see you will not confess! Well, I will now leave you; and then you are undone, body and soul, for ever.' Her brother urged her to confess, and told her that, in so doing, she could not lie: to which she answered, ' Good brother, do not say so; for I shall lie if I confess, and then who shall answer unto God for my lie?' He still asserted it, and said that God would not suffer so many good men to be in such an error about it, and that she would be hanged if she did not confess; and continued so long and so violently to urge and press her to confess, that she thought, verily, that her life would have gone from her, and became so terrified in her mind that she owned, at length, almost any thing that they propounded to her; that she had wronged her conscience in so doing; she was guilty of a great sin in belying of herself, and desired to mourn for it so long as she lived. This she said, and a great deal more of the like nature; and all with such affection, sorrow, relenting, grief, and mourning, as that it exceeds any pen to describe and express the same."

" Goodwife Wilson said that she was in the dark as to some things in her confession. Yet she asserted that, knowingly, she never had familiarity with the Devil; that, knowingly, she never consented to the afflicting of any person, &c. However, she said that truly she was in the dark as to the matter of her being a witch. And being asked how she was in the dark, she replied, that the afflicted persons crying out of her as afflicting them made her fearful of herself; and that was all that made her say that she was in the dark."

" Goodwife Bridges said that she had confessed against herself things which were all utterly false; and that she was brought to her confession by being told that she certainly was a witch, and so made to believe it, — though she had no other grounds so to believe."

Some explanation of the details which those, prevailed upon to confess, put into their testimony, and which seemed, at the time, to establish and demonstrate the truth of their statements, is afforded by what Mary Osgood is reported, by Increase Mather, to have said to him on this occasion : —

" Being asked why she prefixed a time, and spake of her being baptized, &c., about twelve years since, she replied and said, that, when she had owned the thing, they asked the time, to which she answered that she knew not the time. But, being told that she did know the time, and must tell the time, and the like, she considered that about twelve years before (when she had her last child) she had a fit of sickness, and was melancholy; and so thought that that time might be as proper a time to mention as any, and accordingly did prefix the said time. Being asked about

the cat, in the shape of which she had confessed that the
Devil had appeared to her, &c., she replied, that, being told
that the Devil had appeared to her, and must needs appear
to her, &c. (she being a witch), she at length did own that
the Devil had appeared to her; and, being pressed to say in
what creature's shape he appeared, she at length did say
that it was in the shape of a cat. Remembering that, some
time before her being apprehended, as she went out at her
door, she saw a cat, &c.; not as though she any whit suspected the said cat to be the Devil, in the day of it, but
because some creature she must mention, and this came
into her mind at that time."

This poor woman, as well as several others, besides
Goodwife Tyler, who denied and renounced their confessions, manifested, as Dr. Mather affirms, the utmost
horror and anguish at the thought that they could
have been so wicked as to have belied themselves, and
brought injury upon others by so doing. They " be-
wailed and lamented their accusing of others, about
whom they never knew any evil" in their lives. They
proved the sincerity of their repentance by abandoning
and denouncing their confessions, and thus offering
their lives as a sacrifice to atone for their falsehood.
They were then awaiting their trial; and there seemed
no escape from the awful fate which had befallen all
persons brought to trial before, and who had not
confessed or had withdrawn their confession. Fortunately for them, the Court did not meet again in 1692;
and they were acquitted at the regular session, in the
January following.

In one of Calef's tracts, he sums up his views, on the subject of the confessions, as follows : —

" Besides the powerful argument of life (and freedom from hardships, not only promised, but also performed to all that owned their guilt), there are numerous instances of the tedious examinations before private persons, many hours together ; they all that time urging them to confess (and taking turns to persuade them), till the accused were wearied out by being forced to stand so long, or for want of sleep, &c., and so brought to give assent to what they said ; they asking them, ' Were you at such a witch meeting ?' or, ' Have you signed the Devil's book ?' &c. Upon their replying ' Yes,' the whole was drawn into form, as their confession."

This accounts for the similarity of construction and substance of the confessions generally.

Calef remarks :—

" But that which did mightily further such confessions was their nearest relations urging them to it. These, seeing no other way òf escape for them, thought it the best advice that could be given ; hence it was, that the husbands of some, by counsel, often urging, and utmost earnestness, and children upon their knees intreating, have at length prevailed with them to say they were guilty."

One of the most painful things in the whole affair was, that the absolute conviction of the guilt of the persons accused, pervading the community, took full effect upon the minds of many relatives and friends. They did not consider it as a matter of the least possible doubt. They therefore looked upon it as wicked obstinacy not to confess, and, in this sense, an additional and most conclusive evidence of a mind alienated from truth and wholly given over to Satan. This turned natural love and previous friendships into resentment, indignation, and abhorrence, which left the unhappy prisoners in a condition where only the most wonderful clearness of conviction and strength of character could hold them up. And, in many cases where they yielded, it was not from unworthy fear, or for self-preservation, but because their judgment was overthrown, and their minds in complete subjection and prostration.

There can, indeed, hardly be a doubt, that, in some instances, the confessing persons really believed themselves guilty. To explain this, we must look into the secret chambers of the human soul; we must read the history of the imagination, and consider its power over the understanding. We must transport ourselves to the dungeon, and think of its dark and awful walls, its dreary hours, its tedious loneliness, its heavy and benumbing fetters and chains, its scanty fare, and all its dismal and painful circumstances. We must reflect upon their influence over a terrified and agitated, an injured and broken spirit. We must think of the situation of the poor prisoner, cut off from hope; hearing from all quarters, and at all times, morning, noon, and night, that there is no doubt of his guilt; surrounded and overwhelmed by accusations and evidence, gradually but insensibly mingling and confounding the visions and vagaries of his troubled dreams with the reveries of his waking hours, until his reason becomes obscured, his recollections are thrown into derangement, his mind loses the power of distinguishing between what is perpetually told him by others and what belongs to the suggestions of his own memory: his imagination at last gains complete ascendency over his other faculties, and he believes and declares himself guilty of crimes of which he is as innocent as the child unborn. The history of the transaction we have been considering, affords a clear illustration of the truth and reasonableness of this explanation.

The facility with which persons can be persuaded, by perpetually assailing them with accusations of the truth of a charge, in reality not true, even when it is made against themselves, has been frequently noticed. Addison, in one of the numbers of his "Spectator," speaks of it in connection with our present subject: "When an old woman," says he, "begins to dote, and grow chargeable to a parish, she is generally turned into a witch, and fills the whole country with extravagant fancies, imaginary distempers, and terrifying dreams. In the mean time, the poor wretch that is the innocent occasion of so many evils begins to be frighted at herself, and sometimes confesses secret commerces and familiarities that her imagination forms in a delirious old age. This frequently cuts off charity from the greatest objects of compassion, and inspires people with a malevolence towards those poor, decrepit parts of our species in whom human nature is defaced by infirmity and dotage."

This passage is important, in addition to the bearing it has upon the point we have been considering, as describing the state of opinion and feeling in England twenty years after the folly had been exploded here. In another number of the same series of essays, he bears evidence, that the superstitions which here came to a head in 1692 had long been prevalent in the mother-country : " Our forefathers looked upon nature with more reverence and horror before the world was enlightened by learning and philosophy, and loved to astonish themselves with the apprehensions of witchcraft, prodigies, charms, and enchantments. There was not a village in England that had not a ghost in it; the churchyards were all haunted; every large common had a circle of fairies belonging to it; and there was scarce a shepherd to be met with who had not seen a spirit." These fancies still linger in the minds of some in the Old World and in the New.

After allowing for the utmost extent of prevalent superstitions, the exaggerations incident to a state of general excitement, and the fertile inventive faculties of the accusing girls, there is much in the evidence that cannot easily be accounted for. In other cases than that of Westgate, we find the symptoms of that bewildered condition of the senses and imagination not at all surprising or unusual in the experience of men staggering home in midnight hours from tavern haunts. Disturbed dreams were, it is not improbable, a fruitful source of delusion. A large part of the evidence is susceptible of explanation by the supposition, that the witnesses had confounded the visions of their sleeping, with the actual observations and occurrences of their waking hours. At the trial of Susanna Martin, it was in evidence, that one John Kembal had agreed to purchase a puppy from the prisoner, but had afterwards fallen back from his bargain, and procured a puppy from some other person, and that Martin was heard to say, " If I live, I will give him puppies enough." The circumstances seem to me to render it probable, that the following piece of evidence given by Kembal, and to which the Court attached great weight, was the result of a nightmare occasioned by his apprehension and dread of the fulfilment of the reported threat: —

" I, this deponent, coming from his intended house in the woods to Edmund Elliot's house where I dwelt, about the sunset or presently after ; and there did arise a little black cloud in the north-west, and a few drops of rain, and the wind blew pretty hard. In going between the house of John Weed and the meeting-house, this deponent came by several stumps of trees by the wayside ; and he by impulse he can give no reason of, that made him tumble over the stumps one after another, though he had his axe upon his shoulder which put him in much danger, and made him resolved to avoid the next, but could not.

" And, when he came a little below the meeting-house, there did appear a little thing like a puppy, of a darkish color. It shot between my legs forward and backward, as one that were dancing the hay.* And this deponent, being free from all fear, used all possible endeavors to cut it with his axe, but could not hurt it ; and, as he was thus laboring with his axe, the puppy gave a little jump from him, and seemed to go into the ground.

" In a little further going, there did appear a black puppy, somewhat bigger than the first, but as black as a coal to his apprehension, which came against him with such violence as its quick motions did exceed his motions of his axe, do what he could   And it flew at his belly, and away, and then at his throat and over his shoulder one way, and go off, and up at it again another way ; and with such quickness, speed, and violence did it assault him, as if it would tear out his throat or his belly. A good while, he was without fear ; but, at last, I felt my heart to fail and sink under it, that I thought my life was going out. And I recovered myself, and gave a start up, and ran to the fence, and calling upon God and naming the name Jesus Christ, and then it invisibly away. My meaning is, it ceased at once ; but this deponent made it not known to anybody, for fretting his wife." †

* Love's Labour's Lost, act v., sc. 1.

† There are several other depositions in these cases, that may perhaps be explained under the head of nightmare. The following are specimens; that, for instance, of Robert Downer, of Salisbury, who testifies and says, —

"That, several years ago, Susanna Martin, the then wife of George Martin, being brought to court for a witch, the said Downer, having some words with her, this deponent, among other things, told her he believed that she was a witch, by what was said or witnessed against her; at which she, seeming not well affected, said that a, or some, she-devil would fetch him away shortly, at which this deponent was not much moved; but at night, as he lay in his bed in his own house, alone, there came at his win-

We are all exposed to the danger of confounding the impressions left by the imagination, when, set free from all confinement, it runs wild in dreams, with the actual experiences of wakeful faculties in real life.   It is a topic worthy the consideration of writers on evidence, and of legal tribunals.   So also is the effect, upon the personal consciousness, of the continued

dow the likeness of a cat, and by and by came up to his bed, took fast hold of his throat, and lay hard upon him a considerable while, and was like to throttle him.   At length, he minded what Susanna Martin threatened him with the day before.   He strove what he could, and said, 'Avoid, thou she-devil, in the name of the Father, and the Son, and the Holy Ghost!' and then it let him go, and jumped down upon the floor, and went out at the window again."

Susanna Martin, by the boldness and severity of her language, in defending herself against the charge of witchcraft, had evidently, for a long time, rendered herself an object of dread, and seems to have disturbed the dreams of the superstitious throughout the neighborhood. For instance, Jarvis Ring, of Salisbury, made oath as follows : —

"That, about seven or eight years ago, he had been several times afflicted, in the night-time, by some body or some thing coming up upon him when he was in bed, and did sorely afflict him by lying upon him; and he could neither move nor speak while it was upon him, but sometimes made a kind of noise that folks did hear him and come up to him; and, as soon as anybody came, it would be gone.   This it did for a long time, both then and since, but he did never see anybody clearly; but one time, in the night, it came upon me as at other times, and I did then see the person of Susanna Martin, of Amesbury.   I, this deponent, did perfectly see her; and she came to this deponent, and took him by the hand, and bit him by the finger by force, and then came and lay upon him awhile, as formerly, and after a while went away.   The print of the bite is yet to be seen on the little finger of his right hand; for it was hard to heal.   He further saith, that several times he was asleep when it came; but, at that time, he was as fairly awaked as ever he was, and plainly saw her shape, and felt her teeth, as aforesaid."

Barnard Peach made oath substantially as follows : —

repetition of the same story, or of hearing it repeated by others. Instances are given in books, — perhaps can be recalled by our own individual experience or observation, — in which what was originally a delibe-

"That about six or seven years past, being in bed on a Lord's-day night, he heard a scrambling at the window, and saw Susanna Martin come in at the window, and jump down upon the floor. She was in her hood and scarf, and the same dress that she was in before, at meeting the same day. Being come in, she was coming up towards this deponent's face, but turned back to his feet, and took hold of them, and drew up his body into a heap, and lay upon him about an hour and a half or two hours, in all which time this deponent could not stir nor speak; but, feeling himself beginning to be loosened or lightened, and he beginning to strive, he put out his hand among the clothes, and took hold of her hand, and brought it up to his mouth, and bit three of the fingers (as he judges) to the breaking of the bones; which done, the said Martin went out of the chamber, down the stairs, and out of the door. The deponent further declared, that, on another Lord's-day night, while sleeping on the hay in a barn, about midnight the said Susanna Martin and another came out of the shop into the barn, and one of them said, 'Here he is,' and then came towards this deponent. He, having a quarter-staff, made a blow at them; but the roof of the barn prevented it, and they went away: but this deponent followed them, and, as they were going towards the window, made another blow at them, and struck them both down; but away they went out at the shop-window, and this deponent saw no more of them. And the rumor went, that the said Martin had a broken head at that time; but the deponent cannot speak to that upon his own knowledge."

Any one who has had the misfortune to be subject to nightmare will find the elements of his own experience very much resembling the descriptions given by Kembal, Downer, Ring, and Peach. The terrors to which superstition, credulity, and ignorance subjected their minds; the frightful tales of witchcraft and apparitions to which they were accustomed to listen; and the contagious fears of the neighborhood in reference to Susanna Martin, taken in connection with a disordered digestion, an overloaded stomach, and a hard bed, or a strange lodging-place, — are wholly sufficient to account for all the phenomena to which they testified.

rate fabrication of falsehood or of fancy has come, at last, to be regarded as a veritable truth and a real occurrence.

A thorough and philosophical treatise on the subject of evidence is, in view of these considerations, much needed. The liability all men are under to confound the fictions of their imaginations with the realities of actual observation is not understood with sufficient clearness by the community; and, so long as it is not understood and regarded, serious mistakes and inconveniences will be apt to occur in seasons of general excitement. We are still disposed to attribute more importance than we ought to strong convictions, without stopping to inquire whether they may not be in reality delusions of the understanding. The cause of truth demands a more thorough examination of this whole subject. The visions that appeared before the mind of the celebrated Colonel Gardiner are still regarded by the generality of pious people as evidence of miraculous interposition, while, just so far as they are evidence to that point, so far is the authority of Christianity overthrown; for it is a fact, that Lord Herbert of Cherbury believed with equal sincerity and confidence that he had been vouchsafed a similar vision sanctioning his labors, when about to publish what has been pronounced one of the most powerful attacks ever made upon our religion. It is dangerous to advance arguments in favor of any cause which may be founded upon nothing better than the reveries of an ardent imagination!

The phenomena of dreams, of the exercises and convictions which occupy the mind, while the avenues of the senses are closed, and the soul is more or less extricated from its connection with the body, particularly in the peculiar conditions of partial slumber, are among the deep mysteries of human experience. The writers on mental philosophy have not given them the attention they deserve.

The testimony in these trials is particularly valuable as showing the power of the imagination to completely deceive and utterly falsify the senses of sober persons, when wide awake and in broad daylight. The following deposition was given in Court under oath. The parties testifying were of unquestionable respectability. The man was probably a brother of James Bayley, the first minister of the Salem Village parish.

"The Deposition of Joseph Bayley, aged forty-four years. — Testifieth and saith, that, on the twenty-fifth day of May last, myself and my wife being bound to Boston, on the road, when I came in sight of the house where John Procter did live, there was a very hard blow struck on my breast, which caused great pain in my stomach and amazement in my head, but did see no person near me, only my wife behind me on the same horse; and, when I came against said Procter's house, according to my understanding, I did see John Procter and his wife at said house. Procter himself looked out of the window, and his wife did stand just without the door. I told my wife of it; and she did look that way, and could see nothing but a little maid at

the door. Afterwards, about half a mile from the aforesaid
house, I was taken speechless for some short time. My
wife did ask me several questions, and desired me, that,
if I could not speak, I should hold up my hand; which I
did, and immediately I could speak as well as ever. And,
when we came to the way where Salem road cometh into
Ipswich road, there I received another blow on my breast,
which caused so much pain that I could not sit on my horse.
And, when I did alight off my horse, to my understanding,
I saw a woman coming towards us about sixteen or twenty
pole from us, but did not know who it was: my wife could
not see her. When I did get up on my horse again, to my
understanding, there stood a cow where I saw the woman.
After that, we went to Boston without any further molestation; but, after I came home again to Newbury, I was
pinched and nipped by something invisible for some time:
but now, through God's goodness to me, I am well again. —
Jurat in curia by both persons."

Bayley and his wife were going to Boston on election week. It was a good two days' journey from
Newbury, as the roads then were, and riding as they
did. According to the custom of the times, she was
mounted on a pillion behind him. They had probably
passed the night at the house of Sergeant Thomas
Putnam, with whom he was connected by marriage.
It was at the height of the witchcraft delirium.
Thomas Putnam's house was the very focus of it.
There they had listened to highly wrought accounts
of its wonders and terrors, had witnessed the amazing
phenomena exhibited by Ann Putnam and Mercy
Lewis, and their minds been filled with images of

spectres of living witches, and ghosts of the dead. They had seen with their own eyes the tortures of the girls under cruel diabolical influence, of which they had heard so much, and realized the dread outbreak of Satan and his agents upon the lives and souls of men.

They started the next morning on their way through the gloomy woods and over the solitary road. It was known that they were to pass the house of John Procter, believed to be a chief resort of devilish spirits. Oppressed with terror and awe, Bayley was on the watch, his heart in his mouth. The moment he came in sight, his nervous agitation reached its climax; and he experienced the shock he describes. When he came opposite to the house, to his horror there was Procter looking at him from the window, and Procter's wife standing outside of the door. He knew, that, in their proper persons and natural bodies, they were, at that moment, both of them, and had been for six weeks, in irons, in one of the cells of the jail at Boston. Bayley's wife, from her position on the pillion behind him, had her face directed to the other side of the road. He told her what he saw. She looked round to the house, and could see nothing but a little maid at the door. After one or two more fits of fright, he reached the Lynn road, had escaped from the infernal terrors of the infected region, and his senses resumed their natural functions. It was several days before his nervous agitations ceased. Altogether, this is a remarkable case of hallucination:

showing that the wildest fancies brought before the
mind in dreams may be paralleled in waking hours;
and that mental excitement may, even then, close the
avenues of the senses, exclude the perception of reality, and substitute unsubstantial visions in the place
of actual and natural objects.

There may be an interest in some minds to know
who the "little maid at the door" was. The elder
children of John Procter were either married off, or
lived on his farm at Ipswich, with the exception of
Benjamin, his oldest son, who remained with his father
on the Salem farm. Benjamin had been imprisoned
two days before Bayley passed the house. Four days
before, Sarah, sixteen years of age, had also been
arrested, and committed to jail. This left only William, eighteen years of age, who, three days after, was
himself put into prison; Samuel, seven; Abigail, between three and four years of age; and one still
younger. No female of the family was then at the
house older than Abigail. This poor deserted child
was "the little maid." Curiosity to see the passing
strangers, or possibly the hope that they might be her
father and mother, or her brother and sister, brought
her to the door.

In the terrible consequences that resulted from the
mischievous, and perhaps at the outset merely sportive, proceedings of the children in Mr. Parris's family,
we have a striking illustration of the principle, that
no one can foretell, with respect either to himself or
others, the extent of the suffering and injury that may

be occasioned by the least departure from truth, or from the practice of deception. In the horrible succession of crimes through which those young persons were led to pass, in the depth of depravity to which they were thrown, we discern the fate that endangers all who enter upon a career of wickedness.

No one can have an adequate knowledge of the human mind, who has not contemplated its developments in scenes like those that have now been related. It may be said of the frame of our spiritual, even with more emphasis than of our corporeal nature, that we are fearfully and wonderfully made. In the maturity of his bodily and mental organization, health gliding through his veins, strength and symmetry clothing his form, intelligence beaming from his countenance, and immortality stamped on his brow, man is indeed the noblest work of God. In the degradation and corruption to which he can descend, he is the most odious and loathsome object in the creation. The human mind, when all its faculties are fully developed and in proper proportions, reason seated on its rightful throne and shedding abroad its light, memory embracing the past, hope smiling upon the future, faith leaning on Heaven, and the affections diffusing through all their gentle warmth, is worthy of its source, deserves its original title of " image of God," and is greater and better than the whole material universe. It is nobler than all the works of God ; for it is an emanation, a part of God himself, " a ray from the fountain of light." But where, I

ask, can you find a more deplorable and miserable
object than the mind in ruins, tossed by its own re-
bellious principles, and distorted by the monstrously
unequal development of its faculties? You will look
in vain upon the earthquake, the volcano, or the hurricane, for those elements of the awful and terrible
which are manifested in a community of men whose
passions have trampled upon their principles, whose
imaginations have overthrown the government of reason, and who are swept along by the torrent until all
order and security are swallowed up and lost. Such
a spectacle we have now been witnessing. We have
seen the whole population of this place and vicinity
yielding to the sway of their credulous fancies, allowing their passions to be worked up to a tremendous
pitch of excitement, and rushing into excesses of
folly and violence that have left a stain on their
memory, and will awaken a sense of shame, pity, and
amazement in the minds of their latest posterity.

There is nothing more mysterious than the self-
deluding power of the mind, and there never were
scenes in which it was more clearly displayed than
the witchcraft prosecutions. Honest men testified,
with perfect confidence and sincerity, to the most absurd impossibilities; while those who thought themselves victims of diabolical influence would actually
exhibit, in their corporeal frames, all the appropriate
symptoms of the sufferings their imaginations had
brought upon them. Great ignorance prevailed in
reference to the influences of the body and the mind

upon each other. While the imagination was called into a more extensive and energetic action than at any succeeding or previous period, its properties and laws were but little understood: the extent of the connection of the will and the muscular system, the reciprocal influence of the nerves and the fancy, and the strong and universally pervading sympathy between our physical and moral constitutions, were almost wholly unknown. These important subjects, indeed, are but imperfectly understood at the present day.

It may perhaps be affirmed, that the relations of the human mind with the spiritual world will never be understood while we continue in the present stage of existence and mode of being. The error of our ancestors — and it is an error into which men have always been prone to fall, and from which our own times are by no means exempt — was in imagining that their knowledge had extended, in this direction, beyond the boundary fixed unalterably to our researches, while in this corporeal life.

It admits of much question, whether human science can ever find a solid foundation in what relates to the world of spirits. The only instrument of knowledge we can here employ is language. Careful thinkers long ago came to the conclusion, that it is impossible to frame a language precisely and exclusively adapted to convey abstract and spiritual ideas, even if it is possible, as some philosophers have denied, for the mind, in its present state, to have such ideas. All

attempts to construct such a language, though made
by the most ingenious men, have failed. Language
is based upon imagery, and associations drawn from
so much of the world as the senses disclose to us;
that is, from material objects and their relations. We
are here confined, as it were, within narrow walls.
We can catch only glimpses of what is above and
around us, outside of those walls. Such glimpses
may be vouchsafed, from time to time, to rescue us
from sinking into materialism, and to keep alive our
faith in scenes of existence remaining to be revealed
when the barriers of our imprisonment shall be taken
down, and what we call death lift us to a clearer and
broader vision of universal being.

Of the reality of the spiritual world, we are assured
by consciousness and by faith ; but our knowledge of
that world, so far as it can go into particulars, or become the subject of definition or expression, extends
no further than revelation opens the way. In all ages,
men have been awakened to the "wonders of the invisible world;" but they remain "wonders" still.
Nothing like a permanent, stable, or distinct science
has ever been achieved in this department. Man and
God are all that are placed within our ken. Metaphys-
ics and Theology are the names given to the sciences
that relate to them. The greater the number of books
written by human learning and ingenuity to expound
them, the more advanced the intelligence and piety of
mankind, the less, it is confessed, do we know of them
in detail, the more they rise above our comprehension,

the more unfathomable become their depths. Experience, history, the progress of light, all increase our sense of the impossibility of estimating the capacities of the human soul. So also we find that the higher we rise towards the Deity, in the contemplation of his works and word, the more does he continue to transcend our power to describe or imagine his greatness and glory. The revelation which the Saviour brought to mankind is all that the heart of man need desire, or the mind of man can comprehend. We are God's children, and he is our Father. That is all; and, the wiser and better we become, the more we are convinced and satisfied that it is enough.

There are, undoubtedly, innumerable beings in the world of spirits, besides departed souls, the Redeemer, and the Father. But of such beings we have, while here, no absolute and specific knowledge. In every age, as well as in our own, there have been persons who have believed themselves to hold communication with unseen spirits. The methods of entering into such communication have been infinitely diversified, from the incantations of ancient sorcery to the mediums and rappings of the present day. In former periods, particularly where the belief of witchcraft prevailed, it was thought that such communications could be had only with evil spirits, and, mostly, with the Chief of evil spirits. They were accordingly treated as criminal, and made the subject of the severest penalties known to the law. In our day, no such penalties are attached to the practice of seeking spiritual communications. Those who have a fancy for such experiments arc allowed to amuse themselves in this way without reproach or molestation. It is not charged upon them that they are dealing with the Evil One or any of his subordinates. They do not imagine such a thing themselves. I have no disposition, at any time, in any given case, to dispute the reality of the wonderful stories told in reference to such matters. All that I am prompted ever to remark is, that, if spirits do come, as is believed, at the call of those who seek to put themselves into communication with them, there is no evidence, I venture to suggest, that they are good spirits. I have never heard of their doing much good, substantially, to any one. No important truth has been revealed by them, no discovery been made, no science had its field enlarged; no department of knowledge has been brought into a clearer light; no great interest has been promoted; no movement of human affairs, whether in the action of nations or the transactions of men, has been advanced or in any way facilitated; no impulse has been given to society, and no elevation to life and character. It may be that the air is full of spiritual beings, hovering about us; but all experience shows that no benefit can be derived from seeking their intervention to share with us the duties or the burdens of our present probation. The mischiefs which have flowed from the belief that they can operate upon human affairs, and from attempting to have dealings with them, have been illustrated in the course of our narrative. In this view of the subject, no law is needed to prevent real or pretended communication with invisible beings. Enlightened reflection, common sense, natural prudence, would seem to be sufficient to keep men from meddling at all with practices, or countenancing notions, from which all history proclaims that no good has ever come, but incalculable evil flowed.

For the conduct of life, while here in these bodies, we must confine our curiosity to fields of knowledge open to our natural and ordinary faculties, and embraced within the limits of the established condition of things. Our fathers filled their fancies with the visionary images of ghosts, demons, apparitions, and all other supposed forms and shadows of the invisible world; lent their ears to marvellous stories of communications with spirits; gave to supernatural tales of witchcraft and demonology a wondering credence, and allowed them to occupy their conversation, speculations, and reveries. They carried a belief of such things, and a proneness to indulge it, into their daily life, their literature, and the proceedings of tribunals, ecclesiastical and civil. The fearful results shrouded their annals in darkness and shame. Let those results for ever stand conspicuous, beacon-monuments warning us, and coming generations, against superstition in every form, and all credulous and vain attempts to penetrate beyond the legitimate boundaries of human knowledge.

The phenomena of the real world, so far as science discloses them to our contemplation; the records of actual history; the lessons of our own experience; the utterances of the voice within, audible only to ourselves; and the teachings of the Divine Word, — are sufficient for the exercise of our faculties and the education of our souls during this brief period of our being, while in these bodies. In God's appointed time, we shall be transferred to a higher level of vision. Then, but not before, we may hope for re-union with disembodied spirits, for intercourse with angels, and for a nearer and more open communion with all divine beings.

The principal difference in the methods by which communications were believed to be made between mortals and spiritual beings, at the time of the witchcraft delusion and now, is this. Then it was chiefly by the medium of the eye, but at present by the ear. The "afflicted children" professed to have seen and conversed with the ghosts of George Burroughs's former wives and of others. They also professed to have seen the shapes or appearances of living persons in a disembodied form, or in the likeness of some animal or creature. Now it is affirmed by those calling themselves Spiritualists, that, by certain rappings or other incantations, they can summon into immediate but invisible presence the spirits of the departed, hold conferences with them, and draw from them information not derivable from any sources of human knowledge. There is no essential distinction between the old and the new belief and practice. The consequences that resulted from the former would be likely to result from the latter, if it should obtain universal or general credence, be allowed to mix with judicial proceedings, or to any extent affect the rights of person, property, or character.

The " afflicted children " at Salem Village had, by long practice, become wonderful adepts in the art of jugglery, and probably of ventriloquism. They did many extraordinary things, and were believed to have constant communications with ghosts and spectres; but they did not attain to spiritual rapping. If they had possessed that power, the credulity of judges, ministers, magistrates, and people, would have been utterly overwhelmed, and no limit could have been put to the destruction they might have wrought.

If there was any thing supernatural in the witchcraft of 1692, if any other than human spirits were concerned at all, one thing is beyond a doubt: they were shockingly wicked spirits, and led those who dealt with them to the utmost delusion, crime, and perdition; and this example teaches all who seek to consult with spirits, through a medium or in any other way, to be very strict to require beforehand the most satisfactory and conclusive evidence of good character before they put themselves into communication with them. Spirits who are said to converse with people, in these modern ages, cannot be considered as having much claim to a good repute. No valuable discovery of truth, no important guidance in human conduct, no useful instruction, has ever been conveyed to mankind through them; and much

mischief perhaps may have resulted from confiding
in them. It is not wise to place our minds under
the influence of any of our fellow-creatures, in the ordinary guise of humanity, unless we know something
about them entitling them to our acquaintance ; much
less so, to take them into our intimacy or confidence.
Spirits cannot be put under oath, or their credibility
be subjected to tests. Whether they are spirits of
truth or falsehood cannot be known ; and common
caution would seem to dictate an avoidance of their
company. The fields of knowledge opened to us in
the works of mortal men ; the stores of human learning and science ; the pages of history, sacred or profane ; the records of revelation ; and the instructions
and conversation of the wise and good of our fellow-
creatures, while in the body, — are wide enough for our
exploration, and may well occupy the longest lifetime.

In its general outlines and minuter details, Salem
Witchcraft is an illustration of the fatal effects of
allowing the imagination inflamed by passion to take
the place of common sense, and of pushing the curiosity and credence of the human mind, in this stage
of our being, while in these corporeal embodiments,
beyond the boundaries that ought to limit their exercise. If we disregard those boundaries, and try to
overleap them, we shall be liable to the same results.
The lesson needs to be impressed equally upon all
generations and ages of the world's future history.
Essays have been written and books published to
prove that the sense of the miraculous is destined

to decline as mankind becomes more enlightened, and
ascribing a greater or less tendency to the indulgence
of this sense to particular periods of the church, or
systems of belief, or schools of what is called philosophy. It is maintained that it was more prevalent
in the mediæval ages than in modern times. Some
assert that it has had a greater development in Catholic
than Protestant countries; and some, perhaps, insist
upon the reverse. Some attempt to show that it has
manifested itself more remarkably among Puritans
than in other classes of Protestant Christians. The
last and most pretentious form of this dogma is, that
the sense of the miraculous fades away in the progress of what arrogates to itself the name of Rational-
ism. This is one of the delusive results of introducing
generalization into historical disquisitions. History
deals with man. Man is always the same. The race
consists, not of an aggregation, but of individuals, in
all ages, never moulded or melted into classes. Each
individual has ever retained his distinctness from every
other. There has been the same infinite variety in
every period, in every race, in every nation. Society,
philosophy, custom, can no more obliterate these varie-
ties than they can bring the countenances and features
of men into uniformity. Diversity everywhere alike
prevails. The particular forms and shapes in which
the sense of the miraculous may express itself have
passed and will pass away in the progress of civiliza-
tion. But the sense itself remains; just as particular
costumes and fashions of garment pass away, while the

human form, its front erect and its vision towards the heavens, remains. The sense of the miraculous remains with Protestants as much as with Catholics, with Churchmen as much as with Puritans, with those who reject all creeds, equally with those whose creeds are the longest and the oldest. In our day, it must have been generally noticed, that the wonders of what imagines itself to be Spiritualism are rather more accredited by persons who aspire to the character of rationalists than by those who hold on tenaciously to the old landmarks of Orthodoxy.

The truth is, that the sense of the miraculous has not declined, and never can. It will grow deeper and stronger with the progress of true intelligence. As long as man thinks, he will feel that he is himself a perpetual miracle. The more he thinks, the more will he feel it. The mind which can wander into the deepest depths of the starry heavens, and feel itself to be there; which, pondering over the printed page, lives in the most distant past, communes with sages of hoar antiquity, with prophets and apostles, joins the disciples as they walk with the risen Lord to Emmaus, or mingles in the throng that listen to Paul at Mars' Hill, — knows itself to be beyond the power of space or time, and greater than material things. It knows not what it shall be; but it feels that it is something above the present and visible. It realizes the spiritual world, and will do so more and more, the higher its culture, the greater its freedom, and the wider its view of the material nature by which it is environed, while in this transitory stage of its history.

The lesson of our story will be found not to discard spiritual things, but to teach us, while in the flesh, not to attempt to break through present limitations, not to seek to know more than has been made known of the unseen and invisible, but to keep the inquiries of our minds and the action of society within the bounds of knowledge now attainable, and extend our curious researches and speculations only as far as we can here have solid ground to stand upon.

To explain the superstitious opinions that took effect in the witchcraft delusion, it is necessary to consider the state of biblical criticism at that period.   That department of theological learning was then in a very immature condition.

The authority of Scripture, as it appeared on the face of the standard version, seemed to require them to pursue the course they adopted; and those enlarged and just principles of interpretation which we are taught by the learned of all denominations at the present day to apply to the Sacred Writings had not then been brought to the view of the people or received by the clergy.

It was gravely argued, for instance, that there was nothing improbable in the idea that witches had the power, in virtue of their compact with the Devil, of riding aloft through the air, because it is recorded, in the history of our Lord's temptation, that Satan transported him in a similar manner to the pinnacle of the temple, and to the summit of an exceedingly high mountain. And Cotton Mather declares, that, to his apprehension, the disclosures of the wonderful operations of the Devil, upon and through his subjects, that were made in the course of the witchcraft prosecutions, had shed a marvellous light upon the Scriptures! What a perversion of the Sacred Writings to employ them for the purpose of sanctioning the extravagant and delirious reveries of the human imagination! What a miserable delusion, to suppose that the Word of God could receive illumination from the most absurd and horrible superstition that ever brooded in darkness over the mind of man!

One of the sources of the delusion of 1692 was ignorance of many natural laws that have been revealed by modern science. A vast amount of knowledge on these subjects has been attained since that time. In our halls of education, in associations for the diffusion of knowledge, and in a diversified and all-pervading popular literature, what was dark and impenetrable mystery then has been explained, accounted for, and brought within the grasp of all minds. The contemplation of the evils brought upon our predecessors by their ignorance of the laws of nature cannot but lead us to appreciate more highly our opportunities to get knowledge in this department. As we advance into the interior of the physical system to which we belong; are led in succession from one revelation of beauty and grandeur to another, and the field of light and truth displaces that of darkness and mystery ; while the fearful images that disturbed the faith and bewildered the thoughts of our fathers are dissolving and vanishing, the whole host of spirits, ghosts, and demons disappearing, and the presence and providence of God alone found to fill all scenes and cause all effects, — our hearts ought to rise to him in loftier adoration and holier devotion. If, while we enjoy a fuller revelation of his infinite and all-glorious operations and designs than our fathers did, the sentiment of piety which glowed in their hearts like a coal from the altar of God has been permitted to grow dim in ours, no reproach their errors and faults can possibly authorize will equal that which will justly fall upon us.

Another cause of their delusion was too great a dependence upon the imagination. We shall find no lesson more clearly taught by history, by experience, or by observation, than this, that man is never safe while either his fancy or his feeling is the guiding principle of his nature. There is a strong and constant attraction between his imagination and his passions; and, if either is permitted to exercise unlimited sway, the other will most certainly be drawn into co-operation with it, and, when they are allowed to act without restraint upon each other and with each other, they lead to the derangement and convulsion of his whole system. They constitute the combustible elements of our being: one serves as the spark to explode the other. Reason, enlightened by revelation and guided by conscience, is the great conservative principle: while that exercises the sovereign power over the fancy and the passions, we are safe; if it is dethroned, no limit can be assigned to the ruin that may follow. In the scenes we have now been called to witness, we have perceived to what lengths of folly, cruelty, and crime even good men have been carried, who relinquished the aid, rejected the counsels, and abandoned the guidance of their reason.

Another influence that operated to produce the catastrophe in 1692 was the power of contagious sympathy. Every wise man and good citizen ought to be aware of the existence and operation of this power. There seems indeed to be a constitutional, original, sympathy in our nature. When men act in a crowd, their heartstrings are prone to vibrate in unison. Whatever chord of passion is struck in one breast, the same will ring forth its wild note through the whole mass. This principle shows itself particularly in seasons of excitement, and its power rises in proportion to the ardor and zeal of those upon whom it acts. It is for every one who desires to be preserved from the excesses of popular feeling, and to prevent the community to which he belongs from plunging into riotous and blind commotions, to keep his own judgment and emotions as free as possible from a power that seizes all it can reach, draws them into its current, and sweeps them round and round like the Maelstrom, until they are overwhelmed and buried in its devouring vortex. When others are heated, the only wisdom is to determine to keep cool; whenever a people or an individual is rushing headlong, it is the duty of patriotism and of friendship to check the motion.

In this connection it may be remarked—and I should be sorry to bring the subject to a close without urging the thought upon your attention—that the mere power of sympathy, the momentum with which men act in a crowd, is itself capable of convulsing society and overthrowing all its safeguards, without the aid or supposed agency of supernatural beings. The early history of the colony of New York presents a case in point.

In 1741, just half a century after the witchcraft prosecutions in Massachusetts, the city of New York, then containing about nine thousand inhabitants, witnessed a scene quite rivalling, in horror and folly, that presented here. Some one started the idea, that a conspiracy was on foot, among the colored portion of the inhabitants, to murder the whites. The story was passed from one to another. Although subsequently ascertained to have been utterly without foundation, no one stopped to inquire into its truth, or had the wisdom or courage to discountenance its circulation. Soon a universal panic, like a conflagration, spread through the whole community; and the results were most frightful. More than one hundred persons were cast into prison. Four white persons and eighteen negroes were hanged. Eleven negroes were burned at the stake, and fifty were transported into slavery. As in the witchcraft prosecutions, a clergyman was among the victims, and perished on the gallows.

The "New-York Negro Plot," as it was called, was indeed marked by all the features of absurdity in the delusion, ferocity in the popular excitement, and destruction along the path of its progress, which belonged to the witchcraft proceedings here, and shows that any people, given over to the power of contagious passion, may be swept by desolation, and plunged into ruin.

One of the practical lessons inculcated by the history that has now been related is, that no duty is more certain, none more important, than a free and fearless expression of opinion, by all persons, on all occasions. No wise or philosophic person would think of complaining of the diversities of sentiment it is likely to develop. Such diversities are the vital principle of free communities, and the only elements of popular intelligence. If the right to utter them is asserted by all and for all, tolerance is secured, and no inconvenience results. It is probable that there were many persons here in 1692 who doubted the propriety of the proceedings at their commencement, but who were afterwards prevailed upon to fall into the current and swell the tide. If they had all discharged their duty to their country and their consciences by freely and boldly uttering their disapprobation and declaring their dissent, who can tell but that the whole tragedy might have been prevented? and, if it might, the blood of the innocent may be said, in one sense, to be upon their heads.

The leading features and most striking aspects of

the witchcraft delusion have been repeated in places where witches and the interference of supernatural beings are never thought of: whenever a community gives way to its passions, and spurns the admonitions and casts off the restraints of reason, there is a delusion that can hardly be described in any other phrase. We cannot glance our eye over the face of our country without beholding such scenes: and, so long as they are exhibited ; so long as we permit ourselves to invest objects of little or no real importance with such an inordinate imaginary interest that we are ready to go to every extremity rather than relinquish them ; so long as we yield to the impulse of passion, and plunge into excitement, and take counsel of our feelings rather than our judgment, — we are following in the footsteps of our fanatical ancestors. It would be wiser to direct our ridicule and reproaches to the delusions of our own times than to those of a previous age ; and it becomes us to treat with charity and mercy the failings of our predecessors, at least until we have ceased to imitate and repeat them.

It has been my object to collect and arrange all the materials within reach necessary to give a correct and adequate view of the passage of history related and discussed in this work, and to suggest the considerations and conclusions required by truth and justice. It is worthy of the most thoughtful contemplation. The moralist, metaphysician, and political philosopher will find few chapters of human experience more fraught with instruction, and may well ponder upon the lessons it teaches, scrutinize thoroughly all its periods, phases, and branches, analyze its causes, eliminate its elements, and mark its developments. The laws, energies, capabilities, and liabilities of our nature, as exhibited in the character of individuals and in the action of society, are remarkably illustrated. The essential facts belonging to the transaction, gathered from authentic records and reliable testimonies and traditions, have been faithfully presented. THE WITCHCRAFT DELUSION OF 1692, so far as I have been able to recover it from misunderstanding and oblivion, has been brought to view; and I indulge the belief, that the subject will commend itself to, and reward, the study of every meditative mind.

I know not in what better terms the discussion of this subject can be brought to a termination, than in those which express the conclusions to which one of our own most distinguished citizens was brought, after having examined the whole transaction with the eye of a lawyer and the spirit of a judge. The following is from the Centennial Discourse pronounced in Salem on the 18th of September, 1828, by the late Hon. Joseph Story, of the Supreme Court of the United States : —

"We may lament, then," says he, "the errors of the times, which led to these prosecutions. But surely our ancestors had no special reasons for shame in a belief which had the universal sanction of their own and all former ages ; which counted in its train philosophers, as well as enthusiasts ; which was graced

by the learning of prelates, as well as by the countenance of kings ; which the law supported by its man-
dates, and the purest judges felt no compunctions in
enforcing. Let Witch Hill remain for ever memorable
by this sad catastrophe, not to perpetuate our dishonor,
but as an affecting, enduring proof of human infirmity ;
a proof that perfect justice belongs to one judgment-
seat only, — that which is linked to the throne of
God."

In the work which has now reached its close, many
strange phases of humanity have been exposed. We
have beheld, with astonishment and horror, the extent
to which it is liable to be the agent and victim of delusion and ruin. Folly that cannot be exceeded ; wrong,
outrage, and woe, melting the heart that contemplates
them ; and crime, not within our power or province
to measure, — have passed before us. But not the
dark side only of our nature has been displayed.
Manifestations of innocence, heroism, invincible devotion to truth, integrity of soul triumphing over all the
terrors and horrors that can be accumulated in life
and in death, Christian piety in its most heavenly radi-
ance, have mingled in the drama, whose curtain is now
to fall. Noble specimens of virtue in man and woman,
old and young, have shed a light, as from above, upon
its dark and melancholy scenes. Not only the sufferers, but some of those who shared the dread responsibility of the crisis, demand our commiseration, and
did what they could to atone for their error.

The conduct of Judge Sewall claims our particular admiration. He observed annually in private a day of humiliation and prayer, during the remainder of his life, to keep fresh in his mind a sense of repentance and sorrow for the part he bore in the trials. On the day of the general fast, he rose in the place where he was accustomed to worship, the Old South, in Boston, and, in the presence of the great assembly, handed up to the pulpit a written confession, acknowledging the error into which he had been led, praying for the forgiveness of God and his people, and concluding with a request to all the congregation to unite with him in devout supplication, that it might not bring down the displeasure of the Most High upon his country, his family, or himself. He remained standing during the public reading of the paper. This was an act of true manliness and dignity of soul.

The following passage is found in his diary, under the date of April 23, 1720, nearly thirty years afterwards. It was suggested by the perusal of Neal's "History of New England:"—

"In Dr. Neal's 'History of New England,' its nakedness is laid open in the businesses of the Quakers, Anabaptists, witchcraft. The judges' names are mentioned p. 502; my confession, p. 536, vol. ii. The good and gracious God be pleased to save New England and me, and my family!"

There never was a more striking and complete fulfilment of the apostolic assurance, that the prayer of a righteous man availeth much, than in this instance. God has been pleased, in a remarkable manner, to save and bless New England. The favor of Heaven was bestowed upon Judge Sewall during the remainder of his life. He presided for many years on the bench where he committed the error so sincerely deplored by him, and was regarded by all as a benefactor, an ornament, and a blessing to the community: while his family have enjoyed to a high degree the protection of Providence from that day to this; have adorned every profession, and every department of society; have filled with honor the most elevated stations; have graced, in successive generations, the same lofty seat their ancestor occupied; and been the objects of the confidence, respect, and love of their fellow-citizens.

Your thoughts have been led through scenes of the most distressing and revolting character. I leave before your imaginations one bright with all the beauty of Christian virtue, — that which exhibits Judge Sewall standing forth in the house of his God and in the presence of his fellow-worshippers, making a public declaration of his sorrow and regret for the mistaken judgment he had co-operated with others in pronouncing. Here you have a representation of a truly great and magnanimous spirit; a spirit to which the divine influence of our religion had given an expansion and a lustre that Roman or Grecian virtue never knew; a spirit that had achieved a greater victory than warrior ever won, — a victory over itself; a spirit so noble and so pure, that it felt no shame in acknowledging an error, and publicly imploring, for a great wrong done to his fellow-creatures, the forgiveness of God and man.

Our Essex poet, whose beautiful genius has made classical the banks of his own Merrimac, shed a romantic light over the early homes and characters of New England, and brought back to life the spirit, forms, scenes, and men of the past, has not failed to immortalize, in his verse, the profound penitence of the misguided but upright judge : —

> " Touching and sad, a tale is told,
> Like a penitent hymn of the Psalmist old,
> Of the fast which the good man life-long kept
> With a haunting sorrow that never slept,
> As the circling year brought round the time
> Of an error that left the sting of crime,
> When he sat on the bench of the witchcraft courts,
> With the laws of Moses and 'Hale's Reports,'
> And spake, in the name of both, the word
> That gave the witch's neck to the cord,
> And piled the oaken planks that pressed
> The feeble life from the warlock's breast!
> All the day long, from dawn to dawn,
> His door was bolted, his curtain drawn ;
> No foot on his silent threshold trod,
> No eye looked on him save that of God,
> As he baffled the ghosts of the dead with charms
> Of penitent tears, and prayers, and psalms,
> And, with precious proofs from the sacred Word
> Of the boundless pity and love of the Lord,
> His faith confirmed and his trust renewed,
> That the sin of his ignorance, sorely rued,
> Might be washed away in the mingled flood
> Of his human sorrow and Christ's dear blood ! "

SUPPLEMENT.

SUPPLEMENT.

———◆———

[The subject of Salem Witchcraft has been traced to its conclusion, and discussed within its proper limits, in the foregoing work. But whoever is interested in it as a chapter of history or an exhibition of humanity may feel a curiosity, on some points, that reasonably demands gratification. The questions will naturally arise, Who were the earliest to extricate themselves and the public from the delusion? what is known, beyond the facts mentioned in the progress of the foregoing discussion, of the later fortunes of its prominent actors? what the view taken in the retrospect by individuals and public bodies implicated in the transaction? and what opinions on the general subject have subsequently prevailed? To answer these questions is the design of this Supplement.]

IT can hardly be said that there was any open and avowed opposition in the community to the proceedings during their early progress. There is some uncertainty and obscurity to what extent there was an unexpressed dissent in the minds of particular private persons. On the general subject of the existence and power of the Devil and his agency, more or less, in influencing human and earthly affairs, it would be difficult to prove that there was any considerable difference of opinion.

The first undisguised and unequivocal opposition to the proceedings was a remarkable document that has recently come to light. Among some papers which have found their way to the custody of the Essex Institute, is a letter, dated "Salisbury, Aug. 9, 1692," addressed "To the worshipful Jonathan Corwin, Esq., these present at his house in Salem." It is indorsed, "A letter to my grandfather, on account of the condemnation of the witches." Its date shows that it was written while the public infatuation and fury were at their height, and the Court was sentencing to death and sending to the gallows its successive cartloads. There is no injunction of secresy, and no shrinking from responsibility. Although the name of the writer is not given in full, he was evidently well known to Corwin, and had written to him before on the subject. The messenger, in accordance with the superscription, undoubtedly delivered it into the hands of the judge at his residence on the corner of Essex and North Streets. The fact that Jonathan Corwin preserved this document, and placed it in the permanent files of his family papers, is pretty good proof that he appreciated the weight of its arguments. It is not improbable that he expressed himself to that effect to his brethren on the bench, and perhaps to others. What he said, and the fact that he was holding such a correspondence, may have reached the ears of the accusers, and led them to commence a movement against him by crying out upon his mother-in-law.

The letter is a most able argument against the manner in which the trials were conducted, and, by conclusive logic, overthrows the whole fabric of the evidence on the strength of which the Court was convicting and taking the lives of innocent persons. No such piece of reasoning has come to us from that age. Its author must be acknowledged to have been an expert in dialectic subtleties, and a pure reasoner of unsurpassed acumen and force. It requires, but it will reward, the closest attention and concentration of thought in following the threads of the argument. It reaches its conclusions on a most difficult subject with clearness and certainty. It achieves and realizes, in mere mental processes, quantities, and forces, on the points at which it aims, what is called demonstration in mathematics and geometry.

The writer does not discredit, but seems to have received, the then prevalent doctrines relating to the personality, power, and attributes of the Devil; and, from that standpoint, controverts and demolishes the principles on which the Court was proceeding, in reference to the "spectral evidence" and the credibility of the "afflicted children" generally. The letter, and the formal argument appended to it, arrest notice in one or two general aspects. There is an appearance of their having proceeded from an elderly

person, not at all from any marks of infirmity of intellect, but
rather from an air of wisdom and a tone of authority which can only
result from long experience and observation. The circumstance
that an amanuensis was employed, and the author writes the
initials of his signature only, strengthens this impression. At
the same time, there are indications of a free and progressive
spirit, more likely to have had force at an earlier period of life.
In some aspects, the document indicates a theological education,
and familiarity with matters that belong to the studies of a minister ; in others, it manifests habits of mind and modes of expression
and reasoning more natural to one accustomed to close legal statements and deductions. If the production of a trained professional
man of either class, it would justly be regarded as remarkable.
If its author belonged to neither class, but was merely a local magistrate, farmer, and militia officer, it becomes more than remarkable.
There must have been a high development among the founders of
our villages, when the laity could present examples of such a capacity to grasp the most difficult subjects, and conduct such acute
and abstruse disquisitions. [See Appendix.]

The question as to the authorship of this paper may well excite
interest, involving, as it does, minute critical speculations. The
elements that enter into its solution illustrate the difficulties and
perplexities encompassing the study of local antiquities, and attempts to determine the origin and bearings of old documents or to
settle minute points of history. The weight of evidence seems to
indicate that the document is attributable to Major Robert Pike, of
Salisbury. Whoever was its author did his duty nobly, and stands
alone, above all the scholars and educated men of the time, in bearing testimony openly, bravely, in the very ears of the Court, against
the disgraceful and shocking course they were pursuing.*

* The facts and considerations in reference to the authorship of the letter
to Jonathan Corwin may be summarily stated as follows: —

The letter is signed " R. P." Under these initials is written, " Robert
Pain," in a different hand, and, as the ink as well as the chirography shows,
at a somewhat later date. R. P. are blotted over, but with ink of such
lighter hue that the original letters are clearly discernible under it. A Robert Paine graduated at Harvard College, in 1656. But he was probably the
foreman of the grand jury that brought in all the indictments in the witchcraft trials; and therefore could not, from the declarations in the letter itself,
have been its author. The only other person of that name at the time, of

William Brattle, an eminent citizen and opulent merchant of Boston, and a gentleman of education and uncommon abilities, wrote a letter to an unknown correspondent of the clerical profes-

whom we have knowledge, was his father, who seems, by the evidence we have, to have died in 1693. (That date is given in the Harvard Triennial for the death of Robert Paine, the graduate; but erroneously, I think, as signatures to documents, and conveyances of property subsequently, can hardly be ascribed to any other person.) Robert Paine, the father, from the earliest settlement of Ipswich, had been one of the leading men of the town, apparently of larger property than any other, often its deputy in the General Court, and, for a great length of time, ruling elder of the church. " Elder Pain," or Penn, as the name was often spelled, enjoyed the friendship of John Norton, and all the ministers far and near; and religious meetings were often held at his house. We know nothing to justify us in saying that he could not have been the author of this paper; but we also know nothing, except the appearance of his name upon it, to impute it to him.

The document is dated from " Salisbury." So far as we know, Elder Paine always lived in Ipswich; although, having property in the upper county, he may have often been, and possibly in his last years resided, there. It is, it is true, a strong circumstance, that his name is written, although by a late hand, under the initials. It shows that the person who wrote it thought that " R. P." meant Robert Paine; but any one conversant especially with the antiquities of Ipswich, or this part of the county, might naturally fall into such a mistake. The authorship of documents was often erroneously ascribed. The words " Robert Pain " were, probably, not on the paper when the indorsement was made, "A letter to my grandfather," &c. Elder Robert Paine, if living in 1692, was ninety-one years of age. The document under consideration, if composed by him, is truly a marvellous production, — an intellectual phenomenon not easily to be paralleled.

The facts in reference to Robert Pike, of Salisbury, as they bear upon the question of the authorship of the document, are these: He was seventy-six years of age in 1692, and had always resided in " Salisbury." The letter and argument are both in the handwriting of Captain Thomas Bradbury, Recorder of old Norfolk County. On this point, there can be no question. Bradbury and Pike had been fellow-townsmen for more than half a century, connected by all the ties of neighborhood and family intermarriage, and jointly or alternately had borne all the civic and military honors the people could bestow. The document was prepared and delivered to the judge while Mrs. Bradbury was in prison, and just one month before her trial. Pike, as has been shown (p. 226), was deeply interested in her behalf. The original signature (" R. P.") has the marked characteristics of the same initial letters as found in innumerable autographs of his, on file or record. There are interlineations, beyond question in Pike's handwriting. These facts demonstrate that both Pike and Bradbury were concerned in producing the document.

sion, in October, 1692. It is an able criticism upon the methods of procedure at the trials, condemning them in the strongest language ; but it was a confidential communication, and not published

The history of Robert Pike proves that he was a man of great ability, had a turn of mind towards logical exercises, and was, from early life, conversant with disputations. Nearly fifty years before, he argued in town-meeting against the propriety, in view of civil and ecclesiastical law, of certain acts of the General Court. They arraigned, disfranchised, and otherwise punished him for his "litigiousness:" but the weight of his character soon compelled them to restore his political rights; and the people of Salisbury, the very next year, sent him among them as their deputy, and continued him from time to time in that capacity. At a subsequent period, he was the leader and spokesman of a party in a controversy about some ecclesiastical affairs, involving apparently certain nice questions of theology, which created a great stir through the country. The contest reached so high a point, that the church at Salisbury excommunicated him; but the public voice demanded a council of churches, which assembled in September, 1676, and re-instated Major Pike condemning his excommunication, " finding it not justifiable upon divers grounds." On this occasion, as before, the General Court frowned upon and denounced him; but the people came again to his rescue, sending him at the next election into the House of Deputies, and kept him there until raised to the Upper House as an Assistant. He was in the practice of conducting causes in the courts, and was long a local magistrate and one of the county judges.

He does not appear to have been present at any of the trials or examinations of 1692; but his official position as Assistant caused many depositions taken in his neighborhood to be acknowledged and sworn before him. While entertaining the prevalent views about diabolical agency, he always disapproved of the proceedings of the Court in the particulars to which the arguments of the communication to Jonathan Corwin apply, — the "spectre evidence," — and the statements and actings of "the afflicted children." There are indications that sometimes he saw through the folly of the stories told by persons whose depositions he was called to attest. One John Pressy was circulating a wonderful tale about an encounter he had with the spectre of Susanna Martin. Pike sent for him, and took his deposition. Pressy averred, that, one evening, coming from Amesbury Ferry, he fell in with the shape of Martin in the form of a body of light, which "seemed to be about the bigness of a half-bushel." After much dodging and manœuvring, and being lost and bewildered, wandering to and fro, tumbling into holes, — where, as the deposition states, no "such pitts" were known to exist, — and other misadventures, he came to blows with the light, and had several brushes with it, striking it with his stick. At one time, "he thinks he gave her at least forty blows." He finally succeeded in finding "his own house: but, being then seized with fear, could not speak till his wife spoke to him at the door, until many years afterwards. He says that "the witches' meetings, the Devil's baptisms and mock sacraments, which the accusing and confessing witches oft speak of, are nothing else but the effect of their fancy, depraved and deluded by the Devil, and not a reality to be regarded or minded by any wise man." He charges the judges with having taken testimony from the Devil himself, through witnesses who swore to what they said the Devil communicated to them, thus indirectly introducing the Devil as a witness; and he clinches the accusation by quoting the judges themselves, who, when the accusing and confessing witnesses contradicted each other, got over the difficulty by saying that the Devil, in such instances, took away the memory of some of them, for the moment, obscuring their brains, and misleading them. He sums up this part of his reasoning in these words: "If it be thus granted that the Devil is able to represent false ideas to the imaginations of the confessors, what man of sense will regard the confessions, or any of the words of these confessors?" He says that he knows several persons "about the Bay," — men, for understanding, judgment, and piety, inferior to few, if any, in New England, — that do utterly condemn the said proceedings. He repudiates the idea that Salem was, in any sense, exclusively responsible for the transaction; and affirms that "other justices in the country, besides the Salem jus-

and was in such a condition that the family was afraid of him; which story being carried to the town the next day, it was, upon inquiry, understood, that said Goodwife Martin was in such a miserable case and in such pain that they swabbed her body, as was reported." He concludes his deposition by saying, that Major Pike "seemed to be troubled that this deponent had not told him of it in season that she might have been viewed to have seen what her ail was." The affair had happened "about twenty-four years ago." Probably neither Pressy nor the Court appreciated the keenness of the major's expression of regret. It broke the bubble of the deposition. The whole story was the product of a benighted imagination, disordered by fear, filled with inebriate vagaries, exaggerated in nightmare, and resting upon wild and empty rumors. Robert Pike's course, in the case of Mrs. Bradbury, harmonizes with the supposition that he was Corwin's correspondent.

Materials may be brought to light that will change the evidence on the point. It may be found that Elder Paine died before 1692: that would dispose of the question. It may appear that he was living in Salisbury at the time, and acted with Pike and Bradbury, they giving to the paper the authority of his venerable name and years. But all that is now known, constrains me to the conclusion stated in the text.

tices, have issued out their warrants ; " and states, that, of the eight
"judges, commissioned for this Court at Salem, five do belong to
Suffolk County, four of which five do belong to Boston, and therefore I see no reason why Boston should talk of Salem as though
their own judges had had no hand in these proceedings in Salem."

There is one view of the subject, upon which Brattle presses
with much force and severity. There is ground to suspect, that the
proceedings were suffered to go on after some of those appearing
to countenance them had ceased to have faith in the accusations.
He charges, directly, complicity in the escape of Mrs. Carey, Mrs.
English, Captain Alden, Hezekiah Usher, and others, upon the
high officials; and says that while the evidence, upon which so
many had been imprisoned, sentenced, and executed, bore against
Mrs. Thacher, of Boston, she was never proceeded against. "She
was much complained of by the afflicted persons, and yet the
justices would not issue out their warrants to apprehend" her and
certain others ; while at the very same time they were issuing, upon
no better or other grounds, warrants against so many others. He
charges the judges with this most criminal favoritism. The facts
hardly justify such an imputation upon the judges. They did not,
after the trials had begun, it is probable, ever issue warrants :
that was the function of magistrates. With the exception, perhaps, of Corwin, I think there is no evidence of there having been
any doubts or misgivings on the bench. It is altogether too heavy
a charge to bring, without the strongest evidence, upon any one.
To intimate that officials, or any persons, who did not believe in
the accusations, connived at the escape of their friends and relatives, and at the same time countenanced, pretended to believe,
and gave deadly effect to them when directed against others, is
supposing a criminality and baseness too great to be readily admitted. In that wild reign of the worst of passions, this would
have transcended them all in its iniquity. The only excusable
people at that time were those who honestly, and without a doubt,
believed in the guilt of the convicted. Those who had doubts,
and did not frankly and fearlessly express them, were the guilty
ones. On their hands is the stain of the innocent blood that was
shed. It is not probable, and is scarcely possible, that any considerable number could be at once doubters and prosecutors. On this

point, Brattle must be understood to mean, not that judges, or others actively engaged in the prosecutions, warded off proceedings against particular friends or relatives from a principle of deliberate favoritism, but that third parties, actuated by a sycophantic spirit, endeavored to hush up or intercept complaints, when directed too near to the high officials, or thought to gain their favor by aiding the escape of persons in whom they were interested.

Brattle uses the same weapon which afterwards the opponents of Mr. Parris, in his church at Salem Village, wielded with such decisive effect against him and all who abetted him. It is much to be lamented, that, instead of hiding it under a confidential letter, he did not at the time openly bring it to bear in the most public and defiant manner. One brave, strong voice, uttered in the face of the court and in the congregations of the people, echoed from the corners of the streets, and reaching the ears of the governor and magistrates, denouncing the entire proceedings as the damnable crime of familiarity with evil spirits, and sorcery of the blackest dye, might perhaps have recalled the judges, the people, and the rulers to their senses. If the spirit of the ancient prophets of God, of the Quakers of the preceding age, or of true reformers of any age, had existed in any breast, the experiment would have been tried. Brattle says, —

"I cannot but admire that any should go with their distempered friends and relations to the afflicted children, to know what their distempered friends ail, whether they are not bewitched, who it is that afflicts them, and the like. It is true, I know no reason why these afflicted may not be consulted as well as any other, if so be that it was only their natural and ordinary knowledge that was had recourse to: but it is not on this notion that these afflicted children are sought unto, but as they have a supernatural knowledge; a knowledge which they obtain by their holding correspondence with spectres or evil spirits, as they themselves grant. This consulting of these afflicted children, as abovesaid, seems to me to be a very gross evil, a real abomination, not fit to be known in New England; and yet is a thing practised, not only by *Tom* and *John*, — I mean the rude and more ignorant sort, — but by many who profess high, and pass among us for some of the better sort. This is that which aggravates the evil, and makes it heinous and tremendous; and yet this is not the worst of it, — for, as sure as I now write to you, even some of our civil leaders and spiritual teachers, who, I think, should punish and preach down such sorcery and wickedness, do yet allow of, encourage, yea, and practise, this very abomination. I know there are several worthy gentlemen in Salem who account this practice as an abomination, have trembled to see the methods of this nature which others have used, and have declared themselves to think the practice to be very evil and corrupt. But all avails little with the abettors of the said practice."

If Mr. Brattle and the " several worthy gentlemen" to whom he alludes, instead of sitting in " trembling" silence, or whispering in private their disapprobation, or writing letters under the injunction of secrecy, had come boldly out, and denounced the whole thing, in a spirit of true courage, meeting and defying the risk, and carrying the war home, and promptly, upon the ministers, magistrates, and judges, they might have succeeded, and exploded the delusion before it had reached its fatal results.

He mentions, in the course of his letter, among those persons known by him to disapprove of the proceedings, —

" The Hon. Simon Bradstreet, Esq. (our late governor), the Hon. Thomas Danforth, Esq. (our late deputy-governor), the Rev. Mr. Increase Mather, and the Rev. Mr. Samuel Willard. Major N. Saltonstall, Esq., who was one of the judges, has left the court, and is very much dissatisfied with the proceedings of it. Excepting Mr. Hale, Mr. Noyes, and Mr. Parris, the reverend elders, almost throughout the whole country, are very much dissatisfied. Several of the late justices — viz., Thomas Graves, Esq.; N. Byfield, Esq.; Francis Foxcroft, Esq. — are much dissatisfied; also several of the present justices, and, in particular, some of the Boston justices, were resolved rather to throw up their commissions than be active in disturbing the liberty of Their Majesties' subjects merely on the accusations of these afflicted, possessed children."

It is to be observed, that the dissatisfaction was with some of the methods adopted in the proceedings, and not with the prosecutions themselves. Increase Mather and Samuel Willard signed the paper indorsing Deodat Lawson's famous sermon, which surely drove on the prosecutions; and the former expressed, in print, his approbation of his son Cotton's " Wonders of the Invisible World," in which he labors to defend the witchcraft prosecutions, and to make it out that those who suffered were " malefactors."

Dr. Increase Mather is understood to have countenanced the burning of Calef's book, some few years afterwards, in the square of the public grounds of Harvard College, of which institution he was then president. It cannot be doubted, however, that both the elder Mather and Mr. Willard had expressed, more or less distinctly, their disapprobation of some of the details of the proceedings. It is honorable to their memories, and shows that the former was not wholly blinded by parental weakness, but willing to express his dissent, in some particulars, from the course of his distinguished son, and that the latter had an independence of character which enabled him to criticise and censure a court in which three of his parishioners sat as judges.

Brattle relates a story which seems to indicate that Increase Mather sometimes was unguarded enough to express himself with severity against those who gave countenance to the proceedings. "A person from Boston, of no small note, carried up his child to Salem, near twenty miles, on purpose that he might consult the afflicted about his child, which accordingly he did; and the afflicted told him that his child was afflicted by Mrs. Carey and Mrs. Obinson." The "afflicted," in this and some other instances, had struck too high. The magistrates in Boston were unwilling to issue a warrant against Mrs. Obinson, and Mrs. Carey had fled. All that the man got for his pains, in carrying his child to Salem, was a hearty scolding from Increase Mather, who asked him "whether there was not a God in Boston, that he should go to the Devil, in Salem, for advice."

Bradstreet's great age prevented, it is to be supposed, his public appearance in the affair; but his course in a case which occurred twelve years before fully justifies confidence in the statement of Brattle. The tradition has always prevailed, that he looked with disapprobation upon the proceedings, from beginning to end. The course of his sons, and the action taken against them, is quite decisive to the point.

Facts have been stated, which show that Thomas Danforth, if he disapproved of the proceedings at Salem, in October, must have undergone a rapid change of sentiments. No irregularities, improprieties, extravagances, or absurdities ever occurred in the examinations or trials greater than he was fully responsible for in April. Having, in the mean while, been superseded in office, he had leisure, in his retirement, to think over the whole matter; and it is satisfactory to find that he saw the error of the ways in which he had gone himself, and led others.

The result of the inquiry on this point is, that, while some, outside of the village, began early to doubt the propriety of the proceedings in certain particulars, they failed, with the single exception of Robert Pike, to make manly and seasonable resistance. He remonstrated in a writing signed with his own initials, and while the executions were going on. He sent it to one of the judges, and did not shrink from having his action known. No other voice was raised, no one else breasted the storm, while it lasted. The errors which led to the delusion were not attacked from any quarter at any time during that generation, and have remained lurking in many minds, in a greater or less degree, to our day.

There were, however, three persons in Salem Village and its immediate vicinity, who deserve to be for ever remembered in this connection. They resisted the fanaticism at the beginning, and defied its wrath. Joseph Putnam was a little more than twenty-two years of age. He probably did not enter into the question of the doctrines then maintained on such subjects, but was led by his natural sagacity and independent spirit to the course he took. In opposition to both his brothers and both his uncles, and all the rest of his powerful and extensive family, he denounced the proceedings through and through. At the very moment when the excitement was at its most terrible stage, and Mr. Parris held the life of every one in his hands, Joseph Putnam expressed his disapprobation of his conduct by carrying his infant child to the church in Salem to be baptized. This was a public and most significant act. For six months, he kept some one of his horses under saddle night and day, without a moment's intermission of the precaution; and he and his family were constantly armed. It was understood, that, if any one attempted to arrest him, it would be at the peril of life. If the marshal should approach with overwhelming force, he would spring to his saddle, and bid defiance to pursuit. Such a course as this, taken by one standing alone against the whole community to which he belonged, shows a degree of courage, spirit, and resolution, which cannot but be held in honor.

Martha Corey was an aged Christian professor, of eminently devout habits and principles. It is, indeed, a strange fact, that, in her humble home, surrounded, as it then was, by a wilderness, this husbandman's wife should have reached a height so above and beyond her age. But it is proved conclusively by the depositions adduced against her, that her mind was wholly disenthralled from the errors of that period. She utterly repudiated the doctrines of witchcraft, and expressed herself freely and fearlessly against them. The prayer which this woman made "upon the ladder," and which produced such an impression on those who heard it, was undoubtedly expressive of enlightened piety, worthy of being characterized as "eminent" in its sentiments, and in its demonstration of an innocent heart and life.

The following paper, in the handwriting of Mr. Parris, is among the court-files. It has not the ordinary form of a deposition, but somehow was sworn to in Court: —

"The morning after the examination of Goody Nurse, Sam. Sibley met John Procter about Mr. Phillips's, who called to said Sibley as he was going to said Phillips's, and asked how the folks did at the village. He answered, he heard they were very bad last night, but he had heard nothing this morning. Procter replied, he was going to fetch home his jade; he left her there last night, and had rather given forty shillings than let her come up. Said Sibley asked why he talked so. Procter replied, if they were let alone so, we should all be devils and witches quickly; they should rather be had to the whipping-post; but he would fetch his jade home, and thrash the Devil out of her, — and more to the like purpose, crying, 'Hang them! hang them!'"

In another document, it is stated that Nathaniel Ingersoll and others heard John Procter tell Joseph Pope, "that, if he had John Indian in his custody, he would soon beat the Devil out of him."

The declarations thus ascribed to John Procter show that his views of the subject were about right; and it will probably be generally conceded, that the treatment he proposed for Mary Warren and "John Indian," if dealt out to the "afflicted children" generally at the outset, would have prevented all the mischief. A sound thrashing all round, seasonably administered, would have reached the root of the matter; and the story which has now been concluded of Salem witchcraft would never have been told.

When the witchcraft tornado burst upon Andover, it prostrated every thing before it. Accusers and accused were counted by scores, and under the panic of the hour the accused generally confessed. But Andover was the first to recover its senses. On the 12th of October, 1692, seven of its citizens addressed a memorial to the General Court in behalf of their wives and children, praying that they might be released on bond, "to remain as prisoners in their own houses, where they may be more tenderly cared for." They speak of their "distressed condition in prison, — a company of poor distressed creatures as full of inward grief and trouble as they are able to bear up in life withal." They refer to the want of "food convenient" for them, and to "the coldness of the winter season that is coming which may despatch such out of the way that have not been used to such hardships," and represent the ruinous effects of their absence from their families, who were at the same time required to maintain them in jail. On the 18th of October, the two ministers of Andover, Francis Dane and Thomas Barnard, with twenty-four other citizens of Andover, addressed a similar memorial to the Governor and General Court, in which we find the first public expression of condemnation of the proceedings. They call the accusers "distempered persons." They express the opinion that their friends and neighbors have been misrepresented. They bear the strongest testimony in favor of the persons accused, that several of them are members of the church in full communion, of blameless conversation, and "walking as becometh women professing godliness." They relate the methods by which they had been deluded and terrified into confession, and show the worthlessness of those confessions as evidences against them. They use this bold and significant language: "Our troubles we foresee are likely to continue and increase, if other methods be not taken than as yet have been; and we know not who can think himself safe, if the accusations of children and others who are under a diabolical influence shall be received against persons of good fame." On the 2d of January, 1693, the Rev. Francis Dane addressed a letter to a brother clergyman, which is among the files, and was probably designed to reach the eyes of the Court, in which he vindicates Andover against the scandalous reports got up by the accusers, and says that a residence there of forty-four years, and intimacy with the people, enable him to declare that they are not justly chargeable with any such things as witchcraft, charms, or sorceries of any kind. He expresses himself in strong language: "Had charity been put on, the Devil would not have had such an advantage against us, and I believe many innocent persons have been accused and imprisoned." He denounces "the conceit of spectre evidence," and warns against continuing in a course of proceeding that will procure "the divine displeasure." A paper signed by Dudley Bradstreet, Francis Dane, Thomas Barnard, and thirty-eight other men and twelve women of Andover, was presented to the Court at Salem to the same effect.

None of the persons named by Brattle can present so strong a claim to the credit of having opposed the witchcraft fanaticism before the close of the year 1692, as Francis Dane, his colleague Barnard, and the citizens of Andover, who signed memorials to the Legislature on the 18th of October, and to the Court of Trials about the same time. There is, indeed, one conclusive proof that the venerable senior pastor of the Andover Church made his disapprobation of the witchcraft proceedings known at an earlier period, at least in his immediate neighborhood. The wrath of the accusers was concentrated upon him to an unparalleled extent from their entrance into Andover. They did not venture to attack him directly. His venerable age and commanding position made it inexpedient; but they struck as near him, and at as many points, as they dared. They accused, imprisoned, and caused to be convicted and sentenced to death, one of his daughters, Abigail Faulkner. They accused, imprisoned, and brought to trial another, Elizabeth Johnson. They imprisoned, and brought to the sentence of death, his grand-daughter, Elizabeth Johnson, Jr. They cried out against, and caused to be imprisoned, several others of his grandchildren. They accused and imprisoned Deliverance the wife, and also the "man-servant," of his son Nathaniel. There is reason for supposing, as has been stated, that Elizabeth How was the wife of his nephew. Surely, no one was more signalized by their malice and resentment than Francis Dane; and he deserves to be recognized as standing pre-eminent, and, for a time, almost alone, in bold denunciation and courageous resistance of the execrable proceedings of that dark day.

Francis Dane made the following statement, also designed to reach the authorities, which cannot be read by any person of sensibility without feeling its force, although it made no impression upon the Court at the time : —

"Concerning my daughter Elizabeth Johnson, I never had ground to suspect her, neither have I heard any other to accuse her, till by spectre evidence she was brought forth ; but this I must say, she was weak, and incapacious, fearful, and in that respect I fear she hath falsely accused herself and others. Not long before she was sent for, she spake as to her own particular, that she was sure she was no witch. And for her daughter Elizabeth, she is but simplish at the best ; and I fear the common speech, that was frequently spread among us, of their liberty if they would confess, and the like expression used by some, have brought many into a snare. The Lord direct and guide those that are in place, and give us all submissive wills ; and let the Lord do with me and mine what seems good in his own eyes ! "

There is nothing in the proceedings of the Special Court of Oyer and Terminer more disgraceful than the fact, that the regular Court of Superior Judicature, the next year, after the public mind had been rescued from the delusion, and the spectral evidence repudiated, proceeded to try these and other persons, and, in the face of such statements as the foregoing, actually condemned to death Elizabeth Johnson, Jr.

It is remarkable that Brattle does not mention Calef. The understanding has been that they acted in concert, and that Brattle had a hand in getting up some of Calef's arguments. The silence of Brattle is not, upon the whole, at all inconsistent with their mutual action and alliance. As Calef was more perfectly unembarrassed, without personal relations to the clergy and others in high station, and not afraid to stand in the gap, it was thought best to let him take the fire of Cotton Mather. His name had not been connected with the matter in the public apprehension. He was a merchant of Boston, and a son of Robert Calef of Roxbury. His attention was called to the proceedings which originated in Salem Village ; and his strong faculties and moral courage enabled him to become the most efficient opponent, in his day, of the system of false reasoning upon which the prosecutions rested. He prepared several able papers in different forms, in which he discussed the subject with great ability, and treated Cotton Mather and all others whom he regarded as instrumental in precipitating the community into the fatal tragedy, with the greatest severity of language and force of logic, holding up the whole procedure to merited condemnation. They were first printed, at London, in 1700, in a small quarto volume, under the title of "More Wonders of the Invisible World." This publication burst like a bomb-shell upon all who had been concerned in promoting the witchcraft prosecutions. Cotton Mather was exasperated to the highest pitch. He says in his diary: "He sent this vile volume to London to be published, and the book is printed; and the impression is, this day week, arrived here. The books that I have sent over into England, with a design to glorify the Lord Jesus Christ, are not published, but strangely delayed; and the books that are sent over to vilify me, and render me incapable to glorify the Lord Jesus Christ, — these are published." Calef's writings gave a shock to Mather's influence, from which it never recovered.

Great difficulty has been experienced in drawing the story out in its true chronological sequence. The effect produced upon the public mind, when it became convinced that the proceedings had been wrong, and innocent blood shed, was a universal disposition to bury the recollection of the whole transaction in silence, and, if possible, oblivion. This led to a suppression and destruction of the ordinary materials of history. Papers were abstracted from the files, documents in private hands were committed to the flames, and a chasm left in the records of churches and public bodies. The journal of the Special Court of Oyer and Terminer is nowhere to be found. Hutchinson appears to have had access to it. It cannot well be supposed to have been lost by fire or other accident, because the records of the regular Court, up to the very time when the Special Court came into operation, and from the time when it expired, are preserved in order. A portion of the papers connected with the trials have come down in a miscellaneous, scattered, and dilapidated state, in the offices of the Clerk of the Courts in the County of Essex, and of the Secretary of the Commonwealth. By far the larger part have been abstracted, of which a few have been deposited, by parties into whose hands they had happened to come, with the Massachusetts Historical Society in Boston and the Essex Institute at Salem. The records of the parish of Salem Village, although exceedingly well kept before and after 1692 by Thomas Putnam, are in another hand for that year, very brief, and make no reference whatever to the witch-craft transactions. This general desire to obliterate the memory of the calamity has nearly extinguished tradition. It is more scanty and less reliable than on any other event at an equal distance in the past. A subject on which men avoided to speak soon died out of knowledge. The localities of many very interesting incidents cannot be identified. This is very observable, and peculiarly remarkable as to places in the now City of Salem. The reminiscences floating about are vague, contradictory, and few in number. In a community of uncommon intelligence, composed, to a greater degree perhaps than almost any other, of families that have been here from the first, very inquisitive for knowledge, and always imbued with the historical spirit, it is truly surprising how little has been borne down, by speech and memory, in the form of anecdote, personal traits, or local incidents, of this most extraordinary and wonderful occurrence of such world-wide celebrity. Almost all that we know is gleaned from the offices of the Registry of Deeds and Wills.*

* As an illustration of the oblivion that had settled over the details of the transactions and characters connected with the witchcraft prosecutions, it may be mentioned, that when, thirty-five years ago, I prepared the work entitled ' Lectures on Witchcraft; comprising a History of the Delusion in 1692, ' although professional engagements prevented my making the elaborate exploration that has now been given to the subject, I extended the investigation over the ordinary fields of research, and took particular pains to obtain information brought down by tradition, gleaned all that could be gathered from the memories of old persons then living of what they had heard from their predecessors, and sought for every thing that local antiquaries and genealogists could contribute. I find, by the methods of inquiry adopted in the preparation of the present work, how inadequate and meagre was the knowledge then possessed. Most of the persons accused and executed, like Giles Corey, his wife Martha, and Bridget Bishop, were supposed to have been of humble, if not mean condition, of vagrant habits, and more or less despicable repute. By following the threads placed in my hands, in the files of the county-offices of Registry of Deeds and Wills, and documents connected with trials at law, and by a collation of conveyances and the administration of estates, I find that Corey, however eccentric or open to criticism in some features of character and passages of his life, was a large landholder, and a man of singular force and acuteness of intellect; while his wife had an intelligence in advance of her times, and was a woman of eminent piety. The same is found to have been the case with most of those who suffered.

The reader may judge of my surprise in now discovering, that, while

It is remarkable, that the marshal and sheriff, both quite young men, so soon followed their victims to the other world. Jonathan Walcot, the father of Mary, and next neighbor to Parris, removed from the village, and died at Salem in 1699. Thomas Putnam and Ann his wife, the parents of the "afflicted child," who acted so extraordinary a part in the proceedings and of whom further mention will be made, died in 1699, — the former on the 24th of May, the latter on the 8th of June, — at the respective ages of forty-seven and thirty-eight.* There are indications that they saw the errors into which they had been led. If their eyes were at all opened to this view, how terrible must have been the thought of the cruel wrongs and wide-spread ruin of which they had been the cause! Of the circumstances of their deaths, or their last words and sentiments, we have no knowledge. It is not strange, that, in addition to all her woes, the death of her husband was more than Mrs. Ann Putnam could bear, and that

writing the "Lectures on Witchcraft," I was owning and occupying a part of the estate of Bridget Bishop, if not actually living in her house. The hard, impenetrable, all but petrified oak frame seems to argue that it dates back as far as when she rebuilt and renewed the original structure. Little, however, did I suspect, while delivering those lectures in the Lyceum Hall, that we were assembled on the site of her orchard, the scene of the preternatural and diabolical feats charged upon her by the testimony of Louder and others. Her estate was one of the most eligible and valuable in the old town, with a front, as has been mentioned, of a hundred feet on Washington Street, and extending along Church Street more than half the distance to St. Peter's Street. At the same time, her husband seems to have had a house in the village, near the head of Bass River. It is truly remarkable, that the locality of the property and residence of a person of her position, and who led the way among the victims of such an awful tragedy, should have become wholly obliterated from memory and tradition, in a community of such intelligence, consisting, in so large a degree, of old families, tracing themselves back to the earliest generations, and among whom the innumerable descendants of her seven great-grandchildren have continued to this day. It can only be accounted for by the considerations mentioned in the text. Tradition was stifled by horror and shame. What all desired to forget was forgotten. The only recourse was in oblivion; and all, sufferers and actors alike, found shelter under it.

* The looseness and inaccuracy of persons in reference to their own ages, in early times, is quite observable. In depositions, they speak of themselves as 'about' so many years, or as of so many years "or thereabouts." A variance on this point is often found in the statements of the same person

she followed him so soon to the grave. Of the other accusers, we have but little information. Elizabeth Booth was married to Israel Shaw about the year 1700. Mary Walcot was married, somewhere between 1692 and 1697, to a person belonging to Woburn, whose name is torn or worn off from Mr. Parris's records. Of the other "afflicted children" nothing is known, beyond the fact, that the Act of the Legislature of the Province, reversing the judgments, and taking off the attainder from those who were sentenced to death in 1692, has this paragraph: " Some of the principal accusers and witnesses in those dark and severe prosecutions have since discovered themselves to be persons of profligate and vicious conversation;" and Calef speaks of them as "vile varlets," and asserts that their reputations were not without spot before, and that subsequently they became abandoned to open and shameless vice.

A very considerable number of the people left the place. John Shepard and Samuel Sibley sold their lands, and went elsewhere; as did Peter Cloyse, who never brought his family to the village after his wife's release from prison. Edward and Sarah Bishop sold their estates, and took up their abode at Rehoboth. Some of the Raymond family removed to Middleborough. The Haynes family emigrated to New Jersey. No mention is afterwards found of other families in the record-books. The descendants of Thomas and Edward Putnam, in the next generation, were mostly dis-

at different times. Neither are records always to be relied upon as to precision. In the record-book of the village church, Mr. Parris enters the age of Mrs. Ann Putnam, at the date of her admission, June 4, 1691, as "Ann: ætat: 27." But an "Account of the Early Settlers of Salisbury," in the "New-England Historical and Genealogical Register," vol. vii. p. 314, gives the date of her birth " 15, 4, 1661." Her age is stated above according to this last authority; and, if correct, she was not so young, at the time of her marriage, as intimated (vol. i. p. 253), but seventeen years five months and ten days. It is difficult, however, to conceive how Parris, who was careful about such matters, and undoubtedly had his information from her own lips, could have been so far out of the way. Her brother, William Carr, in 1692, deposed that he was then forty-one years of age or thereabouts; whereas, the " Account of the Early Settlers of Salisbury," just referred to, gives the date of his birth " 15, 1, 1648." It is indeed singular, that two members of a family of their standing should have been under an error as to their own age; one to an extent of almost, the other of some months more than, three years.

persed to other places ; but those of Joseph remained on his lands, and have occupied his homestead to this day. It is a singular circumstance, that some of the spots where, particularly, the great mischief was brewed, are, and long have been, deserted. Where the parsonage stood, with its barn and garden and well and pathways, is now a bare and rugged field, without a vestige of its former occupancy, except a few broken bricks that mark the site of the house. The same is the case of the homestead of Jonathan Walcot. It was in these two families that the affair began and was matured. The spots where several others, who figured in the proceedings, lived, have ceased to be occupied; and the only signs of former habitation are hollows in the ground, fragments of pottery, and heaps of stones denoting the location of cellars and walls. Here and there, where houses and other structures once stood, the blight still rests.

Some circumstances relating to the personal history of those who experienced the greatest misery during the prevalence of the dreadful fanaticism, and were left to mourn over its victims, have happened to be preserved in records and documents on file. On the 30th of November, 1699, Margaret Jacobs was married to John Foster. She belonged to Mr. Noyes's parish; but the recollection of his agency in pushing on proceedings which carried in their train the execution of her aged grandfather, the exile of her father, the long imprisonment of her mother and herself, with the prospect of a violent and shameful death hanging over them every hour, and, above all, her own wretched abandonment of truth and conscience for a while, probably under his persuasion, made it impossible for her to think of being married by him. Mr. Greene was known to sympathize with those who had suffered, and the couple went to the village to be united. Some years afterwards, when the church of the Middle Precinct, now South Danvers, was organized, John and Margaret Foster, among the first, took their children there for baptism; and their descendants are numerous, in this neighborhood and elsewhere. Margaret, the widow of John Willard, married William Towne. Elizabeth, the widow of John Procter, married, subsequently to 1696, a person named Richards. Edward Bishop, the husband of Bridget, a few years afterwards was appointed guardian of Susannah Mason, the only child of Christian, who was the only child of Bridget by her former husband Thomas Oliver. Bishop seems to have invested the money of his ward in the lot at the extreme end of Forrester Street, where it connects with Essex Street, bounded by Forrester Street on the north and east, and Essex Street on the south. This was the property of Susannah when she married John Becket, Jr. Bishop appears to have continued his business of a sawyer to a very advanced age, and died in Salem, in 1705.

Sarah Nurse, about two years after her mother's death, married Michael Bowden, of Marblehead; and they occupied her father's house, in the town of Salem, of which he had retained the possession. His family having thus all been married off, Francis Nurse gave up his homestead to his son Samuel, and divided his remaining property among his four sons and four daughters. He made no formal deed or will, but drew up a paper, dated Dec. 4, 1694, describing the distribution of the estate, and what he expected of his children. He gave them immediate occupancy and possession of their respective portions. The provision made by the old man for his comfort, and the conditions required of his children, are curious. They give an interesting insight of the life of a rural patriarch. He reserved his "great chair and cushion;" a great chest; his bed and bedding; wardrobe, linen and woollen; a pewter pot; one mare, bridle, saddle, and sufficient fodder; the whole of the crop of corn, both Indian and English, he had made that year. The children were to discharge all the debts of his estate, pay him fourteen pounds a year, and contribute equally, as much more as might be necessary for his comfortable maintenance, and also to his "decent burial." The labors of his life had closed. He had borne the heaviest burden that can be laid on the heart of a good man. He found rest, and sought solace and support, in the society and love of his children and their families, as he rode from house to house on the road he had opened, by which they all communicated with each other. The parish records show that he continued his interest in its affairs. He lived just long enough to behold sure evidence that justice would be done to the memory of those who suffered, and the authors of the mischief be consigned to the condemnation of mankind. The tide, upon which Mr. Parris had ridden to the destruction of so many, had turned; and it was becoming apparent to all, that he would soon be compelled to disappear from his ministry in the village, before the awakening resentment of the people and the ministers. Francis Nurse died on the 22d of November, 1695, seventy-seven years of age. His sons with their wives, and his daughters with their husbands, went into the Probate Court with the paper before described, and unanimously requested the judge to have the estate divided according to its terms. This is conclusive proof that the father had been just and wise in his arrangements, and that true fraternal love and harmony pervaded the whole family. The descendants, under the names of Bowden, Tarbell, and Russell, are dispersed in various parts of the country: those under the name of Preston, while some have gone elsewhere, have been ever since, and still are, among the most respectable and honored citizens of the village. Some of the name of Nurse have also remained, and worthily represent and perpetuate it.

I have spoken of the tide's beginning to turn in 1695. Sure indications to that effect were then quite visible. It had begun far down in the public mind before the prosecutions ceased; but it was long before the change became apparent on the surface. It was long before men found utterance for their feelings.

Persons living at a distance have been accustomed, and are to this day, to treat the Salem-witchcraft transaction in the spirit of lightsome ridicule, and to make it the subject of jeers and jokes. Not so those who have lived on, or near, the fatal scene. They have ever regarded it with solemn awe and profound sorrow, and shunned the mention, and even the remembrance, of its details. This prevented an immediate expression of feeling, and delayed movements in the way of attempting a reparation of the wrongs that had been committed. The heart sickened, the lips were dumb, at the very thought of those wrongs. Reparation was impossible. The dead were beyond its reach. The sorrows and anguish of survivors were also beyond its reach. The voice of sympathy was felt to be unworthy to obtrude upon sensibilities that had been so outraged. The only refuge left for the individuals who had been bereaved, and for the body of the people who realized that innocent blood was on all their hands, was in humble and soul-subdued silence, and in prayers for forgiveness from God and from each other.

It was long before the public mind recovered from its paralysis. No one knew what ought to be said or done, the tragedy had been so awful. The parties who had acted in it were so numerous, and of such standing, including almost all the most eminent and honored leaders of the community from the bench, the bar, the magistracy, the pulpit, the medical faculty, and in fact all classes and descriptions of persons; the mysteries connected with the accusers and confessors; the universal prevalence of the legal, theological, and philosophical theories that had led to the proceedings ; the utter impossibility of realizing or measuring the extent of the calamity ; and the general shame and horror associated with the subject in all minds; prevented any open movement. Then there was the dread of rekindling animosities which time was silently subduing, and nothing but time could fully extinguish. Slowly, however, the remembrance of wrongs was becoming obscured. Neighborhood and business relations were gradually reconciling the estranged. Offices of civility, courtesy, and good-will were reviving; social and family intimacies and connections were taking effect and restoring the community to a natural and satisfactory condition. Every day, the sentiment was sinking deeper in the public mind, that something was required to be done to avert the displeasure of Heaven from a guilty land. But while some were ready to forgive, and some had the grace to ask to be forgiven, any general movement in this direction was obstructed by difficulties hard to be surmounted.

The wrongs committed were so remediless, the outrages upon right, character, and life, had been so shocking, that it was expecting too much from the ordinary standard of humanity to demand a general oblivion. On the other hand, so many had been responsible for them, and their promoters embraced such a great majority of all the leading classes of society, that it was impossible to call them to account. Dr. Bentley describes the condition of the community, in some brief and pregnant sentences, characteristic of his peculiar style : " As soon as the judges ceased to condemn, the people ceased to accuse. . . . Terror at the violence and guilt of the proceedings succeeded instantly to the conviction of blind zeal ; and what every man had encouraged all professed to abhor. Few dared to blame other men, because

few were innocent. The guilt and the shame became the portion
of the country, while Salem had the infamy of being the place of
the transactions. . . . After the public mind became quiet, few
things were done to disturb it. But a diminished population,
the injury done to religion, and the distress of the aggrieved,
were seen and felt with the greatest sorrow. . . . Every place was
the subject of some direful tale. Fear haunted every street.
Melancholy dwelt in silence in every place, after the sun retired.
Business could not, for some time, recover its former channels ;
and the innocent suffered with the guilty."

While the subject was felt to be too dark and awful to be
spoken of, and most men desired to bury it in silence, occasionally
the slumbering fires would rekindle, and the flames of animosity
burst forth. The recollection of the part he had acted, and the
feelings of many towards him in consequence, rendered the
situation of the sheriff often quite unpleasant; and the resentment
of some broke out in a shameful demonstration at his death, which
occurred early in 1697. Mr. English, representing that class who
had suffered under his official hands in 1692, having a business
demand upon him, in the shape of a suit for debt, stood ready
to seize his body after it was prepared for interment, and prevented the funeral at the time. The body was temporarily deposited on the sheriff's own premises. There were, it is probable,
from time to time, other less noticeable occurrences manifesting
the long-continued existence of the unhappy state of feeling engendered in 1692. There were really two parties in the community,
generally both quiescent, but sometimes coming into open collision ; the one exasperated by the wrongs they and their friends
had suffered, the other determined not to allow those who had
acted in conducting the prosecutions to be called to account for
what they had done. After the lapse of thirty years, and long
subsequent to the death of Mr. Noyes, Mr. English was prosecuted for having said that Mr. Noyes had murdered Rebecca
Nurse and John Procter.

It has been suggested, that the bearing of the executive officers
of the law towards the prisoners was often quite harsh. This resulted from the general feeling, in which these officials would have
been likely to sympathize, of the peculiarly execrable nature of
the crime charged upon the accused, and from the danger that

might attend the manifestation of any appearance of kindly regard for them. So far as the seizure of goods is considered, or the exaction of fees, the conduct of the officials was in conformity with usage and instructions. The system of the administration of the law, compared with our times, was stern, severe, and barbarous. The whole tone of society was more unfeeling. Philanthropy had not then extended its operations, or directed its notice, to the prison. Sheriff Corwin was quite a young man, being but twenty-six years of age at the time of his appointment. He probably acted under the advice of his relatives and connections on the bench. I think there is no evidence of any particular cruelty evinced by him. The arrests, examinations, and imprisonments had taken place under his predecessor, Marshal Herrick, who continued in the service as his deputy.

That individual, indeed, had justly incurred the resentment of the sufferers and their friends, by eager zeal in urging on the prosecutions, perpetual officiousness, and unwarrantable interference against the prisoners at the preliminary examinations. The odium originally attached to the marshal seems to have been transferred to his successor, and the whole was laid at the door of the sheriff. Marshal Herrick does not appear to have been connected with Joseph Herrick, who lived on what is now called Cherry Hill, but was a man of an entirely different stamp. He was thirty-four years of age, and had not been very long in the country. John Dunton speaks of meeting him in Salem, in 1686, and describes him as a " very tall, handsome man, very regular and devout in his attendance at church, religious without bigotry, and having every man's good word." His impatient activity against the victims of the witchcraft delusion wrought a great change in the condition of this popular and "handsome" man, as is seen in a petition presented by him, Dec. 8, 1692, to "His Excellency Sir William Phips, Knight, Captain-general and Governor of Their Majesties' Territories and Dominions of Massachusetts Bay in New England; and to the Honorable William Stoughton, Esq., Deputy-Governor; and to the rest of the Honored Council." It begins thus: " The petition of your poor servant, George Herrick, most humbly showeth." After recounting his great and various services " for the term of nine months, as marshal or deputy-sheriff in apprehending many prisoners, and conveying

them " unto prison and from prison to prison," he complains that
his whole time had been taken up so that he was incapable of
getting any thing for the maintenance of his " poor family : " he
further states that he had become so impoverished that necessity
had forced him to lay down his place ; and that he must certainly
come to want, if not in some measure supplied.   " Therefore I
humbly beseech Your Honors to take my case and condition so
far into consideration, that I may have some supply this hard
winter, that I and my poor children may not be destitute of sustenance, and so inevitably perish ; for I have been bred a gentleman,
and not much used to work, and am become despicable in these
hard times."   He concludes by declaring, that he is not " weary
of serving his king and country," nor very scrupulous as to the
kind of service ; for he promises that " if his habitation " could
thereby be " graced with plenty in the room of penury, there
shall be no services too dangerous and difficult, but your poor
petitioner will gladly accept, and to the best of my power accomplish.   I shall wholly lay myself at Your Honorable feet for
relief."   Marshal Herrick died in 1695.

But, while this feeling was spreading among the people, the
government were doing their best to check it.   There was great
apprehension, that, if allowed to gather force, it would burst over
all barriers, that no limit would be put to its demands for the
restoration of property seized by the officers of the law, and that
it would wreak vengeance upon all who had been engaged in
the prosecutions.   Under the influence of this fear, the following attempt was made to shield the sheriff of the county from
prosecutions for damages by those whose relatives had suffered : —

" *At a Superior Court of Judicature, Court of Assize, and General Jail
    Delivery, held at Ipswich, the fifteenth day of May, anno Domini* 1694.—
    Present, William Stoughton, Esq., *Chief-justice ;* Thomas Danforth,
    Esq. ; Samuel Sewall, Esq.

    " This Court, having adjusted the accounts of George Corwin, Esq.,
high-sheriff for the county of Essex, do allow the same to be just and
true ; and that there remains a balance due to him, the said Corwin,
of £67. 6s. 4d., which is also allowed unto him ; and, pursuant to law,
this Court doth fully, clearly, and absolutely acquit and discharge him,

the said George Corwin, his heirs, executors, and administrators, lands and tenements, goods and chattels, of and from all manner of sum or sums of money, goods or chattels levied, received, or seized, and of all debts, duties, and demands which are or may be charged in his, the said Corwin's, accounts, or which may be imposed by reason of the sheriff's office, or any thing by him done by virtue thereof, or in the execution of the same, from the time he entered into the said office, to this Court."

This extraordinary attempt of the Court to close the doors of justice beforehand against suits for damages did not seem to have any effect; for Mr. English compelled the executors of the sheriff to pay over to him £60. 3s.

At length, the government had to meet the public feeling. A proclamation was issued, "By the Honorable the Lieutenant-Governor, Council, and Assembly of His Majesty's province of the Massachusetts Bay, in General Court assembled." It begins thus : " Whereas the anger of God is not yet turned away, but his hand is still stretched out against his people in manifold judgments ;" and, after several specifications of the calamities under which they were suffering, and referring to the " many days of public and solemn " addresses made to God, it proceeds : " Yet we cannot but also fear that there is something still wanting to accompany our supplications ; and doubtless there are some particular sins which God is angry with our Israel for, that have not been duly seen and resented by us, about which God expects to be sought, if ever he again turn our captivity." Thursday, the fourteenth of the next January, was accordingly appointed to be observed as a day of prayer and fasting, —

" That so all God's people may offer up fervent supplications unto him, that all iniquity may be put away, which hath stirred God's holy jealousy against this land ; that he would show us what we know not, and help us, wherein we have done amiss, to do so no more ; and especially, that, whatever mistakes on either hand have been fallen into, either by the body of this people or any orders of men, referring to the late tragedy, raised among us by Satan and his instruments, through the awful judgment of God, he would humble us therefor, and pardon all the errors of his servants and people that desire to love his name ; that he would remove the rod of the wicked from off the lot of the

righteous; that he would bring in the American heathen, and cause
them to hear and obey his voice.

"Given at Boston, Dec. 17, 1696, in the eighth year of His Majesty's reign.   ISAAC ADDINGTON, *Secretary.*"

The jury had acted in conformity with their obligations and
honest convictions of duty in bringing in their verdicts. They had
sworn to decide according to the law and the evidence. The law
under which they were required to act was laid down with absolute positiveness by the Court. They were bound to receive it,
and to take and weigh the evidence that was admitted; and to their
minds it was clear, decisive, and overwhelming, offered by persons
of good character, and confirmed by a great number of confessions. If it had been within their province, as it always is declared not to be, to discuss the general principles, and sit in
judgment on the particular penalties of law, it would not have
altered the case; for, at that time, not only the common people,
but the wisest philosophers, supported the interpretation of the
law that acknowledged the existence of witchcraft, and its sanction
that visited it with death.

Notwithstanding all this, however, so tender and sensitive were
the consciences of the jurors, that they signed and circulated the
following humble and solemn declaration of regret for the part
they had borne in the trials. As the publication of this paper was
highly honorable to those who signed it, and cannot but be contemplated with satisfaction by all their descendants, I will repeat
their names: —

"We whose names are underwritten, being in the year 1692 called
to serve as jurors in court at Salem, on trial of many who were by
some suspected guilty of doing acts of witchcraft upon the bodies of
sundry persons, — we confess that we ourselves were not capable to
understand, nor able to withstand, the mysterious delusions of the
powers of darkness and Prince of the air, but were, for want of knowledge in ourselves and better information from others, prevailed with to
take up with such evidence against the accused as, on further consideration and better information, we justly fear was insufficient for the
touching the lives of any (Deut. xvii. 6), whereby we fear we have
been instrumental, with others, though ignorantly and unwittingly, to
bring upon ourselves and this people of the Lord the guilt of innocent
blood; which sin the Lord saith in Scripture he would not pardon

(2 Kings xxiv. 4), — that is, we suppose, in regard of his temporal
judgments. We do therefore hereby signify to all in general, and to
the surviving sufferers in special, our deep sense of, and sorrow for,
our errors in acting on such evidence to the condemning of any person; and do hereby declare, that we justly fear that we were sadly
deluded and mistaken, — for which we are much disquieted and distressed in our minds, and do therefore humbly beg forgiveness, first,
of God, for Christ's sake, for this our error, and pray that God would
not impute the guilt of it to ourselves nor others: and we also pray
that we may be considered candidly and aright by the living sufferers,
as being then under the power of a strong and general delusion, utterly
unacquainted with, and not experienced in, matters of that nature.

"We do heartily ask forgiveness of you all, whom we have justly
offended; and do declare, according to our present minds, we would
none of us do such things again, on such grounds, for the whole
world, — praying you to accept of this in way of satisfaction for our
offence, and that you would bless the inheritance of the Lord, that he
may be entreated for the land.

"Thomas Fisk, *Foreman.*	Thomas Pearly, Sr.
William Fisk.	John Peabody.
John Bacheler.	Thomas Perkins.
Thomas Fisk, Jr.	Samuel Sayer.
John Dane.	Andrew Eliot.
Joseph Evelith.	Henry Herrick, Sr."

In 1697, Rev. John Hale, of Beverly, published a work on the
subject of the witchcraft persecutions, in which he gives the reasons
which led him to the conclusion that there was error at the foundation of the proceedings. The following extract shows that he
took a rational view of the subject: —

"It may be queried then, How doth it appear that there was a
going too far in this affair?

"Answer I. — By the number of persons accused. It cannot be
imagined, that, in a place of so much knowledge, so many, in so small
a compass of land, should so abominably leap into the Devil's lap, —
at once.

"Ans. II. — The quality of several of the accused was such as
did bespeak better things, and things that accompany salvation.
Persons whose blameless and holy lives before did testify for them;
persons that had taken great pains to bring up *their children in the
nurture and admonition of the Lord,* such as we had charity for as for our

own souls, — and charity is a Christian duty, commended to us in 1 Cor. xiii., Col. iii. 14, and many other places.

"Ans. III. — The number of the afflicted by Satan daily increased, till about fifty persons were thus vexed by the Devil. This gave just ground to suspect some mistake.

"Ans. IV. — It was considerable, that nineteen were executed, and all denied the crime to the death ; and some of them were knowing persons, and had before this been accounted blameless livers. And it is not to be imagined but that, if all had been guilty, some would have had so much tenderness as to seek mercy for their souls in the way of confession, and sorrow for such a sin.

"Ans. V. — When this prosecution ceased, the Lord so chained up Satan, that the afflicted grew presently well : the accused are generally quiet, and for five years since we have no such molestation by them."

Such reasonings as these found their way into the minds of the whole community ; and it became the melancholy conviction of all candid and considerate persons that innocent blood had been shed. Standing where we do, with the lights that surround us, we look back upon the whole scene as an awful perversion of justice, reason, and truth.

On the 13th of June, 1700, Abigail Faulkner presented a well-expressed memorial to the General Court, in which she says that her pardon "so far had its effect, as that I am yet suffered to live, but this only as a malefactor convict upon record of the most heinous crimes that mankind can be supposed to be guilty of ; " and prays for "the defacing of the record" against her. She claims it as no more than a simple act of justice ; stating that the evidence against her was wholly confined to the "afflicted, who pretended to see me by their spectral sight, and not with their bodily eyes." That "the jury (upon only their testimony) brought me in 'Guilty,' and the sentence of death was passed upon me ; " and that it had been decided that such testimony was of no value. The House of Representatives felt the force of her appeal, and voted that "the prayer of the petitioner be granted." The council declined to concur, but addressed "His Excellency to grant the petitioner His Majesty's gracious pardon ; and His Excellency expressed His readiness to grant the same." Some adverse influence, it seemed, prevailed to prevent it.

On the 18th of March, 1702, another petition was presented to the General Court, by persons of Andover, Salem Village, and Topsfield, who had suffered imprisonment and condemnation, and by the relations of others who had been condemned and executed on the testimony, as they say, of "possessed persons," to this effect: —

"Your petitioners being dissatisfied and grieved that (besides what the condemned persons have suffered in their persons and estates) their names are exposed to infamy and reproach, while their trial and condemnation stands upon public record, we therefore humbly pray this honored Court that something may be publicly done to take off infamy from the names and memory of those who have suffered as aforesaid, that none of their surviving relations nor their posterity may suffer reproach on that account."

[Signed by Francis Faulkner, Isaac Easty, Thorndike Procter, and eighteen others.]

On the 20th of July, in answer to the foregoing petitions, a bill was ordered by the House of Representatives to be drawn up, forbidding in future such procedures, as in the witchcraft trials of 1692; declaring that "no spectre evidence may hereafter be accounted valid or sufficient to take away the life or good name of any person or persons within this province, and that the infamy and reproach cast on the names and posterity of said accused and condemned persons may in some measure be rolled away." The council concurred with an additional clause, to acquit all condemned persons "of the penalties to which they are liable upon the convictions and judgments in the courts, and estate them in their just credit and reputation, as if no such judgment had been had."

This petition was re-enforced by an "address" to the General Court, dated July 8, 1703, by several ministers of the county of Essex. They speak of the accusers in the witchcraft trials as "young persons under diabolical molestations," and express this sentiment: "There is great reason to fear that innocent persons then suffered, and that God may have a controversy with the land upon that account." They earnestly beg that the prayer of the petitioners, lately presented, may be granted. This petition was signed by Thomas Barnard, of Andover; Joseph Green, of Salem Village; William Hubbard, John Wise, John Rogers, and Jabez

Fitch, of Ipswich; Benjamin Rolfe, of Haverhill; Samuel Cheever, of Marblehead; Joseph Gerrish, of Wenham; Joseph Capen, of Topsfield; Zechariah Symmes, of Bradford; and Thomas Symmes, of Boxford. Francis Dane, of Andover, had died six years before. John Hale, of Beverly, had died three years before. The great age of John Higginson, of Salem, — eighty-seven years, — probably prevented the papers being handed to him. It is observable, that Nicholas Noyes, his colleague, is not among the signers.

What prevented action, we do not know; but nothing was done. Six years afterwards, on the 25th of May, 1709, an "humble address" was presented to the General Court by certain inhabitants of the province, some of whom "had their near relations, either parents or others, who suffered death in the dark and doleful times that passed over this province in 1692;" and others "who themselves, or some of their relations, were imprisoned, impaired and blasted in their reputations and estates by reason of the same." They pray for the passage of a "suitable act" to restore the reputations of the sufferers, and to make some remuneration "as to what they have been damnified in their estates thereby." This paper was signed by Philip English and twenty-one others. Philip English gave in an account in detail of what articles were seized and carried away, at the time of his arrest, from four of his warehouses, his wharf, and shop-house, besides the expenses incurred in prison, and in escaping from it. It appears by this statement, that he and his wife were nine weeks in jail at Salem and Boston. Nothing was done at this session. The next year, Sept. 12, 1710, Isaac Easty presented a strong memorial to the General Court in reference to his case. He calls for some remuneration. In speaking of the arrest and execution of his "beloved wife," he says "my sorrow and trouble of heart in being deprived of her in such a manner, which this world can never make me any compensation for." At the same time, the daughters of Elizabeth How, the son of Sarah Wildes, the heirs of Mary Bradbury, Edward Bishop and his wife Sarah, sent in severally similar petitions, — all in earnest and forcible language. Charles, one of the sons of George Burroughs, presented the case of his "dear and honored father;" declaring that his innocence of the crime of which he was accused, and his excellence of character, were shown in "his careful catechising his children, and upholding religion in his family, and by his solemn and savory written instructions from prison." He describes in affecting details the condition in which his father's family of little children was left at his death. One of Mr. Burroughs's daughters, upon being required to sign a paper in reference to compensation, expresses her distress of mind in these words : " Every discourse on this melancholy subject doth but give a fresh wound to my bleeding heart. I desire to sit down in silence." John Moulton, in behalf of the family of Giles Corey, says that they " cannot sufficiently express their grief" for the death, in such a manner, of "their honored father and mother." Samuel Nurse, in behalf of his brothers and sisters, says that their "honored and dear mother had led a blameless life from her youth up. . . . Her name and the name of her posterity lies under reproach, the removing of which reproach is the principal thing wherein we desire restitution. And, as we know not how to express our loss of such a mother in such a way, so we know not how to compute our charge, but leave it to the judgment of others, and shall not be critical." He distinctly intimates, that they do not wish any money to be paid them, unless " the attainder is taken off." Many other petitions were presented by the families of those who suffered, all in the same spirit ; and several besides the Nurses insisted mainly upon the " taking off the attainder."

The General Court, on the 17th of October, 1710, passed an act, that " the several convictions, judgments, and attainders be, and hereby are, reversed, and declared to be null and void." In simple justice, they ought to have extended the act to all who had suffered ; but they confined its effect to those in reference to whom petitions had been presented. The families of some of them had disappeared, or may not have had notice of what was going on ; so that the sentence which the Government acknowledged to have been unjust remains to this day unreversed against the names and memory of Bridget Bishop, Susanna Martin, Alice Parker, Ann Pudeator, Wilmot Read, and Margaret Scott. The stain on the records of the Commonwealth has never been fully effaced. What caused this dilatory and halting course on the part of the Government, and who was responsible for it, cannot be ascertained. Since the presentation of Abigail Faulkner's petition in 1700, the Legislature, in the popular branch at least, and the

Governor, appear to have been inclined to act favorably in the premises; but some power blocked the way. There is some reason to conjecture that it was the influence of the home government. Its consent to have the prosecutions suspended, in 1692, was not very cordial, but, while it approved of "care and circumspection therein," expressed reluctance to allow any "impediment to the ordinary course of justice."

On the 17th of December, 1711, Governor Dudley issued his warrant for the purpose of carrying out a vote of the "General Assembly," "by and with the advice and consent of Her Majesty's Council," to pay "the sum of £578. 12s." to "such persons as are living, and to those that legally represent them that are dead;" which sum was divided as follows:—

John Procter and wife	£150	0	0
George Jacobs	79	0	0
George Burroughs	50	0	0
Sarah Good	30	0	0
Giles Corey and wife	21	0	0
Dorcas Hoar	21	17	0
Abigail Hobbs	10	0	0
Rebecca Eames	10	0	0
Mary Post	8	14	0
Mary Lacy	8	10	0
Ann Foster	6	10	0
Samuel Wardwell and wife	36	15	0
Rebecca Nurse	25	0	0
Mary Easty	20	0	0
Mary Bradbury	20	0	0
Abigail Faulkner	20	0	0
John Willard	20	0	0
Sarah Wildes	14	0	0
Elizabeth How	12	0	0
Mary Parker	8	0	0
Martha Carrier	7	6	0
	£578	12	0

The distribution, as above, according to the evidence as it has come down to us, is as unjust and absurd as the smallness of the amount, and the long delay before it was ordered, are discreditable to the province. One of the larger sums was allowed to William Good, while he clearly deserved nothing, as he was an adverse witness in the examination of his wife, and did what he could to promote the prosecution against her. He did not, it is true, swear that he believed her to be a witch; but what he said tended to prejudice the magistrates and the public against her. Benjamin Putnam acted as his attorney, and received the money for him. Good was a retainer and dependant of that branch of the Putnam family; and its influence gave him so large a proportionate amount, and not the reason or equity of the case. More was allowed to Abigail Hobbs, a very malignant witness against the prisoners, than to the families of several who were executed. Nearly twice as much was allowed for Abigail Faulkner, who was pardoned, as for Elizabeth How, who was executed. The sums allowed in the cases of Parker, Carrier, and Foster, were shamefully small. The public mind evidently was not satisfied; and the Legislature were pressed for a half-century to make more adequate compensation, and thereby vindicate the sentiment of justice, and redeem the honor of the province.

On the 8th of December, 1738, Major Samuel Sewall, a son of the Judge, introduced an order in the House of Representatives for the appointment of a committee to get information relating to "the circumstances of the persons and families who suffered in the calamity of the times in and about the year 1692." Major Sewall entered into the matter with great zeal. The House unanimously passed the order. He was chairman of the committee; and, on the 9th of December, wrote to his cousin Mitchel Sewall in Salem, son of Stephen, earnestly requesting him and John Higginson, Esq., to aid in accomplishing the object. The following is an extract from a speech delivered by Governor Belcher to both Houses of the Legislature, Nov. 22, 1740. It is honorable to his memory.

"The Legislature have often honored themselves in a kind and generous remembrance of such families and of the posterity of such as have been sufferers, either in their persons or estates, for or by the Government, of which the public records will give you many instances. I should therefore be glad there might be a committee appointed by this Court to inquire into the sufferings of the people called Quakers, in the early days of this country, as also into the descendants of such families as were in a manner ruined in the mistaken management of the terrible affair called witchcraft. I really think there is something incumbent on this Government to be done for relieving the estates and reputations of the posterities of the unhappy families that so suffered; and the doing it, though so long afterwards, would doubtless be acceptable to Almighty God, and would reflect honor upon the present Legislature."

On the 31st of May, 1749, the heirs of George Burroughs addressed a petition to Governor Shirley and the General Court, setting forth " the unparalleled persecutions and sufferings " of their ancestor, and praying for " some recompense from this Court for the losses thereby sustained by his family." It was referred to a committee of both Houses. The next year, the petitioners sent a memorial to Governor Spencer Phips and the General Court, stating, that " it hath fell out, that the Hon. Mr. Danforth, chairman of the said committee, had not, as yet, called them together so much as once to act thereon, even to this day, as some of the honorable committee themselves were pleased, with real concern, to signify to your said petitioners." The House immediately passed this order: " That the committee within referred to be directed to sit forthwith, consider the petition to them committed, and report as soon as may be."

All that I have been able to find, as the result of these long-delayed and long-protracted movements, is a statement of Dr. Bentley, that the heirs of Philip English received two hundred pounds. He does not say when the act to this effect was passed. Perhaps some general measure of the kind was adopted, the record of which I have failed to meet. The engrossing interest of the then pending French war, and of the vehement dissensions that led to the Revolution, probably prevented any further attention to this subject, after the middle of the last century.

It is apparent from the foregoing statements and records, that while many individuals, the people generally, and finally Governor Belcher and the House of Representatives emphatically, did what they could, there was an influence that prevailed to prevent for a long time, if not for ever, any action of the province to satisfy the demands made by justice and the honor of the country in repairing the great wrongs committed by the legislative, executive, and judicial branches of the Government in 1692. The only bodies of men who fully came up to their duty on the occasion were the clergy of the county, and, as will appear, the church at Salem Village.

What was done by the First Church in Salem is shown in the following extract from its records : —

"March 2, 1712. — After the sacrament, a church-meeting was appointed to be at the teacher's house, at two of the clock in the afternoon, on the sixth of the month, being Thursday : on which day they accordingly met to consider of the several following particulars propounded to them by the teacher ; viz. : —

"1. Whether the record of the excommunication of our Sister Nurse (all things considered) may not be erased and blotted out. The result of which consideration was, That whereas, on July 3d, 1692, it was proposed by the Elders, and consented to by an unanimous vote of the church, that our Sister Nurse should be excommunicated, she being convicted of witchcraft by the Court, and she was accordingly excommunicated, since which the General Court having taken off the attainder, and the testimony on which she was convicted being not now so satisfactory to ourselves and others as it was generally in that hour of darkness and temptation ; and we being solicited by her son, Mr. Samuel Nurse, to erase and blot out of the church records the sentence of her excommunication, — this church, having the matter proposed to them by the teacher, and having seriously considered it, doth consent that the record of our Sister Nurse's excommunication be accordingly erased and blotted out, that it may no longer be a reproach to her memory, and an occasion of grief to her children. Humbly requesting that the merciful God would pardon whatsoever sin, error, or mistake was in the application of that censure and of that whole affair, through our merciful High-priest, who knoweth how to have compassion on the ignorant, and those that are out of the way.

"2. It was proposed whether the sentence of excommunication against our Brother Giles Corey (all things considered) may not be erased and blotted out. The result was, That whereas, on Sept. 18, 1692, it was considered by the church, that our Brother Giles Corey stood accused of and indicted for the sin of witchcraft, and that he had obstinately refused to plead, and so threw himself on certain death. It was agreed by the vote of the church, that he should be excommunicated for it ; and accordingly he was excommunicated. Yet the church, having now testimony in his behalf, that, before his death, he did bitterly repent of his obstinate refusal to plead in defence of his life, do consent that the sentence of his excommunication be erased and blotted out."

It will be noticed that these proceedings were not had at a regular public meeting, but at a private meeting of the church, on a week-day afternoon, at the teacher's house. The motives that led to them were a disposition to comply with the act of the General Court, and the solicitations of Mr. Samuel Nurse, rather than a profound sense of wrong done to a venerable member of their own body, who had claims upon their protection as such. The language of the record does not frankly admit absolutely that there was sin, error, or mistake, but requests forgiveness for whatsoever there may have been. The character of Rebecca Nurse, and the outrageous treatment she had received from that church, in the method arranged for her excommunication, demanded something more than these hypothetical expressions, with such a preamble.

The statement made in the vote about Corey is, on its face, a misrepresentation. From the nature of the proceeding by which he was destroyed, it was in his power, at any moment, if he "repented of his obstinate refusal to plead," by saying so, to be instantly released from the pressure that was crushing him. The only design of the torture was to make him bring it to an end by "answering" guilty, or not guilty. Somebody fabricated the slander that Corey's resolution broke down under his agonies, and that he bitterly repented; and Mr. Noyes put the foolish scandal upon the records of the church.

The date of this transaction is disreputable to the people of Salem. Twenty years had been suffered to elapse, and a great outrage allowed to remain unacknowledged and unrepented. The credit of doing what was done at last probably belongs to the Rev. George Corwin. His call to the ministry, as colleague with Mr. Noyes, had just been consummated. The introduction of a new minister heralded a new policy, and the proceedings have the appearance of growing out of the kindly and auspicious feelings which generally attend and welcome such an era.

The Rev. George, son of Jonathan Corwin, was born May 21, 1683, and graduated at Harvard College in 1701. Mr. Barnard, of Marblehead, describes his character: "The spirit of early devotion, accompanied with a natural freedom of thought and easy elocution, a quick invention, a solid judgment, and a tenacious memory, laid the foundation of a good preacher; to which his acquired literature, his great reading, hard studies, deep meditation, and close walk with God, rendered him an able and faithful minister of the New Testament." The records of the First Church, in noticing his death, thus speak of him: " He was highly esteemed in his life, and very deservedly lamented at his death; having been very eminent for his early improvement in learning and piety, his singular abilities and great labors, his remarkable zeal and faithfulness. He was a great benefactor to our poor." Those bearing the name of Curwen among us are his descendants. He died Nov. 29, 1717.

The Rev. Nicholas Noyes died Dec. 13, 1717. He was a person of superior talents and learning. He published, with the sermon preached by Cotton Mather on the occasion, a poem on the death of his venerable colleague, Mr. Higginson, in 1708; and also a poem on the death of Rev. Joseph Green, in 1715. Although an amiable and benevolent man in other respects, it cannot be denied that he was misled by his errors and his temperament into the most violent course in the witchcraft prosecutions; and it is to be feared that his feelings were never wholly rectified in reference to that transaction.

Jonathan, the father of the Rev. George Corwin, and whose part as a magistrate and judge in the examinations and trials of 1692 has been seen, died on the 9th of July, 1718, seventy-eight years of age.

It only remains to record the course of the village church and people in reference to the events of 1692. After six persons, including Rebecca Nurse, had suffered death; and while five others, George Burroughs, John Procter, John Willard, George Jacobs, and Martha Carrier, were awaiting their execution, which was to take place on the coming Friday, Aug. 19, — the facts, related as follows by Mr. Parris in his record-book, occurred: —

" Sabbath-day, 14th August, 1692. — The church was stayed after the congregation was dismissed, and the pastor spake to the church after this manner: —

" ' Brethren, you may all have taken notice, that, several sacrament days past, our brother Peter Cloyse, and Samuel Nurse and his wife, and John Tarbell and his wife, have absented from communion with us at the Lord's Table, yea, have very rarely, except our brother Samuel Nurse, been with us in common public worship: now, it is needful that the church send some persons to them to know the reason of their absence. Therefore, if you be so minded, express yourselves.'

"None objected. But a general or universal vote, after some discourse, passed, that Brother Nathaniel Putnam and the two deacons should join with the pastor to discourse with the said absenters about it.

"31st August. — Brother Tarbell proves sick, unmeet for discourse ; Brother Cloyse hard to be found at home, being often with his wife in prison at Ipswich for witchcraft; and Brother Nurse, and sometimes his wife, attends our public meeting, and he the sacrament, 11th September, 1692 : upon all which we choose to wait further."

When it is remembered that the individuals aimed at all belonged to the family of Rebecca Nurse, whose execution had taken place three weeks before under circumstances with which Mr. Parris had been so prominently and responsibly connected, this proceeding must be felt by every person of ordinary human sensibilities to have been cruel, barbarous, and unnatural. Parris made the entry in his book, as he often did, some time after the transaction, as the inserted date of Sept. 11, shows. What his object was in commencing disciplinary treatment of this distressed family is not certain. It may be that he was preparing to get up such a feeling against them as would make it safe to have the " afflicted " cry out upon some of them. Or it may be that he wished to get them out of his church, to avoid the possibility of their proceeding against him, by ecclesiastical methods, at some future day. He could not, however, bring his church to continue the process. This is the first indication that the brethren were no longer to be relied on by him to go all lengths, and that some remnants of good feeling and good sense were to be found among them.

But Mr. Parris was determined not to allow the public feeling against persons charged with witchcraft to subside, if he could help it ; and he made one more effort to renew the vehemence of the prosecutions. He prepared and preached two sermons, on the 11th of September, from the text, Rev. xvii. 14 : " These shall make war with the Lamb, and the Lamb shall overcome them : for he is

Lord of lords, and King of kings; and they that are with him are called and chosen and faithful." They are entitled, "The Devil and his instruments will be warring against Christ and his followers." This note is added, "After the condemnation of six witches at a court at Salem, one of the witches, viz., Martha Corey, in full communion with our church." The following is a portion of "the improvement" in the application of these discourses : —

"It may serve to reprove such as seem to be so amazed at the war the Devil has raised amongst us by wizards and witches, against the Lamb and his followers, that they altogether deny it. If ever there were witches, men and women in covenant with the Devil, here are multitudes in New England. Nor is it so strange a thing that there should be such; no, nor that some church-members should be such. Pious Bishop Hall saith, ' The Devil's prevalency in this age is most clear in the marvellous number of witches abounding in all places. Now hundreds (says he) are discovered in one shire; and, if fame deceive us not, in a village of fourteen houses in the north are found so many of this damned brood. Heretofore, only barbarous deserts had them; but now the civilized and religious parts are frequently pestered with them. Heretofore, some silly, ignorant old woman, &c.; but now we have known those of both sexes who professed much knowledge, holiness, and devotion, drawn into this damnable practice.' "

The foregoing extract is important as showing that some persons at the village had begun to express their disbelief of the witchcraft doctrine of Mr. Parris, "altogether denying it." The title and drift of the sermons in connection with the date, and his proceedings, the month before, against Samuel Nurse, Tarbell, and Cloyse, members of his church, give color to the idea that he was designing to have them "cried out" against, and thus disposed of. It is a noticeable fact, that, about this time, Cotton Mather was also laying his plans for a renewal, or rather continuance, of witchcraft prosecutions. Nine days after these sermons were preached by Parris, Mather wrote the following letter to Stephen Sewall of Salem : —

BOSTON, Sept. 20, 1692.

MY DEAR AND MY VERY OBLIGING STEPHEN, — It is my hap to be continually . . . with all sorts of objections, and objectors against the . . . work now doing at Salem; and it is my further good hap to do some little service for God and you in my encounters.

But that I may be the more capable to assist in lifting up a standard against the infernal enemy, I must renew my most importunate request, that you would please quickly to perform what you kindly promised, of giving me a narrative of the evidences given in at the trials of half a dozen, or if you please a dozen, of the principal witches that have been condemned. I know 'twill cost you some time; but, when you are sensible of the benefit that will follow, I know you will not think much of that cost; and my own willingness to expose myself unto the utmost for the defence of my friends with you makes me presume to plead something of merit to be considered.

I shall be content, if you draw up the desired narrative by way of letter to me; or, at least, let it not come without a letter, wherein you shall, if you can, intimate over again what you have sometimes told me of the awe which is upon the hearts of your juries, with . . . unto the validity of the spectral evidences.

Please also to . . . some of your observations about the confessors and the credibility of what they assert, or about things evidently preternatural in the witchcrafts, and whatever else you may account an entertainment, for an inquisitive person, that entirely loves you and *Salem*. Nay, though I will never lay aside the character which I mentioned in my last words, yet I am willing, that, when you write, you should imagine me as obstinate a Sadducee and witch-advocate as any among us: address me as one that believed nothing reasonable; and when you have so knocked me down, in a spectre so unlike me, you will enable me to box it about among my neighbors, till it come — I know not where at last.

But assure yourself, as I shall not wittingly make what you write prejudicial to any worthy design which those two excellent persons, Mr. Hale and Mr. Noyse, may have in hand; so you shall find that I shall be, sir, your grateful friend,   C. MATHER.

P. S. — That which very much strengthens the charms of the request which this letter makes you is, that His Excellency the Governor laid his positive commands upon me to desire this favor of you; and the truth is, there are some of his circumstances with reference to this affair, which I need not mention, that call for the expediting of your kindness, — *kindness,* I say, for such it will be esteemed as well by him as by your servant,   C. MATHER.

In order to understand the character and aim of this letter, it will be necessary to consider its date. It was written Sept. 20, 1692. On the 19th of August, but one month before, Dr. Mather was acting a conspicuous part under the gallows at Witch-hill, at the execution of Mr. Burroughs and four others, increasing the power of the awful delusion, and inflaming the passions of the people. On the 9th of September, six more miserable creatures received sentence of death. On the 17th of September, nine more received sentence of death. On the 19th of September, Giles Cory was crushed to death. And, on the 22d of September, eight were executed. These were the last that suffered death. The letter, therefore, was written while the horrors of the transaction were at their height, and by a person who had himself been a witness of them, and whose " good hap " it had been to " do some little service " in promoting them. The object of the writer is declared to be, that he might be " more capable to assist in lifting up a standard against the infernal enemy." The literal meaning of this expression is, that he might be enabled to get up another witchcraft delusion under his own special management and control. Can any thing be imagined more artful and dishonest than the plan he had contrived to keep himself out of sight in all the operations necessary to accomplish his purpose ? " Nay, though I will never lay aside the character which I mentioned in my last words, yet I am willing, that, when you write, you should imagine me as obstinate a Sadducee and witch-advocate as any among us : address me as one that believed nothing reasonable ; and when you have so knocked me down, in a spectre so unlike me, you will enable me to box it about among my neighbors, till it come — I know not where at last."

Upon obtaining the document requisite to the fulfilment of his design, he did " box it about " so effectually among his neighbors, that he succeeded that next summer in getting up a wonderful case of witchcraft, in the person of one Margaret Rule, a member of his congregation in Boston. Dr. Mather published an account of her long-continued fastings, even unto the ninth day, and of the incredible sufferings she endured from the " infernal enemy." " She was thrown," says he, " into such exorbitant convulsions as were astonishing to the spectators in general. They that could behold the doleful condition of the poor family without sensible compassions might have entrails, indeed, but I am sure they could have no true bowels in them." So far was he successful in spreading the delusion, that he prevailed upon six men to testify that they had seen Margaret Rule lifted bodily from her bed, and raised by an invisible power " so as to touch the garret floor ; " that she was entirely removed from the bed or any other material support; that she continued suspended for several minutes; and that a strong man, assisted by several other persons, could not effectually resist the mysterious force that lifted her up, and poised her aloft in the air! The people of Boston were saved from the horrors intended to be brought upon them by this dark and deep-laid plot, by the activity, courage, and discernment of Calef and others, who distrusted Dr. Mather, and, by watching his movements, exposed the imposture, and overthrew the whole design.

Mr. Parris does not appear to have produced much effect by his sermons. The people had suffered enough from the " war between the Devil and the Lamb," as he and Mather had conducted it ; and it could not be renewed.

Immediately upon the termination of the witchcraft proceedings, the controversy between Mr. Parris and the congregation, or the inhabitants, as they were called, of the village, was renewed, with earnest resolution on their part to get rid of him. The parish neglected and refused to raise the means for paying his salary ; and a majority of the voters, in the meetings of the " inhabitants," vigilantly resisted all attempts in his favor. The church was still completely under his influence ; and, as has been stated in the First Part, he made use of that body to institute a suit against the people. The court and magistrates were wholly in his favor, and peremptorily ordered the appointment, by the people, of a new committee. The inhabitants complied with the order by the election of a new committee, but took care to have it composed exclusively of men opposed to Mr. Parris ; and he found himself no better off than before. He concluded not to employ his church any longer as a principal agent in his lawsuit against the parish ; but used it for another purpose.

After the explosion of the witchcraft delusion, the relations of parties became entirely changed. The prosecutors at the trials were put on the defensive, and felt themselves in peril. Parris saw his danger, and, with characteristic courage and fertility of resources, prepared to defend himself, and carry the war upon any quarter from which an attack might be apprehended. He continued, on his own responsibility, to prosecute, in court, his suit against the parish, and in his usual trenchant style. As the law then was, a minister, in a controversy with his parish, had a secure advantage, and absolutely commanded the situation, if his church were with him. From the time of his settlement, Parris had shaped his policy on this basis. He had sought to make his church an impregnable fortress against his opponents. But, to be impregnable, it was necessary that there should be no enemies within it. A few disaffected brethren could at any time demand, and have a claim to, a mutual council; and Mr. Parris knew, that, before the investigations of such a council, his actions in the witchcraft prosecutions could not stand. This perhaps suggested his movements, in August, 1692, against Samuel Nurse, John Tarbell, and Peter Cloyse. He did not at that time succeed in getting rid of them; and they remained in the church, and, with the exception of Cloyse, in the village. They might at any time take the steps that would lead to a mutual council; and Mr. Parris was determined, at all events, to prevent that. It was evident that the members of that family would insist upon satisfaction being given them, in and through the church, for the wrongs he had done them. Although, in the absence of Cloyse, but two in number, there was danger that sympathy for them might reach others of the brethren. Thomas Wilkins, a member in good standing, son of old Bray Wilkins, and a connection of John Willard, an intelligent and resolute man, had already joined them. Parris felt that others might follow, and that whatever could be done to counteract them must be done quickly. He accordingly initiated proceedings in his church to rid himself of them, if not by excommunication, at least by getting them under discipline, so as to prevent the possibility of their dealing with him.

This led to one of the most remarkable passages of the kind in the annals of the New-England churches. It is narrated in detail by Mr. Parris, in his church record-book. It would not be easy to find anywhere an example of greater skill, wariness, or ability in a conflict of this sort. On the one side is Mr. Parris, backed by his church and the magistrates, and aided, it is probable, by Mr. Noyes; on the other, three husbandmen. They had no known backers or advisers; and, at frequent stages of the fencing match, had to parry or strike, without time to consult any one. Mr. Parris was ingenious, quick, a great strategist, and not over-scrupulous as to the use of his weapons. Nurse, Tarbell, and Wilkins were cautious, cool, steady, and persistent. Of course, they were wholly inexperienced in such things, and liable to make wrong moves, or to be driven or drawn to untenable ground. But they will not be found, I think, to have taken a false step from beginning to end. Their line of action was extremely narrow. It was necessary to avoid all personalities, and every appearance of passion or excitement; to make no charge against Mr. Parris that could touch the church, as such, or reflect upon the courts, magistrates, or any others that had taken part in the prosecutions. It was necessary to avoid putting any thing into writing, with their names attached, which could in any way be tortured into a libel. Parris lets fall expressions which show that he was on the watch for something of the kind to seize upon, to transfer the movement from the church to the courts. Entirely unaccustomed to public speaking, these three farmers had to meet assemblages composed of their opponents, and much wrought up against them; to make statements, and respond to interrogatories and propositions, the full and ultimate bearing of which was not always apparent: any unguarded expression might be fatal to their cause. Their safety depended upon using the right word at the right time and in the right manner, and in withholding the statement of their grievances, in adequate force of language, until they were under the shelter of a council. If, during the long-protracted conferences and communications, they had tripped at any point, allowed a phrase or syllable to escape which might be made the ground of discipline or censure, all would be lost; for Parris could not be reached but through a council, and a council could not even be asked for except by brethren in full and clear standing. It was often attempted to ensnare them into making charges against the church; but they kept their eye on Parris, and, as they told him more than once in the presence of the whole body of the people, on him alone. Limited as the ground was on which they could stand, they held it steadfastly, and finally drove him from his stronghold.

On the first movement of Mr. Parris offensively upon them, they commenced their movement upon him. The method by which alone they could proceed, according to ecclesiastical law and the platform of the churches, was precisely as it was understood to be laid down in Matt. xviii. 15–17. Following these directions, Samuel Nurse first called alone upon Mr. Parris, and privately made known his grievances. Parris gave him no satisfaction. Then, after a due interval, Nurse, Tarbell, and Wilkins called upon him together. He refused to see them together, but one at a time was allowed to go up into his study. Tarbell and Nurse each spent an hour or more with him, leaving no time for Wilkins. In these interviews, he not only failed to give satisfaction, but, according to his own account, treated them in the coolest and most unfeeling manner, not allowing himself to utter a soothing word, but actually reiterating his belief of the guilt of their mother; telling them, as he says, "that he had not seen sufficient grounds to vary his opinion." Cloyse came soon after to the village, and had an interview with him for the same purpose. Parris saw them one only at a time, in order to preclude their taking the second step required by the gospel rule; that is, to have a brother of the church with them as a witness. He also took the ground that they could not be witnesses for each other, but that he should treat them all as only one person in the transaction. A sense of the injustice of his conduct, or some other consideration, led William Way, another of the brethren, to go with them as a witness. Nurse, Tarbell, Wilkins, Cloyse, and Way went to his house together. He said that the four first were but one person in the case; but admitted that Way was a distinct person, a brother of accredited standing, and a witness. He escaped, however, under the subterfuge that the gospel rule required "two or *three* witnesses." In this way, the matter stood for some time; Parris saying that they had not complied with the conditions in Matt. xviii., and they maintaining that they had.

The course of Parris was fast diminishing his hold upon the public confidence. It was plain that the disaffected brethren had done what they could, in an orderly way, to procure a council. At length, the leading clergymen here and in Boston, whose minds were open to reason, thought it their duty to interpose their advice. They wrote to Parris, that he and his church ought to consent to a council. They wrote a second time in stronger terms. Not daring to quarrel with so large a portion of the clergy, Parris pretended to comply with their advice, but demanded a majority of the council to be chosen by him and his church. The disaffected brethren insisted upon a fair, mutual council; each party to have three ministers, with their delegates, in it. To this, Parris had finally to agree. The dissatisfied brethren named, as one of their three, a church at Ipswich. Parris objected to the Ipswich church. The dissenting brethren insisted that each side should be free to select its respective three churches. Parris was not willing to have Ipswich in the council. The other party insisted, and here the matter hung suspended. The truth is, that the disaffected brethren were resolved to have the Rev. John Wise in the council. They knew Cotton Mather would be there, on the side of Parris; and they knew that John Wise was the man to meet him. The public opinion settled down in favor of the dissatisfied brethren, on the ground that each party to a mutual council ought to — and, to make it really mutual, must — have free and full power to nominate the churches to be called by it. Parris, being afraid to have a mutual council, and particularly if Mr. Wise was in it, suddenly took a new position. He and his church called an *ex parte* council, at which the following ministers, with their delegates, were present: Samuel Checkley of the New South Church, James Allen of the First Church, Samuel Willard of the Old South, Increase and Cotton Mather of the North Church, — all of Boston; Samuel Torrey of Weymouth; Samuel Phillips of Rowley, and Edward Payson, also of Rowley. Among the delegates were many of the leading public men of the province. The Result was essentially damaging to Mr. Parris. The tide was now strongly set against him. The Boston ministers advised him to withdraw from the contest. They provided a settlement for him in Connecticut, and urged him to quit the village, and go there. But he refused, and prolonged the struggle. In the course of it, papers were drawn up and signed, one by his friends, another by his opponents, together embracing nearly all the men and women of the village. Those who did not sign either paper were understood to sympathize with the disaffected brethren. Many who signed the paper favorable to him acted undoubtedly from the motive stated in the heading; viz., that the removal of Mr. Parris could do no good, "for we have had three ministers removed already, and by every removal our differences have been rather aggravated." Another removal, they thought, would utterly ruin them. They do not express any particular interest in Mr. Parris, but merely dread another change. They preferred to bear the ills they had, rather than fly to others that they knew not of. It is a very significant fact, that neither Mrs. Ann Putnam nor the widow Sarah Houlton signed either paper (the Sarah Houlton whose name appears was the wife of Joseph Houlton, Sr.). There is reason to believe that they regretted the part they had taken, particularly against Rebecca Nurse, and probably did not feel over favorably to the person who had led them into their dreadful responsibility.

In the mean time, the controversy continued to wax warm among the people. Mr. Parris was determined to hold his place, and, with it, the parsonage and ministry lands. The opposition was active, unappeasable, and effective. The following paper, handed about, illustrates the methods by which they assailed him: —

"As to the contest between Mr. Parris and his hearers, &c., it may be composed by a satisfactory answer to Lev. xx. 6: 'And the soul that turneth after such as have familiar spirits, and after wizards, to go a-whoring after them, I will set my face against that soul, and will cut him off from among his people.' 1 Chron. x. 13, 14: 'So Saul died for his transgression which he committed against the Lord, — even against the word of the Lord, which he kept not, — and also for asking counsel of one who had a familiar to inquire of it, and inquired not of the Lord: therefore he slew him,'" &c.

Mr. Parris mirrored, or rather daguerrotyped, his inmost thoughts upon the page of his church record-book. Whatever feeling happened to exercise his spirit, found expression there. This gives it a truly rare and singular interest. Among a variety of scraps variegating the record, and thrown in with other notices of deaths, he has the following: —

"1694, Oct. 27. — Ruth, daughter to Job Swinnerton (died), and buried the 28th instant, being the Lord's Day; and the corpse carried by the meeting-house door in time of singing before meeting afternoon, and more at the funeral than at the sermon."

This illustrates the state of things. The Swinnerton family were all along opposed to Mr. Parris, and kept remarkably clear from the witchcraft delusion. Originally, it was not customary to have prayers at funerals. At any rate, all that Mr. Parris had to do on the occasion was to witness and record the fact, which he indites in the pithy manner in which he often relieves his mind, that more people went to the distant burial-ground than came to hear him preach. The procession was made up of his opponents; the congregation, of his friends. At last, Captain John Putnam proposed that each party should choose an equal number from themselves to decide the controversy; and that Major Bartholomew Gedney, from the town, should be invited to act as moderator of the joint meeting. Both sides agreed, and appointed their representatives. Major Gedney consented to preside. But this movement came to nothing, probably owing to the refractoriness of Mr. Parris; for, from that moment, he had no supporters. The church ceased to act: its members were merged in the meeting of the inhabitants. There was no longer any division among them. The party that had acted as friends of Mr. Parris united thenceforward with his opponents to defend the parish in the suit he had brought against it in the courts. The controversy was quite protracted. The Court was determined to uphold him, and expressed its prejudice against the parish, sometimes with considerable severity of manner and action.*

* The following passage is from the parish records:—

"On the 3d of February, 1693, a warrant was issued for a meeting of the inhabitants of the village, signed by Thomas Preston, Joseph Pope, Joseph Houlton, and John Tarbell, of the standing annual committee, to be held Feb. 14, "to consider and agree and determine who are capable of voting in our public transactions, by the power given us by the General-court order at our first settlement; and to consider of and make void a vote in our book of records, on the 18th of June, 1689, where there is a salary of sixty-six pounds stated to Mr. Parris, he not complying with it; also to consider of and make void several votes in the book of records on the 10th of October, 1692, where our ministry house and barn and two acres of land seem to be conveyed from us after a fraudulent manner."

At this meeting, it was voted, that "all men that are ratable, or hereafter shall be living within that tract of land mentioned in our General-court order, shall have liberty in nominating and appointing a committee, and voting in any of our public concerns."

By referring to the account, in the First Part, of the controversy between the inhabitants of the village and Mr. Bayley, "the power" above alluded to, "given us by the General Court," will be seen fully described. In its earnestness to fasten Mr. Bayley upon "the inhabitants," the Court elaborately ordained the system by which they should be constrained to provide for him, and compelled to raise the means of paying his salary. As no church

The parish heeded not the frowns of the Court, but persisted inexorably in its purpose to get rid of Mr. Parris. After an obstinate contest, it prevailed. In the last stage of the controversy, it appointed four men, as its agents or attorneys, whose names indicate the spirit in which it acted, — John Tarbell, Samuel Nurse, Daniel Andrew, and Joseph Putnam. His dauntless son did not follow the wolf through the deep and dark recesses of his den with a more determined resolution than that with which Joseph Putnam pursued Samuel Parris through the windings of the law, until he ferreted him out, and rid the village of him for ever.

Finally, the inferior court of Common Pleas, before which Mr. Parris had carried the case, ordered that the matters in controversy between him and the inhabitants of Salem Village should be referred to arbitrators for decision. The following statement was laid before them by the persons representing the inhabitants : —

" *To the Honorable Wait Winthrop, Elisha Cook, and Samuel Sewall, Esquires, Arbitrators, indifferently chosen, between Mr. Samuel Parris and the Inhabitants of Salem Village.*

" *The Remonstrances of several Aggrieved Persons in the said Village, with further Reasons why they conceive they ought not to hear Mr. Parris, nor to own him as a Minister of the Gospel, nor to contribute any Support to him as such for several years past, humbly offered us fit for consideration.*

" We humbly conceive that, having, in April, 1693, given our reasons why we could not join with Mr. Parris in prayer, preaching, or sacrament, if these reasons are found sufficient for our withdrawing (and we cannot yet find but they are), then we conceive ourselves virtually discharged, not only in conscience, but also in law, which re-

had then been organized, the General Court fastened the duty upon " householders." The fact had not been forgotten, and the above vote showed that the parish intended to hold on to the power then given them. This highly incensed the Court of Sessions. It ordered the parish book of records to be produced before it, and caused a condemnation of such a claim of right to be written out, in open Court, on the face of the record, where it is now to be seen. It is as follows : —

" At the General Sessions of the Peace holden at Ipswich, March the 28th, 1693. This Court having viewed and considered the above agreement or vote contained in the last five lines, finding the same to be repugnant to the laws of this province, do declare the same to be null and void, and that this order be recorded with the records of this Court.

" Attest, STEPHEN SEWALL, *Clerk.*"

quires maintenance to be given to such as are orthodox and blameless; the said Mr. Parris having been teaching such dangerous errors, and preached such scandalous immoralities, as ought to discharge any (though ever so gifted otherways) from the work of the ministry, particularly in his oath against the lives of several, wherein he swears that the prisoners with their looks knock down those pretended sufferers. We humbly conceive that he that swears to more than he is certain of, is equally guilty of perjury with him that swears to what is false. And though they did fall at such a time, yet it could not be known that they did it, much less could they be certain of it; yet did swear positively against the lives of such as he could not have any knowledge but they might be innocent.

"His believing the Devil's accusations, and readily departing from all charity to persons, though of blameless and godly lives, upon such suggestions; his promoting such accusations; as also his partiality therein in stifling the accusations of some, and, at the same time, vigilantly promoting others, — as we conceive, are just causes for our refusal, &c.

"That Mr. Parris's going to Mary Walcot or Abigail Williams, and directing others to them, to know who afflicted the people in their illnesses, — we understand this to be a dealing with them that have a familiar spirit, and an implicit denying the providence of God, who alone, as we believe, can send afflictions, or cause devils to afflict any : this we also conceive sufficient to justify such refusal.

"That Mr. Parris, by these practices and principles, has been the beginner and procurer of the sorest afflictions, not to this village only, but to this whole country, that did ever befall them.

"We, the subscribers, in behalf of ourselves, and of several others of the same mind with us (touching these things), having some of us had our relations by these practices taken off by an untimely death; others have been imprisoned and suffered in our persons, reputations, and estates, — submit the whole to your honors' decision, to determine whether we are or ought to be any ways obliged to honor, respect, and support such an instrument of our miseries; praying God to guide your honors to act herein as may be for his glory, and the future settlement of our village in amity and unity.

"JOHN TARBELL,
SAMUEL NURSE,
JOSEPH PUTNAM,
DANIEL ANDREW,
Attorneys for the people of the Village.

Boston, July 21, 1697."

The arbitrators decided that the inhabitants should pay to Mr. Parris a certain amount for arrearages, and also the sum of £79. 9s. 6d. for all his right and interest in the ministry house and land, and that he be forthwith dismissed; and his ministerial relation to the church and society in Salem Village dissolved. The parish raised the money with great alacrity. Nathaniel Ingersol, who had, as has been stated, made him a present at his settlement of a valuable piece of land adjoining the parsonage grounds, bought it back, paying him a liberal price for it, fully equal to its value; and he left the place, so far as appears, for ever.

On the 14th of July, 1696, in the midst of his controversy with his people, his wife died. She was an excellent woman; and was respected and lamented by all. He caused a stone slab to be placed at the head of her grave, with a suitable inscription, still plainly legible, concluding with four lines, to which his initials are appended, composed by him, of which this is one: " Farewell, best wife, choice mother, neighbor, friend." Her ashes rest in what is called the Wadsworth burial ground.

Mr. Parris removed to Newton, then to Concord; and in November, 1697, began to preach at Stow, on a salary of forty pounds, half in money and half in provisions, &c. A grant from the general court was relied upon from year to year to help to make up the twenty pounds to be paid in money. Afterwards he preached at Dunstable, partly supported by a grant from the general court, and finally in Sudbury, where he died, Feb. 27, 1720. His daughter Elizabeth, who belonged, it will be remembered, to the circle of " afflicted children " in 1692, then nine years of age, in 1710 married Benjamin Barnes of Concord. Two other daughters married in Sudbury. His son Noyes, who graduated at Harvard College in 1721, became deranged, and was supported by the town. His other son Samuel was long deacon of the church at Sudbury, and died Nov. 22, 1792, aged ninety-one years.

In the " Boston News Letter," No. 1433, July 15, 1731, is a notice, as follows: —

" Any person or persons who knew Mr. Samuel Parris, formerly of Barbadoes, afterwards of Boston in New England, merchant, and after that minister of Salem Village, &c., deceased to be a son of Thomas Parris of the island aforesaid, Esq. who deceased 1673, or sole heir by will to all his estate in said island, are desired to give or send notice thereof to the printer of this paper; and it shall be for their advantage."

Whether the identity of Mr. Parris, of Salem Village, with the son of Thomas Parris, of Barbadoes, was established, we have no information. If it was, some relief may have come to his descendants. There is every reason to believe, that, after leaving the village, he and his family suffered from extremely limited means, if not from absolute poverty. The general ill-repute brought upon him by his conduct in the witchcraft prosecutions followed him to the last. He had forfeited the sympathy of his clerical brethren by his obstinate refusal to take their advice. They earnestly, over and over again, expostulated against his prolonging the controversy with the people of Salem Village, besought him to relinquish it, and promised him, if he would, to provide an eligible settlement elsewhere. They actually did provide one. But he rejected their counsels and persuasions, in expressions of ill-concealed bitterness. So that, when he was finally driven away, they felt under no obligations to befriend him; and with his eminent abilities he eked out a precarious and inadequate maintenance for himself and family, in feeble settlements in outskirt towns, during the rest of his days.

It is difficult to describe the character of this unfortunate man. Just as is the condemnation which facts compel history to pronounce, I have a feeling of relief in the thought, that, before the tribunal to which he so long ago passed, the mercy we all shall need, which comprehends all motives and allows for all infirmities, has been extended to him, in its infinite wisdom and benignity.

He was a man of uncommon abilities, of extraordinary vivacity and activity of intellect. He does not appear to have been wilfully malevolent; although somewhat reckless in a contest, he was not deliberately untruthful; on the contrary, there is in his statements a singular ingenuousness and fairness, seldom to be found in a partisan, much more seldom in a principal. Although we get almost all we know of the examinations of accused parties in the witchcraft proceedings, and of his long contentions with his parish, from him, there is hardly any ground to regret that the parties on the other side had no friends to tell their story. A transparency

of character, a sort of instinctive incontinency of mind, which
made him let out every thing, or a sort of blindness which prevented his seeing the bearings of what was said and done, make
his reports the vehicles of the materials for the defence of the very
persons he was prosecuting. I know of no instance like it. His
style is lucid, graphic, lively, natural to the highest degree; and
whatever he describes, we see the whole, and, as it were, from all
points of view. Language flowed from his pen with a facility,
simplicity, expressiveness, and accuracy, not surpassed or often
equalled. He wrote as men talk, using colloquial expressions
without reserve, but always to the point. When we read, we
hear him; abbreviating names, and clipping words, as in the
most familiar and unguarded conversation. He was not hampered
by fear of offending the rules which some think necessary to dig-
nify composition. In his off-hand, free and easy, gossiping entries
in the church-book, or in his carefully prepared productions, like
the "Meditations for Peace," read before his church and the dissatisfied brethren, we have specimens of plain good English, in its
most translucent and effective forms. Considering that his aca-
demic education was early broken off, and many intermediate
years were spent in commercial pursuits, his learning and attainments are quite remarkable. The various troubles and tragic
mischiefs of his life, the terrible wrongs he inflicted on others, and
the retributions he brought upon himself, are traceable to two or
three peculiarities in his mental and moral organization.

He had a passion for a scene, a ceremony, an excitement. He
delighted in the exercise of power, and rejoiced in conflicts or
commotions, from the exhilaration they occasioned, and the opportunity they gave for the gratification of the activity of his nature.
He pursued the object of getting possession of the ministry house
and land with such desperate pertinacity, not, I think, from ava-
ricious motives, but for the sake of the power it would give him
as a considerable landholder. His love of form and public excitement led him to operate as he did with his church. He kept it in
continual action during the few years of his ministry. He had at
least seventy-five special meetings of that body, without counting
those which probably occurred without number, but of which
there is no record, during the six months of the witchcraft period.
Twice, the brethren gave out, wholly exhausted; and the powers

of the church were, by vote, transferred to a special committee, to
act in its behalf, composed of persons who had time and strength
to spare. But Mr. Parris, never weary of excitement, would have
been delighted to preside over church-meetings, and to be a par-
ticipator in vehement proceedings, every day of his life. The
more noisy and heated the contention, the more he enjoyed it.
During all the transactions connected with the witchcraft prosecutions, he was everywhere present, always wide awake, full of
animation, if not cheerfulness, and ready to take any part to carry
them on. These propensities and dispositions were fraught with
danger, and prolific of evil in his case, in consequence of what
looks very much like a total want in himself of many of the natural
human sensibilities, and an inability to apprehend them in others.
Through all the horrors of the witchcraft prosecutions, he never
evinced the slightest sensibility, and never seemed to be aware
that anybody else had any. It was not absolute cruelty, but the
absence of what may be regarded as a natural sense. It was not
a positive wickedness, but a negative defect. He seemed to be
surprised that other people had sentiments, and could not understand why Tarbell and Nurse felt so badly about the execution of
their mother. He told them to their faces, without dreaming of
giving them offence, that, while they thought she was innocent, and
he thought she was guilty and had been justly put to death, it was a
mere difference of opinion, as about an indifferent matter. In his
" Meditations for Peace," presented to these dissatisfied brethren,
for the purpose and with an earnest desire of appeasing them, he
tells them that the indulgence of such feelings at all is a yielding
to " temptation," being under " the clouds of human weakness,"
and " a bewraying of remaining corruption." Indeed, the theology
of that day, it must be allowed, bore very hard upon even the best
and most sacred affections of our nature. The council, in their
Result, allude to the feelings of those whose parents, and other
most loved and honored relatives and connections, had been so
cruelly torn from them and put to death, as " infirmities discovered by them in such an heart-breaking day," and bespeak for
their grief and lamentations a charitable construction. They ask
the church, whose hands were red with the blood of their innocent
and dearest friends, not to pursue them with " more critical and
vigorous proceedings" in consequence of their exhibiting these

natural sensibilities on the occasion, but "to treat them with bowels of much compassion." These views had taken full effect upon Mr. Parris, and obliterated from his breast all such "infirmities." This is the only explanation or apology that can be made for him.

Of the history of Cotton Mather, subsequently to the witchcraft prosecutions, and more or less in consequence of his agency in them, it may be said that the residue of his life was doomed to disappointment, and imbittered by reproach and defeat. The storm of fanatical delusion, which he doubted not would carry him to the heights of clerical and spiritual power, in America and everywhere, had left him a wreck. His political aspirations, always one of his strongest passions, were wholly blasted; and the great aim and crown of his ambition, the Presidency of Harvard College, once and again and for ever had eluded his grasp. I leave him to tell his story, and reveal the state of his mind and heart in his own most free and full expressions from his private diary for the year 1724.

"1. What has a gracious Lord helped me to do for the *seafaring tribe*, in prayers for them, in sermons to them, in books bestowed upon them, and in various projections and endeavors to render the sailors a happy generation? And yet there is not a man in the world so reviled, so slandered, so cursed among sailors.

"2. What has a gracious Lord helped me to do for the instruction and salvation and comfort of the poor negroes? And yet some, on purpose to affront me, call their negroes by the name of COTTON MATHER, that so they may, with some shadow of truth, assert crimes as committed by one of that name, which the hearers take to be *Me*.

"3. What has a gracious Lord given me to do for the profit and honor of the female sex, especially in publishing the virtuous and laudable characters of holy women? And yet where is the man whom the female sex have spit more of their venom at? I have cause to question whether there are twice ten in the town but what have, at some time or other, spoken *basely* of me.

"4. What has a gracious Lord given me to do, that I may be a blessing to my relatives? I keep a catalogue of them, and not a week passes me without some good devised for some or other of them, till I have taken all of them under my cognizance. And yet where is the man who has been so tormented with such *monstrous* relatives? Job said, ' *I am a brother to dragons.*'

" 5. What has a gracious Lord given me to do for the vindication and reputation of the Scottish nation? And yet no Englishman has been so vilified by the tongues and pens of Scots as I have been.

" 6. What has a gracious Lord given me to do for the good of the country, in applications without number for it in all its interests, besides publications of things useful to it and for it? And yet there is no man whom the country so loads with disrespect and calumnies and manifold expressions of aversion.

" 7. What has a gracious Lord given me to do for the upholding of the government, and the strengthening of it, and the bespeaking of regards unto it? And yet the discountenance I have almost perpetually received from the government! Yea, the indecencies and indignities which it has multiplied upon me are such as no other man has been treated with.

" 8. What has a gracious Lord given me to do, that the COLLEGE may be owned for the bringing forth such as are somewhat known in the world, and have read and wrote as much as many have done in other places? And yet the College for ever puts all possible marks of disesteem upon me. If I were the greatest blockhead that ever came from it, or the greatest blemish that ever came to it, they could not easily show me more contempt than they do.

" 9. What has a gracious Lord given me to do for the study of *a profitable conversation?* For nearly fifty years together, I have hardly ever gone into any company, or had any coming to me, without some explicit contrivance to speak something or other that they might be the wiser or the better for. And yet my company is as little sought for, and there is as little resort unto it, as any minister that I am acquainted with.

" 10. What has a gracious Lord given me to do in *good offices,* wherever I could find opportunities for the doing of them? I for ever entertain them with alacrity. I have offered pecuniary recompenses to such as would advise me of them. And yet I see no man for whom all are so loth to do good offices. Indeed I find some cordial friends, *but how few!* Often have I said, What would I give if there were any one man in the world to do for me what I am willing to do for every man in the world!

" 11. What has a gracious Lord given me to do in the writing of many books for the advancing of piety and the promoting of his kingdom? There are, I suppose, more than three hundred of them. And yet I have had more books written against me, more pamphlets to traduce and reproach me and belie me, than any man I know in the world.

" 12. What has a gracious Lord given me to do in a variety of *services?* For many lustres of years, not a day has passed me, without some devices, even written devices, to be serviceable. And yet my sufferings! They seem to be (as in reason they should be) more than my services. Everybody points at me, and speaks of me as by far the most afflicted minister in all New England. And many look on me as the greatest sinner, because the greatest sufferer; and are pretty arbitrary in their conjectures upon my punished miscarriages."

"*Diary, May* 7, 1724. — The sudden death of the unhappy man who sustained the place of President in our College will open a door for my doing singular services in the best of interests. I do not know that the care of the College will now be cast upon me, though I am told that it is what is most generally wished for. If it should be, I shall be in abundance of distress about it; but, if it should not, yet I may do many things for the good of the College more quietly and more hopefully than formerly.

"*June* 5. — The College is in great hazard of dissipation and grievous destruction and confusion. My advice to some that have some influence on the public may be seasonable.

"*July* 1, 1724. — This day being our *insipid, ill-contrived anniversary,* which we call the *Commencement,* I chose to spend it at home in supplications, partly on the behalf of the College that it may not be foolishly thrown away, but that God may bestow such a President upon it as may prove a rich blessing unto it and unto all our churches."

On the 18th of November, 1724, the corporation of Harvard College elected the Rev. Benjamin Colman, pastor of the Brattle-street Church in Boston, to the vacant presidential chair. He declined the appointment. The question hung in suspense another six months. In June, 1725, the Rev. Benjamin Wadsworth, pastor of the First Church in Boston, was elected, accepted the office, and held it to his death, on the 16th of March, 1737. It may easily be imagined how keenly these repeated slights were felt by Cotton Mather. He died on the 13th of February, 1728.

From the early part of the spring of 1695, when the abortive attempt to settle the difficulty between Mr. Parris and the people of the village, by the umpirage of Major Gedney, was made, it evidently became the settled purpose of the leading men, on both sides, to restore harmony to the place. On all committees, persons who had been prominent in opposition to each other were joined together, that, thus co-operating, they might become reconciled.

64

This is strikingly illustrated in the " seating of the meeting-house,"
as it was called.   In 1699, in a seat accommodating three persons,
John Putnam the son of Nathaniel, and John Tarbell, were two of
the three.   Another seat for three was occupied by James and John
Putnam, sons of John, and by Thomas Wilkins.   Thomas Putnam
and Samuel Nurse were placed in the same seat; and so were the
wives of Thomas Putnam and Samuel Nurse, and the widow
Sarah Houlton.   The widow Preston, daughter of Rebecca Nurse,
was seated with the widow Walcot, mother of Mary, one of the
accusing girls.

We see in this the effect of the wise and decisive course adopted
by Mr. Parris's successor, the Rev. Joseph Green.   Immediately
upon his ordination, Nov. 10, 1698, he addressed himself in earnest to the work of reconciliation in that distracted parish.   From
the date of its existence, nearly thirty years before, it had been
torn by constant strife.   It had just passed through scenes which
had brought all hearts into the most terrible alienation.   A man
of less faith would not have believed it possible, that the horrors
and outrages of those scenes could ever be forgotten, forgiven, or
atoned for, by those who had suffered or committed the wrongs.
But he knew the infinite power of the divine love, which, as a minister of Christ, it was his office to inspire and diffuse.   He knew
that, with the blessing of God, that people, who had from the first
been devouring each other, and upon whose garments the stain of
the blood of brethren and sisters was fresh, might be made " kind
one to another, tender-hearted, forgiving one another, even as
God for Christ's sake hath forgiven" them.   In this heroic and
Christ-like faith, he entered upon and steadfastly adhered to his
divine work.   He pursued it with patience, wisdom, and courageous
energy.   No ministry in the whole history of the New-England
churches has had a more difficult task put upon it, and none has
more perfectly succeeded in its labors.   I shall describe the administration of this good man, as a minister of reconciliation, in his
own words, transcribed from his church records: —

" Nov. 25, 1698, being spent in holy exercises (in order to our preparation for the sacrament of the Lord's Supper), at John Putnam,
Jr.'s, after the exercise, I desired the church to manifest, by the usual
sign, that they were so cordially satisfied with their brethren, Thomas
Wilkins, John Tarbell, and Samuel Nurse, that they were heartily

desirous that they would join with us in all ordinances, that so we might all live lovingly together. This they consented unto, and none made any objection, but voted it by lifting up their hands. And further, that whatever articles they had drawn up against these brethren formerly, they now looked upon them as nothing, but let them fall to the ground, being willing that they should be buried for ever.

"Feb. 5, 1699. — This day, also our brother John Tarbell, and his wife, and Thomas Wilkins and his wife, and Samuel Nurse's wife, joined with us in the Lord's Supper; which is a matter of thankfulness, seeing they have for a long time been so offended as that they could not comfortably join with us.

"1702. — In December, the pastor spake to the church, on the sabbath, as followeth: 'Brethren, I find in your church-book a record of Martha Corey's being excommunicated for witchcraft; and, the generality of the land being sensible of the errors that prevailed in that day, some of her friends have moved me several times to propose to the church whether it be not our duty to recall that sentence, that so it may not stand against her to all generations; and I myself being a stranger to her, and being ignorant of what was alleged against her, I shall now only leave it to your consideration, and shall determine the matter by a vote the next convenient opportunity.'

"Feb. 14, 170⅔. — The major part of the brethren consented to the following: 'Whereas this church passed a vote, Sept. 11, 1692, for the excommunication of Martha Corey, and that sentence was pronounced against her Sept. 14, by Mr. Samuel Parris, formerly the pastor of this church; she being, before her excommunication, condemned, and afterwards executed, for supposed witchcraft; and there being a record of this in our church-book, page 12, we being moved hereunto, do freely consent and heartily desire that the same sentence may be revoked, and that it may stand no longer against her; for we are, through God's mercy to us, convinced that we were at that dark day under the power of those errors which then prevailed in the land; and we are sensible that we had not sufficient grounds to think her guilty of that crime for which she was condemned and executed; and that her excommunication was not according to the mind of God, and therefore we desire that this may be entered in our church-book, to take off that odium that is cast on her name, and that so God may forgive our sin, and may be atoned for the land; and we humbly pray that God will not leave us any more to such errors and sins, but will teach and enable us always to do that which is right in his sight.'

"There was a major part voted, and six or seven dissented.

"J. Gr., *Pr.*"

The First Church in Salem rescinded its votes of excommunication of Rebecca Nurse and Giles Corey, in March, 1712. The
church at the village was nearly ten years before it, in this act of
justice to itself and to the memory of the injured dead. Mr.
Green did not wait until the public sentiment drove him to it.
He regarded it as his duty to lead, and keep in front of that sentiment, in the right direction. He did not wait until everybody
demanded it to be done, but instantly began to prepare his people
for it. At the proper time, he gave notice that he was about to
bring the question before them; and he accordingly did so. He
had no idea of allowing a few narrow-minded, obstinate individuals
to keep the blot any longer upon the records of his church. His
conduct is honorable to his name, and to the name of the village.
By wise, prudent, but persistent efforts, he gradually repaired
every breach, brought his parish out from under reproach, and set
them right with each other, with the obligations of justice, and
with the spirit of Christianity. It is affecting to read his ejaculations of praise and gratitude to God for every symptom of the
prevalence of harmony and love among the people of his charge.

The man who extinguished the fires of passion in a community
that had ever before been consumed by them deserves to be held
in lasting honor. The history of the witchcraft delusion in Salem
Village would, indeed, be imperfectly written, if it failed to present
the character of him who healed its wounds, obliterated the traces
of its malign influence on the hearts and lives of those who acted,
and repaired the wrongs done to the memory of those who suffered,
in it. Joseph Green had a manly and amiable nature. He was
a studious scholar and an able preacher. He was devoted to
his ministry and faithful to its obligations. He was a leader of his
people, and shared in their occupations and experiences. He was
active in the ordinary employments of life and daily concerns of
society. Possessed of independent property, he was frugal and
simple in his habits, and liberal in the use of his means. The parsonage, while he lived in it, was the abode of hospitality, and
frequented by the best society in the neighborhood. By mingled
firmness and kindliness, he met and removed difficulties. He had
a cheerful temperament, was not irritated by the course of events,
even when of an unpleasant character. While Mr. Noyes was
disturbed, even to resentment, by encroachments upon his parish,

in the formation of new societies in the middle precinct of Salem, now South Danvers, and in the second precinct of Beverly, now Upper Beverly, Mr. Green, although they drew away from him as many as from Mr. Noyes, went to participate in the raising of their meeting-houses. Of a genial disposition, he countenanced innocent amusements. He was fond of the sports of the field. The catamount was among the trophies of his sure aim, and he came home with his huntsman's bag filled with wild pigeons. He would take his little sons before and behind him on his horse, and spend a day with them fishing and fowling on Wilkins's Pond; and, when Indians threatened the settlements, he would shoulder his musket, join the brave young men of his parish, and be the first in the encounter, and the last to relinquish the pursuit of the savage foe.

He was always, everywhere, a peacemaker; by his genial manner, and his genuine dignity and decision of character, he removed dissensions from his church and neighborhood, and secured the respect while he won the love of all. That such a person was raised up and placed where he was at that time, was truly a providence of God.

The part performed in the witchcraft tragedy by the extraordinary child of twelve years of age, Ann Putnam, has been fully set forth. As has been stated, both her parents (and no one can measure their share of responsibility, nor that of others behind them, for her conduct) died within a fortnight of each other, in 1699. She was then nineteen years of age; a large family of children, all younger than herself, was left with her in the most melancholy orphanage. How many there were, we do not exactly know: eight survived her. Although their uncles, Edward and Joseph, were near, and kind, and able to care for them, the burden thrown upon her must have been great. With the terrible remembrance of the scenes of 1692, it was greater than she could bear. Her health began to decline, and she was long an invalid. Under the tender and faithful guidance of Mr. Green, she did all that she could to seek the forgiveness of God and man. After consultations with him, in visits to his study, a confession was drawn up, which she desired publicly to make. Upon conferring with Samuel Nurse, it was found to be satisfactory to him, as the representative of those who had suffered from her testimony. It was her desire to offer this confession and a profession of religion at the same time. The day was fixed, and made known to the public. On the 25th of August, 1706, a great concourse assembled in the meeting-house. Large numbers came from other places, particularly from the town of Salem. The following document, having been judged sufficient and suitable, was written out in the church-book the evening before, and signed by her. It was read by the pastor before the congregation, who were seated; she standing in her place while it was read, and owning it as hers by a declaration to that effect at its close, and also acknowledging the signature.

"The Confession of Anne Putnam, when she was received to Communion, 1706.

"I desire to be humbled before God for that sad and humbling providence that befell my father's family in the year about '92; that I, then being in my childhood, should, by such a providence of God, be made an instrument for the accusing of several persons of a grievous crime, whereby their lives were taken away from them, whom now I have just grounds and good reason to believe they were innocent persons; and that it was a great delusion of Satan that deceived me in that sad time, whereby I justly fear I have been instrumental, with others, though ignorantly and unwittingly, to bring upon myself and this land the guilt of innocent blood; though what was said or done by me against any person I can truly and uprightly say, before God and man, I did it not out of any anger, malice, or ill-will to any person, for I had no such thing against one of them ; but what I did was ignorantly, being deluded by Satan. And particularly, as I was a chief instrument of accusing of Goodwife Nurse and her two sisters, I desire to lie in the dust, and to be humbled for it, in that I was a cause, with others, of so sad a calamity to them and their families ; for which cause I desire to lie in the dust, and earnestly beg forgiveness of God, and from all those unto whom I have given just cause of sorrow and offence, whose relations were taken away or accused.

[Signed]   *anne Putnam.*

"This confession was read before the congregation, together with her relation, Aug. 25, 1706 ; and she acknowledged it.

"J. GREEN, *Pastor.*

This paper shows the baleful influence of the doctrine of Satan then received. It afforded a refuge and escape from the compunctions of conscience. The load of sin was easily thrown upon the back of Satan. This young woman was undoubtedly sincere in her penitence, and was forgiven, we trust and believe; but she failed to see the depth of her iniquity, and of those who instigated and aided her, in her false accusations. The blame, and the deed, were wholly hers and theirs. Satan had no share in it. Human responsibility cannot thus be avoided.

While, in a certain sense, she imputes the blame to Satan, this declaration of Ann Putnam is conclusive evidence that she and her confederate accusers did not believe in any communications having been made to them by invisible spirits of any kind. Those persons, in our day, who imagine that they hold intercourse, by rapping or otherwise, with spiritual beings, have sometimes found arguments in favor of their belief in the phenomena of the witchcraft trials. But Ann Putnam's confession is decisive against this. If she had really received from invisible beings, subordinate spirits, or the spirits of deceased persons, the matters to which she testified, or ever believed that she had, she would have said so. On the contrary, she declares that she had no foundation whatever, from any source, for what she said, but was under the subtle and mysterious influence of the Devil himself.

She died at about the age of thirty-six years. Her will is dated May 20, 1715, and was presented in probate June 29, 1716. Its preamble is as follows : —

"In the name of God, amen. I, Anne Putnam, of the town of Salem, single woman, being oftentimes sick and weak in body, but of a disposing mind and memory, blessed be God! and calling to mind the mortality of my body, and that it is appointed for all men once to die, do make this my last will and testament. First of all, I recommend my spirit into the hands of God, through Jesus Christ my Redeemer, with whom I hope to live for ever; and, as for my body, I commit it to the earth, to be buried in a Christian and decent manner, at the discretion of my executor, hereafter named, nothing doubting but, by the mighty power of God, to receive the same again at the resurrection."

She divided her land to her four brothers, and her personal estate to her four sisters.

It seems that she was frequently the subject of sickness, and her bodily powers much weakened. The probability is, that the long-continued strain kept upon her muscular and nervous organization, during the witchcraft scenes, had destroyed her constitution. Such uninterrupted and vehement exercise, to their utmost tension, of the imaginative, intellectual, and physical powers, in crowded and heated rooms, before the public gaze, and under the feverish and consuming influence of bewildering and all but delirious excitement, could hardly fail to sap the foundations of health in so young a child. The tradition is, that she had a slow and fluctuating decline. The language of her will intimates, that, at intervals, there were apparent checks to her disease, and rallies of strength, — " oftentimes sick and weak in body." She inherited from her mother a sensitive and fragile constitution ; but her father, although brought to the grave, probably by the terrible responsibilities and trials in which he had been involved, at a comparatively early age, belonged to a long-lived race and neighborhood. The opposite elements of her composition struggled in a protracted contest, — on the one side, a nature morbidly subject to nervous excitability sinking under the exhaustion of an overworked, overburdened, and shattered system ; on the other, tenacity of life. The conflict continued with alternating success for years ; but the latter gave way at last. Her story, in all its aspects, is worthy of the study of the psychologist. Her confession, profession, and death point the moral.

The Rev. Joseph Green died Nov. 26, 1715. The following tribute to his memory is inscribed on the records of the church. It is in the handwriting, and style of thought and language, of Deacon Edward Putnam.

" Then was the choicest flower and greenest olive-tree in the garden of our God here cut down in its prime and flourishing estate at the age of forty years and two days, who had been a faithful ambassador from God to us eighteen years. Then did that bright star set, and never more to appear here among us ; then did our sun go down ; and now what darkness is come upon us ! Put away and pardon our iniquities, O Lord ! which have been the cause of thy sore displeasure, and return to us again in mercy, and provide yet again for this thy flock a pastor after thy own heart, as thou hath promised to thy people in thy word ; on which promise we have hope, for we are called by thy name ; and, oh, leave us not ! "

The Rev. Peter Clark was ordained June 5, 1717. The termination of the connection between the Salem Village church and the witchcraft delusion, and all similar kinds of absurdity and wickedness, is marked by the following record, which fully and for ever redeems its character. If Samuel Parris had been as wise and brave as Peter Clark, he would, in the same decisive manner, have nipped the thing in the bud.

" Salem Village Church Records.

"Sept. 5, 1746. — At a church meeting appointed on the lecture, the day before, on the occasion of several persons in this parish being reported to have resorted to a woman of a very ill reputation, pretending to the art of divination and fortune-telling, &c., to make inquiry into that matter, and to take such resolutions as may be thought proper on the occasion, the brethren of the church then present came into the following votes; viz., That for Christians, especially church-members, to seek to and consult reputed witches or fortune-tellers, this church is clearly of opinion, and firmly believes on the testimony of the Word of God, is highly impious and scandalous, being a violation of the Christian covenant sealed in baptism, rendering the persons guilty of it subject to the just censure of the church.

"No proof appearing against any of the members of this church (some of whom had been strongly suspected of this crime), so as to convict them of their being guilty, it was further voted, That the pastor, in the name of the church, should publicly testify their disapprobation and abhorrence of this infamous and ungodly practice of consulting witches or fortune-tellers, or any that are reputed such; exhorting all under their watch, who may have been guilty of it, to an hearty repentance and returning to God, earnestly seeking forgiveness in the blood of Christ, and warning all against the like practice for the time to come.

" Sept. 7. — This testimony, exhortation, and warning, voted by the church, was publicly given by the pastor, before the dismission of the congregation."

The Salem Village Parish, when its present pastor, the Rev. Charles B. Rice, was settled, Sept. 2, 1863, had been in existence a hundred and ninety-one years. During its first twenty-five years, it had four ministers, whose aggregate period of service was eighteen years. During the succeeding hundred and sixty-six years, it had four ministers, whose aggregate period of service was one hundred and fifty-eight years. They had all been well educated, several were men of uncommon endowments, and without exception they possessed qualities suitable for success and usefulness in their calling.

The first period was filled with an uninterrupted series of troubles, quarrels, and animosities, culminating in the most terrific and horrible disaster that ever fell upon a people. The second period was an uninterrupted reign of peace, harmony, and unity; no religious society ever enjoying more comfort in its privileges, or exhibiting a better example of all that ought to characterize a Christian congregation.

The contrast between the lives of its ministers, in the two periods respectively, is as great as between their pastorates. The first four suffered from inadequate means of support, and, owing to the feuds in the congregation, rates not being collected, were hardly supplied with the necessaries of life. There is no symptom in the records of the second period of there having ever been any difficulty on this score. The prompt fulfilment of their contracts by the people, and the favor of Providence, placed the ministers above the reach or approach of inconvenience or annoyance from that quarter.

The history of the New-England churches presents no epoch more melancholy, distressful, and stormy than the first, and none more united, prosperous, or commendable than the second period in the annals of the Salem Village church.

The contrast between the fortunes and fates of the ministers of these two periods is worthy of being stated in detail.

James Bayley began to preach at the Village at the formation of the society, when he was quite a young man, within three years from receiving his degree at Harvard College. After about seven years, during which he buried his wife and three children, and encountered a bitter and turbulent opposition, — so far as we can see, most causeless and unreasonable, — he relinquished the ministry altogether, and spent the residue of his life in another profession elsewhere.

The ministry of George Burroughs, at the Village, lasted about two years. The violence of both parties to the controversy by which the parish had been rent was concentrated upon his innocent and unsheltered head. He was, at a public assembly of his people, in his own meeting-house, arrested, and taken out in the custody of the marshal of the county, a prisoner for a debt incurred to meet the expenses of his wife's recent funeral, of an amount less than the salary then due him, and which, in point of fact, he had paid at the time by an order upon the parish treasurer. From such outrageous ill-treatment, he escaped by resigning his ministry. He was followed to his retreat in a remote settlement, and while engaged there, a laborious, self-sacrificing, and devoted minister, was. by the malignity of his enemies at the Village, suddenly seized, all unconscious of having wronged a human creature, snatched from the table where he was taking his frugal meal in his humble home, torn from his helpless family, hurried up to the Village; overwhelmed in a storm of falsehood, rage, and folly; loaded with irons, immured in a dungeon, carried to the place of execution, consigned to the death of a felon; and his uncoffined remains thrown among the clefts of the rocks of Witch Hill, and left but half buried, — for a crime of which he was as innocent as the unborn child.

Deodat Lawson, a great scholar and great preacher, after a two years' trial, and having buried his wife and daughter at the Village, abandoned the attempt to quell the storm of passion there. He found another settlement on the other side of Massachusetts Bay, which he left without taking leave, and was never heard of more by his people. Eight years afterwards, he re-appeared in the reprint, at London, of his famous Salem Village sermon, and then vanished for ever from sight. A cloud of impenetrable darkness envelopes his name at that point. Of his fate nothing is known, except that it was an "unhappy" one.

Samuel Parris, after a ministry of seven years, crowded from the very beginning with contention and animosity, and closed in desolation, ruin, and woes unutterable, havoc scattered among his people and the whole country round, was driven from the parish, the blood of the innocent charged upon his head, and, for the rest of his days, consigned to obscurity and penury. The place of his abode has upon it no habitation or structure of man; and the only vestiges left of him are his records of the long quarrel with his congregation, and his inscription on the headstone, erected by him, as he left the Village for ever, over the fresh grave of his wife.

Surely, the annals of no church present a more dismal, shocking, or shameful history than this.

Joseph Green, on the 26th of November, 1715, terminated with his life a ministry of eighteen years, as useful, beneficent, and honorable as it had been throughout harmonious and happy. Peter Clark died in office, June 10, 1768, after a service of fifty-one years. He was recognized throughout the country as an able minister and a learned divine. Peace and prosperity reigned, without a moment's intermission, among the people of his charge. Benjamin Wadsworth, D.D., also died in office, Jan. 18, 1826, after a service of fifty-four years. Through life he was universally esteemed and loved in all the churches. Milton P. Braman, D.D., on the 1st of April, 1861, terminated by resignation a ministry of thirty-five years. He always enjoyed universal respect and affection, and the parish under his care, uninterrupted union and prosperity. He did not leave his people, but remains among them, participating in the enjoyment of their privileges, and upholding the hands of his successor. His eminent talents are occasionally exercised in neighboring pulpits, and in other services of public usefulness. He lives in honored retirement on land originally belonging to Nathaniel Putnam, distant only a few rods, a little to the north of east, from the spot owned and occupied by his first predecessor, James Bayley.

It can be said with assurance, of this epoch in the history of the Salem Village church and society, that it can hardly be paralleled in all that indicates the well-being of man or the blessings of Heaven. No such contrast, as these two periods in the annals of this parish present, can elsewhere be found.

Prosecutions for witchcraft continued in the older countries after they had been abandoned here; although it soon began to be difficult, everywhere, to procure the conviction of a person accused of witchcraft. In 1716, a Mrs. Hicks and her daughter, the latter aged nine years, were hanged in Huntingdon, in England, for witchcraft. In the year 1720, an attempt, already alluded to, was made to renew the Salem excitement in Littleton, Mass., but it failed: the people had learned wisdom at a price too dear to allow them so soon to forget it. In a letter to Cotton Mather, written Feb. 19, 1720, the excellent Dr. Watts, after having expressed his doubts respecting the sufficiency of the spectral evidence for condemnation, says, in reference to the Salem witchcraft, " I am much persuaded that there was much immediate agency of the Devil in these affairs, and perhaps there were some real witches too." Not far from this time, we find what was probably the opinion of the most liberal-minded and cultivated people in England expressed in the following language of Addison : " To speak my thoughts freely, I believe, in general, that there is and has been such a thing as witchcraft, but, at the same time, can give no credit to any particular instance of it."

There was an execution for witchcraft in Scotland in 1722. As late as the middle of the last century, an annual discourse, commemorative of executions that took place in Huntingdon during the reign of Queen Elizabeth, continued to be delivered in that place. An act of a Presbyterian synod in Scotland, published in 1743, and reprinted at Glasgow in 1766, denounced as a national sin the repeal of the penal laws against witchcraft.

Blackstone, the great oracle of British law, and who flourished in the latter half of the last century, declared his belief in witchcraft in the following strong terms : " To deny the possibility, nay, the actual existence, of witchcraft and sorcery, is at once flatly to contradict the revealed Word of God, in various passages both of the Old and New Testament ; and the thing itself is a truth to which every nation in the world hath in its turn borne testimony, either by examples seemingly well attested, or by prohibitory laws, which at least suppose the possibility of commerce with evil spirits."

It is related, in White's " Natural History of Selborne," that, in the year 1751, the people of Tring, a market town of Hertfordshire, and scarcely more than thirty miles from London, " seized on two superannuated wretches, crazed with age and overwhelmed with infirmities, on a suspicion of witchcraft." They were carried to the edge of a horse-pond, and there subjected to the water ordeal. The trial resulted in the acquittal of the prisoners ; but they were both drowned in the process.

A systematic effort seems to have been made during the eighteenth century to strengthen and renew the power of superstition. Alarmed by the progress of infidelity, many eminent and excellent men availed themselves of the facilities which their position at the head of the prevailing literature afforded them, to push the faith of the people as far as possible towards the opposite extreme of credulity. It was a most unwise, and, in its effects, deplorable policy. It was a betrayal of the cause of true religion. It was an acknowledgment that it could not be vindicated before the tribunal of severe reason. Besides all the misery produced by filling the imagination with unreal objects of terror, the restoration to influence, during the last century, of the fables and delusions of an ignorant age, has done incalculable injury, by preventing the progress of Christian truth and sound philosophy ; thus promoting the cause of the very infidelity it was intended to check. The idea of putting down one error by setting up another cannot have suggested itself to any mind that had ever been led to appreciate the value or the force of truth. But this was the policy of Christian writers from the time of Addison to that of Johnson. The latter expressly confesses, that it was necessary to maintain the credit of the belief of the existence and agency of ghosts, and other supernatural beings, in order to help on the argument for a future state as founded upon the Bible.

Dr. Hibbert, in his excellent book on the " Philosophy of Apparitions," illustrates some remarks similar to those just made, by the following quotation from Mr. Wesley : —

" It is true, that the English in general, and indeed most of the men in Europe, have given up all accounts of witches and apparitions as mere old wives' fables. I am sorry for it ; and I willingly take this opportunity of entering my solemn protest against this violent compliment, which so many that believe the Bible pay to those who do not believe it. I owe them no such service. I take knowledge, these are at the bottom of the outcry which has been raised, and with such insolence spread throughout the nation, in direct opposition, not only to the Bible, but to the suffrage of the wisest and best men in all ages and nations. They well know (whether Christians know it or not), that the giving up witchcraft is, in effect, giving up the Bible. And they know, on the other hand, that, if but one account of the intercourse of men with separate spirits be admitted, their whole castle in the air (Deism, Atheism, Materialism) falls to the ground. I know no reason, therefore, why we should suffer even this weapon to be wrested out of our hands. Indeed, there are numerous arguments besides, which abundantly confute their vain imaginations. But we need not be hooted out of one : neither reason nor religion requires this."

The belief in witchcraft continued to hold a conspicuous place among popular superstitions during the whole of the last century. Many now living can remember the time when it prevailed very generally. Each town or village had its peculiar traditionary tales, which were gravely related by the old, and deeply impressed upon the young.

The legend of the "Screeching Woman" of Marblehead is worthy of being generally known. The story runs thus: A piratical cruiser, having captured a Spanish vessel during the seventeenth century, brought her into Marblehead harbor, which was then the site of a few humble dwellings. The male inhabitants were all absent on their fishing voyages. The pirates brought their prisoners ashore, carried them at the dead of the night into a retired glen, and there murdered them. Among the captives was an English female passenger. The women who belonged to the place heard her dying outcries, as they rose through the midnight air, and reverberated far and wide along the silent shores. She was heard to exclaim, "O mercy, mercy! Lord Jesus Christ, save me! Lord Jesus Christ, save me!" Her body was buried by the pirates on the spot. The same piercing voice is believed to be heard at intervals, more or less often, almost every year, in the stillness of a calm starlight or clear moonlight night. There is something, it is said, so wild, mysterious, and evidently superhuman in the sound, as to strike a chill of dread into the hearts of all who listen to it. The writer of an article on this subject, in the "Marblehead Register" of April 3, 1830, declares, that "there are not wanting, at the present day, persons of unimpeachable veracity and known respectability, who still continue firmly to believe the tradition, and to assert that they themselves have been auditors of the sounds described, which they declare were of such an unearthly nature as to preclude the idea of imposition or deception."

When "the silver moon unclouded holds her way," or when the stars are glistening in the clear, cold sky, and the dark forms of the moored vessels are at rest upon the sleeping bosom of the harbor; when no natural sound comes forth from the animate or inanimate creation but the dull and melancholy rote of the sea along the rocky and winding coast, — how often is the watcher startled from the reveries of an excited imagination by the pite-

ous, dismal, and terrific screams of the unlaid ghost of the murdered lady!

A negro died, fifty years ago, in that part of Danvers called
originally Salem Village, at a very advanced age. He was supposed to have reached his hundredth year. He never could be
prevailed upon to admit that there was any delusion or mistake in
the proceedings of 1692. To him, the whole affair was easy of
explanation. He believed that the witchcraft was occasioned by
the circumstance of the Devil's having purloined the church-book,
and that it subsided so soon as the book was recovered from his
grasp. Perhaps the particular hypothesis of the venerable African
was peculiar to himself; but those persons must have a slight
acquaintance with the history of opinions in this and every other
country, who are not aware that the superstition on which it was
founded has been extensively entertained by men of every color,
almost, if not quite, up to the present day. If the doctrines of
demonology have been completely overthrown and exterminated
in our villages and cities, it is a very recent achievement; nay, I
fear that in many places the auspicious event remains to take
place.

In the year 1808, the inhabitants of Great Paxton, a village of
Huntingdonshire, in England, within sixty miles of London, rose
in a body, attacked the house of an humble, and, so far as appears,
inoffensive and estimable woman, named Ann Izard, suspected of
bewitching three young females, — Alice Brown, Fanny Amey,
and Mary Fox, — dragged her out of her bed into the fields,
pierced her arms and body with pins, and tore her flesh with their
nails, until she was covered with blood. They committed the
same barbarous outrage upon her again, a short time afterwards;
and would have subjected her to the water ordeal, had she not
found means to fly from that part of the country.

The writer of the article "Witchcraft," in Rees's "Cyclo-
pædia," gravely maintains the doctrine of "ocular fascination."

Prosecutions for witchcraft are stated to have occurred, in the
first half of the present century, in some of the interior districts of
our Southern States. The civilized world is even yet full of necromancers and thaumaturgists of every kind. The science of
"palmistry" is still practised by many a muttering vagrant; and
perhaps some in this neighborhood remember when, in the days

of their youthful fancy, they held out their hands, that their future fortunes might be read in the lines of their palms, and their wild and giddy curiosity and anxious affections be gratified by information respecting wedding-day or absent lover.

The most celebrated fortune-teller, perhaps, that ever lived, resided in an adjoining town. The character of "Moll Pitcher" is familiarly known in all parts of the commercial world. She died in 1813. Her place of abode was beneath the projecting and elevated summit of High Rock, in Lynn, and commanded a view of the wild and indented coast of Marblehead, of the extended and resounding beaches of Lynn and Chelsea, of Nahant Rocks, of the vessels and islands of Boston's beautiful bay, and of its remote southern shore. She derived her mysterious gifts by inheritance, her grandfather having practised them before in Marblehead. Sailors, merchants, and adventurers of every kind, visited her residence, and placed confidence in her predictions. People came from great distances to learn the fate of missing friends, or recover the possession of lost goods; while the young of both sexes, impatient of the tardy pace of time, and burning with curiosity to discern the secrets of futurity, availed themselves of every opportunity to visit her lowly dwelling, and hear from her prophetic lips the revelation of the most tender incidents and important events of their coming lives. She read the future, and traced what to mere mortal eyes were the mysteries of the present or the past, in the arrangement and aspect of the grounds or settlings of a cup of tea or coffee. Her name has everywhere become the generic title of fortune-tellers, and occupies a conspicuous place in the legends and ballads of popular superstition. Her renown has gone abroad to the farthest regions, and her memory will be perpetuated in the annals of credulity and imposture. An air of romance is breathed around the scenes where she practised her mystic art, the interest and charm of which will increase as the lapse of time removes her history back towards the dimness of the distant past.

The elements of the witchcraft delusion of 1692 are slumbering still in the bosom of society. We hear occasionally of haunted houses, cases of second-sight, and communications from the spiritual world. It always will be so. The human mind feels instinctively its connection with a higher sphere. Some will ever be impatient of the restraints of our present mode of being, and prone to break away from them; eager to pry into the secrets of the invisible world, willing to venture beyond the bounds of ascertainable knowledge, and, in the pursuit of truth, to aspire where the laws of evidence cannot follow them. A love of the marvellous is inherent to the sense of limitation while in these terrestrial bodies; and many will always be found not content to wait until this tabernacle is dissolved and we shall be clothed upon with a body which is from Heaven.

APPENDIX.

APPENDIX.

———◆———

I.

PREFATORY ADDRESS.

[From the edition of Deodat Lawson's Sermon printed in London, 1704.]

To all my Christian Friends and Acquaintance, the Inhabitants of Salem Village.

CHRISTIAN FRIENDS, — The sermon here presented unto you was delivered in your audience by that unworthy instrument who did formerly spend some years among you in the work of the ministry, though attended with manifold sinful failings and infirmities, for which I do implore the pardoning mercy of God in Jesus Christ, and entreat from you the covering of love. As this was prepared for that particular occasion when it was delivered amongst you, so the publication of it is to be particularly recommended to your service.

My heart's desire and continual prayer to God for you all is, that you may be saved in the day of the Lord Jesus Christ; and, accordingly, that all means he is using with you, by mercies and afflictions, ordinances and providences, may be sanctified to the building you up in grace and holiness, and preparing you for the kingdom of glory. We are told by the apostle (Acts xiv. 22), that through many tribulations we must enter into the kingdom of God.* Now, since (besides your share in the common calamities, under the burden whereof this poor people are groaning at this time) the righteous and holy God hath been pleased to permit a sore and grievous affliction to befall you, such as can hardly be said to be common to men; viz., by giving liberty to Satan to range and rage amongst you, to the torturing the bodies and distracting the minds of some of the visible sheep and lambs of the Lord Jesus Christ. And (which is yet more astonishing) he who is the accuser of the brethren endeavors to introduce as criminal some of the visible subjects of Christ's kingdom, by whose sober and godly conversation in times past we could draw no other conclusions than that they were real members of his mystical body, representing them as the instruments of his malice against their friends and neighbors.

I thought meet thus to give you the best assistance I could, to help you out of your distresses. And since the ways of the Lord, in his permissive as well as effective providence, are unsearchable, and his doings past finding out, and pious souls are at a loss what will be the issue of these things, I therefore bow my knees unto the God and Father of our Lord Jesus Christ, that he would cause all grace to abound to you and in you, that your poor place may be delivered from those breaking and ruining calamities which are threatened as the pernicious consequences of Satan's malicious operations; and that you may not be left to bite and devour one another in your sacred or civil society, in your relations or families, to the destroying much good and promoting much evil among you, so as in any kind to weaken the hands or discourage the heart of your reverend and pious pastor, whose family also being so much under the influence of these troubles, spiritual sympathy cannot but stir you up to assist him as at all times, so especially at such a time as this; he, as well as his neighbors, being under such awful circumstances. As to this discourse, my humble desire and endeavor is, that it may appear to be according to the form of sound words, and in expressions every way intelligible to the meanest capacities. It pleased God, of his free grace, to give it some acceptation with those that heard it, and some that heard of it desired me to transcribe it, and afterwards to give way to the printing of it. I present it therefore to your acceptance, and commend it to the divine benediction; and that it may please the Almighty God to manifest his power in putting an end to your sorrows of this nature, by bruising Satan under your feet shortly, causing these and all other your and our troubles to work together for our good now, and salvation in the day of the Lord, is the unfeigned desire, and shall be the uncessant prayer, of —

Less than the least, of all those that serve,

In the Gospel of our Lord Jesus,

DEODAT LAWSON.

II.

DEODAT LAWSON'S NARRATIVE.

[Appended to his Sermon, London edition, 1704.]

AT the request of several worthy ministers and Christian friends, I do here annex, by way of appendix to the preceding sermon, some brief account of these amazing things which occasioned that discourse to be delivered. Let the reader please therefore to take it in the brief remarks following, and judge as God shall incline him.

It pleased God, in the year of our Lord 1692, to visit the people at a place called Salem Village, in New England, with a very sore and grievous affliction, in which they had reason to believe that the sovereign and holy God was pleased to permit Satan and his instruments to affright and afflict those poor mortals in such an astonishing and unusual manner.

Now, I having for some time before attended the work of the ministry in that village, the report of those great afflictions came quickly to my notice, and the more readily because the first person afflicted was in the minister's family who succeeded me after I was removed from them. In pity, therefore, to my Christian friends and former acquaintance there, I was much concerned about them, frequently consulted with them, and fervently, by divine assistance, prayed for them; but especially my concern was augmented when it was reported, at an examination of a person suspected for witchcraft, that my wife and daughter, who died three years before, were sent out of the world under the malicious operations of the infernal powers, as is more fully represented in the following remarks. I did then desire, and was also desired by some concerned in the Court, to be there present, that I might hear what was alleged in that respect; observing, therefore, when I was amongst them, that the case of the afflicted was very amazing and deplorable, and the charges brought against the accused such as were ground of suspicions, yet very intricate, and difficult to draw up right conclusions about them; I thought good, for the satisfaction of myself and such of my friends as might be curious to inquire into those mysteries of God's providence and Satan's malice, to draw up and keep by me a brief account of the most remarkable things that came to my knowledge in those affairs, which remarks were afterwards (at my request) revised and corrected by some who sat judges on the bench in those matters, and were now transcribed from the same paper on which they were then written. After this, I being by the providence of God

called over into England in the year 1696, I then brought that paper of remarks on the witchcraft with me; upon the sight thereof some worthy ministers
and Christian friends here desired me to reprint the sermon, and subjoin the
remarks thereunto in way of appendix; but for some particular reasons I did
then decline it. But now, forasmuch as I myself had been an eye and ear witness of most of those amazing things, so far as they came within the notice
of human senses, and the requests of my friends were renewed since I came
to dwell in London, I have given way to the publishing of them, that I may
satisfy such as are not resolved to the contrary, that there may be (and are)
such operations of the powers of darkness on the bodies and minds of mankind by divine permission, and that those who sat judges on those cases may,
by the serious consideration of the formidable aspect and perplexed circumstances of that afflictive providence, be in some measure excused, or at least
be less censured, for passing sentence on several persons as being the instruments of Satan in those diabolical operations, when they were involved in
such a dark and dismal scene of providence, in which Satan did seem to spin
a finer thread of spiritual wickedness than in the ordinary methods of witchcraft: hence the judges, desiring to bear due testimony against such diabolical
practices, were inclined to admit the validity of such a sort of evidence as was
not so clearly and directly demonstrable to human senses as in other cases is
required, or else they could not discover the mysteries of witchcraft. I presume not to impose upon my Christian or learned reader any opinion of
mine how far Satan was an instrument in God's hand in these amazing
afflictions which were on many persons there about that time; but I am
certainly convinced, that the great God was pleased to lengthen his chain to
a very great degree for the hurting of some and reproaching of others, as far
as he was permitted so to do. Now, that I may not grieve any whose relations were either accused or afflicted in those times of trouble and distress,
I choose to lay down every particular at large, without mentioning any
names or persons concerned (they being wholly unknown here); resolving to
confine myself to such a proportion of paper as is assigned to these remarks
in this impression of the book, yet, that I may be distinct, shall speak briefly
to the matter under three heads; viz.: —

1. Relating to the afflicted.
2. Relating to the accused. And,
3. Relating to the confessing witches.

To begin with the afflicted. —

1. One or two of the first that were afflicted complaining of unusual illness, their relations used physic for their cure; but it was altogether in
vain.

2. They were oftentimes very stupid in their fits, and could neither hear
nor understand, in the apprehension of the standers-by; so that, when prayer
hath been made with some of them in such a manner as might be audible in
a great congregation, yet, when their fit was off, they declared they did not
hear so much as one word thereof.

3. It was several times observed, that, when they were discoursed with about God or Christ, or the things of salvation, they were presently afflicted at a dreadful rate; and hence were oftentimes outrageous, if they were permitted to be in the congregation in the time of the public worship.

4. They sometimes told at a considerable distance, yea, several miles off, that such and such persons were afflicted, which hath been found to be done according to the time and manner they related it; and they said the spectres of the suspected persons told them of it.

5. They affirmed that they saw the ghosts of several departed persons, who, at their appearing, did instigate them to discover such as (they said) were instruments to hasten their deaths, threatening sorely to afflict them if they did not make it known to the magistrates. They did affirm at the examination, and again at the trial of an accused person, that they saw the ghosts of his two wives (to whom he had carried very ill in their lives, as was proved by several testimonies), and also that they saw the ghosts of my wife and daughter (who died above three years before); and they did affirm, that, when the very ghosts looked on the prisoner at the bar, they looked red, as if the blood would fly out of their faces with indignation at him. The manner of it was thus: several afflicted being before the prisoner at the bar, on a sudden they fixed all their eyes together on a certain place of the floor before the prisoner, neither moving their eyes nor bodies for some few minutes, nor answering to any question which was asked them: so soon as that trance was over, some being removed out of sight and hearing, they were all, one after another, asked what they saw; and they did all agree that they saw those ghosts above mentioned. I was present, and heard and saw the whole of what passed upon that account, during the trial of that person who was accused to be the instrument of Satan's malice therein.

6. In this (worse than Gallick) persecution by the dragoons of hell, the persons afflicted were harassed at such a dreadful rate to write their names in a Devil-book presented by a spectre unto them: and one, in my hearing, said, "I will not, I will not write! It is none of God's book, it is none of God's book: it is the Devil's book, for aught I know;" and, when they steadfastly refused to sign, they were told, if they would but touch, or take hold of, the book, it should do; and, lastly, the diabolical propositions were so low and easy, that, if they would but let their clothes, or any thing about them, touch the book, they should be at ease from their torments, it being heir consent that is aimed at by the Devil in those representations and operations.

7. One who had been long afflicted at a stupendous rate by two or three spectres, when they were (to speak after the manner of men) tired out with tormenting of her to force or fright her to sign a covenant with the Prince of Darkness, they said to her, as in a diabolical and accursed passion, "Go your ways, and the Devil go with you; for we will be no more pestered and plagued about you." And, ever after that, she was well, and no more afflicted, that ever I heard of.

67

8. Sundry pins have been taken out of the wrists and arms of the afflicted; and one, in time of examination of a suspected person, had a pin run through both her upper and her lower lip when she was called to speak, yet no apparent festering followed thereupon, after it was taken out.

9. Some of the afflicted, as they were striving in their fits in open court, have (by invisible means) had their wrists bound fast together with a real cord, so as it could hardly be taken off without cutting. Some afflicted have been found with their arms tied, and hanged upon an hook, from whence others have been forced to take them down, that they might not expire in that posture.

10. Some afflicted have been drawn under tables and beds by undiscerned force, so as they could hardly be pulled out; and one was drawn half-way over the side of a well, and was, with much difficulty, recovered back again.

11. When they were most grievously afflicted, if they were brought to the accused, and the suspected person's hand but laid upon them, they were immediately relieved out of their tortures; but, if the accused did but look on them, they were instantly struck down again. Wherefore they used to cover the face of the accused, while they laid their hands on the afflicted, and then it obtained the desired issue: for it hath been experienced (both in examinations and trials), that, so soon as the afflicted came in sight of the accused, they were immediately cast into their fits; yea, though the accused were among the crowd of people unknown to the sufferers, yet, on the first view, were they struck down, which was observed in a child of four or five years of age, when it was apprehended, that so many as she could look upon, either directly or by turning her head, were immediately struck into their fits.

12. An iron spindle of a woollen wheel, being taken very strangely out of an house at Salem Village, was used by a spectre as an instrument of torture to a sufferer, not being discernible to the standers-by, until it was, by the said sufferer, snatched out of the spectre's hand, and then it did immediately appear to the persons present to be really the same iron spindle.

13. Sometimes, in their fits, they have had their tongues drawn out of their mouths to a fearful length, their heads turned very much over their shoulders; and while they have been so strained in their fits, and had their arms and legs, &c., wrested as if they were quite dislocated, the blood hath gushed plentifully out of their mouths for a considerable time together, which some, that they might be satisfied that it was real blood, took upon their finger, and rubbed on their other hand. I saw several together thus violently strained and bleeding in their fits, to my very great astonishment that my fellow-mortals should be so grievously distressed by the invisible powers of darkness. For certainly all considerate persons who beheld these things must needs be convinced, that their motions in their fits were preternatural and involuntary, both as to the manner, which was so strange as a well person could not (at least without great pain) screw their bodies into,

and as to the violence also, they were preternatural motions, being much beyond the ordinary force of the same persons when they were in their right minds; so that, being such grievous sufferers, it would seem very hard and unjust to censure them of consenting to, or holding any voluntary converse or familiarity with, the Devil.

14. Their eyes were, for the most part, fast closed in their trance-fits, and when they were asked a question they could give no answer; and I do verily believe, they did not hear at that time; yet did they discourse with the spectres as with real persons, asserting things and receiving answers affirmative or negative, as the matter was. For instance, one, in my hearing, thus argued *with*, and railed *at*, a spectre: "Goodw—, begone, begone, begone! Are you not ashamed, a woman of your profession, to afflict a poor creature so? What hurt did I ever do you in my life? You have but two years to live, and then the Devil will torment your soul for this. Your name is blotted out of God's book, and it shall never be put into God's book again. Begone! For shame! Are you not afraid of what is coming upon you? I know, I know what will make you afraid, — the wrath of an angry God: I am sure that will make you afraid. Begone! Do not torment me. I know what you would have" (we judged she meant her soul): "but it is out of your reach; it is clothed with the white robes of Christ's righteousness." This sufferer I was well acquainted with, and knew her to be a very sober and pious woman, so far as I could judge; and it appears that she had not, in that fit, voluntary converse with the Devil, for then she might have been helped to a better guess about that woman abovesaid, as to her living but two years, for she lived not many months after that time. Further, this woman, in the same fit, seemed to dispute with a spectre about a text of Scripture: the apparition seemed to deny it; she said she was sure there was such a text, and she would tell it; and then said she to the apparition, "I am sure you will be gone, for you cannot stand before that text." Then was she sorely afflicted, — her mouth drawn on one side, and her body strained violently for about a minute; and then said, "It is, it is, it is," three or four times, and then was afflicted to hinder her from telling; at last, she broke forth, and said, "It is the third chapter of the Revelations." I did manifest some scruple about reading it, lest Satan should draw any thereby superstitiously to improve the word of the eternal God; yet judging I might do it once, for an experiment, I began to read; and, before I had read through the first verse, she opened her eyes, and was well. Her husband and the spectators told me she had often been relieved by reading texts pertinent to her case, — as Isa. 40, 1, ch. 49, 1, ch. 50, 1, and several others. These things I saw and heard from her.

15. They were vehemently afflicted, to hinder any persons praying with them, or holding them in any religious discourse. The woman mentioned in the former section was told by the spectre I should not go to prayer; but she said I should, and, after I had done, reasoned with the apparition, "Did not I say he should go to prayer?" I went also to visit a person afflicted in

Boston; and, after I was gone into the house to which she belonged, she being abroad, and pretty well, when she was told I was there, she said, " I am loath to go in; for I know he will fall into some good discourse, and then I am sure I shall go into a fit." Accordingly, when she came in, I advised her to improve all the respite she had to make her peace with God, and sue out her pardon through Jesus Christ, and beg supplies of faith and every grace to deliver her from the powers of darkness; and, before I had uttered all this, she fell into a fearful fit of diabolical torture.

16. Some of them were asked how it came to pass that they were not affrighted when they saw the *black-man*: they said they were at first, but not so much afterwards.

17. Some of them affirmed they saw the *black-man* sit on the gallows, and that he whispered in the ears of some of the condemned persons when they were just ready to be turned off, even while they were making their last speech.

18. They declared several things to be done by witchcraft, which happened before some of them were born, — as strange deaths of persons, casting away of ships, &c.; and they said the spectres told them of it.

19. Some of them have sundry times seen a *white-man* appearing amongst the spectres, and, as soon as he appeared, the *black-witches* vanished: they said this white-man had often foretold them what respite they should have from their fits, as sometimes a day or two or more, which fell out accordingly. One of the afflicted said she saw him, in her fit, and was with him in a glorious place which had no candle nor sun, yet was full of light and brightness, where there was a multitude in white, glittering robes, and they sang the song in Rev. 5, 9; Psal. 110, 149. She was loath to leave that place, and said, " *How long shall I stay here? Let me be along with you.*" She was grieved she could stay no longer in that place and company.

20. A young woman that was afflicted at a fearful rate had a spectre appeared to her with a white sheet wrapped about it, not visible to the standers-by until this sufferer (violently striving in her fit) snatched at, took hold, and tore off a corner of that sheet. Her father, being by her, endeavored to lay hold upon it with her, that she might retain what she had gotten; but, at the passing-away of the spectre, he had such a violent twitch of his hand as if it would have been torn off: immediately thereupon appeared in the sufferer's hand the corner of a sheet, — a real cloth, *visible* to the spectators, which (as it is said) remains still to be seen.

REMARKABLE THINGS RELATING TO THE ACCUSED.

1. A woman, being brought upon public examination, desired to go to prayer. The magistrates told her they came not there to hear her pray, but to examine her in what was alleged against her relating to suspicions of witchcraft.

2. It was observed, both in times of examination and trial, that the

accused seemed little affected with what the sufferers underwent, or what was charged against them as being the instruments of Satan therein, so that the spectators were grieved at their unconcernedness.

3. They were sometimes their *own image*, and not always practising upon poppets made of clouts, wax, or other materials, (according to the old methods of witchcraft); for *natural* actions in them seemed to produce preternatural impressions on the afflicted, as biting their lips in time of examination and trial caused the sufferers to be bitten so as they produced the marks before the magistrates and spectators: the accused pinching their hands together seemed to cause the sufferers to be *pinched;* those again *stamping* with their feet, *these* were tormented in their legs and feet, so as they *stamped fearfully.* After all this, if the accused did but lean against the bar at which they stood, some very sober women of the afflicted complained of their breasts, as if their bowels were torn out; thus, some have since confessed, they were wont to afflict such as were the objects of their malice.

4. Several were accused of having familiarity with the *black-man* in time of examination and trial; and that he whispered in their ears, and therefore they could not hear the magistrates; and that one woman accused rid (in her shape and spectre) by the place of judicature, behind the black man, in the very time when she was upon examination.

5. When the suspected were standing at the bar, the afflicted have affirmed that they saw their shapes in other places suckling a yellow bird; sometimes in one place and posture, and sometimes in another. They also foretold that the spectre of the prisoner was going to afflict such or such a sufferer, which presently fell out accordingly.

6. They were accused by the sufferers to keep days of hellish fasts and thanksgivings; and, upon one of their fast-days, they told a sufferer she must not eat, it was fast-day. She said she would: they told her they would choke her then, which, when she did eat, was endeavored.

7. They were also accused to hold and administer diabolical sacraments; viz., a mock-baptism and a Devil-supper, at which cursed imitations of the sacred institutions of our blessed Lord they used forms of words to be trembled at in the very rehearsing: concerning baptism I shall speak elsewhere. At their cursed supper, they were said to have red bread and red drink; and, when they pressed an afflicted person to eat and drink thereof, she turned away her head, and spit at it, and said, " I will not eat, I will not drink: it is blood. That is not the bread of life, that is not the water of life; and I will have none of yours." Thus horribly doth Satan endeavor to have his kingdom and administrations to resemble those of our Lord Jesus Christ.

8. Some of the most *sober* afflicted persons, when they were well, did affirm the spectres of such and such as they did complain of in their fits did appear to them, and could relate what passed betwixt them and the apparitions, after their fits were over, and give account after what manner they were hurt by them.

9. Several of the accused would neither in time of examination nor trial

confess any thing of what was laid to their charge: some would not admit of any minister to pray with them, others refused to pray for themselves. It was said by some of the confessing witches, that such as have received the Devil-sacrament can never confess: only one woman condemned, after the death-warrant was signed, freely confessed, which occasioned her re-prieval for some time; and it was observable this woman had one lock of hair of a very great length, viz., four foot and seven inches long by measure. This lock was of a different color from all the rest, which was short and gray. It grew on the hinder part of her head, and was matted together like an elf-lock. The Court ordered it to be cut off, to which she was very un-willing, and said she was told if it were cut off she should die or be sick; yet the Court ordered it so to be.

10. A person who had been frequently transported to and fro by the devils for the space of near two years, was struck dumb for about nine months of that time; yet he, after that, had his speech restored to him, and did de-pose upon oath, that, in the time while he was dumb, he was many times bodily transported to places where the witches were gathered together, and that he there saw feasting and dancing; and, being struck on the back or shoulder, was thereby made fast to the place, and could only see and hear at a distance. He did take his oath that he did, with his bodily eyes, see some of the accused at those witch-meetings several times. I was present in court when he gave his testimony. He also proved by sundry persons, that, at those times of transport, he was bodily absent from his abode, and could nowhere be found, but being met with by some on the road, at a distance from his home, was suddenly conveyed away from them.

11. The afflicted persons related that the spectres of several eminent per-sons had been brought in amongst the rest; but, as the sufferers said the Devil could not hurt them in their shapes, but two witches seemed to take them by each hand, and lead them or force them to come in.

12. Whiles a godly man was at prayer with a woman afflicted, the daughter of that woman (being a sufferer in the like kind) affirmed that she saw two of the persons accused at prayer to the Devil.

13. It was proved by substantial evidences against one person accused, that he had such an unusual strength (though a very little man), that he could hold out a gun with one hand behind the lock, which was near seven foot in the barrel, being as much as a lusty man could command with both hands after the usual manner of shooting. It was also proved, that he lifted barrels of meat and barrels of molasses out of a canoe alone, and that putting his fingers into a barrel of molasses (full within a finger's length according to custom) he carried it several paces; and that he put his finger into the muzzle of a gun which was more than five foot in the barrel, and lifted up the butt-end thereof, lock, stock, and all, without any visible help to raise it. It was also testified, that, being abroad with his wife and his wife's brother, he occasionally staid behind, letting his wife and her brother walk forward; but, suddenly coming up with them, he was angry with his wife for what

discourse had passed betwixt her and her brother: they wondering how he should know it, he said, "I know your thoughts;" at which expression, they, being amazed, asked him how he could do that; he said, "My God, whom I serve, makes known your thoughts to me."

I was present when these things were testified against him, and observed that he could not make any plea for himself (in these things) that had any weight: he had the liberty of challenging his jurors before empanelling, according to the statute in that case, and used his liberty in challenging many; yet the jury that were sworn brought him in guilty.

14. The magistrates privately examined a child of four or five years of age, mentioned in the remarks of the afflicted, sect. 11: [p. 530] and the child told them it had a little snake which used to suck on the lowest joint of its forefinger; and, when they (inquiring where) pointed to other places, it told them not *there* but *here*, pointing on the lowest joint of the forefinger, where they observed a deep red spot about the bigness of a flea-bite. They asked it who gave it that snake, whether the black man gave it : the child said no, its mother gave it. I heard this child examined by the magistrates.

15. It was proved by sundry testimonies against some of the accused, that, upon their malicious imprecations, wishes, or threatenings, many observable deaths and diseases, with many other odd inconveniences, have happened to cattle and other estate of such as were so threatened by them, and some to the persons of men and women.

REMARKABLE THINGS CONFESSED BY SOME SUSPECTED OF BEING GUILTY OF WITCHCRAFT.

1. It pleased God, for the clearer discovery of those mysteries of the kingdom of darkness, so to dispose, that several persons, men, women, and children, did confess their hellish deeds, as followeth: —

2. They confessed against themselves that they were witches, told how long they had been so, and how it came about that the Devil appeared to them; viz., sometimes upon discontent at their mean condition in the world, sometimes about fine clothes, sometimes for the gratifying other carnal and sensual lusts. Satan then, upon his appearing to them, made them fair (though false) promises, that, if they would yield to him, and sign his book, their desires should be answered to the uttermost, whereupon they signed it; and thus the accursed confederacy was confirmed betwixt them and the Prince of Darkness.

3. Some did affirm that there were some hundreds of the society of witches, considerable companies of whom were affirmed to muster in arms by beat of drum. In time of examinations and trials, they declared that such a man was wont to call them together from all quarters to witch-meetings with the sound of a diabolical trumpet.

4. Being brought to see the prisoners at the bar upon their trials, they did affirm in open court (I was then present), that they had oftentimes seen

them at witch-meetings, where was feasting, dancing, and jollity, as also at Devil-sacraments; and particularly that they saw such a man —— amongst the rest of the cursed crew, and affirmed that he did administer the sacrament of Satan to them, encouraging them to go on in their way, and they should certainly prevail. They said also that such a woman —— was a deacon, and served in distributing the diabolical elements: they affirmed that there were great numbers of the witches.

5. They affirmed that many of those wretched souls had been baptized at Newbury Falls, and at several other rivers and ponds; and, as to the manner of administration, the great Officer of Hell took them up by the body, and, putting their heads into the water, said over them, " Thou art mine, I have full power over thee: and thereupon they engaged and covenanted to renounce God, Christ, their sacred baptism, and the whole way of Gospel salvation, and to use their utmost endeavors to oppose the kingdom of Christ, and to set up and advance the kingdom of Satan.

6. Some, after they had confessed, were very penitent, and did wring their hands, and manifest a distressing sense of what they had done, and were by the mercies of God recovered out of those snares of the kingdom of darkness.

7. Several have confessed against their own mothers, that they were instruments to bring them into the Devil's covenant, to the undoing of them, body and soul; and some girls of eight or nine years of age did declare, that, after they were so betrayed by their mothers to the power of Satan, they saw the Devil go in their own shapes to afflict others.

8. Some of those that confessed were immediately afflicted at a dreadful rate, after the same manner with the other sufferers.

9. Some of them confessed, that they did afflict the sufferers according to the time and manner they were accused thereof ; and, being asked what they did to afflict them, some said that they pricked pins into poppets made with rags, wax, and other materials: one that confessed after the signing the death-warrant said she used to afflict them by clutching and pinching her hands together, and wishing in what part and after what manner she would have them afflicted, and it was done.

10. They confessed the design was laid by this witchcraft to root out the interest of Christ in New England, and that they began at the Village in order to settling the kingdom of darkness and the powers thereof ; declaring that such a man —— was to be head conjurer, and for his activity in that affair was to be crowned king of hell, and that such a woman —— was to be queen of hell.

Thus I have given my reader a brief and true account of those fearful and amazing operations and intrigues of the Prince of Darkness: and I must call them so; for, let some persons be as incredulous as they please about the powerful and malicious influence of evil angels upon the minds and bodies of mankind, *sure I am* none that observed those things above mentioned could refer them to any other head than the sovereign permission of the holy God, and the malicious operations of his and our implacable enemy. I have here related nothing more than what was acknowledged to be true by the judges that sat on the bench, and other credible persons there, which I have without prejudice or partiality represented.

I therefore close all with my uncessant prayers, that the great and everlasting Jehovah would, for the sake of his blessed Son, our most glorious intercessor, rebuke Satan, and so vanquish him, from time to time, that his power may be more and more every day suppressed, his kingdom destroyed; and that all his malicious and accursed instruments in those spiritual wickednesses may gnash their teeth, melt away, and be ashamed in their secret places, till they come to be judged and condemned unto the place of everlasting burnings prepared for the Devil and his angels, that they may there be tormented with him for ever and ever.

68

III.

LETTER FROM R. P. TO JONATHAN CORWIN.

SALISBURY, Aug. 9, 1692.

HONORED SIR, — According as in my former to you I hinted that I held myself obliged to give you some farther account of my rude though solemn thoughts of that great case now before you, the happy management whereof do so much conduce to the glory of God, the safety and tranquillity of the country, besides what I have said in my former and the enclosed, I further humbly present to consideration the doubtfulness and unsafety of admitting spectre testimony against the life of any that are of blameless conversation, and plead innocent, from the uncertainty of them and the incredulity of them; for as for diabolical visions, apparitions, or representations, they are more commonly false and delusive than real, and cannot be known when they are real and when feigned, but by the Devil's report; and then not to be believed, because he is the father of lies.

1. Either the organ of the eye is abused and the senses deluded, so as to think they do see or hear some thing or person, when indeed they do not, and this is frequent with common jugglers.

2. The Devil himself appears in the shape and likeness of a person or thing, when it is not the person or thing itself; so he did in the shape of Samuel.

3. And sometimes persons or things themselves do really appear, but how it is possible for any one to give a true testimony, which possibly did see neither shape nor person, but were deluded; and if they did see any thing, they know not whether it was the person or but his shape. All that can be rationally or truly said in such a case is this, — that I did see the shape or likeness of such a person, if my senses or eyesight were not deluded: and they can honestly say no more, because they know no more (except the Devil tells them more); and if he do, they can but say he told them so. But the matter is still incredible: first, because it is but their saying the Devil told them so; if he did so tell them, yet the verity of the thing remains still unproved, because the Devil was a liar and a murtherer (John viii. 44), and may tell these lies to murder an innocent person.

But this case seems to be solved by an assertion of some, that affirm that the Devil do not or cannot appear in the shape of a godly person, to do hurt: others affirm the contrary, and say that he can and often have so done, of which they give many instances for proof of what they say; which if granted, the case remains yet unsolved, and yet the very hinge upon which that weighty case depends. To which I humbly say: First, That I do lament that such a point should be so needful to be determined, which seems not probable, if possible, to be determined to infallible satisfaction for want of clear Scripture to decide it by, though very rational to be believed according to rules; as, for instance, if divers examples are alleged of the shape of persons that have been seen, of whom there is ample testimony that they lived and died in the faith, yet, saith the objecter, 'tis possible they may be hypocrites, therefore the proof not infallible: and as it may admit of such an objection against the reasons given on the affirmative, much more may the same objection be made against the negative, for which they can or do give no reason at all, nor can a negative be proved (therefore difficult to be determined to satisfy infallibly); but, seeing it must be discussed, I humbly offer these few words: First, I humbly conceive that the saints on earth are not more privileged in that case than the saints in heaven; but the Devil may appear in the shape of a saint in heaven, namely, in the shape of Samuel (1 Sam. xxviii. 13, 14); therefore he can or may represent the shape of a saint that is upon the earth. Besides, there may be innocent persons that are not saints, and their innocency ought to be their security, as well as godly men's; and I hear nobody question but the Devil may take their shape.

Secondly, It doth not hurt any man or woman to present the shape or likeness of an innocent person, more than for a limner or carver to draw his picture, and show it, if he do not in that form do some evil (nor then neither) if the laws of man do not oblige him to suffer for what the Devil doth in his shape, the laws of God do not.

Thirdly, The Devil had power, by God's permission, to take the very person of our Lord Jesus Christ, in the day or time of his humiliation, and carry him from place to place, and tempted him with temptations of horrid blasphemy, and yet left him innocent. Why may we not suppose the like may be done to a good man? And why not much more appear in his shape (or make folk think it is his shape, when indeed it is not), and yet the person be innocent, being far enough off, and not knowing of it, nor would consent if he had known it, his profession and conversation being otherwise?

Fourthly, I suppose 'tis granted by all, that the person of one that is dead cannot appear, because the soul and body are separated, and so the person is dissolved, and so ceaseth to be: and it is as certain that the person of the living cannot be in two places at one time, but he that is at Boston cannot be at Salem or Cambridge at the same time; but as the malice and envy in the Devil makes it his business to seek whom he may devour, so no question but he doth infuse the same quality into those that leave Jesus Christ to embrace him, that they do envy those that are innocent, and upon that account be as ready to say and swear that they did see them as the Devil is to present their shape to them. Add but this also, that, when they are once under his power, he puts them on headlong (they must needs go whom the Devil drives, saith the proverb), and the reason is clear, — because they are taken captive by him, to do his will. And we see, by woful and undeniable experience, both in the afflicted persons and the confessors, some of them, that he torments them at his pleasure, to force them to accuse others. Some are apt to doubt they do but counterfeit; but, poor souls! I am utterly of another mind, and I lament them with all my heart; but, take which you please, the case is the same as to the main issue. For, if they counterfeit, the wickedness is the greater in them, and the less in the Devil: but if they be compelled to it by the Devil, against their wills, then the sin is the Devil's, and the sufferings theirs; but if their testimonies be allowed of, to make persons guilty by, the lives of innocent persons are alike in danger by them, which is the solemn consideration that do disquiet the country.

Now, that the only wise God may so direct you in all, that he may have glory, the country peace and safety, and your hands strengthened in that great work, is the desire and constant prayer of your humble servant, **R. P.,** who shall no further trouble you at present.

Position. — That to put a witch to death is the command of God, and therefore the indispensable duty of man, — namely, the magistrate (Ex. xxii. 18); which, granted, resolves two questions that I have heard made by some: —

First, Whether there are any such creatures as witches in the world. Secondly, If there be, whether they can be known to be such by men: both which must be determined on the affirmative, or else that commandment were in vain.

Position Second. — That it must be witches that are put to death, and not innocent persons: " Thou shalt not condemn the innocent nor the righteous " (Ex. xxiii. 7).

Query. — Which premised, it brings to this query, — namely, how a witch may be known to be a witch.

Answer. — First, By the mouth of two or three witnesses (Deut. xix. 15; Matt. xviii. 16; Deut. xvii. 6). Secondly, They may be known by their own confession, being *compos mentis,* and not under horrid temptation to self-murther (2 Sam. xvi.; Josh. vii. 16).

Query Second. — What is it that those two or three witnesses must swear? Must they swear that such a person is a witch? Will that do the thing, as is vulgarly supposed?

Answer. — I think that is too unsafe to go by, as well as hard to be done by the advised: First, because it would expose the lives of all alike to the pleasure or passion of those that are minded to take them away; secondly, because that, in such a testimony, the witnesses are not only informers in matter of fact, but sole judges of the crime, — which is the proper work of the judges, and not of witnesses.

Query Third. — What is it that the witnesses must testify in the case, to prove one to be a witch?

Answer. — They must witness the person did put forth some act which, if true, was an act of witchcraft, or familiarity with the Devil, the witness attest the fact to be upon his certain knowledge, and the judges to judge that fact to be such a crime.

Query Fourth. — What acts are they which must be proved to be committed by a person, that shall be counted legal proof of witchcraft, or familiarity with the Devil?

Answer. — This I do profess to be so hard a question, for want of light from the Word of God and laws of men, that I do not know what to say to it; and therefore humbly conceive, that, in such a difficulty, it may be more safe, for the present, to let a guilty person live till further discovery, than to put an innocent person to death.

First, Because a guilty person may afterward be discovered, and so put to death; but an innocent person to be put to death cannot be brought again to life when once dead.

Secondly, Because secret things belong to God only, but revealed things to us and to our children. And though it be so difficult sometimes, yet witches there are, and may be known by some acts or other put forth by them, that may render them such; for Scripture examples, I can remember but few in the Old Testament, besides Balaam (Num. xxii. 6, xxxi. 16).

First, The sorcerers of Egypt could not tell the interpretation of Pharaoh's dream, though he told them his dream (Gen. xli 8): his successors afterwards had sorcerers, that by enchantments did, first, turn their rods into serpents (Exod. vii. 11, 12); second, turned water into blood; thirdly, brought frogs upon the land of Egypt (Exod. viii. 7).

Thirdly, Nebuchadnezzar's magicians said that they would tell him the interpretation, if he would tell them his dream (Dan. iv. 7); but the king did not believe them (ver. 8, 9).

Fourthly, The Witch of Endor raised the Devil, in the likeness of Samuel, to tell Saul his fortune; and Saul made use of him accordingly (1 Sam. xxviii. 8, 11–15); and, as for New Testament, I see very little of that nature. Our Lord Jesus Christ did cast out many devils, and so did his disciples, both while he was upon earth and afterward, of which some were dreadfully circumstanced (Mark ix. 18; Mark v. 2–5); but of witches, we only read of four mentioned in the apostles' time: first, Simon Magus (Acts viii. 9, 11); secondly, Elymas the sorcerer (Acts xiii. 6, 8); thirdly, the seven sons of Sceva, a Jew, that were vagabond Jews, — exorcists (Acts xix. 13–16); fourthly, the girl which, by a spirit of divination, brought her master much gain (Acts xvi. 16), whether it were by telling fortunes or finding out lost things, as our cunning men do, is not said; but something it was that was done by that spirit which was in her, which, being cast out, she could not do. Now, whatever was done by any of these, by the help of the Devil, or by virtue of familiarity with him, or that the Devil did do by their consent or instigation, it is that which, the like being now proved to be done by others, is legal conviction of witchcraft, or familiarity with the Devil.

As I remember, Mr. Perkins apprehends witchcraft may be sometimes committed by virtue of an implicit covenant with the Devil, though there be not explicit covenant visibly between them; namely, by using such words and gestures whereby they do intimate to the Devil what they would have him do, and he doth it.

3. To tell events contingent, or to bring any thing to pass by supernatural means, or by no means.

I have heard of some that make a circle, and mumble over some uncouth words; and some that have been spiteful and suspicious persons, that have sent for a handful of thatch from the house or barn of him that they have owed a spite to, and the house have been burnt as they had burnt the thatch that they fetched.

When Captain Smith was cast away in the ship built by Mr. Stevens at Gloucester, many years ago, it was said that the woman that was accused for doing it did put a dish in a pail of water, and sent her girl several times to see the motion of the dish, till at last it was turned over, and then the woman said, " Now Smith is gone," *or* " is cast away."

A neighbor of mine, who was a Hampshire man, told me that a suspected woman desired something of some of the family, which being denied, she either muttered or threatened, and some evil suddenly followed, and they put her into a cart to carry her to Winchester; and, when they had gone a little way, the team could not move the cart, though in plain ground. The master commanded to carry a knitch of straw, and burn her in the cart; which to avoid, she said they should go along, and they did. This they did several times before they came to Winchester, of which passages the men that went with her gave their oaths, and she was executed.

Some have been transformed into dogs, cats, hares, hogs, and other creatures; and in those shapes have sometimes received wounds which have made them undeniably guilty, and so confessed. Sometimes having their imps sucking them, or infallible tokens that they are sucked, in the search of which great caution to be given, because of some superfluities of nature, and diseases that people are incident unto, as the piles, &c., of which the judges are, upon the testimony of the witnesses, to determine what of crime is proved by any of these circumstances, with many other, in which God is pleased many times, by some overt acts, to bring to light that secret wickedness to apparent conviction, sometimes by their own necessitated confession, whereby those that he hath commanded to be put to death may be known to be such, which, when known, then it is a duty to put them to death, and not before, though they were as guilty before as then.

There are two queries more with respect to what is proper to us in this juncture of time, of which we have no account of the like being common at other times, or in other places; namely, these, —

Query Fifth. — The fifth query is, what we are to think of those persons at Salem, or the Village, before whom people are brought for detection, or otherwise to be concerned with them, in order to their being apprehended or acquitted.

Answer. — That I am, of all men, the least able to give any conjecture about it, because I do not know it, having myself never seen it, nor know nothing of it but by report, in which there must be supposed a possibility of some mistake, in part or in whole; but that which I have here heard is this: First, That they do tell who are witches, of which some they know, and some they do not. Secondly, They tell who did torment such and such a person, though they know not the person. Thirdly, They are tormented themselves by the looks of persons that are present, and recovered again by the touching of them. Fourthly, That, if they look to them, they fall down tormented; but, if the persons accused look from them, they recover, or do not fall into that torment. Fifthly, They can tell when a person is coming before they see them, and what clothes they have, and some what they have done for several years past, which nobody else ever accused them with, nor do not yet think them guilty of. Sixthly, That the dead out of their graves do appear unto them, and tell them that they have been murdered, and require them to see them to be revenged on the murtherers, which they name to them; some of which persons are well known to die their natural deaths, and publicly buried in the sight of all men. Now, if these things be so, I thus affirm, —

First, That whatsoever is done by them that is supernatural, is either divine or diabolical.

Secondly, That nothing is, or can be, divine, but what have God's stamp upon it, to which he refers for trial (Isa. viii. 19, 20): "If they speak not according to these, there is no light in them."

Thirdly, And by that rule none of these actions of theirs have any warrant in God's word, but condemned wholly.

First, It is utterly unlawful to inquire of the dead, or to be informed by them (Isa. viii. 19). It was an act of the Witch of Endor to raise the dead, and of a reprobate Saul to inquire of him (1 Sam. xxviii. 8, 11–14; Deut. xviii. 11).

Secondly, It is a like evil to seek to them that have familiar spirits (Lev. xix. 31). It was the sin of Saul in the forementioned place (1 Sam. xxviii. 8); and of wicked Manasses (2 Kings, xxi. 6).

Thirdly, No more is it likely that their racking and tormenting should be done by God or good angels, but by the Devil, whose manner have ever been to be so employed. Witness his dealing with the poor child (Mark ix. 17, 19, 20–22); and with the man that was possessed by him (Mark v. 2–5); besides what he did to Job (Job ii. 7); and all the lies that he told against him to the very face of God.

Fourthly, The same may be rationally said of all the rest. Who should tell them things that they do not see, but the Devil; especially when some things that they tell are false and mistaken?

Query Sixth. — These things premised, it now comes to the last and greatest question or query; namely, How shall it be known when the Devil do any of these acts of his own proper motion, without human concurrence, consent, or instigation, and when he doth it by the suggestion or consent of any person? This question, well resolved, would do our business.

First, That the Devil can do acts supernatural without the furtherance of him by human consent or concurrence; but men or women cannot do them without the help of the Devil (must be granted). That granted, it follows, that the Devil is always the doer, but whether abetted in it by anybody is uncertain.

Secondly, Will it be sufficient for the Devil himself to say such a man or woman set him a work to torment such a person by looking upon him? Is the Devil a competent witness in such a case?

Thirdly, Or are those that are tormented by him legal witnesses to say that the Devil doth it by the procurement of such a person, whenas they know nothing about it but what comes to them from the Devil (that torments them)?

Fourthly, May we believe the witches that do accuse any one because they say so (can the fruit be better than the tree)? If the root of all their knowledge be the Devil, what must their testimony be?

Fifthly, Their testimony may be legal against themselves, because they know what themselves do, but cannot know what another doth but by information from the Devil: I mean in such cases when the person accused do deny it, and his conversation is blameless (Prov. xviii. 5; Prov. xix. 5).

First, It is directly contrary to the use of reason, the law of nature, and principles of humanity, to deny it, and plead innocent, when accused of witchcraft, and yet, at the same time, to be acting witchcraft in the sight of all men, when they know their lives lie at stake by doing it. Self-interest teaches every one better.

Secondly, It is contrary to the Devil's nature, or common practice, to accuse witches. They are a considerable part of his kingdom, which would fall, if divided against itself (Matt. xii. 26); except we think he that spake the words understood not what he said (which were blasphemy to think); or that those common principles or maxims are now changed; or that the Devil have changed his nature, and is now become a reformer to purge out witches out of the world, out of the country, and out of the churches; and is to be believed, though a liar and a murtherer from the beginning, and also though his business is going about continually, seeking whom he may destroy (1 Pet. v. 8); and his peculiar subject of his accusation are the brethren: called the accuser of the brethren.

Objection. — God do sometimes bring things to light by his providence in a way extraordinary.

Answer. — It is granted God have so done, and brought hidden things to light, which, upon examination, have been proved or confessed, and so the way is clear for their execution; but what is that to this case, where the Devil is accuser and witness?

IV.

EXTRACTS FROM MR. PARRIS'S CHURCH RECORDS.

[The following passages are taken from the records of the Salem Village Church, as specimens of Mr. Parris's style of narrative in that interesting document, and as shedding some light upon the subject of these volumes : —]

SAB: 4 Nov. [1694]. — After sermon in the afternoon, it was propounded to the brethren, whether the church ought not to inquire again of our dissenting brethren after the reason of their dissent. Nothing appearing from any against it, it was put to vote, and carried in the affirmative (by all, as far as I know, except one brother, Josh: Rea), that Brother Jno. Tarbell should, the next Lord's Day, appear and give in his reasons in public; the contrary being propounded, if any had aught to object against it. But no dissent was manifested; and so Brother Nathaniel Putnam and Deacon Ingersoll were desired to give this message from the church to the said Brother Tarbell.

Sab: 11 Nov. — Before the evening blessing was pronounced, Brother Tarbell was openly called again and again; but, he not appearing, application was made to the abovesaid church's messengers for his answer: whereupon said Brother Putnam reported that the said Brother Tarbell told him he did not know how to come to us on a Lord's Day, but desired rather that he might make his appearance some week-day. Whereupon the congregation was dismissed with the blessing: and the church stayed, and, by a full vote, renewed their call of said Brother Tarbell to appear the next Lord's Day for the ends abovesaid; and Deacon Putnam and Brother Jonathan Putnam were desired to be its messengers to the said dissenting brother.

Sab: 18 Nov. — The said brother came in the afternoon; and, after sermon, he was asked the reasons for his withdrawing: whereupon he produced a paper, which he was urged to deliver to the pastor to communicate to the church; but he refused it, asking who was the church's mouth. To which, when he was answered, " The pastor," he replied, Not in this case, because his offence was with him. The pastor demanded whether he had offence against any of the church besides the pastor. He answered, " No." So at length we suffered a non-member, Mr. Jos: Hutchinson, to read it. After

69

which the pastor read openly before the whole congregation his overtures for peace and reconciliation. After which said Tarbell, seemingly (at least) much affected, said, that, if half so much had been said formerly, it had never come to this. But he added that others also were dissatisfied besides himself: and therefore he desired opportunity that they might come also, which was immediately granted; viz., the 26 instant, at two o'clock.

26 Nov. — At the public meeting above appointed at the meeting-house, after the pastor had first sought the grace of God with us in prayer, he then summed up to the church and congregation (among which were several strangers) the occasion of our present assembling, as is hinted the last meeting. Then seeing, together with Brother Tarbell, two more of our dissenting brethren, viz., Sam: Nurse, and Thomas Wilkins (who had, to suit their designs, placed themselves in a seat conveniently together), the church immediately, to save further sending for them, voted that said Brother Wilkins and Brother Nurse should now, together with Brother Tarbell, give in their reasons of withdrawing from the church. Then the pastor applied himself to all these three dissenters, pressing the church's desire upon them. So they produced a paper, which they much opposed the coming into the pastor's hands, and his reading of it; but at length they yielded to it. Whilst the paper was reading, Brother Nurse looked upon another (which he said was the original): and, after it was read throughout, he said it was the same with what he had. Their paper was as followeth: —

"The reasons why we withdraw from communion with the church of Salem Village, both as to hearing the word preached, and from partaking with them at the Lord's Table, are as followeth: —
"1. Why we attend not on public prayer and preaching the word, these are, (1.) The distracting and disturbing tumults and noises made by the persons under diabolical power and delusions, preventing sometimes our hearing and understanding and profiting of the word preached; we having, after many trials and experiences, found no redress in this case, accounted ourselves under a necessity to go where we might hear the word in quiet. (2.) The apprehensions of danger of ourselves being accused as the Devil's instruments to molest and afflict the persons complaining, we seeing those whom we had reason to esteem better than ourselves thus accused, blemished, and, of their lives bereaved, foreseeing this evil, thought it our prudence to withdraw. (3.) We found so frequent and positive preaching up some principles and practices by Mr. Parris, referring to the dark and dismal mysteries of iniquity working amongst us, as was not profitable, but offensive. (4.) Neither could we, in conscience, join with Mr. Parris in many of the requests which he made in prayer, referring to the trouble then among us and upon us; therefore thought it our most safe and peaceable way to withdraw.
"2. The reasons why we hold not communion with them at the Lord's

Table are, first, we esteem ourselves justly aggrieved and offended with the officer who doth administer, for the reasons following: (1.) From his declared and published principles, referring to our molestation from the invisible world, differing from the opinion of the generality of the Orthodox ministers of the whole country. (2.) His easy and strong faith and belief of the affirmations and accusations made by those they call the afflicted. (3.) His laying aside that grace which, above all, we are required to put on; namely, charity toward his neighbors, and especially towards those of his church, when there is no apparent reason for the contrary. (4.) His approving and practising unwarrantable and ungrounded methods for discovering what he was desirous to know referring to the bewitched or possessed persons, as in bringing some to others, and by and from them pretending to inform himself and others who were the Devil's instruments to afflict the sick and pained. (5.) His unsafe and unaccountable oath, given by him against sundry of the accused. (6.) His not rendering to the world so full, if true, an account of what he wrote on examination of the afflicted. (7.) Sundry unsafe, if sound, points of doctrine delivered in his preaching, which we esteem not warrantable, if Christian. (8.) His persisting in these principles, and justifying his practices, not rendering any satisfaction to us when regularly desired, but rather further offending and dissatisfying ourselves.

" John Tarbell.
Tho: Wilkins.
Sam: Nurse."

When the pastor had read these charges, he asked the dissenters above mentioned whether they were offended with none in the church besides himself. They replied, that they articled against none else. Then the officer asked them if they withdrew from communion upon account of none in the church besides himself. They answered, that they withdrew only upon my account. Then I read them my "Meditations for Peace," mentioned 18 instant; viz.: —

"Forasmuch as it is the undoubted duty of all Christians to pursue peace (Ps. xxxiv. 14), even unto a reaching of it, if it be possible (Rom. xii. 18, 19); and whereas, through the righteous, sovereign, and awful Providence of God, the Grand Enemy to all Christian peace has, of late, been most tremendously let loose in divers places hereabouts, and more especially amongst our sinful selves, not only to interrupt that partial peace which we did sometimes enjoy, but also, through his wiles and temptations and our weaknesses and corruptions, to make wider breaches, and raise more bitter animosities between too many of us, in which dark and difficult dispensation we have been all, or most of us, of one mind for a time, and afterwards of differing apprehensions, and, at last, are but in the dark, — upon serious thoughts of all, and after many prayers, I have been moved to present to you (my beloved flock) the following particulars, in way of contribution towards a regaining of Christian concord (if so be we are not altogether unappeasable, irreconcilable, and so destitute of the good spirit which is first pure, then peaceable, gentle, and easy to be entreated, James iii. 17); viz., (1.) In that the Lord ordered the late horrid calamity (which afterwards, plague-like, spread in many other places) to break out first in my family, I cannot but look upon as a very sore rebuke, and humbling providence, both to myself and mine, and desire so we may improve it. (2.) In that also in my family were some of both parties, viz., accusers and accused, I look also upon as an aggravation of the rebuke, as an addition of wormwood to the gall. (3.) In that means were used in my family (though totally unknown to me or mine, except servants, till afterwards) to raise spirits and create apparitions in no better than a diabolical way, I do look upon as a further rebuke of Divine Providence. And by all, I do humbly own this day, before the Lord and his people, that God has been righteously spitting in my face (Num. xii. 14). And I desire to lie low under all this reproach, and to lay my hand upon my mouth. (4.) As to the management of those mysteries, as far as concerns myself, I am very desirous (upon farther light) to own any errors I have therein fallen into, and can come to a discerning of. In the mean while, I do acknowledge, upon after-considerations, that, were the same troubles again, (which the Lord, of his rich mercy, for ever prevent), I should not agree with my former apprehensions in all points; as, for instance, (1.) I question not but God sometimes suffers the Devil (as of late) to afflict in the shape of not only innocent but pious persons, or so delude the senses of the afflicted that they strongly conceit their hurt is from such persons, when, indeed, it is not. (2.) The improving of one afflicted to inquire by, who afflicts the others, I fear may be, and has been, unlawfully used, to Satan's great advantage. (3.) As to my writing, it was put upon me by authority; and therein I have been very careful to avoid the wronging of any (a). (4.) As to my oath, I never meant it, nor do I know how it can be otherwise construed, than as vulgarly and every one understood; yea, and upon inquiry, it may be found so worded also. (5.) As to any passage in preaching or prayer, in that sore hour of distress and darkness, I always intended but due justice on each hand, and that not according to man, but God (who knows all things most perfectly), however, through weakness or sore exercise, I might sometimes, yea, and possibly sundry times, unadvisedly expressed myself. (6.) As to several that have confessed against themselves, they being wholly strangers to me, but yet of good account with better men than myself, to whom also they are well known, I do not pass so much as a secret condemnation upon them; but rather, seeing God has so amazingly lengthened out Satan's chain in this most formidable outrage, I much more incline to side with the opinion of those that have grounds to hope better of them. (7.) As to all that have unduly suffered in these matters (either in their persons or relations), through the clouds of human weakness, and Satan's wiles and sophistry, I do truly sympathize with them; taking it for granted that such as drew themselves clear of this great transgression, or that have sufficient grounds so to look upon their dear friends, have hereby been under those sore trials and temptations, that not an ordinary measure of true grace would be sufficient to prevent a bewraying of remaining corruption. (8.) I am very much in the mind, and abundantly persuaded, that God (for holy ends, though for what in particular is best known to himself) has suffered the evil angels to delude us on both hands, but how far on the one side or the other is much above me to say. And, if we cannot reconcile till we come to a full discerning of these things, I fear we shall never come to agreement, or, at soonest, not in this world. Therefore (9), in fine, The matter being so dark and perplexed as that there is no present appearance that all God's servants should be altogether of one mind, in all circumstances touching the same, I do most heartily, fervently, and humbly beseech pardon of the merciful God, through the blood of Christ, of all my mistakes and trespasses in so weighty a matter; and also all your forgiveness of every offence in this and other affairs, wherein you see or conceive I have erred and offended; professing, in the presence of the Almighty God, that what I have done has been, as for substance, as I apprehended was duty, — however through weakness, ignorance, &c., I may have been mistaken; I also, through grace, promising each of you the like of me. And so again, I beg, entreat, and beseech you, that Satan, the devil, the roaring lion, the old dragon, the enemy of all righteousness, may no longer be served by us, by our envy and strifes, where every evil work prevails whilst these bear sway (Isa. iii. 14–16); but that all, from this day forward, may be covered with the mantle of love, and we may on all hands forgive each other heartily, sincerely, and thoroughly, as we do hope and pray that God, for Christ's sake, would forgive each of ourselves (Matt. xviii. 21 *ad finem;* Col. iii. 12, 13). Put on, therefore, as the elect of God, holy and beloved, bowels of mercies, kindness, humbleness of mind, meekness, long-suffering, forbearing one another, and forgiving one another. If any man have a quarrel against any, even as Christ forgave you, so also do ye (Eph. iv. 31, 32). Let all bitterness and wrath and anger and clamor and evil-speaking be put away from you, with all malice; and be ye kind one to another, tenderhearted, forgiving one another, even as God, for Christ's sake, hath forgiven you. Amen, amen.   SAM: PARRIS.

"26 Nov., 1694."

[In the record, off against (*a*) as above, the following is in Mr. Parris's writing:]

(*a*) Added, by the desire of the council, this following paragraph; viz., Nevertheless, I fear, that, in and through the throng of the many things written by me, in the late confusions, there has not been a due exactness always used; and, as I now see the inconveniency of my writing so much on those difficult occasions, so I would lament every error of such writings. — Apr. 3, 1695. Idem. S. P.

[The above passage (*a*) is inserted in a marginal space left for it on a page containing the record of a meeting, Nov. 26, 1694, while it is dated April 3, 1695, and purports to be added "by the desire of the council," which met at the last-named date. There are other indications, that the record of Mr. Parris's controversy with the dissatisfied brethren, consequent upon the proceedings in 1692, was made originally on separate sheets of paper, and then compiled, and inscribed in the church-book, as it there appears. There are several other entries, which refer to dates ahead. He probably made out his record near the close of the struggle which resulted in his dismission, and left it, on the pages of the book, as his history of the case. After giving his " Meditations for Peace," the record goes on : —]

After I had read these overtures abovesaid, I desired the brethren to declare themselves whether they remained still dissatisfied. Brother Tarbell answered, that they desired to consider of it, and to have a copy of what I had read. I replied, that then they must subscribe their reasons (above mentioned), for as yet they were anonymous : so at length, with no little difficulty, I purchased the subscription of their charges by my abovesaid overtures, which I gave, subscribed with my name, to them, to consider of; and so this meeting broke up. Note that, during this agitation with our dissenting brethren, they entertained frequent whisperings with comers and goers to them and from them; particularly Dan: Andrews, and Tho: Preston from Mr. Israel Porter, and Jos: Hutchinson, &c.

Nov. 30, 1694. — Brother Nurse and Brother Tarbell (bringing with them Joseph Putnam and Tho: Preston) towards night came to my house, where they found the two deacons and several other brethren; viz., Tho: Putnam, Jno. Putnam, Jr., Benj. Wilkins, and Ezek: Cheever, besides Lieutenant Jno. Walcot. And Brother Tarbell said they came to answer my paper, which they had now considered of, and their answer was this; viz., that they remained dissatisfied, and desired that the church would call a council, according to the advice we had lately from ministers.

[An account has been given, p. 493, of the attempts of the " dissatisfied brethren " to procure a mutual council to decide the controversy between them and Mr. Parris. On the 14th of June, 1694, a letter was addressed to him, advising him to agree to the call of such a council, signed by John Higginson, of the First Church in Salem ; James Allen, of the First Church in Boston ; John Hale, of the church in Beverly ; Samuel Willard, of the Old South Church in Boston ; Samuel Cheever, of the church in Marblehead ; and Joseph Gerrish, of the church in Wenham. Nicholas Noyes joined in the advice, " with this proviso, that he be not chosen one of the council." Mr. Parris contrived to avoid following the advice. On the 10th of September, Messrs. Higginson, Allen, Willard, Cheever, and Gerrish again, in earnest and quite peremptory terms, renewed their advice in another letter to Mr. Parris. No longer venturing to resist their authority, he yielded, and consented to a mutual council, upon certain terms, one of which was, that neither of the churches whose ministers had thus forced him to the measure should be of the council. The following passages give the conclusion of the matter, as related by Mr. Parris in his record-book : —]

Feb. 12 [1695]. — The church met again, as last agreed upon; and, after a while, our dissenting brethren, Tho: Wilkins, Sam: Nurse, and Jno. Tarbell, came also. After our constant way of begging the presence of God with us, we desired our dissenting brethren to acquaint us whether they would accept of our last proposals, which they desired to this day to consider of. They answered, that they were willing to drop the six churches from whose elders we had had the advice abovesaid, dated 14 June last; but they were not free to exclude Ipswich. This they stuck unto long, and then desired that they might withdraw a little to confer among themselves about it, which was granted. But they quickly returned, as resolved for Ipswich as before. We desired them to nominate the three churches they would have sent to: and, after much debate, they did; viz., Rowley, Salisbury, and Ipswich. Whereupon we voted, by a full consent, Rowley and Salisbury churches for a part of the council, and desired them to nominate a third church. But still they insisted on Ipswich, which we told them they were openly informed, the last meeting, that we had excepted against. Then they were told that we would immediately choose three other churches to join with the two before nominated and voted, if they saw not good to nominate any more; or else we would choose two other churches to join with the aforesaid two, if they pleased. They answered, they would be willing to that, if Ipswich might be one of them. Then it was asked them, if a dismission to some other Orthodox church, where they might better please themselves, would content them. Brother Tarbell answered, "Ay, if we could find a way to remove our livings too." Then it was propounded, whether we could not unite amongst ourselves. The particular answer hereunto I remember not; but (I think) such hints were given by them as if it were impossible. Thus much time being gone, it being well towards sunset, and we concluding that it was necessary that we should do something ourselves, if they would not (as the elders had heretofore desired) accept of our joining with them, we dismissed them; and, by a general agreement amongst ourselves, read and voted letters to the churches at North Boston, Weymouth, Malden, and Rowley, for their help in a council.

[Mr. Parris's plan of finding refuge in an *ex-parte* council was utterly frustrated. On the 1st of March, the "reverend elders in the Bay accounted it advisable," as he expresses it in his records, that the First Church and the Old South Church in Boston should be added to the council. They wrote to him to that effect, and he had to comply. This brought James Allen and Samuel Willard into the council, and determined the character of the result, which, coming from a tribunal called by him to adjudicate the case, and hearing only such evidence as he laid before it, so far as it bore against him, was decisive and fatal. It was as follows: —]

The elders and messengers of the churches — met in council at Salem Village, April 3, 1695, to consider and determine what is to be done for the composure of the present unhappy differences in that place, — after solemn invocation of God in Christ for his direction, do unanimously declare and advise as followeth: —

I. We judge that, albeit in the late and the dark time of the confusions, wherein Satan had obtained a more than ordinary liberty to be sifting of this plantation, there were sundry unwarrantable and uncomfortable steps taken by Mr. Samuel Parris, the pastor of the church in Salem Village, then under the hurrying distractions of amazing afflictions; yet the said Mr. Parris, by the good hand of God brought unto a better sense of things, hath so fully expressed it, that a Christian charity may and should receive satisfaction therewith.

II. Inasmuch as divers Christian brethren in the church of Salem Village have been offended at Mr. Parris for his conduct in the time of the difficulties and calamities which have distressed them, we now advise them charitably to accept the satisfaction which he hath tendered in his Christian acknowledgments of the errors therein committed; yea, to endeavor, as far as 'tis possible, the fullest reconciliation of their minds unto communion with him, in the whole exercise of his ministry, and with the rest of the church (Matt. vi. 12–14; Luke xvii. 3; James v. 16).

III. Considering the extreme trials and troubles which the dissatisfied brethren in the church of Salem Village have undergone in the day of sore temptation which hath been upon them, we cannot but advise the church to treat them with bowels of much compassion, instead of all more critical or rigorous proceedings against them, for the infirmities discovered by them in such an heart-breaking day. And if, after a patient waiting for it, the said brethren cannot so far overcome the uneasiness of their spirits, in the remembrance of the disasters that have happened, as to sit under his ministry, we advise the church, with all tenderness, to grant them a dismission unto any other society of the faithful whereunto they may desire to be dismissed (Gal. vi. 1, 2; Ps. ciii. 13, 14; Job xix. 21).

IV. Mr. Parris having, as we understand, with much fidelity and integrity acquitted himself in the main course of his ministry since he hath been pastor to the church in Salem Village, about his first call whereunto, we look upon all contestations now to be both unreasonable and unseasonable; and our Lord having made him a blessing unto the souls of not a few, both old and young, in this place, we advise that he be accordingly respected, honored, and supported, with all the regards that are due to a painful minister of the gospel (1 Thess. v. 12, 13; 1 Tim. v. 17).

V. Having observed that there is in Salem Village a spirit full of contentions and animosities, too sadly verifying the blemish which hath heretofore lain upon them, and that some complaints brought against Mr. Parris have been either causeless and groundless, or unduly aggravated, we do, in the name and fear of the Lord, solemnly warn them to consider, whether, if they continue to devour one another, it will not be bitterness in the latter end; and beware lest the Lord be provoked thereby utterly to deprive them of those which they should account their precious and pleasant things, and abandon them to all the desolations of a people that sin away the mercies of the gospel (James iii. 16; Gal. v. 15; 2 Sam. ii. 26; Isa. v. 4, 5, 6; Matt. xxi. 43).

VI. If the distempers in Salem Village should be (which God forbid!) so incurable, that Mr. Parris, after all, find that he cannot, with any comfort and service, continue in his present station, his removal from thence will not expose him unto any hard character with us, nor, we hope, with the rest of the people of God among whom we live (Matt. x. 14; Acts xxii. 18).

All which advice we follow with our prayers that the God of peace would bruise Satan under our feet. Now, the Lord of peace himself give you peace always by all means.

INCREASE MATHER, *Moderator.*

* JOSEPH BRIDGHAM.	* EPHRAIM HUNT.
* SAMUEL CHECKLEY.	* NATHLL. WILLIAMS.
* WILLIAM TORREY.	SAMUEL PHILLIPS.
* JOSEPH BOYNTON.	JAMES ALLEN.
* RICHARD MIDDLECOT.	SAMUEL TORREY.
* JOHN WALLEY.	SAMUEL WILLARD.
* JER: DUMMER.	EDWARD PAYSON.
* NEHEMIAH JEWET.	COTTON MATHER.

[The names of the lay members of the Council are marked thus, *. They were persons of high standing in civil life. Samuel Checkley was not (as stated [Supplement, p. 494], through an inadvertence, of which, I trust, not many such instances can be found in these volumes) the Rev. Mr. Checkley, but his father, Col. Samuel Checkley, a citizen of Boston, of much prominence at the time.

The foregoing document is skilfully drawn. While kindly in its tone towards Mr. Parris, it is, in reality, a strong condemnation of his course, especially in Article I., as also in the paragraph marked (*a*), (p. 549), "added by the desire of the Council" to his "Meditations for Peace." Article III. discountenances the proceedings of his church in its censure of "the dissatisfied brethren," and requires that they should be recognized and treated as members in good standing. The fifth article administers rebuke with an equal hand to both sides, while the sixth and last recommends the removal of Mr. Parris, if the alienation of his opponents should prove "incurable."

As an authoritative condemnation of the proceedings related in this work, pronounced at the time, it is a fitting final close of the presentation of this subject.]

THE END.